BIOGRAPHIES

OF

DISTINGUISHED SCIENTIFIC MEN.

BIOGRAPHIES

OF

DISTINGUISHED SCIENTIFIC MEN.

BY FRANCOIS ARAGO,

MEMBER OF THE INSTITUTE.

TRANSLATED BY

ADMIRAL W. H. SMYTH, D.C.L., F.R.S., &c.

THE REV. BADEN POWELL, M.A., F.R.S., &c.

AND

ROBERT GRANT, ESQ., M.A., F.R.A.S.

SECOND SERIES.

BOSTON:

TICKNOR AND FIELDS.

M DCCC LIX.

RIVERSIDE, CAMBRIDGE:
PRINTED BY H. O. HOUGHTON AND COMPANY.

CONTENTS.

CARNOT.

MALUS.

JAMES WATT.

LIVES

OF

DISTINGUISHED SCIENTIFIC MEN.

CARNOT

BIOGRAPHY READ AT A PUBLIC ASSEMBLY OF THE ACADEMY OF SCIENCES, ON THE 21ST OF AUGUST, 1837.

CHILDHOOD OF CARNOT.—HIS EDUCATION.

LAZARE-NICOLAS-MARGUERITE CARNOT was born at Nolay (Côte-d'Or), in the ancient duchy of Burgundy that had already been the cradle of three of the greatest ornaments of which the Academies could boast: Bossuet, Vauban, and Buffon. His father was an advocate, and exercised that noble profession with a great deal of talent (which is not uncommon) and with very great disinterestedness (which is said to be not so common). The advocate, Claude-Abraham Carnot, had eighteen children; so that, according to the old adage, which promises prosperity to a numerous family, he might expect a happy future for each of his children. Indeed, at one period, he might have counted, in this numerous family, two lieutenant-generals of the French armies; a councillor at the court of repeal; an attorney-general of the *cour royale;* the directress of the hospice de Nolay; a municipal magistrate much esteemed whilst he was administering the affairs of his corporation, and still more esteemed, if possible, when, after twenty-three years' exercise of his functions, he submitted to be brutally deposed sooner than fail in his duty. I must mention that, like an affectionate and provident father, the advocate of Nolay had not trusted unreservedly to the virtue of the proverb, but always presided personally over the early education of his sons. Lazare Carnot, the subject of this biography, only left his father's house to go, as it was then called, through his Rhetoric and Philosophy.

The childhood of those privileged men who, under various claims, have acted a brilliant part on the stage of the world, has always attracted the attention of every biographer. The "know thyself" of an ancient philosopher would be but poorly interpreted if only looked on as a maxim of prüdence; the maxim is susceptible of a juster and wider interpretation: it presents to us, I think, the whole human race, as a body, for the most important species of study that we can undertake. Therefore, Gentlemen, let us carefully examine how those extraordinary minds are indicated, are born, and grow, which, on their complete development, are destined to open out for themselves unknown paths. These characteristics should be collected with all the more interest, because they become daily more rare. In our modern schools, modelled on exactly the same pattern from north to south and from east to west; subjected to the same regulations and to a uniform discipline; where children enter moreover at the age of nine or ten years, and do not leave until they are eighteen or twenty, individual character is effaced, or disappears, or is covered with the mask of conventionality. The agriculturist would never go into a hothouse to learn the character, the form, or the appearance of those admirable plants which are the ornament of our ancient forests. Neither is it in our regiments that one might hope to trace out the true types of the peasants of Brittany, Normandy, Lorraine, or Franche-Comté. Our "school-regiments" (if I may be allowed the expression) would lead moralists quite as much astray. There, a sort of mean is established, about which, with very slight variations, all the youth of the present day is grouped. Is this for good or for evil? Far be it from me to open such a discussion here; I merely say that such is the fact, and this fact will explain why I have collected various particulars of the childhood of our colleague, which might otherwise have appeared trifling.

Carnot was only ten years old when his mother, in a journey to Dijon, took him with her, and, to reward him for the thoughtful docility which he always showed, took him to the theatre. A piece was represented that day, in which evolutions of troops and battles succeeded one another without intermission. The young scholar followed with sustained attention the series of events which were developed before him; but, all on a sudden, he gets up, he is agitated, and, in spite of the endeavours of his mother, calls out in terms hardly polite, to an actor who had just come on the stage. This person was the acting general of the troops on whose side the young Carnot was interested; by his cries, the child was warning the unskilful chief that the artillery was badly placed; that the gunners, being without cover, must necessarily be killed by the first fire of musketry from the ramparts of the fortress which they were about to attack; that, on the other hand, by establishing the battery behind a rock, which he pointed out, both by word of mouth and by gesture, the men would be much less exposed. The astonished actors did not know what to do; Madame Carnot was distressed at the disturbance which her son was occasioning; the audience burst out laughing; every one was puzzled as to the cause of such an unusual criticism; and the supposed frolic was nothing else than the revelation of a superior military talent, the first symptom of that powerful genius which, despising beaten tracks, created, a few years later, new tactics, and proposed to replace the scientifically and ingeniously combined fortifications of Vauban, by an altogether different system.

From the age of twelve to fifteen, Carnot pursued the course of studies at the College at Autun. He made himself remarkable there by a lively, original turn of mind, and by a rare degree of intelligence. He next entered the "little seminary" of the same town. At sixteen years of age he had finished his Philosophy. The firmness which we shall find in him in the course of a most stormy career, was already the leading feature in his character. The timid professors of the seminary of Autun, had a troublesome experience of it on the day when their scholar had to support his thesis.

This ceremony always took place in public. According to regulations, the liberality of which would, at the present day, appear excessive to the authorities of our universities, every one of the audience had the right of making objections. This criticism might be applied both to the principles and to the style. Thus the *amour propre* of the master ran as much risk as that of the pupil, and the reputation of a large establishment lay at the mercy of some heedless young fellow. Thence came the custom of starting the competitors in the arena accompanied by a Mentor, who came to the assistance of their treacherous memories, and who, by a word put in at the proper moment, brought them back into the right path as soon as they began to wander from it; and the Mentor was often himself drawn into the discussion on his own account. According to this custom, the teachers of the Seminary of Autun were proceeding towards the *salle des exercises,* where a large concourse of people was assembled, when the young Carnot signified his intention to ascend to the rostrum alone, that he would not be accompanied by a prompter, that he would not keep at all to the routine they had assigned him, and that he would speak alone or not at all. This resolution was combated by alternate entreaties and threats, but in vain: they were obliged to submit, whether they liked it or not, to this unprecedented caprice of the pupil. However, the most brilliant success soon justified it, even in the eyes of the irritated professors. A curious incident rendered the meeting remarkable: a lady, the wife of a doctor of medicine, became the most formidable adversary of the young rhetorician: she argued against him, in Latin, with a force of logic, with an ease, a grace, and an elegance of expression, which the more astonished Carnot and the audience, inasmuch as no indiscreet display had hitherto made them even suspect that Madame l'Homme had carried her studies farther than the *Cuisinière bourgeoise*, the *Almanach de Liége*, or the *Petit Paroissien.*

Carnot had so thoroughly taken, not only to the principle of religion, but, moreover (and they are not the same things), to the minute practices of devotion scrupulously followed at the little seminary of Autun, that some of his friends thought at one time of putting him into holy orders. They were strengthened in this idea by the recollection of the great number of ecclesiastical dignitaries of which this honourable family could boast, amongst whom figured canons, *vicaires-généraux* of the diocese of Châlon, doctors of the Sorbonne, and an abbé of Cîteaux. However, the career of military engineer carried the day, and young Carnot was sent to Paris to a special school, there to prepare for his examination. The comrades whom he met there had certainly not been brought up at the Seminary; for the profound piety of the new scholar, of which he would by no means make a mystery, became the subject of their continual sarcasms. Sarcasms are not reasons. Carnot was not therefore staggered by them; but he felt the necessity of maturing, by reflection and study, ideas and sentiments to which his pure and candid soul had hitherto given itself up with perfect goodwill and confidence. Theology, then, became, for some months, the only occupation of an *apprenti-officier*, or military novice. No one can tell what was the effect of these meditations; for, at all periods of his life, Carnot carefully avoided, even in the intimacy of the domestic circle, any discussions,—nay, more, any simple conversations—relating to religion. We only know that he professed principles now adopted by all good and enlightened minds. "Universal tolerance," said he, when, proscribed and wandering in a foreign land, he had to ward off the spiteful darts of calumny,—"universal tolerance, that is the dogma which I decidedly profess . . . . . I abhor fanaticism, and I believe that the fanaticism of irreligion, brought into fashion by such men as Marat and Père Duchêsne, is the most fatal of all. We must not kill men to force them to believe: we must not kill them to prevent their believing; let us compassionate the weaknesses of others, since every one has his own; and let us allow prejudices to wear away by time when we cannot obviate them by reason."

After theology, scientific studies, especially those of geometry and algebra, had their turn, and, as at Nolay and Autun, his success was rapid and brilliant. M. de Longpré, director of the preparatory school, was acquainted with D'Alembert. The illustrious geometer was not above going amongst very young scholars, to encourage rising merit by his approbation. In one of his visits he particularly distinguished Carnot, and addressed to him flattering and prophetic words, which our colleague would repeat with emotion, even during those periods when fortune had rendered him one of the arbiters of the destinies of Europe.

Perhaps this is an opportunity, Gentlemen, for regretting that, in our society, such as half a century of revolutions has made it, the personal intercourse which formerly existed between the professors and distinguished scholars of great schools, has totally disappeared, and has become indeed, to a certain degree, impossible. Now-a-days, at the hour set down in the programmes, illustrious men of learning or of literature arrive in spacious amphitheatres. A crowd is waiting for them. During entire hours, all that is profound, intricate, or new, in science or literature, is developed with system, clearness, and eloquence; but, the lesson finished, the professor retires, without even knowing the names of those who have listened to him. Nevertheless, in the midst of such an audience (I will confine myself, Gentlemen, to a single example), Fourcroy found, in an apothecary's boy who had come furtively to hear him, the devoted, exact, indefatigable, and ingenious coöperator whom, by these traits, each of you has already recognized—he discovered Vauquelin!

ENTRANCE OF CARNOT INTO THE SCHOOL OF MÉZIÈRES AS SECOND LIEUTENANT OF ENGINEERS.

At the time when Carnot quitted the establishment of M. de Longpré, the "ordonnance" in virtue of which a genealogist coöperated with a geometer in the examination of the future officers of engineers was not in force. In 1771 any Frenchman might still be admitted at the school of Mézières without showing any parchments, on condition always that neither his father nor mother had endeavoured to enrich their family and their country by commerce or by manual labour. The young aspirant displayed unusual mathematical knowledge before the examiner, Bossut. His father, in obedience to the sad exigencies of the period, proved on his part that no ship of his had ever been to distant countries to exchange the fruits of the French soil or of French industry, for productions reserved by nature to other climates; that his hands had never put together the movable types of Gutenberg, even for the purpose of reproducing the Bible or the Gospel; that he had not personally coöperated in the construction of any of those admirable instruments which measure time, or which sound the depths of space.

After legal proof of these negative merits, young Carnot was declared of sufficiently good family to wear an epaulette, and received without delay that of a second lieutenant.

Decorated with this so-much-desired epaulette, Carnot, at the age of eighteen years, came to the School of Engineers. There, under the auspices of Monge, he doubtless cultivated descriptive geometry and the physical sciences with his habitual success; but on this point it must be owned, we are reduced to mere conjecture; for in carrying to an extreme the natural desire to conceal from strangers the knowledge, then but little spread, of the art of making and destroying fortifications, the celebrated school of Mézières had been made a sort of conclave of which the secrets were never penetrated by the profane.

CARNOT A FIRST LIEUTENANT ON SERVICE IN FORTRESSES.

On the 12th of January, 1773, Carnot, having become a first lieutenant, was sent to Calais. The works of a place where the periodical oscillations of the ocean add a new and important condition to the already very complicated data of the problem of fortification, were very interesting to the young officer. He thus overleaped without hindrance, the passage, generally so troublesome, from learned theories to tiresome practice; from the brilliant illusions which amuse us in schools, to the sad realities of life.

The *Mémorial de Saint Hélène* says that in his youth "Carnot was looked on by his comrades as an original." This title Napoleon had borrowed from Carnot himself. I find it in the answer to Bailleul, but explained and commented on, and deprived of that vagueness which leaves it to be taken either as a compliment or a reproach. Carnot, at twenty years of age, was, to the officers of the garrison of Calais, an "original," or a "philosopher," (these words were equivalent,) because he did not join them either in their turbulence or in any of their wild pranks; because he passed his time in the libraries rather than at the café; because, he read Thucydides, Polybius, and Cæsar, rather than the licentious works of that period; because, if he were intimate with the Prince de Croy, Commandant-General of Picardy, it was not for the sake of obtaining leave from, or alleviations of, duty, but in order to assist him in delicate geographical researches, and to work at charts of the Southern Hemisphere, showing the latest nautical discoveries. Carnot, nevertheless, was anything but an ill-natured judge of others. Severe towards himself, he had an inexhaustible fund of indulgence to every one else. He employed his hours of leisure or relaxation in composing little poems, all impressed with a gentle and social gayety. To have quoted ballads in the biography of a geometer would certainly have had great novelty, and this weak merit, quite within my grasp, had almost persuaded me to do so; a little reflection has caused me to give it up. A great poet in our country having stamped that nature of composition with his immortal seal, song should no longer be lightly quoted.

THE FIRST COMMUNICATION BETWEEN CARNOT AND THE ACADEMY OF SCIENCES.—AIR-BALLOONS.

The first direct communication between Carnot and the Academy of Sciences (this fact will be a novelty to every one) was brought about by a problem which not only has not yet been solved, but which, according to many physical philosophers, appears as if it never can be—"the problem of guiding balloons."

Scientific discoveries, even those from which mankind might expect the greatest advantages—such, for instance, as those of the mariner's compass and the steam-engine—

were received on their first appearance with disdainful indifference. Political and military events exclusively enjoy the privilege of exciting the public. There have been, however, two exceptions to this rule. You will all know by this hint, that I allude to America and air-balloons, Christopher Columbus and Montgolfier. The discoveries of these two men of genius, so different hitherto in their results, had, at their birth, similar fortunes. Gather, in fact, from the *Historia del Almirante* the marks of the general enthusiasm which the discovery of certain islands excited amongst the Andalusians, the Catalonians, the Arragonese, and the Castilians; read the account of the unheard-of honours which they hastened to render, as well in the largest cities as in the smallest hamlets, not only to the leader of the enterprise, but even to the very sailors of the caravels La Santa Maria, La Pinta, and La Niña, which were the first to reach the western shores of the Atlantic; you may then save yourselves the trouble of searching in the writings of the period what sort of sensation air-balloons produced amongst our compatriots: the processions at Seville and Barcelona were faithful representations of the fêtes which took place at Lyons and Paris. In 1783, just as it happened two centuries before, warm imaginations were not at the trouble of confining themselves to the limits of facts or of probabilities. In the one instance, there was not a Spaniard who did not wish, after the example of Columbus, himself also to tread lands where, in a few days, he might collect as great a quantity of gold and precious stones as was formerly the possession of the richest potentates. In France each individual, following the favourite direction of his ideas, made different but charming applications of the new faculty—I had almost said of the new organs—which man had just received from the hands of Montgolfier. The physical philosopher, transported into the region of meteors, and catching Nature in the act, penetrated at a glance the mystery of the formation of lightning, of snow, and of hail. The geographer, profiting by a favourable wind, was to explore, without danger or fatigue, as well those polar zones which the accumulated ice of centuries seems to wish to conceal for ever from our curiosity, as those central parts of Africa, New Holland, Java, Sumatra, and Borneo, forbidden to our enterprises not less by a deadly climate than by the fierce animals and tribes which live there. Certain generals thought it an urgent duty to study the systems of fortification and artillery which it would be necessary to oppose to enemies moving in balloons; others elaborated new principles of tactics applicable to aërial battles. One would say that projects such as these, which might have been fathered on Ariosto, should certainly have satisfied the most adventurous and enthusiastic spirits: such was not the case, however. The discovery of balloons, notwithstanding the brilliant accessories with which each one enthusiastically surrounded it, appeared to be only the forerunner of still greater discoveries; henceforward nothing was to be impossible to one who had conquered the atmosphere. This idea was continually reproducing itself; it put on every shape; youth seized it with joy; old age made it the text of a thousand bitter regrets. See the Maréchale de Villeroi, an octogenarian and an invalid: she is led to one of the windows of the Tuileries almost by force, for she does not believe in balloons; the balloon nevertheless detaches itself from its moorings; our colleague, Charles, seated in the cradle, gaily salutes the spectators, and soars majestically into the air. Oh! on the instant passing without transition from the most complete incredulity to an unbounded confidence in the powers of the human mind, the old Maréchale falls on her knees, and, her eyes bathed in tears, gasps forth these sad words: "Yes, it is decided, now it is certain; THEY will discover the secret of never dying, *but it will be when I am dead!*"

Carnot, being of a rigorous turn of mind (though he was not yet eighty years of age), took good care not to go so far as the Maréchale de Villeroi. Nevertheless, he appeared in the ranks of the enthusiasts. He then believed, and always did so afterwards, in the possibility of directing balloons, and consequently in the applications which science and the art of war had hoped from them. The archives of the Academy ought to contain a paper in which Captain Carnot of the engineers submitted to the authorities an arrangement of light oars, which, in his opinion, should attain the desired end. This paper has not yet been discovered. I will continue my researches for it, and if the work seems likely to add to the reputation of our fellow academician, the public shall not be deprived of it. Perhaps I shall join with it a memoir of the same nature, also unpublished, by another academician, the illustrious Meunier.

ÉLOGE OF VAUBAN BY CARNOT.—HIS DISCUSSIONS WITH M. DE MONTALEMBERT.

A certain literary society of a very small town once on a time gave itself the title, on its own full authority, of *Daughter of the French Academy*. Voltaire thought that they should not refuse it this title: "Indeed, I esteem her," said he, "as a very virtuous daughter, since she has never given occasion for any talk about her."

Such an epigram would not have been applicable to the Academy of Dijon. This celebrated society did not shun the public gaze, either when it proposed the question, "Whether the reëstablishment of the arts and sciences had cóntributed to the refinement of manners," nor, more especially, when it rewarded the discourse in which Jean-Jacques pronounced in the negative. Time has done ample justice to the paradox; but it ought not to have effaced the remembrance of the generous proceeding which, in giving to Rousseau an unexpected celebrity, attached him for ever to the brilliant career in which he met with competitors and rivals, but not with a master.

To the merit which I have just related, the Academy of Dijon can add that of having called forth the first production of Carnot's which the press took possession of,—the *Éloge of Vauban.*

The intrepidity, the disinterestedness, and the science of the illustrious marshal had already received, from the tongue of Fontenelle, an homage to which it seemed difficult to add. What speech indeed could more worthily characterize a military life than these few figures? "Vauban caused work to be done at 300 fortresses; he constructed 33 new ones; he conducted 53 sieges; he was present at 140 actions of importance." And does not this other sentence seem as though borrowed from Plutarch? "The morals of Vauban held out perfectly against the most brilliant dignities, and never even wavered. In a word, he was a Roman whom it seemed as if our age had stolen from the best times of the Republic!"

The éloge from which these two passages are taken had always appeared to me so eloquent and true, that, at the moment when I first discovered an oration on Vauban amongst the productions of our colleague, I burst out into heartfelt abuse at the academic programme which, taking advantage of the inexperience of a young man, had exposed him to so formidable a comparison. Indeed, I should not have been more uneasy, if I had discovered that Carnot had endeavoured to rewrite *La Mécanique* of Lagrange, *Athalie*, or the *Fables* of La Fontaine. These fears were superfluous. The Burgundian members of the Academy of Dijon were right in thinking that the Burgundian Vauban might still become an interesting subject of study, even after the brilliant portrait traced by Fontenelle. And, in truth, the Secretary of the Academy of Sciences had prudently left in the shade one of the finest points of the illustrious marshal.

It would seem that the éloge of Vauban, from the pen of an officer of engineers, must consist principally of an exact appreciation of the means of attack and defence with which the illustrious marshal endowed the art of war. This was not the plan, however, which Carnot adopted. It was principally for the qualities of the heart, for virtue, and for patriotism, that Vauban seemed to him worthy of admiration. "He was," said he, "one of those men whom nature gives to the world formed entirely for benevolence; gifted, like the bee, with an innate activity for the general welfare; who cannot separate their lot from that of the Republic, and who, intimate members of society, live and flourish, or suffer and languish, with it."

Prince Henry of Prussia was present at the assembly

of the Academy of Dijon, at which the éloge of Vauban was read and rewarded. He expressed, in the most unequivocal terms, the great pleasure that the discourse had given him; and assured the author of his profound esteem, both verbally and in writing. Piqued with emulation, the Prince de Condé, who presided at the assembly, as governor of Burgundy, outdid the marks of favour which were shown to the young engineer officer by the brother of Frederic the Great.

Had Carnot then flattered the prejudices of the nobles? Were his principles in 1784 so different from those which afterwards directed all his actions, as necessarily to receive the suffrages of the great? Listen, Gentlemen, and judge!

The *Dîme Royale* (the King's Tithe), that writing which, under Louis XIV., brought about the complete disgrace of Vauban, and of which Fontenelle had the prudence not even to mention the title, in enumerating the works of the illustrious marshal, was called by Carnot a simple and pathetic exposition of facts; a work in which "every thing is striking by its precision and truthfulness." The assessment of the taxes, in France, in the eyes of the young officer, was "barbarous;" the manner of gathering them "more barbarous still." According to him, the true object of a government is to oblige every individual of the State to labour; the method which he points out for obtaining this result would be (I quote from the text) to cause riches to pass from those hands where they are superfluous, into those where they are necessary. Carnot gives his adhesion unreservedly to this precept of Vauban's; the laws ought to prevent the frightful misery of the one class and the excessive opulence of the other; he sets his face against the odious multiplicity of privileges from which the more numerous classes of the population had then so much to suffer; finally, after having divided mankind into two categories, the workers and the idlers, he goes so far as to say of these latter, who alone, according to him, have been taken into account in the constitution of modern society, that "they do not begin to be useful till the moment in which they die, for they do not vivify the earth except by reëntering it." Such, Gentlemen, are the bold opinions which an Academy rewarded in 1784; which called forth from Buffon, who certainly cannot be accused of having been an innovator in matters of government, these words so flattering to the successful orator:—"Your style is noble and flowing; you have done, sir, an agreeable and useful work;" and which inspired the brother of an absolute king with the desire of attaching Carnot, whose "friend" he declared himself to be, to the service of Prussia; which gained for the young officer the favour of the prince whom Worms and Coblentz witnessed a few years afterwards at the head of the emigration! Who then will dare to call our revolution of 1789 an effect without a cause, a meteor of whose arrival there had been no warning? The moral transformations of society are subjected to the law of continuity; they rise and grow like the productions of the earth, by imperceptible gradations.

Each century develops, discusses, and adapts to itself, in some degree, truths—or, if you prefer it, principles—of which the conception belonged to the preceding century; this work of the mind usually goes on without being perceived by the vulgar; but when the day of application arrives, when principles claim their part in practice, when they aim at penetrating into political life, the ancient interests, if they have only this same antiquity to invoke in their favour, become excited, resist, and struggle, and society is shaken to its foundations. The tableau will be complete, Gentlemen, when I add that, in these obstinate conflicts, it is never the principles that succumb.

Carnot, as I have already remarked, had but lightly touched on the technical part of Vauban's works, in his éloge; yet, in the few sentences which he wrote on this subject, he took occasion to say that "*a certain vulgar, ignorant, person*" took an erroneous view of fortification in reducing it to the art of tracing on paper lines subjected to certain, more or less, systematic conditions. These words, in their general sense, seemed as if they might have passed unnoticed; but an unfortunate concurrence of circumstances gave to them an importance which was not foreseen, and still less desired by their author. In 1783, a general of infantry, member of this Academy, M. le Marquis de Montalembert, published, under the title of *Perpendicular Fortification*, an entirely new system of defence of fortresses. This system was outrageously opposed by almost the whole corps of military engineers. The scion of an illustrious family, the general officer of the French army, the academician, might assuredly, without too much vanity, believe himself not included in the *ignorant vulgar* that the author of the eulogy had lightly designated; but M. de Montalembert was determined to apply these expressions to himself, and to revenge himself he published an edition of Vauban's éloge accompanied by notes, in which offence and gross affront were carried to the utmost. There was enough in this pamphlet to upset the mind of a young man a thousand times; nevertheless, under these difficult circumstances, Carnot already showed himself such as he always was afterwards—frank, just, and completely insensible to undeserved abuse.

"If your suspicions were well founded," wrote he to his fiery antagonist, "I should have forgotten the first duties of propriety and decency; I should have been wanting, above all, in the infinite respect which military men owe to a distinguished general: be assured that there is not a single officer of engineers who has not learnt with the same pleasure, from M. le Marquis de Montalembert, how to fortify places well, as from the brave D'Essé to defend them well."

The appositeness and delicacy of this quotation will be appreciated when I mention that the brave D'Essé, who, in 1543, after three months of an heroic resistance, compelled the whole forces of the emperor to raise the siege of Landrecies, was an ancestor of M. de Montalembert.

Moderation and politeness are almost infallible means of success against violence and affront; moreover, in the quarrels of the press, they must often be looked upon as the simple result of calculation, and as proofs of ability. But Carnot's letter allowed no misapprehension as to the sincerity of his sentiments. "Your work," he wrote to him who had just criticized so bitterly the principle, the style, and I might almost add, the punctuation, of his éloge, "your work *is full of genius. . . . . Now that your casemates are known and proved, fortification will put on a new face; it will become a new art.* It will be no longer allowable to employ the revenues of the State to construct something tolerable, when you have taught us to construct something good. . . . . Although the corps of engineers has not the advantage of possessing you, we do not the less consider that we have a right to reckon you amongst its most illustrious members. Whoever extends our knowledge, whoever furnishes us with new means of being useful to France, becomes our comrade, our chief, and our benefactor." M. de Montalembert did not resist such explicit and flattering testimony. The most formal disavowal of the unlucky pamphlet quickly followed Carnot's answer; on the other hand, it must be confessed that the higher authorities of the engineers were so irritated at the praises which a simple captain had allowed himself to bestow on systems which they had authoritatively rejected, that a "lettre de cachet" and the Bastille signified to our member that, on the eve of our great revolution, liberty of discussion, that precious conquest of modern philosophy, had not yet penetrated amongst military usages. Such rigour seems inexplicable, even when one makes every allowance for the requirements of *esprit de corps* and the susceptibilities of self-esteem; Carnot had shown himself, indeed, both in his éloge and in his letter to Montalembert, the warmest defender of the department to which he belonged, and which, said he, "professes to sacrifice its time and its life for the State." Had this man then, I demand, forgotten the duties of his position, who, when called on to judge between the services of a regimental officer and those of the engineer on whom devolves the dangerous honour of tracing parallels, of commanding in the trench, or of directing the head of a sap, expressed himself so nobly: "The officer of engineers is in the midst of peril, but he is there alone and silent; he sees death, but he must gaze on it with coolness; he may not rush on it like the heroes of battle; he sees it approach with tranquillity; he seeks the spot where the lightning bursts forth, not to act but to observe; not to get excited, but to deliberate."

Perhaps, Gentlemen, I should not have insisted at such length on this painful episode in Carnot's life, if I had not had opportunity of perceiving how far removed are such times from ours; if I had not seen, when accompanying our most illustrious officers of engineers in the inspection of some fortified towns, in the discussion of the amelioration they might be susceptible of, the simple *sous-lieutenant* freely oppose his ideas, reflections, and systems, with full liberty, to the opinions of the generals; surrender only after having been victoriously refuted; and come forth from the animated contest, not, as formerly, to go to the Bastille, but with fresh chances of advancement.

Those on whom the duty devolves of incessantly referring to the ameliorations of which our social state is susceptible, would become discouraged, Gentlemen, if, when occasion presents itself, we did not show the public that their endeavours have been sometimes crowned with success.

ESSAY ON MACHINES.—NEW THEOREM ON THE LOSS OF POWER.

The first—nay, more, the principal—scientific production of Carnot, bears the date of the year 1783; it is entitled *Essay on Machines in general.*

They who would seek in the essay of our member the technical description or special study of any one of the machines in particular, simple or composite, from which man has been able to derive so many advantages, would labour to no purpose. Such was not, indeed, the end which the author had in view.

A machine, considered generally, is the assemblage of a more or less considerable number of fixed or movable pieces, by the aid of which forces of all sorts ordinarily produce effects which their direct action could not bring about. Take, for instance, the stone-mason with his hand on the handle of a very simple machine, the winch of the lifting-jack or the roller; he turns about enormous blocks, or inclines them to suit his convenience, or raises them to the summit of the highest buildings, when, without the machine, he could not stir them a hair's breadth.

At sight of these effects, the ignorant make great outcry at the marvel; they persuade themselves that machines multiply force, and this false idea, radically false, leads them into fantastic and generally very complicated conceptions, which take away an immense quantity of capital every year, in pure loss, from agriculture, and manufacturing industry, and commerce.

With a force of any nature whatsoever, that which must be valued in money, that which the fabricator buys from the engineer, may be easily referred to a very simple effect, of which every one has a clear idea. Let the force be supposed directly applied to the raising of a weight; the height to which the force raises the weight in a certain time is observed, and these two data from experiment, the weight and the height, multiplied together form a product which is the exact value of the force employed. This product, indeed, for a given time and the same height, cannot be augmented or diminished without the force augmenting or diminishing in the same proportion; so that, for example, if it becomes double, triple, or decuple, it is the result of the force being multiplied by two, three, or ten.

The product, which gives the direct measure of a force, serves equally to measure it when it exercises its action against a resisting body by an intermediate machine; well, endow this machine, if you please, with the power of thought and all the perfections imaginable, and the product of the weight multiplied by the height it will have passed through in a given time, will be exactly equal to that obtained by the employment of the same force without any intermediate operation. The real effect, then—or, to speak more strongly, the effect of any machine when properly estimated—will never surpass that which the motive force was capable of producing naturally. Doubtless you can, if you like, with a machine, raise enormous masses, of millions or thousands of millions of pounds; but since the product of the weight, multiplied by the height, must remain constant, the height to which these masses can be raised in a minute will be millions or thousands of millions of times smaller than that to which your hand might have raised one pound in the same time.

Every one will now understand the true meaning of that aphorism in mechanics, Machines lose in time or velocity what they gain in power! Give me a point of support situated outside the earth, cried Archimedes, and I will, with the aid of a lever, raise this earth, so large and massive, by the mere effort of my hand. The exclamation of the immortal geometer was marvellously characteristic of machines, in so far as they give to man the means of realizing effects otherwise millions of millions of times beyond his natural strength; but antiquity would no doubt have admired it much less if any one, analyzing phenomena more closely, as we have just done, had added: Yes, doubtless, mathematically speaking, with his fulcrum and lever Archimides might raise the globe; but, after forty million centuries of continuous effort (for such a calculation is not, at the present day, beyond the limits of science), the movement effected would be hardly the breadth of a hair.

If the ideal machine, the machine endowed with all imaginable perfections, adds nothing to the force which puts it in action, at any rate it takes nothing away from it; it transforms the effects by rigorous equivalents. It is not thus with a real machine; in this case the power and the resistance communicate with one another by means of pieces which we had supposed inflexible, and which are not so; by means of chains and cords whose roughness cannot but be injurious; the movable parts, moreover, turn in collars or sockets where great friction takes place; all these causes united absorb in pure loss a very noticeable part of the motive force; so that the effect of a machine must always be inferior to that which would have been engendered by the power acting directly on the resistance.

These results of theory, which are, moreover, completely confirmed by experience, yet allow that, under certain points of view, some particular machine may be recommended without paradox; that it may be useful and often even indispensable. For instance, considerations of solidity or ornament necessitate the carrying to the summit of certain edifices blocks of stone or marble whose weight is beyond the strength of the most vigorous workman; suppress the windlass and analogous machines, and one man will no longer be able to execute the work which the architect has conceived; it will be necessary to unite the strength of thousands of arms at the same point; the narrowness of space will prevent that; the character of grandeur will disappear from all the monuments of architecture; the triumphal arch, the palace, will only be constructed, like the humble cottage, of little rough stones.

You see, Gentlemen, that there are cases, it cannot be too often repeated, in which we must resign ourselves, whether we will or no, to the loss of force consequent on machines, since, without their help, certain works would become impossible.

The losses of force which depend on the flexibility of the materials of which machines are composed, on the roughness of cords, and on friction, had been remarked by the most ancient mechanicians; modern ones have gone farther; their experiments enable them to appreciate these losses and value them in numbers with tolerable exactness. Science had arrived thus far, when Carnot published his Essay. In this work, our member, looking on machines, and even more generally on every system of movable bodies, from an entirely new point of view, indicates a cause unperceived, or at any rate imperfectly analyzed, by his predecessors, and which in certain cases must also give rise to considerable losses; he shows that we ought, by all means, to avoid abrupt changes of velocity. Carnot does more; he finds the mathematical expression of the loss of active force which such changes occasion; he shows that it is equal to the active force by which all the various bodies of the system would be animated, if each of them were endowed with the complete velocity which it lost at the instant of the abrupt change being affected.

Such is, Gentlemen, the enunciation of the principle which, under the name of "Carnot's Theorem," plays so great a part in the calculation of the effect of machines.

This beautiful and valuable theorem is now well known to all engineers; it guides them in practice, and secures them from the gross faults committed by their precursors.

To give an idea of its importance to the generality of the world, I should be inclined to say, notwithstanding the fantastic appearance of the comparison, that Carnot has extended to the material world a proverb whose truth was only established, before his time, in the moral world; that "much noise * and little work" is a saying henceforth quite as applicable to the effective labours of machines, as to the enterprises of certain individuals whose petulance gives rise to the hope of wonders destined not to be realized. In addressing men of learning, I would beg them to distinguish carefully between the invention of the material organs by whose aid forces transmit their action from one point to another, and the discovery of those primordial truths which are applicable indistinctively to all imaginable systems; I will endeavour to show that in this first respect the ancients were perhaps not inferior to us. The screw of Archimedes, the series of toothed wheels of Ctésibius, the hydrostatic fountains of Heron of Alexandria, the steam rotating machine of the same engineer, a great number of warlike machines, and amongst them the balista, might all be brought forward to strengthen my view. In the field of theoretical truths, on the contrary, the preponderance of the moderns would show itself incontestable.† There we should see successively, in all their brilliancy, in Hol-

* The proverb does not fit at all neatly, unless "noise" be taken to mean "irregularity;" some good machines are very noisy.—*Translator*.

† The question is rather unfairly stated against the ancients; for Arago speaks as if Archimedes, &c., had only *made* their machines, and not been masters of the principles, which involved as much primordial truth as any other discoveries. A fairer distinction seems to be, that the moderns launched out into realms where *theory* alone could point out the way; the ancients were led on by *experiment* and *observation*.—*Translator*.

land, Stévin and Huyghens; in Italy, Galileo and Torricelli; in England, Newton and Maclaurin; in Switzerland, Bernouilli and Euler; in France, Pascal, Varignon, D'Alembert, Lagrange, and Laplace.

Well, Gentlemen, those are the illustrious personages amongst whom Carnot made a place for himself by his beautiful theorem.

Perhaps, indeed, I ought to be afraid that, by insisting any longer on the inconvenience of abrupt changes, I may inspire my audience with the desire that I should, notwithstanding every inconvenience, pass "abruptly" to another subject; nevertheless, I will hazard a few more words.

We have just been talking frequently of lost force; the expression is correct when we compare the actual effect of a machine with that which it might have produced if, all other circumstances remaining the same, the constructor had carefully avoided sudden changes of speed; but it must not be imagined that any force, or fraction of a force, can be ever annihilated, in the grammatical acceptation of the word; all that which is not found in the useful effect produced by the motive power, nor in the amount of force which it retains after having acted, must have gone towards the shaking and destroying of the machine.

This last remark was necessary for the appreciation of the eminent and incontestable services which Carnot's theorem has already rendered and will render more and more to art and industry. If I were not afraid of the incredulity which would, at first sight, attach itself to my words, I would add that this same theorem of analysis and mechanics has also played a great part in the numerous events of our Revolution, whose character Carnot's determinations were able to change. However, I have said too much not to complete the idea.

In my youth, encouraged by the good-will and friendship with which Carnot was kind enough to honour me, I sometimes took the liberty of calling his recollection to those great epochs of our revolutionary annals, when parties, in their frenzied convulsions, were destroyed, conquered, or merely appeased, by abrupt and violent measures, by real coups d'état. Then I would ask our colleague how he, alone amongst all the others, had constantly hoped to arrive at the goal without shocks, and without infringement of the laws; his answer, always the same, had become deeply graven on my memory; but what was my surprise when, emerging one day from the round of studies which a young astronomer should always impose on himself, I found, word for word, this constant answer which we have just been discussing in the enunciation of a theorem of mechanics; when I saw that our colleague had always discoursed with me on the political organization of society precisely in the same manner as he speaks in his work of a machine, in which abrupt changes necessarily involve great losses of force, and sooner or later bring about the complete dislocation of the system!*

Can it then be true, Gentlemen, that in the weakness of the human race, the loftiest spirits have been so little convinced of the goodness and truth of the determinations which their hearts inspire them with, that they have found it necessary to confirm and corroborate them with more or less forced assimilations?

* This parallel cannot be deemed exact: in the Revolution they wanted to destroy one machine altogether, and supply quite another; so the rules applicable to steady machinery, or government, do not apply.—*Translator.*

This doubt will not astonish you if I add that one of the learned men whose works have conferred the greatest distinction on this Academy, conducted himself on all difficult occasions (so we are to believe) according to the following assuredly very convenient maxim: "Water takes exactly the form of the vase which contains it; a wise mind should as faithfully model itself on the circumstances of the moment."

I might quote also another of our colleagues, equally celebrated, of whom a certain personage asked one day in my presence, by what secret he had passed through the terrible periods of our civil discords without mishap: "Every country in a state of revolution," answered he, "is a carriage of which the horses have taken the bit between their teeth; to wish to stop the horses is to rush on a catastrophe from gayety of heart; he who leaps from the carriage exposes himself to being crushed under the wheels; the best plan is to abandon one's self to the movement, and shut one's eyes; so did I!"*

In the work whose analysis has carried me farther than I expected, Carnot has devoted some lines to the question of perpetual motion! He shows not only that every machine, of whatever form, abandoned to itself will stop, but he moreover assigns the moment at which that must happen.

The arguments of our colleague are excellent; no geometer will dispute their exactness; may we yet hope that they will nip in the bud the numerous projects which every year, or rather "every spring," sees burst into flower?

This is what we cannot hope for. The contrivers of

* If the horses could not be stopped, surely an attempt should be made to guide them.—*Translator.*

perpetual movements would no more comprehend the work of Carnot, than the discoverers of the quadrature of the circle or the trisection of the angle understand the geometry of Euclid.* Science is not needed by them; they owe their discovery to a sudden supernatural inspiration. Moreover, nothing discourages them, nothing undeceives them; take, for example, that artist, otherwise highly estimable, who, without perceiving any thing innocently burlesque in the terms of his request, begged me to go and see "*why all his perpetual movements had stopped.*"

CARNOT A POLITICIAN AND ONE OF THE JUDGES OF LOUIS XVI.

Carnot was one of the first officers of the French army that loyally and enthusiastically embraced the regenerative views of the National Assembly. Nevertheless, the annals of the Revolution only commence making mention of him in 1791.

Certain writers wrongly take the spirit of proselytism as the just measure of the sincerity of political convictions; they do not understand how a retired and studious life may ally itself to a profound desire for social reforms; Carnot's two years of inaction seem to them quite a phenomenon. Now, guess how they deemed it advisable to explain it. They place our member amongst the émigrés of Coblentz; thus his republican tendencies would only date from the period at which he furtively reëntered France. I will not offend you, Gentlemen, by refuting such a ridiculous supposition.

In 1791 Carnot was in garrison at Saint-Omer, and

* Not quite a just comparison. There is no reason why these geometric feats *must* be impossible, as is the case with perpetual motion. —*Translator.*

there married Mademoiselle Dupont, daughter of a military administrator born in that country. His political principles, the moderation of his conduct, and his varied knowledge, shortly procured him the honour of representing the department of the Pas-de-Calais in the Legislative Assembly. From this period Carnot gave himself up entirely to the imperious duties which were imposed on him, either by the choice of his fellow-citizens, or the voice of his colleagues. The public character almost entirely absorbed that of the geometer: this last only showed itself henceforth at long intervals.

Here, Gentlemen, two roads present themselves to me; one is smooth and open, the other bordered by precipices. If I listened to some persons whose good will towards me has rendered them timid, I should not hesitate to choose the first. To take the other would be to incur, I am well aware, the reproach of imprudence and blindness. Heaven keep me from supposing that I am strong enough to struggle against such clear and decided opinions; but wretched considerations of self-love will always vanish from my sight before the sentiment of duty. Now, I ask, should I not deeply wound the public conscience if, in this area consecrated to the arts, letters, and sciences, I confined myself to speaking of Carnot as an academician? Without doubt one might, whilst developing before you the long series of discoveries of this or that illustrious savant, endowed during his life with the title of senator, legitimately—very legitimately—cry out that posterity would not preserve any recollection of functions without effect, and which, moreover, descending from one degradation to another, had ended by reducing themselves to a monthly communication with the treasury; but it would be an antinational and ungrateful act to apply such words to the great shade of Carnot. I am desired, wished, and almost ordered to do this. Well! I consent, I will not speak of the drama whose "dénouement" was the tragic death of the successor of a hundred kings, and the overthrow of the monarchy; nevertheless I, a decided partisan of the abolition of the punishment of death, do not perceive the supposed difficulties of position which should have hindered me from abandoning myself here publicly to the inspirations of my conscience; nor do I see any better, why I should have abstained from rendering this assembly aware of the deep aversion which I profess for every political decree issued by a political body. Must I say it, in a word?—a fraternal solicitude for the memory of Carnot did not appear to me to require the sacrifice which is imposed upon me. Is it forgotten how contemporaneous history would have furnished me with accusing documents against the thousand courtiers whose interested, hypocritical, and antinational manœuvres cast the monarch into a labyrinth without exit, caused him to be unanimously declared culpable by the national representatives, and were much more instrumental than the ardent democratical ideas of the Convention in rendering the catastrophe of the 21st of January inevitable? If from these high moral considerations I had descended to a minute appreciation and technical discussion of facts, such as one has to submit to a court of appeal or of repeal, I should, in company with all upright minds—with our Daunou, for example,—have found the illegality of the celebrated trial, less in the nature of the sentence, less in the severity of the punishment inflicted, than in the very composition of the tribunal, or in the usurpation of power which had given birth to it. Now, Gentlemen, —and this is a point I should not have failed to remark on,—when the Convention was investing itself with the right of pronouncing on the fate of Louis XVI.; when after this stroke it was regulating its jurisprudence; when it was simultaneously attributing to itself the functions of accuser and judge, Carnot was absent from Paris; he was fulfilling with the armies one of those important missions, the difficulties of which his ardent patriotism always found the secret of surmounting.

CARNOT A MEMBER OF THE COMMITTEE OF PUBLIC SAFETY.

The concession which was required of me, if I con formed exactly to it, nevertheless authorizes me to show myself less docile on the subject of another period of Carnot's life, which is still more stormy and difficult. Let us avoid—I willingly consent to it—carrying our attention back to certain irritating phases of our civil discords; for my own part, I will only put one condition on it; that is, that the memory of none of our members shall suffer by it. Well, Gentlemen, suppose for a moment that I be now silent concerning the "Member of the Committee of Public Safety;" would it not be concluded from my silence—nay more, would it not be right to conclude from thence—that I have recognized the impossibility of repelling the violent, numerous, and *trenchant* attacks of which he was the object? These attacks Carnot, whilst living, was able to disdain; in me, on the contrary, it was incumbent to seek for their origin, and conscientiously weigh their value. I say it without exaggeration, no human power should have decided me to cause the name of Carnot to reëcho here, unless I had discovered the honourable and patriotic causes of certain acts which the most atrocious of calumnies, political calumny, had soiled with its infected slaver. My work, furthermore, was not without some difficulties. Perhaps no one henceforth will have the opportunity to reunite its elements. In a few years, indeed, the colleagues and fellow labourers of Carnot, from whom I have been able to gather some lights and evidences, will have paid the debt of nature.

In 1793 the convention was the only organized power in the State, capable of opposing an effective dyke against the overflow of enemies, who came from all parts of Europe to cast themselves on France, and menace her nationality. The nationality of a people is like honour: the slightest wound to it becomes mortal. Such were, Gentlemen, the sentiments of very many members of the Convention, whose memory France reveres; such were the ties which attached them to the perilous post whither election had called them.

In creating the "Committee of Public Safety," (6th April 1793,) the Convention had reserved to itself the choice of its members. Up to the famous 31st of May, it counted only neutral members, or at any rate such as were strangers to the factions of the Assembly who were combating each other to the death. After several partial renewals it was composed, on the 11th September 1793, of Robespierre, Saint-Just, Couthon, Collot d'Herbois, Billaud-Varennes, Prieur (of the Marne), Prieur (of the Côte-d'Or), Carnot, Jean-bon Saint-André, Barère, Hérault de Séchelles, and Robert Lindet.

The Convention, when it delegated such great powers to the Committee of Public Safety, desired that every affair should be a subject of profound discussion and deliberation in that committee; that the majority of voices should decide. The decisions, to acquire the force of law, under pain of being null, must be furnished with a certain number of signatures. These prescriptions had the greatest of all faults, that of being completely impracticable. Man has discovered in our days the secret of going ten times as fast when he travels, of using less force when he acts, and of casting his searching gaze into the regions of infinity; but he has not yet discovered the means of reading a page of manuscript in less time than it formerly occupied. We must allow that in that respect, the most humble merchant's clerk would advance equally with Cæsar or Cicero, Descrates or Bossuet. The innumerable dispatches which the Committee of Public Safety received daily, from all points of the frontiers menaced or invaded, from all the towns and villages of the interior where the promoters of a new political organization were in violent conflict with the prejudices and interests of the privileged classes, could not be maturely examined. Zeal, activity, and devotion were not sufficient to expedite so many weighty affairs; a reform was indispensable; it concerned the safety of France. Two different ways presented themselves: they could demand the reorganization of the Committee, or divide the work amongst its various members. The reorganization of the Committee, in presence of a powerful enemy, and in the midst of unheard-of difficulties (such as no period of the history of nations had given an example of), would have excited in the Convention new ferments of disorder, enervated its magic power, and compromised the defence of the territory. The division of labour should prevail, and it did prevail. Carnot was charged with the organization of the armies and with their operations; Prieur (of the Côte-d'Or) with arming them; Robert Lindet with provisioning them;

Robespierre, Saint-Just, Couthon, Billaud-Varennes, and Collot d'Herbois, reserved to themselves politics, general police, and measures of security. In each species of subject one signature alone was important, and carried responsibility; the others, though required by law, were to be regarded as the accomplishment of a simple formality: it was evident, indeed, that they would have to be given without discussion and even without examination.

Such were, Gentlemen, the bases of the agreement which Robert Lindet, for his personal security, caused to be put down in a written declaration, and by the aid of which the members of the Committee of Public Safety expected to be able, without passing beyond the terms of their mandate, to exorcise the storms which were menacing the country from all sides. This confiding arrangement will doubtless be blamed: some will cry out at its illegality, others at its imprudence. I will remind the first, that the members of the Committee, entangled in a faulty organization, were every day at issue with an impossibility, and that the word *impossible* is French, whatever national *amour propre* may have said of it at a period when the admirable triumphs of our armies seemed to warrant all hyperbolic speeches. The reproach of imprudence I admit without reserve. I add that, on the part of Carnot, this imprudence was voluntary; that in resigning himself to signing, without examination, the decisions of all his colleagues, he wittingly made the greatest of all sacrifices to France; that he placed his honour in the hands of several of his declared enemies; that, counting eventually on the tardy justice of posterity, he hoisted that almost superhuman motto of one of the most powerful organizations which the Revolution brought to land from the waves of the people,—that motto which moreover every sincere patriot endowed with any warmth of soul might avow : *Perish my reputation sooner than my country.*

You will have already understood, Gentlemen, that my design is to divide into two distinct categories the members of the Committee of Public Safety, and the long series of its acts.

The terrible Committee contributed powerfully to the defence of the territory: thanks to the Committee! There was no other way of resisting the thousand passions let loose, than by vigour of determination; by energy of will; by seizing everywhere with a grasp of iron the barbarians who, auxiliaries of the foreigner, would have torn out the entrails of their country; the Committee showed itself energetic and vigorous; it often showed the grasp of iron: all praise to the Committee!

But, Gentlemen, firmness soon degenerates into frenzy; soon they immolate the rich for the sole reason that they are rich; soon terror reigns through France from one end to the other; terror carries mourning and despair without distinction, as well into the family of the common soldier as into that of the general; she seizes her victims equally in the humble dwelling of the artisan, as in the gilded palace of the former duke and peer; she spares neither age nor sex; she strikes blindly all shades of opinion; finally, adding dissimulation to cruelty, she parodies the forms of justice! Ah! Gentlemen, at this spectacle the heart grows faint, and hope withers; the liveliest and most ardent sympathies gives place to profound grief.

I am aware that attempts have been made to explain,

even to excuse, those bloody saturnalia, by referring them to the will of the people. But if I judge of the people of 1793, whom I have not known, by that which I saw in action in 1830, the explanation is false. I do not hesitate to say so. The people in a moment of effervescence and blindness, sometimes fall into culpable actions, but it has never associated itself with daily barbarities. It is degrading the people to say, that fear only could drive it to meet inimical hordes: nor are its sentiments better known, when it is insinuated that it wished for the death ot one of the members of this Academy who honoured France by his genius; and the death of another of our co-academicians, who did honour to human nature by his virtue. No, Gentlemen; no! in the noble country of France, the death of Lavoisier, the death of Malesherbes, could not be ordered by considerations for the public good. No excuses for such crimes; they must be branded to-day, they must be branded to-morrow; they must be branded for ever. Devoted by sentiment, by conviction, by the irresistible power of logic to the worship of liberty, let us repel far from us the execrable thought, that the scaffold is the inevitable auxiliary of democracy.

The crimes that I have been openly denouncing have been in some measure personified by France, by Europe, by the whole world: these crimes are Robespierre! Some young, some estimable writers, who are now despoiling our revolutionary annals with the indefatigable patience of the Benedictines of former ages, think they have discovered that public opinion is quite wrong. According to them, Robespierre and his partisans have much less contributed to the sanguinary acts of terror, than the Billaud-Varennes, the Collot d'Herbois, or the

Heberts. There is courage, Gentlemen, in coming forward as the defenders of a man, who for nearly half a century has been regarded as the symbol, the type, of political cruelty. On this claim alone the new historians hope to be listened to without prejudice: an honourable character, joined to incontestable talent, gives them no less a right to the serious attention of the public. For my part, I have no business here to try to pierce those thick clouds; my subject does not require it; I will absolve Carnot from all participation in great crimes, without examining whether they should be imputed to Collot d'Herbois, or to Billaud-Varennes, rather than to Robespierre, Saint-Just, and Couthon.

In no instance of his long political career, was Carnot a party-man. Never was he found to try to bring forward his opinions, his systems, his principles, by tortuous ways that honour, that justice, that probity, could not have acknowledged.

In reporting on the 9th of June 1792, on the commission charged to propose some reparation in favour of the families of Theobald Dillon and of Berthois, who were massacred by their own troops before Lille, he does not coquette with his rigorous duty. Any other man, in such harassing times, might perhaps have thought it requisite to consider the susceptibility of the army; but he seemed to think no words too severe to brand such an odious act of wrong-headedness: he exclaimed, "I will not remind you of the circumstances of that atrocity. Posterity, in reading our history, will deem it rather the crime of a horde of cannibals, than that of a free people."

In 1792, some National Guards, under the name of *confederates*, assembled in great numbers at Soissons, and already formed there the nucleus of an army of reserve. All at once a report was spread at Paris, that the bread of those volunteers had been poisoned, that some monsters had mixed pounded glass with all the flour furnished to them, that two hundred soldiers had died already, and the hospitals were overflowing with sick men. The exasperation of the Parisian populace rose to its highest pitch: the depôt at Soissons was formed against the royal will; the crime then must be imputed to the King, to the Queen, to all their adherents. Before acting, they only awaited the report of the commissary who had been sent to the camp. This commissary was Carnot. His truthful examination reduced all this phantasmagoria to nothing: there were no men dead: there were no men sick: the flour was not poisoned; but some panes of glass, broken by the wind, or by the ball of some recruit, had fallen from the window of an old church, and happened (not pulverized, but in large pieces,) to lie on one single bag of flour. The upright testimony of the honest man calmed the popular tempest.

He was not a *party-man* (understood of course in its unfavourable meaning); but one who, often charged with important missions to the armies and to the interior, fulfilled his duties with such moderation, that he could safely, when circumstances required it, without fear of being contradicted, publicly render to himself the testimony of never having caused the arrest of any one. By searching into the offices of the Committee of Safety, we should there find equally clear proofs of the benevolent indulgence of Carnot towards persons professing different political opinions from his, provided always that they were united to honest dealing, and a warm antipathy to the intervention of foreigners in the internal affairs of France. Thus we shall see, under the name of Michaux, amidst the fellow labourers of our academician, the celebrated Darçon, who had emigrated, but returned to his country. Still, what occasion is there to drag our audience through individual instances, when a general reflection will lead to the same result? The Convention was the arena where the chiefs of the factions that divided the country, went to combat; yet it was in the *Clubs* that they created those adherents, and obtained that bodily strength, whose action, and even whose mere presence, often sufficed to annul the effects of the most eloquent discourses. If the Convention saw the thunder-cloud burst, it was outside its walls that it began to threaten, that it swelled, that it acquired an irresistible power. Men could not then acquire political influence without attending daily either at the Jacobins or at the Cordeliers, and mixing and taking part in all their debates: well, Gentlemen, Carnot did not belong to any of those associations; never did a word of his echo in those Clubs. In those troublous times, Carnot made himself exclusively *a man of the nation.*

The character was high, but not without danger. Robespierre especially was jealous of him, and exclaimed in one of his harangues: "To have taken the command of all the military operations, is decidedly *an act of egotism;* obstinately refusing to take any part in the affairs of internal police, is contriving means of accommodation with the enemies of the country."—He said to Cambon on another occasion: "I am in despair at not comprehending anything of the intersection of lines and tints, that I see on those maps. Ah! if I had studied the military art in my youth, I should not now be obliged, whenever our armies are treated of, to submit to the supremacy of the odious Carnot." This animosity began from the epoch when our fellow academician blamed the *coup d'état* (as such) under which the Gironde fell. About the same time, Saint-Just accused him of *moderatism,* and demanded that he should be tried for having refused, while with the army of the North, to put his signature to the order for arresting General O'Moran. Carnot always came out safe and sound from these terrible crises; not from a sentiment of justice or affection, but because every one, friend as well as foe, felt the impossibility of replacing him effectually in his special military character by any other *conventionalist!*

Similar relations between the co-members of a council would now appear fabulous! Is it *my* fault then, if our weak patriotism cannot conceive all the extent of the sacrifices that our fathers imposed on themselves to save our country?

You will remember, Gentlemen, that I did not hesitate to place in the first rank of these sacrifices the obligation which our colleague felt, of blindly signing a quantity of decrees issued by his colleagues. I have explained how this necessity had *manifested* itself; well, it was so abused, that on one occasion, Carnot was made to sign the order for arresting his own secretary; another time that for arresting the *restaurateur* in whose house he took his meals. The word *infernal* seems to me really too feeble for characterizing such acts; and yet, to the honour of our colleague, we must almost congratulate ourselves that they occurred, since they yield an insurmountable and speaking proof of the written arrangement which was agreed to in committee, in the name of *the safety of the country.*

I had read, even in royalist works, and I had read also in some writings published by republicans, that Carnot had saved, in the Committee of Public Safety, more men than his colleagues had immolated. Carnot, then, did not absent himself from the meetings except when military affairs entirely absorbed his time; Carnot, then, sometimes attended the deliberations of the Committee, and on those occasions innocence could depend on an advocate full of feeling and firmness. Only a few days ago, chance enabled me to discover that the part of volunteer defender was not the only one that Carnot took upon himself.

There is amongst you, Gentlemen, a venerable academician equally versed in theoretical and in applied mathematics; he has gloriously attached his name to some useful labours, and to some vast projects that the future, perhaps, will realize. He has gone through a long career, without making, certainly without deserving, an enemy! and yet his head was once menaced, and some wretches wished to make it fall, at the very time that he was projecting one of the scientific monuments that have reflected most honour on the revolutionary era. An anonymous letter informed our colleague of his danger. The storm is dissipated, but it may gather again in an instant; the friendly hand traces out a line of conduct; rules of prudence point out the necessity of preparing a retreat. Nor will it leave the work unfinished, but will again take up the pen if the danger reappears.

The anonymous writer, Gentlemen, was Carnot; the geometer whom he thus preserved to science, and to our affections, was M. de Prony. At that epoch Prony and Carnot had never seen each other.

The years 1793 and 1794 were characterized by two sorts of *terror:* the terror of the interior, I have just proved, Gentlemen, our colleague was always a stranger to, as to any thing criminal in it; but the terror which the French soldiers inspired in the innumerable enemies that came from every part of Europe to assail our frontiers,—this sort of terror was indeed the work of Carnot; it was glorious; the recollection of it will be immortal; I claim it for the memory of our colleague; I claim it also for the honour of the Academy. You will not refuse, Gentlemen, again to follow Carnot in this fine and brilliant phase of his public career. I am assured in this hope by your devotion to our country.

CARNOT ENTRUSTED WITH THE ORGANIZATION AND DIRECTION OF OUR ARMIES.

At divers epochs, in France as well as in other countries, simple administrators have been seen successfully to occupy the eminent positions of Minister of War, and Minister of Marine. The General-in-chief, the Admiral, was then entrusted with a command, with *carte blanche* as to the operations, and the ministers had nothing farther to do than to send regular and opportune provisions and reinforcements. Would you believe it, Gentlemen? it was in this confined circle that bad faith and envy wished to confine the decisive influence that Carnot exercised on our destinies. But it will be easy for us in a few words to tear to pieces this web of hideous ingratitude.

When our colleague became, in August 1793, member of the Committee of Public Safety, France was passing through a frightful crisis. The wreck of Dumouriez's army was repulsed from one position to another; Valenciennes, Condé, opened their gates to the enemy; Mayence, pressed by famine, and without the hope of relief, capitulated; two Spanish armies invaded our territory; 20,000 Piedmontese were crossing the Alps; the 40,000 Vendéans of Cathelineau were taking Bressuire, Thouars, Saumur, Angers; they menaced Tours, le Mans, and attacked Nantes on the right bank of the Loire, whilst Charette manœuvred on the opposite bank; Toulon received an English fleet into its port; in a word, our principal cities, Marseilles, Caen, Lyons, separated themselves violently from the central government.

You have now before your eyes, Gentlemen, a faint image of the dangers which menaced our country; and have some people dared to pretend that the Convention, that the terrible Convention, hoped to escape from the imminent catastrophe that almost all Europe thought inevitable, without even establishing a certain connection in the operations of its generals? and can it have been imagined that, in entrusting one of its members with the almost sovereign direction of its military affairs, it expected from him only the methodical measures and regulations compassed by a purveyor or *intendant* of an army? No, no! no one could possibly in good faith adopt such ideas.

Do not, however, believe that I undervalue Carnot's administrative services. I admire, on the contrary, their noble simplicity. There was not, assuredly, at that time in his administration, either that inextricable series of scribbling which the smallest affair entails on us in the present day; nor that artistic network entangling every one, from the junior clerk of the office up to the head of the department, in so intricate a manner, that the firmest and boldest hand could not hope to break a link or separate the elements. The chief used then to take a responsible, personal, and direct cognizance of the despatches that were addressed to him; the conceptions of the chosen man were not then exposed to perish under the blows of an envious multitude of poor intellects; a mere sergeant of infantry, then, (young Hoche) did not work only on the dusty papers in the archives, when he composed *A Memoir on the Means of penetrating into Belgium;* then, the perusal of this work drew from Carnot this prophetic exclamation: "That is a sergeant of infantry who will make his way." Then this sergeant, watched by the eye in all his actions, became, in the space of a few months, captain, colonel, brigadier-general, general of division, and general in chief; it was not then only a small class that was invested with the privilege of furnishing the chiefs of our armies; then, both in fact and by right, each soldier had promotions in his cartridge-box: splendid actions brought them out; yet the military force then, notwithstanding the important services that it rendered to the country, notwithstanding the disorders of that epoch, respectfully lowered its fasces before the civil authority, the proxy of the nation.

Let us cast a glance towards another phase of the military administration, and Carnot will not appear to us either less great or less successful.

There was a want of pure copper; at the cry of the distressed nation, science discovered in the bells of the convents, of the churches, of the public clocks, an inexhaustible mine, whence she might extract, without delay, all the metal that England, Sweden, and Russia refused her. There was no saltpetre; some lands, where formerly only enough of this substance would have been sought to add certainty to some delicate chemical analysis, furnish enough for all the requirements of our armies and our fleets. The preparation of shoe-leather used to require whole months of labour; such long delays did not suit the wants of our soldiers, and consequently the tanner's art received unhoped-for improvements; days will now take the place of months. The manufacture of arms is so minute, that its slowness seems inevitable; but immediately some mechanical aids are brought into action to strengthen, to direct, to take the place of the workman; the products increase in proportion to the demand for them. Until the year 1794, balloons had been only a mere object of curiosity; but at the battle of Fleurus, a balloon carries General Morlot into the region of the clouds; from thence the smallest manœuvres of the enemy are perceived, are signalized instantly, and this invention of purely French origin procures a splendid triumph for our army. Graphite pencils (black lead) are the pen and ink of an officer on a campaign; it is with the pencil that he writes a few words on the pummel of his saddle, which send thousands of infantry, of cavalry, of artillery-men into the thickest of the fight; graphite is one of the substances that Nature seems to have denied to our soil; the Committee of Public Safety orders it to be created of all sizes, and this order to make a discovery is executed without delay; thus the country is enriched with a new branch of industry. To be brief, for I must resign myself to not saying every thing, the first ideas of the telegraph are drawn from some folio books, wherein they had lain useless for ages; they are perfected, they are extended, they are applied, and from that moment the armies receive their orders in a few minutes; the Committee of Public Safety in Paris is enabled to follow all the events of the war, to the east, the north, the west, as if it were seated in the midst of the combatants.

These somewhat spontaneous creations, these patriotic directions given to so many noble intellects, this art, now lost, of exciting genius, of dragging it from its habitual indolence, will always occupy a large place in the annals of the Committee of Public Safety, and in the history of our colleague's life. Without departing, moreover, from the subject that now occupies us, we might still register many other services.

Carnot was one of that very small number of men who, in 1793, firmly believed that the Republic would sooner or later triumph over its innumerable enemies. Thus, although he gave to the present as large a portion of attention as circumstances demanded, yet having an eye to the future in his administration, he enriched France with many great institutions, the happy effects of which can only be slowly developed.

If time allowed me, I should have to cite amongst the great establishments towards the formation of which Carnot contributed, the first Normal School, the Polytechnic School, the Museum of Natural History, the Conservatory of Arts and Trades; and amongst the labours that he encouraged by his suffrage, was the measurement of the earth, the establishment of the new system of weights and measures, and the great, the incomparable statistic tables.

These are noble titles, Gentlemen, for an era of destruction.

The Convention put into the hands of Carnot the colossal, but incoherent mass of the *requisition*. It was requisite to organize it, to discipline it, to instruct it; Carnot produced from it *fourteen armies*. It was also requisite to create for it some able chiefs: our colleague knew, with a certain Athenian general, that *an army of Deer commanded by a Lion, would be worth more than an army of Lions commanded by a Deer.* Carnot dug without intermission in the fruitful and inexhaustible mine of junior officers; as I before said, his penetrating eye sought in the most obscure ranks for talent united with courage, with disinterestedness, and elevated it rapidly to the highest grades. It was necessary to coördinate so many various movements! Carnot, like Atlas in the fable, carried alone, during several years, the weight of all the military events in Europe; he wrote with his own hand to the generals; he gave them detailed orders, wherein all the eventualities were minutely foreseen; his plans, the one that he addressed to Pichegru, for instance, on the 21 Ventose, year II., seemed the result of real *divination.* Facts occurred so entirely justifying the forethought of our colleague, that to write an account of the memorable campaign of 1794, there would be scarcely a few proper names of villages to be altered in the instructions that he addressed to the commander-in-chief. The places where attacks were to be made, those where they were to limit themselves to demonstrations, to skirmishes; the strength of each garrison, of each post, all is indicated, all is regulated with admirable precision. It was by orders from Carnot that Hoche one day disappeared from before the Prussian army, traversed the Vosges, and, uniting himself to the army of the Rhine, went to strike a decisive blow on Wurmsur, which occasioned the deliverance of Alsace.

In 1793, while the enemy was expecting, according to the classic principles of strategy, to see our troops advance from the Moselle to the Rhine; whilst he was accumulating formidable means of resistance on the latter river, Carnot, without troubling himself about old theories, detached unawares 40,000 men from the army of the Moselle, and sent them to the Meuse by forced marches. Such was the celebrated manœuvre which decided the success of the campaign of 1793, during which the Austrian and Dutch generals had the double chagrin of being constantly beaten, and this against all rules. Yes, Gentlemen, the national tribune was but just, on the day when it echoed these noble words, which have now become historical: "*Carnot has organized victory.*"

CARNOT ON THE FIELD OF BATTLE AT WATTIGNIES.

It might be said of the French armies, as of certain painters, that they have had *various styles*. On the day of battle, it is true, the imperial armies and the republican armies precipitated themselves on the enemy with the same intrepidity; with this exception all else was different. The imperial soldier saw his country only in the ARMY; it was for the honour, for the glory of the army, that he shed his blood at Wagram, at Sommo-Sierra, at the Moscowa. The republican soldier fought for his COUNTRY; the national independence was the thought that, above all others, animated him in the combat; as to recompenses, he did not even dream of them.

Follow those same soldiers into private life, and you will see this dissimilitude continue. The imperialist remains a soldier both in his sentiments and in his manners; the republican, confounded in the mass of the population, becomes soon undistinguishable from an artisan, from a labourer, who had never quitted his workshop or his plough.

It is these shades, cleverly seized, artistically reproduced, that from the first day struck the public with such a lively admiration for the productions of David. One day, an officer of the Empire, known for his brilliant valour, said to me in the library of the Institute, "I cannot reconcile myself to seeing General Carnot in a man dressed *in short breeches and blue stockings.*" I took the opposite view; upon which he added, "Well, be it so! blue stockings may suit a general who was never *baptized by fire!*" Yesterday, also, with less roughness it is true, in word, one of our co-academicians reproduced in my presence the same thought. I shall then fulfil a duty by proving that, when occasion required, the man in blue stockings knew well how to risk his life.

The Prince of Cobourg, at the head of sixty thousand men, occupied all the outlets of the forest of Mormale, and blockaded Maubeuge. This town once taken, the Austrians would have met with no more serious obstacles to their reaching Paris. Carnot perceives the danger; he persuades his colleagues in the Committee of Public Safety that our army, notwithstanding its numerical inferiority, can give battle; that it must attack the enemy in its apparently impregnable positions. It was one of those critical moments that decide the fate, the existence of nations. General Jourdan hesitates under such a terrible responsibility. Carnot goes to the army; in a few hours all is arranged, all is agreed upon; the troops open out, they fall upon their enemies; but the latter are so numerous, they occupy so well chosen a position, they have dug so many entrenchments, they have furnished them so formidably with artillery, that success is uncertain. At the close of the day, our right wing had gained some ground; but the left wing had perhaps lost more. It had moreover left some guns in possession of the Austrians. Let us strengthen the left wing, exclaimed the old tacticians. No, no, replied Carnot; what signifies by which wing we triumph. It was necessary, with good will or ill will, to yield to the authority of the people's representative! The night is employed in breaking up the wing already compromised; its principal troops are marched to the right, and when the sun rose, it was in some measure a new army that Cobourg found opposed to him. The battle recommenced with fresh fury. Shut up in their redoubts, protected by woods, by palisades, by quickset hedges, the Austrians resist valiantly; one of our attacking columns is repulsed, and begins to disperse! Oh! who could describe the cruel anguish that Carnot experienced. Doubtless his imagination already represents to him the enemy penetrating into the capital, defiling along the boulevards, and abandoning themselves to those acts of Vandalism, with which in so many proclamations, in so many insolent manifestoes, we had been threatened! These distracting thoughts, however, do not abate his courage: Carnot rallies his soldiers, reforms them on a plot of ground; solemnly, before the whole army, degrades the general who, in disobeying positive orders, had allowed himself to be defeated; seizes the musket of a grenadier, and marches at the head of the column, in the civil costume of the representative of the nation. Nothing could now withstand the impetuosity of our troops; the charges of the Austrian cavalry are repelled with the bayonet; all who enter into the excavated roads around Wattignies are sure to meet with death. Carnot finally penetrated into the village, the very key of the position of the enemy's army, over heaps of dead bodies, and from that moment the siege of Maubeuge was at an end.

It will be asked, no doubt, where Carnot had gained this firmness, this vigour, the military *coup d'œil,* that knowledge of troops? Seek not for the source but in his ardent patriotism. It was at Wattignies that for the first time he heard the musketry and cannon of the enemy. But I am mistaken, Gentlemen; it is the second, and not the first time: the first time, Carnot, marching as at Wattignies, musket in hand, at the head of a new levy of soldiers, carried the town of Furnez by assault, then occupied by the English.

The battle of Wattignies, considered as to its results, will always occupy one of the foremost places in the annals of the French Revolution. I should probably be less positive on the difficulties of that day, compared with so many others, if I could not support myself by the opinion of the Prince of Cobourg himself. When he saw the French battalions begin to break, that general could not find terms too strong to express, in presence of his staff, the confidence that he felt in the number and ardour of his troops, and in the obstacles of all sorts, both natural and artificial, that the uneven ground occupied by the Austrians presented to the assailants. He exclaimed: "The Republicans are excellent soldiers; but if they dislodge me from this position, I will consent to become a Republican myself." Certainly nothing more decided or more energetic could issue from the mouth of Cobourg. For my part, I could not conceive a more glorious bulletin of the battle of Wattignies!

The German author from whom I have borrowed this anecdote does not say whether, after having dislodged him, the French summoned the Austrian general to keep his word. I have some reason to suppose that, notwithstanding their spirit of propaganda, they disdained a recruit who would have submitted, but whose vocation seemed very uncertain.

STATISTICS OF THE OPERATIONS OF THE ARMIES.

Carnot felt the propriety, the want, of showing towards the national armies a deference from which absolute governments formerly felt themselves free, whilst their soldiers were enrolled at a money price: each year he had to unroll to the eyes of the nation a detailed table of the battles given by our legions, and of the effects that had thence resulted. Here follows the conclusion of the recital of the campaign of seventeen months, during which the troops of the Republic never laid down their arms for a single day.

Twenty-seven victories, eight of which were pitched battles; 120 combats of minor importance; 80,000 enemies killed; 91,000 prisoners; 116 fortresses or strong towns taken, 36 of which had required to be besieged or blockaded; 230 forts or redoubts taken; 3,800 guns of various sizes; 70,000 muskets; 1,900 *milliers* (*tons*) of gunpowder; 90 flags. Let people, if they dare, after reading this table, say that statistics are not eloquent!

CARNOT, NAMED BY FOURTEEN DEPARTMENTS, ENTERS THE COUNCIL OF THE ELDERS, AND THEN THE EXECUTIVE DIRECTORY.—HOCHE SENT TO LA VENDÉE, MOREAU AND JOURDAN TO THE RHINE, AND BONAPARTE TO ITALY.

Carnot quitted the Council of Public Safety shortly before the insurrection of the Parisian sections against the Convention. Carry back your recollection towards the military events that followed the forced, though legal retreat of our colleague, and you will see almost everywhere that victory abandoned the standards of the Republic, and reverses succeeded each other, as triumphs did before; all the springs were unbent, mistrust and discouragement took possession of every mind; and you will then understand, better than by an uninterrupted series of brilliant successes, of what importance the genius of one man alone may be to the destiny of nations.

Carnot was called to the legislature which succeeded to the National Convention by *fourteen departments.* If I were allowed to express a personal sentiment, I would say how pleased I have been to find the name of the department of the Eastern Pyrenees, in the list of those which tried to reward our great citizen for the outrages that a handful of members, excited by the butcher Legendre, cast upon him on several occasions. A short time after he entered the Council of the Elders, Carnot, on the refusal of Sieyès, became one of the five members of the Executive Directory.

At the moment when he for the second time was thus called to direct our armies, the Republic had reached the verge of an abyss. The public treasury was empty. The Directory had great trouble even in procuring clerks and servants in their office, so much was it thought to be insolvent. The despatching of a courier was often delayed on account of the impossibility of providing for the expenses of the journey; the generals themselves no longer received the *eight francs* (I AM NOT MISTAKEN), the *eight francs per month* "en numéraire," (in cash,) that had been granted to them, as a supplement to their pay in assignats; the agricultural producers no longer supplied the markets; the manufacturers refused to sell their products, because there was a right to pay for them in paper-money, and paper-money then was of no value. From one end of France to the other, famine had thrown people into an extreme state of irritation, which daily manifested itself in sanguinary disorders. The army offered a no less deplorable aspect: it was deficient in means of transport, in clothing, in shoes, in munitions. Misery had engendered a want of discipline. Pichegru was weaving criminal relations with the Prince of Condé, allowed himself to be beaten at Heidelberg, compromised the army of Jourdan, evacuated Mannheim, raised the siege of Mayence, and ceded the frontier of the Rhine to the Austrians. War recommenced in La Vendée; the English threatened us with a descent in the Pays-Bas, and on our own coasts. In a word, on our Alpine frontier, Scherer and Kellermann painfully sustained a defensive war against the united forces of the Emperor of Austria, the King of Sardinia, and the confederated Italian princes.

Gentlemen, the great strength of mind, united to the most ardent patriotism, was requisite, under such cruel circumstances, to induce men to accept the burden of public affairs. Let us add that Carnot was so little blind to the faults of the Constitution of the year III., and, above all, to the inconveniences of a multiple executive power, that he had publicly pointed them out in the midst of the Convention, at the time when this constitution was discussed. He then exclaimed: "The destinies of the state will henceforward depend only on the personal character of five men. The more these characters differ, the more dissimilar will be the views of these five directors, and the more will the state have to suffer from their alternate influence." The majority disdained these just apprehensions; faithful to a line of conduct from which he was never seen to swerve, Carnot submitted without a murmur; and, as soon as the new government had received the legal sanction, he served it with the same energy, zeal, and devotion that he had before displayed as a member of the Committee of Public Safety.

La Vendée was on fire; Hoche receives orders from Carnot to pacify it, together with a new system of operations. This republican general complies, triumphs over Charette, takes possession of Stofflet, and clears the Morbihan of the numerous bands of *chouans* who ravaged it. In less than eight months, the civil war, that impious war, in which, however, great courage was displayed on both sides, ceased to desolate our territory.

On the Rhine, our armies are placed under the command of Jourdan and Moreau. A scientific and profound plan of the campaign connected the movements of those two generals, and soon carried their victorious troops into the heart of Germany.

In La Vendée, in Germany, on the Rhine, Carnot, as we have shown, had infused confidence into officers already celebrated by memorable triumphs. The command of the army of Italy he gave, on the contrary, to a general only twenty-five years of age, whose known claims were then restricted to some secondary services that he achieved during the siege of Toulon, and to the easy defeat of the Parisian Sectionaries, on the 13th Vendémiaire, year III., on the humble fields of battle of the Pont Royal and the Rue St.-Honoré, and the steps of St.-Roch. I here claim for Carnot the honour of having personally pointed out and selected the young General Bonaparte for the command of our third army, because it legitimately belongs to him; because this choice was long unjustly considered as the result of a boudoir intrigue; and because every one, I think, must be glad to see the history of the incomparable campaign of Italy purified from such a stain. I have thought, in short, that I ought not to neglect to show you your colleague discerning with infinite perspicacity the hero of Rivoli, of Arcole, of Castiglione, through the bark of timidity, of reserve,—let us out with the true word, of awkwardness,—that everybody then remarked in the *protégé* of Barras.

I foresee all the incredulity I should meet with, if I were to venture on still farther extending the limits of the influence that our colleague exercised over the Italian campaign; and yet, should I not have found, even in the small number of official documents already known to the public, under date of the 10th Floréal, year IV., for example, a despatch from the head-quarters of Chérasco, in which Bonaparte writes to Carnot:—"The armistice concluded between the King of Sardinia and ourselves, enables me to communicate through Turin, that is to say, to spare half the journey; *I could therefore quickly receive* YOUR ORDERS AND LEARN YOUR INTENTIONS, AS TO THE DIRECTION TO BE GIVEN TO THE ARMY." A letter to the Minister of Finance, of the 2d Prairial, year IV., dated from head-quarters at Milan, would afford the following sentence:—"The Executive Directory, who named me to the command of this army, HAS ARRANGED A PLAN OF OFFENSIVE WARFARE which requires prompt measures and extraordinary resources."

The 2d of Prairial, year IV. (May 21, 1796,) Carnot wrote thus to the young general:—"Attack Beaulieu before reinforcements can reach him; do not neglect any thing to prevent this junction; you must not weaken yourself before him, and above all, do not, by disastrously dividing your force, give him the means of beating us in detail, and retaking the ground he has lost. After the defeat of Beaulieu, you will make the expedition to Leghorn. . . . . The intention of the Directory is, that the army shall not pass beyond the Tyrol, until after the expedition to the south of Italy."

Doubtless, these general orders are not the campaign of Italy. No human intelligence could foresee either the route that General Beaulieu would follow after his separation from the Piedmontese army, nor the manœuvres of Wurmsur, nor the long resistance made at Mantua by that old general, nor the marches of Alvinzi, nor many glorious incidents which I abstain from recalling; without doubt it required all the hardihood and genius of Bonaparte, and the coöperation of such officers as Masséna, Augereau, Lannes, Murat, Rampon, to annihilate in a few months three large Austrian armies. Finally, all that I have wished to say is, that it would be unjust to entirely omit the name of Carnot in reciting those immortal campaigns.

I should have a right to say even more were we studying another phase of those wars,—their moral and civilizing phase. Who does not remember those treaties of peace, in which masterpieces of painting and of sculpture were inducements to pardon perfidy and treachery in our enemies, and the official visits of our victorious generals to diffident learned men, rendered illustrious by important discoveries? Well, Gentlemen, all this, whatever people may say of it, was prescribed by Carnot. Will any doubts still be entertained if I transcribe the following letter from our colleague, dated

"24th of Prairial, year IV.

"General, in recommending you, by our letter of the

26th Floréal, to visit and receive the celebrated artists of the countries in which you happen to be, we have especially designated the great astronomer Oriani, of Milan, as deserving of being protected and honoured by the republican troops. The Directory will learn with satisfaction that you have fulfilled its intentions respecting this learned and distinguished man, and it requests you consequently to relate what you have done to prove to citizen Oriani the interest and the esteem that the French have always felt for him, and to testify that they know how to unite the love of glory and liberty with a love for the arts and for talent."

PUBLICATION OF THE WORK ENTITLED "REFLECTIONS ON THE METAPHYSICS OF THE INFINITESIMAL CALCULUS."

The word science, which the series of events has just brought to my pen, reminds me that this epoch is that of the publication of one of Carnot's mathematical works. I am aware how fatiguing it will be to you to listen to the analysis of it; but it is quite necessary that the *savant* also should be occasionally represented in this assembly. The early and very remarkable work on machines of which we gave an idea, has sufficiently indicated how much we may expect from the firm, lucid, and penetrating mind of Carnot. It was then a brilliant and glorious future which the young officer brought as an offering to his country, when, obeying the voice of his fellow-citizens, he exchanged the smooth, tranquil life of the mathematician, for the adventurous and rock-bestrewn career of the tribune. This sacrifice, moreover, he did not make without regret; for geometry was always his favourite relaxation. Debarred by imperious daily duties from the pleasure of "*measuring himself with*" the grand problems whose solution requires years of continuous and persevering effort, Carnot chose those difficult but circumscribed questions which may be taken up, abandoned, and taken up again, by fits and starts; which an elevated mind capable of coping with difficult subjects, develops and fathoms without paper or pencil, either during a walk, in the midst of the excitements of a crowd, the gayeties of a banquet, or the vigils of laborious nights; in a word, he directed his meditations towards the "*metaphysics of the calculus.*" In the present day such researches would be, I fear, but little relished; nevertheless, if we recur to the times when mathematical studies gradually led to the consideration of quantities of such different natures, we shall be amply aware of the apprehension with which they inspired exact philosophers, and must acknowledge that, on many points, it is rather habit than true science which has rendered us more confident.

Amongst the quantities to which I have alluded, the "*irrational*" presented themselves first. The ancients scrupulously avoided using them; the moderns would also have wished to avoid the use of them; "*but they*" (the quantities) "*gained the day by their numbers,*" says the ingenious author of the "*Geometry of Infinites.*"

To the quantities which were not numerically assignable, succeeded the impossible quantities, the "*imaginary quantities,*" regular symbols of which it would be vain to attempt to give, not only the exact values, but even mere approximations. These imaginaries are nevertheless used in combination by addition and subtraction; they are multiplied and divided, the one by the other in the same manner as real quantities; at the end of the calculation the imaginaries sometimes disappear amongst the transformations which they undergo, and the result is then held to be quite as certain as if it had been arrived at without the help of these algebraic hieroglyphics. It must be confessed that, though thousands on thousands of applications of the calculus justify this confidence, few geometers fail to take credit to themselves for the absence of imaginary quantities in the demonstrations where they have been able to avoid them.

The "*infinite*" first made its irruption into geometry on the day when Archimedes determined the approximate proportion of the diameter to the circumference by assimilating the circle to a polygon "*with an infinite number of sides.*" Bonaventura Cavalieri afterwards went much farther in the same field of research; various considerations led him to distinguish some "*infinitely great* quantities" of several orders, from some *infinite quantities* which were nevertheless *infinitely smaller* than other quantities. Can we be astonished that, at sight of such results, and notwithstanding his lively predilection for combinations, which had led him to veritable discoveries, the ingenious Italian author should have exclaimed, in the style of that period, "*Here are difficulties of which even the arms of Achilles could make nothing!*"

The "*infinitely small*" quantities had, for their part, slipped into geometry even before the "*infinitely great*," and this not only to facilitate or abridge such and such demonstrations, but as the immediate and necessary result of certain elementary properties of curves.

Let us examine, in effect, the properties of the most simple of all—the circumference of a circle; and by that we will not understand the rugged clumsy curve which we should succeed in drawing by the aid of our compasses or best geometrical drawing-pens; but really the circumference of a circle endowed with an ideal perfection, really a curve without thickness and without roughness of any sort. Let us, in imagination, draw a tangent to this curve. At the point where the tangent and the curve touch one another, they will form an angle, which has been called the "*angle of contact.*" This angle, since the first origin of mathematical science, has been the object of the most serious reflections of geometers. Since two thousand years ago it has been rigorously demonstrated that no straight line, drawn from the apex of the angle of contact, can be included between its two sides, and that it cannot pass between the curve and the tangent. Well, I ask, what else is that angle into which an infinitely fine straight line cannot be introduced or insinuated, but an infinitely small quantity.

The infinitely small angle of contact, into which no straight line can be introduced, may nevertheless include between its two sides millions of circumferences of circles, all greater than the first. This truth is established by reasoning of an incontestable and uncontested force. Here, then, we have, in the very heart of elementary geometry, an infinitely small quantity, and, what is still more incomprehensible, susceptible of being divided as much as we please! The human intellect was humiliated and lost in face of such results; but, at any rate, these were results, and it submitted.

The infinitely small quantities which Leibnitz introduced into his differential calculus excited more scruples. This great geometer distinguished several orders of them, those of the second order might be neglected in relation with the infinitely small of the first; these infinitely small of the first order in their turn disappeared before finite quantities. At each transformation of the formulæ it might be possible, according to this hierarchy, to disembarrass one's self of fresh quantities; and, nevertheless, one was obliged to believe, to admit, that the definitive results were rigorously exact; that the infinitesimal calculus was not merely a mere method of approximation. Such was, considering the whole thing, the origin of the strong and tenacious opposition which the new calculus raised up at its birth; such was also the difficulty which a man equally celebrated as a geometer and a theologian, Berkeley, bishop of Cloyne, had in view when he exclaimed, addressing himself to the incredulous in matters of religion, "Look at the science of mathematics; does it not admit mysteries more incomprehensible than those of religion?"

These mysteries at the present day, exist no longer for those who desire to become initiated in the knowledge of the methods which constitute the differential calculus in Newton's theory of fluxions; in a paper wherein D'Alembert introduces the consideration of the limits towards which the ratios of the finite differences of functions converge; or, indeed, in Lagrange's *Theory of Analytical Functions.* Nevertheless, Leibnitz's course has prevailed, because it is more simple, easier to recollect, and more convenient in practice. It is, then, important to study it in itself, to penetrate into its essence, and to assure one's self of the perfect exactness of the rules which it furnishes, without the necessity of corroborating them by the results of the calculus of fluxions, or of limits, or of functions. That task,—I mean the search for the true spirit of differential analysis,—forms the principal object of the book which Carnot published, in 1799, under the modest title of *Reflections on the*

Metaphysics of the Infinitesimal Calculus. I am bold enough to assert that the authors, otherwise so excellent, of the best treatises on the differential calculus, have not sufficiently consulted the work of our colleague. The advantages which ought to result from the immediate introduction of infinitely small or elementary quantities into formulas; the considerations by help of which it may be proved that the calculator, by afterwards throwing aside these quantities, will arrive nevertheless at mathematically exact results, by means of certain compensations for errors; in a word, the fundamental and characteristic traits of Leibnitz's method, are analyzed by Carnot, with a clearness, a certainty of judgment, and an ingenuity, which we should look for in vain elsewhere, though the question has been the object of the reflections and researches of the greatest geometers of Europe.

CARNOT BEING "FRUCTIDORISÉ" IS OBLIGED TO RECUR TO FLIGHT.—HE IS ERASED FROM THE LIST OF THE INSTITUTE, AND SUCCEEDED BY GENERAL BONAPARTE.

France has always shown itself an idolater of military glory. Satisfy this passion largely in a national war, and you need not be uneasy about the administration of the interior, however imperfect it may be. The sympathies of the people, and in case of need even their entire submission, may be gained by any government that takes care to adorn itself monthly with a new victory over its external enemies. I perceive but one exception to this rule in our annals. It is also requisite, however, that, by an assimilation, too often deceitful, the legal representatives of the country should be considered as the faithful interpreters of the wishes, the sentiments, the opinions of the majority. The exception to which I am about to allude, will be furnished by our Directorial government.

When the elections of the year V. brought a reinforcement of royalists to the two minorities of the Council of Five-Hundred, and of the Elders, who till then had limited themselves to making a very moderate opposition to the Directory; when, strong in what they thought the popular support, the minority, fancying that they had become the majority, took off the mask so far as to name for the presidency of the Council of Five-Hundred that same Pichegru, who not long before had branded with treason the laurels that he had gained in Holland in the name of the Republic; when the enemies of the Directorial power openly unveiled their projects in the saloons of the celebrated Clichy Club; when the recriminations, the reciprocal accusations, that had reached the utmost violence, were already succeeded by deeds of violence against patriots, and the gainers of national property,—our troops were yet everywhere triumphant. The army of the Rhine and Moselle under the orders of Moreau, the army of the Sambre and Meuse, commanded by Jourdan, had gloriously crossed the Rhine; they were marching into the heart of Germany; the army of Italy was only twenty leagues from Vienna; at Leoben, Bonaparte signed the preliminaries of the much wished-for treaty of peace. Without compromising the negotiations, he could show himself touchy about mere questions of etiquette; he could BLUNTLY refuse to let the name of the Emperor of Germany precede that of the French Republic in the protocols; he could also, when General Meerwald, and the Marquis del Gallo talked to him about gratitude, answer, without a boast, in the following memorable words: "The French Republic does not require to be recognized; it is in Europe what the sun is on the horizon: so much the worse for those who will not see and profit by it." Is it then surprising, Gentlemen, I ask you, that in so favourable a position of our foreign affairs, Carnot believed in the possibility of a conciliation between the political parties into which the country was divided; that he refused (I purposely use his own words) to exorcise danger by going beyond the limits of the Constitution; that he firmly repelled any thought of a *coup-d'état*,—a very convenient way assuredly of getting out of a scrape; but a dangerous way, and one that almost always ends by becoming injurious to the very persons who expected to benefit by it?

I should have much wished, Gentlemen, to have entered more deeply into an examination of the part that Carnot acted at that critical epoch of the Revolution. I have not neglected any thing to raise at least a corner of the veil which still covers an event that so greatly influenced the fate of our colleague, and that of the country; but my efforts, I acknowledge, have been unsuccessful. Documents are not wanting, but they almost all emanate from writers too much interested, either in excusing or in branding the 18th of Fructidor, not to be suspected. The recriminations full of bitterness, of violence against each other, to which some old colleagues then abandoned themselves, have reminded me of that wise declaration by Montesquieu: "Do not listen either to Father Tournemine or to me, when we are speaking of each other, for we have ceased to be friends." The antecedents, the opinions, the character, the known and avowed actions of the various persons who caused the *coup-d'état*,—or became the victims of it, would not have been any better guide. I should have seen Hoche march at one moment against his constant and zealous protector, against him who had saved his life under the rule of Robespierre, and who, in 1793, transformed the trimmings of the young sergeant into the epaulettes of a full general. I should have found Bonaparte contributing by his delegate Augereau, to the upsetting, and to the proscription of the only Director with whom he had continued intimately connected during the campaign of Italy. I should have seen him on his journey to Geneva have the banker Bontemps arrested, under pretext that he had favoured the escape of that same Carnot to whom a few months before, he, Bonaparte, wrote from Plaisance (20th of Floréal, year IV.), from Milan (the 20th of Prairial, the same year), from Verona (the 9th of Pluviose, year V.) : "I owe you special thanks for the attention that you kindly show to my wife ; I recommend her to you ; she is a sincere patriot, and I love her to madness . . . . I will deserve your esteem ; I beg of you to continue your friendship for me. . . . . The sweetest recompense for the fatigues, the dangers, the chances of this profession, is the approbation of the small number of men whom we appreciate. . . . . . I have always had to rejoice in the marks of friendship that you have shown to me and mine, and I shall always be truly grateful to you for them. . . . . The esteem of a small number of persons like yourself, that of my brother officers, of the soldier, interest me deeply."

Of the two sincere Republicans included in the executive Directory, I should have met one among the *Fructidorisants*, the other among the *Fructidorisés ;* the satrap Barras—of whom it might have been said, without exciting contradiction, that he was always sold, and always for sale—would have offered himself to me as the friend, as the ally, or at least as the intimate confidant, of the austere, the honest La Révellière; I should have seen that same Barras, who already, perhaps, at that epoch, corresponded directly with the Count de Provence, surrounded by a crowd of myrmidons, of whom none, be it said in passing, afterwards refused the imperial livery,—upset, by incessant accusations of royalty, the only man of our assemblies who, always constant in his convictions, battled foot by foot against the insatiable ambition of Bonaparte.

Seeking in the sequel by facts, and only by facts, whether the majority of the counsellors was really factious; whether the counter-revolution could not be avoided but by a *coup-d'état;* in a word, whether the 18th of Fructidor was inevitable, I should have found, and this notwithstanding the mutual concessions which the authors of the proscription no doubt made, as in the time of Octavius, of Lepidus, of Anthony,—I should have found an elimination, or, if you will, a filtering of forty-one members only, in the Council of the Five-Hundred, and of eleven in the Council of the Elders.

The thread that could safely guide the historian in this labyrinth of contradictory facts, I repeat it, I have not found. The memoirs snatched from the family of Barras by order of Louis XVIII.; the memoirs that were left by La Révellière, and of which it is so desirable that the public should be no longer deprived; the confessions which on the other hand, we have a right to expect on the part of some of the victims of the Directorial *coup-d'état,* may, perhaps, dissipate all the clouds. Would to God, for the honour of the country, that in the end, the violent and illegal mutilation of the national representation may not appear to be the exclusive result of the animosities and personal antipathies excited, or, at least, in great measure fostered, by the intrigues of several notorious women. Still the investigations of future historians, however extended and complicated they may be, can never militate against the perfect uprightness of our co-academician. Already there remain no vestiges of the accusations detailed in the official report presented in the year VI. to the Council of the Five-Hundred: in a few pages, Carnot reduced them to nought. All that malevolence or mere preconception dares to borrow now from the pamphlet elaborated with so much artifice by Bailleul, is reduced to an empty reproach coarsely expressed, and which I should have disdained to mention, had not Carnot himself indicated on what conditions he accepted it.

Political hacks call by the name of simpletons, all men who would disdain such advantages as are bought at the expense of good faith, honesty, and morality. But we must not be deceived; *simpleton* is the polite epithet; *blockhead* is preferred when we do not feel ourselves bound to keep within limits or to adhere to the language of good society. This epithet, disdainfully cast by Bailleul in the official report, had cruelly mortified Carnot; it is ironically repeated in almost every page of our colleague's answer. He says in one part: "Yes! the blockhead Aristides is chased from his country; the blockhead Socrates drank hemlock; the blockhead Cato is reduced to commit suicide; the blockhead Cicero is assassinated by order of the triumvirs. Yes! the blockhead Phocion is also led to the scaffold, but glorying in having to undergo the fate reserved in all ages for those who serve their country well."

Carnot escaped from the Luxembourg at the moment that the myrmidons were entering his room, to arrest him. A family of Burgundian artisans received and concealed him. Those whose life is an uninterrupted series of privations, know well how to compassionate misfortune. Our colleague afterwards sought refuge in the house of M. Oudot, a great partisan of the *coup-d'état* on the 18th Fructidor; and where, from that date, no one would have thought of seeking the proscribed Director. Carnot had not yet left Paris, when his name was erased from the list of the members of that national Institute, to the creation of which he had so much contributed.

Some laws proclaimed on the 19th and 20th of Fructidor, year V., declared all the places vacant that had been held by the citizens struck by the *coup-d'état* of the 18th. The Minister of the Interior, Letourneux, therefore wrote to the Institute enjoining it to proceed to the naming of a successor to Carnot. The three classes then proceeded to the nomination of the members of each class. *One hundred and four* voters took part in the election; but the urn did not receive one white ball!

I know, Gentlemen, how much, in Revolutionary times, the most upright, the most firm minds, are influenced by public opinion; I know that after the lapse of time that separates us from the 18th of Fructidor, no one can conceive that he has a right to blame the Institute at all for having yielded to the ministerial orders; still, I will here express freely my regret, that imperious circumstances did not permit our honourable predecessors, since the Fructidorian era, to draw a marked line of distinction between the politician and the philosopher. Under the Regency, in the affair of the Abbé Saint-

Pierre, Fontenelle had already, by a courageous stroke, protested against the powers attempting to confound that which the interests of science, of literature, and of art bid us keep for ever apart. If, in the year V. of the Republic, fifty-three voters had had the manliness to imitate Fontenelle, the Institute would not have suffered such cruel mutilations at the Restoration; deprived of the support afforded by unfortunate precedents, certainly not many ministers would have entertained the unpardonable thought of creating an Academy of Sciences at Paris without Monge, an Academy of Fine Arts without David!

You are surprised, no doubt, that I have not yet informed you of the name of the person who succeeded Carnot in the first class of the Institute; well, Gentlemen, it is because I have refrained, as much as possible, from performing a painful duty. When it proceeded to elect a successor to one of its founders, to one of its most illustrious members, the Institute obeyed, at least, an established law proceeding from the powers of the State; but is there, I ask you, any consideration in the world that should induce a man to accept the academic spoils of a learned victim of party rage, and especially so, when that man is General Bonaparte? Like all of you, Gentlemen, I have often indulged in a just feeling of pride, on seeing the admirable proclamations of the army of the East, signed: MEMBER OF THE INSTITUTE, *General-in-Chief;* but a heart-grief followed the first sensation, when it occurred to my mind, that the *Member of the Institute* had arrayed himself with a title which had been torn from his first patron and friend.

I have never thought, Gentlemen, that it was useful to create beings of ideal perfection, at the expense of truth; and this is the reason why, notwithstanding some friendly advice, I have persisted in divulging what you have just heard, relative to the nomination of General Bonaparte to the Institute. "But," said a Napoleonist to me, "coming from you, the story has no weight; for does not all the world know that you astronomers seek to find spots in the sun!" Thus, Gentlemen, my position has given me the privilege of telling truth without offending any one, which, by the by, is extremely rare!

I regret not being able to discover the name of the generous citizen who snatched Carnot from his retreat, and carried him safely in his postchaise to Geneva.

On arriving in that city, Carnot engaged lodgings at a laundryman's, under the name of Jacob. Prudence required his being entirely unknown; but the wish of getting certain news from his beloved country carried the day; he went out, he was recognized in the street by some spies of the Directory, who followed him, discovered his retreat, and immediately set a watch on it. Some French agents who had influence in the Genevese Republic, exclaimed loudly that he ought to be given up to the laws of his country, and even made an official representation to the Genevese Government. The magistrate into whose hands this diplomatic affair fell, was fortunately a man of feeling, and conscientious withal, and who felt what a great blemish would be inflicted on his country thereby. This magistrate was named M. Didier. On such an occasion, Gentlemen, it would be a crime not to cite a name known also in literature, thus connected with a humane action. M. Didier wrote to Carnot; he warned him of his danger, entreated him to quit the house immediately, and directed him to a spot on the lake where a boatman would await him, to take him over to Nyon. It was already very late; the constables of the Directory were watching their prey. Our colleague goes direct to his host, and, without any preamble, asks pardon for having introduced himself into his house under a false name. "I am proscribed, I am Carnot, they are going to arrest me; my fate is in your hands: will you save me?" said he. The honest laundryman replied, "Without any doubt." Immediately he muffled up Carnot with a blouse, with a cotton cap, with a *dossier;* he lays on his head a large loose bundle of dirty linen, which hung down to the shoulders of the pretended Jacob, and hid his figure. By favour of such a disguise, the man who a short time before by writing a few lines could scatter or arrest in their march armies commanded by a Marceau, a Hoche, a Moreau, a Bonaparte; to shed hope or fear at Naples, at Rome, at Vienna; now—melancholy vicissitude of things here below,—having borrowed the trappings of a laundryman's labourer, reaches in safety the little boat, in which he is to escape from being sent a prisoner back to France. In the boat, a new and strange emotion awaited Carnot. In the boatman appointed by M. Didier he recognizes that same Pichegru, whose culpable intrigues had perhaps rendered the 18th Fructidor inevitable. During all the time occupied in crossing the lake, not a single word was exchanged between the two proscribed men. Indeed, the time, the place, the circumstances were not suitable for political debates, for recriminations! Carnot, moreover, had soon to congratulate himself on his reserve; on reading the French journals at Nyon, he learnt that he had been deceived by a fortuitous resemblance; that his travelling companion, far from being a general, had never manœuvred any thing more than his frail boat, and that Pichegru, being arrested by Augereau, was expecting to be taken back to one of the prisons in Paris. Carnot was still at Nyon when Bonaparte, returning from Italy, passed through that little town on his way to Rastadt. Like all the other inhabitants, he illuminated his windows to do homage to the general.

If the plan that I have proposed to myself were to allow me at present to speak of Carnot's rare and sincere modesty, I hope his little illumination at Nyon would not be opposed to me. When he placed two candles in his window, in honour of victories to which he had contributed by his orders, or at least, by his counsels, Carnot proscribed, Carnot labouring under the menace of a forced journey back to Paris, and then of exile in the deserts of Guyana, must certainly have been agitated by far different sentiments; nor can we presume that pride showed itself in any of them.

18TH BRUMAIRE.—RETURN OF CARNOT TO FRANCE.—HIS NOMINATION TO BE MINISTER OF WAR.—HIS DISMISSAL.—HIS APPOINTMENT TO THE TRIBUNATE.

During upwards of two years, Carnot had disappeared from the arena of politics; during upwards of two years he had lived at Augsbourg under a feigned name, exclusively occupied in the cultivation of the sciences and of literature, when General Bonaparte returned from Egypt, and with a breath reversed the 18th Brumaire, a government that had never been able to take root in the country. One of his first acts was his recalling the illustrious exile, and nominating him to be Minister of War. The enemy was then at our gates. Carnot did not hesitate to accept; but a few months after, when the immortal victories of Marengo and of Hohenlinden had given an incontestable superiority to our arms, when the independence of the country was again assured, Carnot resigned his appointment. He would not consent to appear an accomplice in the changes that were preparing in the form of the government. Accordingly, on the 16th Vendémiaire, year IX., he wrote as follows: "Citizen Consuls, I again send you my resignation; I beg you will not defer accepting it."

It is not from a trifling cause that people part thus laconically. The letter I have just given was a corollary of the earnest disputes that were daily occurring between the Republic and the Empire, in the persons of *the First Consul and the Minister of War.*

Recalled to public affairs as a Tribune in 1802, Carnot opposed the creation of the Legion of Honour. He thinks—I was going to say, he foresees—that a distinction bestowed without inquiry by the uncontrolled will of one man, will end, notwithstanding its imposing title, and according to the natural course of things in this world, by no longer being any more than the means of attaching followers, and reducing to silence a swarm of little vanities. Carnot also with all his might opposed the creation of a Consulate for life; but it was especially at the moment when it was proposed to raise Bonaparte to the Imperial Throne, that he redoubled his energy and ardour. History has already recorded his noble words; she will also say, that surrounded by old Jacobins, surrounded even by those same men who, on the 18th Fructidor, had persecuted him as a royalist, Carnot remained standing nearly *alone* in the midst of the general apostasy, as if at least to prove to the world that political conscience is not quite an empty word.

The Tribunate was soon suppressed. Carnot retired

again into private life; I will not say with joy, Gentlemen, for in our colleague's bosom the virtues of a citizen always occupied the principal place; for he had hoped, that, like another Washington, General Bonaparte would avail himself of this unique opportunity to found in France order and liberty on a stable basis; for no man initiated in public affairs, and endowed with some foresight, could without uneasiness see the reins of government placed beyond control, and without guarantee, in the hands of an ambitious soldier. I shall be able at least to show you that Carnot's leisure was nobly and gloriously employed.

PUBLICATION OF THE GEOMETRY OF POSITION.

There is a story told of a young student who, almost discouraged with some difficulties inherent in the first elements of mathematics, went to consult D'Alembert, when this great geometer answered him, "*Go on, sir, go on, and faith will come to you.*" *

The advice was good, and geometers have followed it generally: they "*go on,*" also; they perfect methods, and multiply the applications of them, without preoccupying themselves about the two or three points where the metaphysics of the science offer obscurities. Shall it be said on that account that the filling up of

* D'Alembert's advice requires much explanation; as it stands it would be a good motto for Jesuits. It reads altogether contrary to the spirit of mathematics, where one step is made sure of before looking out for another,—where the self-secured truth is in place of any *faith*. It is meant, perhaps, to encourage the student to disregard contingent apparent puzzles; it should then be rendered, "Hold on in the path whose truth is evident to you, and after a time you will get a clearer view of those collateral circumstances which now confuse you, while looking every way at once."—*Translator*.

these gaps should be altogether neglected? Such was not Carnot's view. We have already seen him devoting the short moments of repose which his Directorial duties left him to the metaphysics of the Infinitesimal Calculus; the suppression of the Tribunate will permit him to submit to similar investigations an equally arduous question —that of negative quantities.

It often happens that, after having reduced a problem to the form of an equation, analysis offers you some negative numbers amongst the solutions sought for; for example *minus* 10, *minus* 50, *minus* 100; these solutions the ancient analysts did not know how to interpret. Vièta himself neglected them as absolutely useless and insignificant. By degrees they got into the habit of regarding negative numbers as quantities less than zero. Newton and Euler gave no other definition of them (*Universal Arithmetic*, and *Introduction to Infinitesimal Analysis*). This notion has in modern times introduced itself into the vulgar tongue: the merchant on the most petty scale understands exactly the position of a correspondent who announces to him negative profits; poetry has also given its sanction to the same thought, as we see in these two verses, by which Chénier stigmatized his political enemies, the editors of the *Mercure de France*:—

> "Which these lettered dwarfs have done, who without literature,
> *Beneath nonentity*, sustain the *Mercure*." *

Well, Gentlemen, it is a notion thus supported by the authority of the greatest geometers of modern times, consecrated by the assent of one who has, they say, more

* "Qu'ont fait ces nains lettrés qui, sans littérature,
Au-dessous du néant, soutiennent le *Mercure*."

talent than Voltaire, or Rousseau, or Bonaparte, and by the assent of the generality of the public, that Carnot has combated with the keen weapons of logic.

Certainly nothing is more simple than the notion of a negative quantity, when it is attached to a positive quantity greater than itself; but a detached negative quantity, a detached quantity looked upon as isolated, must it be really considered less than zero, and *à fortiori*, inferior to a positive quantity? Carnot, agreeing on this point with D'Alembert, who, most amongst the great mathematicians of the last century, occupied himself with the philosophy of science, maintains that negative isolated quantities figure in operations admitted by everybody, and in which, nevertheless, it would be impossible to suppose them beneath zero. Notwithstanding the dryness of such details, I will quote one of these operations. No one denies that

$$+ 10 \text{ is to } - 10 \text{ as } - 10 \text{ is to } + 10.$$

In order that four numbers should form a proportion, it is necessary, and, in fact, it suffices that, if the four numbers are fittingly ranged in order, the product of the extremes should be equal to that of the means. We must not be startled at this, Gentlemen; the principle I call in here, is no other than that of the famous *rule of three* of the teachers of writing and arithmetic; it is the principle of the calculation which is executed some hundreds of thousands of times daily in the shops of the metropolis. Now, in the proportion which I have just cited, the product of the extremes is + 100, as it is also of the means; therefore

$$+ 10 : - 10 :: - 10 : + 10.$$

Nevertheless, if + 10, the first term of the proportion, surpasses the second term — 10, it is impossible to suppose at the same time that — 10, the first term of the second ratio, surpasses + 10, the second term of the same ratio; — 10 cannot be, at the same time, both inferior and superior to + 10.*

Such is, in substance, one of the principal arguments on which our member grounds his view, that the notion of absolute or comparative magnitude should not be applied to negative quantities any more than to imaginary ones; that we cannot examine whether they are greater or less than zero; that they must be considered "*as creations of our reason, as mere algebraical forms.*"

When the genius of Descartes had shown that the positions of all possible curves, their forms, and the whole of their properties, might be exactly included in analytical equations, the question of negative quantities presented itself under an entirely new light. The illustrious philos-

* — 10 is neither inferior nor superior to + 10; it is equal to it; though not algebraically =; but in taking, as our author does, the sense of mathematical formulæ, — 10 is just as good and as strong in its way as + 10 in its other way. Indeed — and + are merely symbols of action one way or the other; notwithstanding the ordinary translation of minus, — being "less," whereas it simply means negative, the opposite of positive. And though it is most habitual to our ideas to consider every thing in a positive light, the negative value is just as real; a correct appreciation of it only requiring the knowledge of *where the zero of the peculiar subjects treated of is placed*, which should always be one of the data in a mathematical question; thus 10 feet below the level of the sea are just as efficient as 10 feet above, and 10 degrees below any level in the thermometer are a perfect match for 10 degrees above. In fact, — 10 may be less than + 10 in our usual manner of viewing positive things; yet mathematically and truly it is not less, nor greater, but just as great. Perhaps calling a — quantity less than nothing, has occasioned a confusion of terms; for it is merely a quantity on the other side of zero, which is only a symbol of equilibrium, or of no power one way or the other. The place and value of zero depend on the class of subjects treated of, and are previously known from experience.—*Translator.*

opher himself established in principle, that in geometry these quantities only differ from the positive in the direction of the lines on which they ought to be reckoned. This profound and simple view is unfortunately subject to some exceptions. Let us suppose, for example, that it is proposed to draw from a point without a circle, a straight line so situated that the portion comprised within the circle shall have a given length. If the distance between the point from which the line is to be drawn, and the point in the circumference which it will first meet, be taken as unknown, the calculation gives two values: the one, *positive*, corresponds with the first point of the intersection of the straight line sought with the circle; the other, *negative*, determines the place of the second intersection. Now who does not see * that these two lengths, the one positive, the other negative, must be measured from the same side of the point from which the straight line was drawn?

Carnot proposed to himself to cause these exceptions to disappear. He does not admit isolated negative solutions in geometry any more than in algebra. To him these solutions, taking away their signs, are the differences of two other absolute quantities; the one of those quantities which was the greatest in the case reasoned on, only becomes the smallest when the negative root

* "Who does not see?" We cannot say that we do, nor can anybody else, perhaps, who has not the calculation before him. There are many ways of measuring distances about a circle; and two different lines in it amounting to the same effect can be so often drawn, that those wishing to be convinced would prefer hearing more about it; at any rate it is easier to suppose there is some thing misunderstood in the working of the problem, or in the meaning of its solution, than that the whole system of notation, on which all former results depend, should be wrong.—*Translator*.

appears. In geometry then, as in algebra, the negative root taken with the sign +, is the solution of a different question from that which was put, or, at any rate, from that which it was exclusively desired to put, in the equation. How is it now that problems foreign to the particular one which the geometer wished to resolve, mix themselves up with it: that analysis answers with deplorable fertility to questions which have not been put to it; that if its aid is sought, for example, to determine the ellipse whose area is a maximum amongst all those which can be drawn through four stated points, it gives three solutions, whilst evidently there is only one good, admissible, and capable of application; that without the knowledge and against the will of the calculator, it thus groups, in this particular case, a problem relating to the limited area of the ellipse with one concerning the hyperbola, a curve with indefinite branches, and therefore with indefinite area? Here is what required clearing up, here is that of which the theory of the *co-relation of figures* and the *Geometry of Position*, which Carnot has connected with his very ingenious views on negative quantities, give generally easy solutions.

Since these labours of our member, every one thus applies without scruple, the formula established on one particular state of any curve, to all the different forms which that curve may take. Those who will read the works of the ancient mathematicians, the collection of Pappus, for example; those who will observe, even in the last century, two celebrated geometers, Simson and Stewart, giving as many demonstrations of a proposition as the figure to which it related could take different positions or forms by the disarrangement of its parts; they will, I say, estimate Carnot's service to geometry as very high. I wish I could say, with the same truth, that the views of our member had more or less filtered into that multitude of elementary treatises which appears every year, and that they had contributed towards perfecting instruction; but on this point I can only express my regret. In the present day the philosophical part of science is very much neglected; the means of shining in an examination, or an assembly, hold the first place; with some rare exceptions, professors think much more of familiarizing their pupils with the mechanism of the calculus, than of causing them to penetrate to its principles. In fact, I almost think we might say of certain persons, that they employ analysis in the same manner as most manufacturers do the steam-engine, without reflecting on its mode of action. And let it not be supposed that this faulty style of instruction is a necessary sacrifice to the reigning passion of our age, the rage for going fast in every thing. Have not illustrious members of this Academy shown, in justly celebrated works on geometry and statics, that extreme exactness does not exclude conciseness?

Carnot's *Geometry of Position* would not have the high merit which I have attributed to it, with regard to the metaphysics of science, if it were not also the origin and base of the progress which geometry, cultivated after the manner of the ancients, has made in the last thirty years in France and Germany. The numerous properties of space which our member has discovered, show to all eyes the power and fecundity of the new methods with which he has endowed science. Permit me to justify by some quotations the favourable opinion which I have formed of the methods of investigation discovered by Carnot.

"If at a given point there be imagined three planes

perpendicular to one another which intersect a sphere, the sum of the areas of the three circles forming the intersections will always be the same, whatever direction be given to these planes: provided that they all three cut the sphere."

"In every trapezium, the sum of the squares of the diagonals is equal to the sum of the squares of the sides which are not parallel, plus twice the product of the parallel sides."

"In every (plane or uneven quadrilateral figure) the sum of the square of the two diagonals is double the sum of the squares of the two straight lines which join the centres of the opposite sides."

I shall have attained my end if these quotations, which I could multiply to any amount, inspire professors of mathematics with the desire of seeing for themselves, in Carnot's *Geometry of Position*, how easily all these curious theorems flow from the methods of our illustrious member.

CARNOT INVENTOR OF A NEW SYSTEM OF FORTIFICATION.

There would be a gap in this biography which would justly attract your criticism, if, notwithstanding the many different points of view from which I have already considered the imposing figure of Carnot, I should neglect to speak to you of the military engineer, of the inventor of a new system of fortification.

You doubtless recollect the violent arguments which Carnot had to sustain, from the time of his entering on the military career, with the chiefs of the army to which he belonged. An upright and inflexible character already made him repel the heavy yoke of *esprit de corps*.

Mature age did not contradict so honourable a début. Carnot also found, in his exalted mind, the secret of extricating himself from the sometimes rather burlesque preoccupations of men exclusively given up to one special pursuit. Even officers of engineers have not always avoided these inconsistencies. They also sometimes extend to exaggeration the consequences of an excellent principle. Some have been seen—I am certain at least of having heard so—some have been seen, who do not cross one valley, who do not surmount one hill, who do not rise over one ridge of ground, without forming the project of establishing there a large fortification, or a crenated castle, or a simple redoubt. The idea that with the existing facilities of communication each point of the territory may become a field of battle, unceasingly besets them; it is on this account that they oppose the opening out of roads, the construction of bridges, the cutting down of woods, the draining of marshes. Fortified towns never appear complete to them; each year they add new and expensive erections to those that centuries had already accumulated. The enemy would doubtlessly have a great deal to do to overcome all the narrow and tortuous defiles, all the crenated gates, all the drawbridges, all the palisades, all the sluices for managing the water, all the ramparts, all the demilunes which unite modern fortresses; but in awaiting an enemy who may never appear, the inhabitants of some fifty large cities are deprived, from generation to generation, of certain enjoyments, of certain conveniences which render life sweeter, and which are freely enjoyed in the most obscure village.

As to the rest, harsh words shall never proceed from me, blaming the prejudices, if they are prejudices, inspired by the most noble of sentiments, the love of national independence. In every thing, however, moderation is requisite. Does not economy when pushed to the extreme become hideous avarice? Does not pride degenerate into vanity; politeness into affectation; freedom into rudeness? It is by weighing in exact scales the good and the evil resulting from all human inventions, that we keep the path of true wisdom. It is thus that, despite the sovereignty of example and habit, despite the influence, generally so powerful, of uniform, the officer of engineers, Carnot, always studied important problems of fortification.

In 1788, some French officers, enthusiastic to delirium respecting Frederic the Great's campaigns, loudly proclaim the entire inutility of fortresses. Government seems to accede to this strange opinion; it does not yet order the demolition of those ancient and glorious walls; but it allows them to fall of themselves. Carnot withstands the general bias, and sends a memoir to M. de Brienne, Minister of War, in which the question is examined in all its phases with a boldness of thought, an ardour of patriotism so much the more worthy of remark, because such examples had then become very rare. It shows that in a defensive war, the only sort that he advises, the only one that he thinks legitimate, our northern fortresses might be regarded as equal to the aid of a hundred thousand men of the regular army; that a kingdom surrounded by rival nations is always in a precarious state when it has troops only without fortresses. Then, entering on the financial question, Carnot affirms (this result I am sure will astonish my audience, as it astonished me also), Carnot repeatedly affirms, that far from being a gulf into which the treasures of the state were continually being lavished, the numerous fortresses of the kingdom from the beginning of monarchy, from the foundation of the oldest, have not cost as much as the cavalry alone of the French army during twenty-six years; and pray remark that at the time when Carnot wrote this memoir, exactly twenty-six years had elapsed without our cavalry having drawn their swords.

Well, Gentlemen, having become a member of the Legislative Assembly, this ardent advocate for fortresses proposed, whatever may have been said about it, not the complete destruction of the special and independent fortifications, backed by cities and called citadels, but the demolition only of those ramparts that before isolated them. Assuredly the certainty of there being a place of safe retreat must, in a time of siege, excite the soldier to prolong the defence and run the hazardous chance of assaults; but by the side of this advantage, citadels appeared to the mind like real Bastilles, the garrisons of which could thunder on the towns, claim ransom from them, or make them submit to any of their caprices. This reflection prevailed in the mind of Carnot, who was an eminently good citizen. The officer of engineers proscribed citadels, and, despite loud clamours, his conscientious opinion prevailed.

This is not quite the case with the new systems of fortifications, and of defence, proposed by our colleague. They have only thus far made proselytes among foreigners. Is it wrong, or is it reasonable, that our cleverest officers should reject them? God forbid that I should venture to cut short this question.* All that I

* Probably the author is alarmed at the difficulty and responsibility of deciding; otherwise he ought, as a biographer, necessarily to give some estimate of the value of all the works of the subject of his memoir.—*Translator.*

can undertake is, to show in what it consists, and even to be understood I shall have to make a fresh appeal to your indulgent attention.

The most ancient fortifications, the earliest ramparts, were simple walls, more or less thick, encircling towns, and thus forming continuous inclosures pierced with a small number of gates, for the entrance and exit of the inhabitants. In order to render escalading them difficult, these ramparts were very high on the outer side towards the country; besides this, a ditch, capable of being filled with water, generally divided them from it.

The very ramparts themselves, even in their highest portion, were of a certain breadth. It was there that the population of the towns collected in cases of attack. It was from thence that, partly hidden behind a low wall now called a *parapet*, they threw a shower of missiles on the assailants. The most timid even had the advantage of not descrying the enemy but through narrow apertures, that are still seen in modern fortifications under the name of loopholes or *meurtrières*.

The besieger did not begin to be redoubtable but from the moment when, having reached the foot of the ramparts, he could, by means of tools, engines, or machines, sap their foundations. To act then freely and vigorously against him was, for the besieged, an indispensable condition of a good defence. Now, let us imagine to ourselves a soldier placed on the summit of the wall; he will evidently not be able to perceive the foot of it without leaning forward, without leaving nearly his whole body exposed, without losing the advantages offered him by the parapet, without the shelter of which he could not have thrown his arrows but by exposing himself to the well-aimed shots of the enemy below.

Let us add that, in such an uneasy position, a man has neither power nor address. To remedy some of these inconveniences, they crowned this sort of wall with a construction which the architects called corbels, and upon which the salient parapets rested. Then the hollows, the openings, or if we must recur to the technical term, the *machicolations* comprehended between the parapet and the rampart, became a means of throwing down stones and burning substances, &c. on those who were trying to sap the walls or escalade them.

To strike the enemy unremittingly, when he reaches the foot of the rampart of a town, is undoubtedly excellent; but to prevent his advancing so far would be still better. They approached this better method, without, however, entirely attaining it, by constructing at various distances, along the wall of the city, large round or polygonal towers, forming very salient points. If we in imagination carry ourselves behind the parapet of the platforms with which those towers were crowned, it will be easy to perceive that without leaning forward, without much exposure, by much less exposure than the assailants undergo, the garrison of each tower could observe the next tower from top to bottom, and moreover a certain portion of the intermediate wall. Of that part of the wall which is now called the *curtain*, at least one half was visible down to the base by the garrison in the tower to the right, and the other half by the garrison in the tower to the left, so that there was no longer any one portion of the wall of which the besieger could approach the base, without exposing himself to the direct attack of the besieged. It is in this that *flanking* consists.

The invention of gunpowder occasioned deep-founded

modifications in the system of fortification, as to the nature of attack and defence. By the aid of this invention and by that of guns of various kinds, which arose from it, the besieger, while still at a great distance, could breach the walls by his artillery. On the other hand, the besieged gained the means of annoying the enemy long before he had reached the walls by his covert ways. Vast banks then rested against the walls, on which the largest guns could be easily worked. Thence arose the necessity of giving to the walls thus destined an immense and expensive thickness, that they might resist the thrust of these accumulations of earth. They at the same time protected the outward base of the ramparts towards the open country, by banks ingeniously contrived so as to agree with the undulations of the ground. By thus defilading the ramparts, they deprived the besieger of the possibility of making a breach from afar; they obliged him to approach very near to the body of the place, before he could expect much effect from his cannon against the walls of the besieged surmounted with guns.

It is recounted that Soliman II. held a consultation with his generals, relative to the best way of besieging Rhodes. One among them, an experienced man, explained the difficulties of the enterprise. The only answer the Sultan made was: "Advance up to me, but remember that if thou puttest only the point of thy foot on the carpet in the midst of which I am sitting, thy head shall fall." After some hesitation the Ottoman general thought best to raise the fearful carpet, and roll it on itself, in proportion as he advanced. He thus safely got closely up to his master, who then exclaimed: "I have now nothing further to teach thee; thou knowest the art of besieging." Such is, in fact, the faithful image of the first movements of the besieger, who wants to get possession of a fortress by a regular attack. The ground represents the Sultan's carpet.* His life is endangered unless he advances under cover; but let him dig the earth; let him heap up the rubbish in front of him; let him unceasingly roll up a little of the carpet as he advances; and behind this movable shelter the besiegers, carrying with them a powerful artillery, approach the ramparts of a fortress very soon in full force, without being seen by the besieged.

The problem of fortification may, indeed, be considered at bottom as a particular case of the geometrical theory of polygonal stars. This assemblage, apparently so inextricable, of salient and of reëntering angles, of bastions, of curtains, of demilunes and ténailles, &c., of which modern fortresses consist, is the solution of the very old question of flanking. We may in some points vary the construction, but the aim is always the same. The abstract principles of the art have become clear and evident. The illustrious corps of officers who at the present day are at liberty to apply them to the defence of the country, have had the good sense to abandon the mystery with which it was before surrounded, and with which it has been so severely reproached. Fortification is taught like other sciences; it is founded on the most elementary geometry; a mere amateur can familiarize himself with the theory in a few lessons.

* This is scarcely a "faithful image," and unless the story could be improved, it is hardly worth preserving. The gradual increase of labour and cover in advancing, and the total absence of cover at the commencement, are features foreign to a regular siege; there cover is obtained at first, and they go steadily on, making no more or less than the requisite cover all the way. The story, however, might be applied to an old fortress with very lofty towers, which would require more cover as you got nearer.—*Translator.*

Let us now remark, that modern fortification has the defect of being extremely expensive. It was this ruinous defect that Carnot wished to remove, by substituting curved (*or vertical*) fire for the direct.* Carnot surrounds a fortress by a simple wall, not faced, but furnished with scarp and counterscarp. The wall does not require a great thickness, because it has not to resist the thrust of the earth destined to bear artillery on it. Behind this wall he places mortars, howitzers, and *pierriers* which are to carry curved fire into the country; the results of which, according to him, must be much more effective than those of direct firing, and oppose obstacles to the enemy's advance, more and more efficacious in proportion to his approach. The wall is defiladed against the direct fire of the besieger, by the earthen counterscarp, forming one of the faces of the ditch. It seems, then, that to make a breach, it is requisite, as in the present system of fortification, to crown the covered way; an operation which, according to the author, would be eminently galling to the assailant. This supposes that a breach could not be made in Carnot's wall but at a very short distance, and within *le tir de plein fouet*, or point-blank range. Foreign experiments, it is said, contradict this hypothesis; by employing curved fire, a breach might be made at a sufficiently great distance, provided the projectiles were of very large calibre. The question then is not yet solved;† the new mode proposed by

* The word "curved fire" is employed, though "vertical" is the usual term in English technical language, because *curved* includes more—as the vertical, the ricochet, and every thing between those two. It might possibly be rendered "elevated fire;" and it should be remembered that Carnot intended to use a sort of ricochet fire as well as the vertical.—*Translator.*

† We should say, the question *is* now solved; the experiments made by *foreigners* are to be relied on, and are kept on record; at

Carnot seems to call for a more thorough examination; but meanwhile we must applaud our illustrious colleague

least that part which he speaks of, namely—the impossibility of breaching Carnot's wall from a distance. In the experiments made at Woolwich, a wall well-built, and having had time to consolidate, *was breached* with expedition and certainty; though of course with a very large expenditure of ammunition, on account of the uncertain nature of the fire; that is, throwing heavy shot over an earthen bank, down against the wall on the opposite side. The vertical fire question does not admit of quite so easy a solution; but Carnot certainly miscalculated the effect of the very small balls he proposed to shower down, as is immediately evident theoretically, and has been tested practically. He said that, a large ball fired at a certain angle with a certain velocity, being found to penetrate on falling into hard earth, about its own diameter, his small balls fired under like angles and velocities would also penetrate to the amount of their diameters; but this is fallacious, he having forgotten the resistance of the air, which retards balls of different sizes in the proportion of the *squares* of their diameters, while their force, or power of retaining momentum, is in proportion to the *cubes* of their diameters. This is an immense difference when it is recollected that Carnot's given experiment was with a ball of some five or six inches diameter, while those he proposed would have been about one inch; and that in vertical fire this resistance of the air acts on the ball through a lengthened route both ascending and descending. Experiment with the proposed balls at Woolwich, has shown that the wounds inflicted by these balls would be seldom disabling, unless they struck a man on the head: their force being only somewhat greater than the strongest effort of a strong man. It has also been shown, that they are given to scatter so much, that the *outworks* in the neighbourhood must be abandoned as soon as this fire is used from the *body* of the place; in fact, by making vertical fire the whole of his defence, Carnot forfeits all the time which the use of direct fire used to cause the assailant to expend in approaching to the summit of the covered way, as a very slight application of raw hides, &c., supported above the approaches, would protect the assailants; and when there, the neighbouring works could not assist in defence, as they must be abandoned from the scattering fire from the body of the place.

Still vertical fire is often good and effective, especially in the latter parts of sieges; and all writers on fortification recommend its extensive use both in defence and attack. Its use has been restricted by

for his endeavour to render the means of defence as efficacious as the means of attack, which were due to the genius of Vauban.

PUBLICATION OF THE TREATISE ON THE DEFENCE OF FORTRESSES.

Napoleon was greatly irritated in 1809, at the slight resistance that several fortified places made to the attacks of the enemy; and therefore he caused Carnot to be asked, towards the end of that year, to write a special code of instructions on this important branch of the military art, from which the governors of citadels might learn the responsibility of their functions, and the full extent of their duty. In this mission Carnot saw a fresh opportunity of rendering himself useful to his country, and did not hesitate to accept it, although his health then occasioned some serious inquietude.

In the eyes of the Emperor, perhaps *working fast* was more esteemed than *working well.* On this occasion, however, his hopes did not go so far as to imagine that the composition of a considerable work that might require ten or twelve large plates, and in which some well-selected historical examples should accompany and support the precepts, could be executed in less than a year. Well, Gentlemen, four months scarcely elapsed from the moment that Carnot knew Napoleon's desire, to the publication of the celebrated Treatise on the Defence of Fortresses.

the difficulty of transporting ammunition, or the train being borrowed from ships, or its being incomplete; but the advantage is allowed by all writers, though only as a part of the system. Carnot's principal novelty was the *theory* of making it take the place of every thing else; and that theory has been ably demolished by the practical arguments of Sir Howard Douglas.—*Translator.*

CARNOT AN ACADEMICIAN.

From 1807 to 1814 Carnot had lived in retirement; he scrupulously fulfilled his duties as an academician. This title had been restored to him the 5th Germinal, year VIII., after the decease of Le Roy. Nearly all the Memoirs on Mechanics submitted to the judgment of the First Class of the Institute, were referred to him. His rare sagacity, with luminous clearness and remarkable precision, pointed out and characterized the new and salient portions. I could cite a certain author on machines, who did not fully conceive his own discovery, until after it had had the good fortune to pass through the filter of that learned critic. He had, besides, a sort of merit that is not always the auxiliary of high science: he knew when to doubt; to his eye theoretical results were not always infallible.

EVENTS OF 1813.—CARNOT APPOINTED TO THE COMMAND AT ANTWERP.

We have now reached the events of 1813. Carnot was not rich enough to subscribe to the newspapers. Every day at the same hour, we see him come to the Library of the Institute, approach the fire, and read with visible anxiety the news of the progress of our enemies. On the 24th of January, 1814, the interest he felt appeared greater than ever; he asked for some paper, and as fast as the pen could trace, wrote the following letter, which you will no doubt like to hear read:—

"SIRE,—As long as success crowned your enterprises, I abstained from offering to your Majesty services which I did not think were agreeable to you; now, that ill-fortune puts your constancy to a severe proof, I no longer hesitate to offer you the small means that remain to me. It is little, certainly, to offer a sexagenary arm; but I have thought that the example of a soldier whose patriotic sentiments are known, might rally to your Eagles many men who are undecided what line to adopt, and who may allow themselves to be persuaded, that in abandoning them, they were serving their country.

"There is still time for you, Sire, to conquer a glorious peace, and *to have the love of the great people restored to you.*—I am, &c."

The details that I have thought it right to give you, relative to the circumstances connected with the writing of this letter, will, I trust, undeceive those who, accustomed to concentrate all their affections on the person of Napoleon, fancied in Carnot's concluding words, a cruel attack from the old democrat, prepared at long-shot distance, against the man who had confiscated the Republic to his own advantage. In truth, Gentlemen, it required a man to be very determined to substitute personal questions for the national weal, to blame the illustrious sexagenarian's offer to defend a fortress, when otherwise he had, relative to capitulations, not long since resumed his idea, expressed in the noble words of the famous Blaise de Montluc to Marshal de Brissac: *I would rather be dead than see my name in such writings.*

Carnot started from Paris for Antwerp at the end of January, without having even seen the Emperor. It was time, Gentlemen, for the new governor could not reach the fortress on the morning of the 2d of February, but by threading the enemy's bivouacs. The bombardment of the town, or rather the bombardment of our fleet, for there were some English among the besiegers, began the next day; it lasted throughout the day of the 3d, and of the 4th, with part of the 6th. Fifteen hundred bombs, eight hundred cannon balls, many red-hot balls and fusees, were thrown on our ships. The enemy then retired; the experience of three days had sufficed to give him the estimate of the rough tilter he had to deal with.

I will borrow from the journal of the siege kept by M. Ransonnet, Carnot's aide-de camp, some details that may be interesting, and which will show the strictness of the man and of the times.

On the 10th of February, the new governor of Antwerp wrote to the Mayor of the town:—

"I am very much surprised that the person charged with ordering the furnishing of my quarters, did not restrict himself to what was necessary.

"I also desire that any demands of this nature, made on my account, may not have the character of a forced requisition.

"All the effects enumerated in the annexed list are unnecessary."

The necessities of the Belgian campaign, having suggested to the Emperor the idea of borrowing some troops from the garrison of Antwerp for the army, Carnot wrote a despatch to the General-in-Chief, Maison, dated the 27th of March, whence I have extracted the following passages:—

"In obeying the orders of the Emperor, I am obliged to declare to you, the Commander-in-Chief, that these orders are equivalent to ordering Antwerp to be ceded . . . . The circumference of this place is immense, and there would be at least fifteen thousand good troops required to defend it. How could His Majesty suppose that with three thousand sailors, the greater part of whom have never seen fire, I could keep the fortress of Antwerp with the eight dependent forts? . . . .

"It only remains then here, for us to disgrace ourselves or to die; I beg you to be believe that we are all determined to prefer the latter . . . .

"I think, Sir, that if you could take upon yourself to leave me at least the infantry and the artillery (there was at Antwerp a detachment of the Imperial Guard), you will render a very great service to His Majesty; but all will be ready to depart to-morrow, unless I receive a counter-order from you, which I shall await with the greatest impatience and the greatest anxiety."

Besides the despatch to General Maison, I find under the same date a letter to the Minister of War, the Duke de Feltre; and I remark the following passage in it:—

"When I offered to serve His Majesty, I was willing to sacrifice my life to him, but not my honour. Your Grace knows that I am not in the habit of dissimulating the truth, because I do not seek favour. The truth is, that the state to which your orders reduce me, is a hundred times worse than death, because I have no chance of saving the place confided to me, but in the cowardice of my enemies."

Bernadotte having wished to dissuade Carnot from the line of conduct that he had laid down for himself, received from him the following answer:—

"10th April, 1814.

"PRINCE,—It is in the name of the French Government that I command in the fortress of Antwerp. That Government alone has the right to fix the termination of my duties: as soon as it shall be incontestably established on a new basis, I shall hasten to obey its orders. This resolution cannot fail of obtaining the approbation of a

Prince born a Frenchman, and who knows so well the laws prescribed by honour."

After the events of Paris, after the institution of a Provisional Government, the Minister of War, Dupont, sent one of his aides-de-camp to Antwerp. The following is the letter that Carnot wrote to him on this occasion:—

"15th April, 1814.

"I must acknowledge, my Lord Count, that your having sent me an aide-de-camp with a white cockade is a calamity: some wished to adopt it instantly, others have sworn to defend Bonaparte; a sanguinary conflict would have immediately resulted in Antwerp itself, if, with the advice of my Council, I had not determined to defer my adhesion, and that of all the armed force . . . . Is civil war then wished for? is it wished that the enemy should become master of all our strongholds? and because the city of Paris has been forced to accept the rule of the conqueror, that therefore all France shall receive it? It is evident that the Provisional Government is only transmitting the orders of the Emperor of Russia. Who will ever absolve us from having obeyed such orders? What! you do not allow us even to preserve our honour; you yourself become an accomplice of desertion, promoter of the most monstrous anarchy! The lessons of 1792 and 1793 are lost upon the new chiefs of the State. They first seek to catch our adhesion by surprise, by affirming to us that Napoleon had abdicated, and now they contradict it. After having given us a tyrant instead of anarchy, they put anarchy in place of the tyrant. When shall we see the end of these cruel oscillations? Paris is enjoying only a momentary peace; a perfidious calm which presages to us the most horrible tempests. Oh, afflicting and withering days, happy those who have not witnessed you!"

The sentiments with which Carnot was able to inspire the population of Antwerp are known to the whole world. I cannot resist the pleasure, however, of citing at least some passages from a letter that was delivered to him the day he departed for Paris; after having been thus ordered by the government under the elder branch of the Bourbons, who had remounted the throne. The authorities and inhabitants of the suburb of Borgerhout, the destruction of which had been resolved on, but which he thought he could preserve without detriment to the general defence, thus expressed themselves:—

"You are going to quit us; we feel deeply afflicted by it; we would wish to possess you still a little longer; we solicit this great favour most earnestly . . . . . The inhabitants of Saint Willebrord and of Borgerhout request permission to inquire once a year, of the person who may be appointed to govern them, after the health of General Carnot . . . . . We may, perhaps, never see you again. If some day General Carnot allows his portrait to be painted, and would permit a copy of it to be made for us . . . . . this precious present would be deposited in the church of Saint Willebrord."

I will not commit the fault, Gentlemen, of weakening such naïve and touching expressions by a cold commentary.

CONDUCT OF CARNOT DURING THE HUNDRED DAYS.

The conduct of Carnot during the Hundred Days, appears to me to have been well and honourably epitomized in those memorable words that Napoleon addressed to him, after the battle of Waterloo: "CARNOT, I HAVE KNOWN YOU TOO LATE!"

But, as I am writing a biography and not a panegyric, I will frankly say that Carnot, as member of the Provisional Government of that epoch, laboured under the injurious and anti-national influence of the Duke of Otranto, which led him to give his adhesion to measures that were stamped with evident feebleness, and to others over which every heart animated by patriotic sentiments would gladly throw a thick veil.

And yet, can we very warmly reproach Carnot with having allowed himself to be fascinated by the intrigues of Fouché, when we see Napoleon, notwithstanding the strongest suspicions of treason, retain that man in his Council?

Amidst the reproaches ostensibly addressed to Carnot, respecting that period of our annals, there is one on which I can give some personal explanation. I have heard the austere Conventional severely blamed for having accepted the title of *Count of the Empire;* happily my memory can faithfully repeat some words of our colleague's which clear up this point in his life, and which were related to me by an officer the very day that he heard them.

They were at table, at the Minister of the Interior's house. A letter arrives; the minister breaks the seal, and almost instantly exclaims: "Well, Gentlemen, see me here a *Count of the Empire!* I can, however, easily guess *whence the blow comes.* It is my dismissal that is wished for, that is demanded; I will not give *him* that satisfaction; I will remain, because I think I can be useful to my country. The day will come, I hope, when I shall be allowed to explain myself fully respecting this perfidy ; at present, I will content myself with disdaining this vain title, with never annexing it to my name, and especially with never accepting the diploma, however much I may be pressed to do it. From this moment, Gentlemen, you may rest assured that Carnot will not long remain Minister after our enemies have been repulsed."

I must have made you ill-appreciate our colleague, Gentlemen, if these words had appeared to require farther explanation.

CARNOT IN EXILE.—HIS DEATH.

Of all the ministers of the Hundred Days, Carnot was the only one whose name apeared on the list of *proscription* prepared on the 24th of July, 1815, by the second Restoration. Whether this special rigour was the consequence of the patriotic ardour with which our colleague disputed with foreigners the last remnants of the French territory, or of his persisting (though unfortunately without good result) to point out to the Emperor the traitor, who, under the favour of his former reputation for talent, had insinuated himself into the Ministry, still his glory will not be tarnished by it.

Already, on the evening of the 24th July, Carnot had received a passport from the Emperor Alexander. He used it, however, only in Germany. Obliged to travel under a feigned name, he would not forego the title of a Frenchman as long as he could avoid it. It was therefore again as a Frenchman that he traversed the great river in a melancholy mood, to the very banks of which he had had the supreme honour of extending our frontiers, and he went to Warsaw.

In a certain country not far from ours, a stranger is always received with this matter-of-course formula :

"My house, and all that it contains are yours;" but at the same moment, I must acknowledge, it is not rare, through a signal that the servants perfectly well understand, for the supposed new *proprietor* to be ever after shown the door of the habitation so liberally offered to him. The reception of Carnot in Poland, however, must not be included in this category. Our excellent friends, the brave Poles, did not confine themselves to mere forms of politeness towards the illustrious exile. General Krasinski made over to him a mayoralty in land of 8,000 francs per annum, that he held from Napoleon; the Count de Paç wished him to accept the possession of several domains. Although Carnot was not a Freemason, all the Masonic Lodges of the kingdom joined in a subscription that produced a considerable sum; finally, and of all these offers that he refused, the following went most directly to the heart of Carnot; a Frenchman, poor himself, established at Warsaw for many years, went to him one morning, carrying a bag with the savings of his whole life!

The severity of the Polish climate, the wish to be nearer to France, determined our colleague to accept the kind offers of the Prussian Government; he settled at Magdebourg, where he passed his latter years in study, in meditation, and in the company of one of his sons, whose education he superintended. It was, Gentlemen, a fine spectacle to see the whole of Europe, above all to see the absolute monarchs, forced in some measure to render homage to one of the greatest, most noble, most striking men in the French Revolution; even to one of the judges of Louis XVI., even to a member of the *Committee of Public Safety.*

Carnot died at Magdebourg, the 2d of August, 1823, aged 70 years.

PORTRAIT OF CARNOT.—ANECDOTES RELATIVE TO HIS POLITICAL AND PRIVATE LIFE.

If *iconography* is not now considered by anybody as a futile science, if some very distinguished minds have made it the object of their earnest study, it may be permitted me here to say, that Carnot was of tall stature, of manly and regular features, a wide and calm forehead, lively and penetrating blue eyes, a polite demeanour, but circumspect and cold; that at the age of sixty, there was still perceptible in him, even in a civilian's costume, something of the military air to which he had been accustomed in his youth.

I have considered him in all his phases,—as a member of the Conventional Government, of the Committee of Public Safety, of the Executive Directory, the Minister of War, a Military Engineer, the Exile, the Academician. Still, many essential traits would be wanting to the portrait, however comprehensive it be already, if I did not also speak of the private man. I shall not swerve, in this latter portion of my picture, from the style that I adopted in the beginning; I shall advance always proof in hand. It is thus I think that a geometer should be praised; I mistake, it is thus that everybody should be praised; seeing how rare honour, disinterestedness, and true patriotism are among the living; and how common, on the contrary, among the dead, according to their funeral eulogies and their epitaphs; the public has come to the wise conclusion of no longer believing either the one or the other.

I have read somewhere that Carnot was an ambitious man. I will not stop to combat this opinion in form, but I will relate, and you yourselves shall judge.

The member of the Committee of Public Safety, who, in 1793, organized the fourteen armies of the Republic, who arranged all their movements, who named and appointed generals, who, at need, as at Wattignies, degraded them during the battle under the enemy's cannon,—was only a Captain of Engineers.

And later, when the Council of the Five Hundred, and the Council of the Elders of the Republic of the year III., unanimously called Carnot to the Executive Directory; when having again become the supreme arbiter of our military operations, he sent Hoche to la Vendée, Jourdan to the Meuse, and Moreau to the Rhine, instead of Pichegru; when, by the most fortunate inspiration, he confided the command of the army of Italy to Bonaparte, our colleague gained a step, but only one step; he had become chef de bataillon *by seniority!*

Carnot still held only this humble rank, when the coup d'état of the 18th Fructidor banished him from France.

The extremely hierarchical ideas of the First Consul could never have reconciled themselves to a mere chef de bataillon being Minister of War. Wherefore in the year IX., he did not elevate Carnot to that eminent post until after he had named him Inspector General of Reviews. Still, it was only turning the obstacle aside, instead of removing it. The semi-military, semi-civil, grade of Inspector General of Reviews, did not prevent the Minister of War, under the government of the Consuls, from being a simple *chef de bataillon* in the Corps of Engineers.

Carnot quitted the Ministry the 16th Vendémiaire, year IX. Twelve days after, his successor asked for the

5*

illustrious citizen's name to be inserted in the list about to be formed of the Generals of Division of the French army. The Report recalled in appropriate terms, and even with a degree of vivacity, all that our colleague had done for the national glory and independence. The Minister went, even in the name of *justice*, of *esteem* and of *friendship*, to invoke the *magnanimity* of the Consuls; the magnanimity was at fault; they did not answer the Report, and the dismissed Minister remained in his old rank.

When it was requisite, in 1814, to send orders to the new Governor of Antwerp, the clerks of the War-office, in order to write the address, sought for the official titles of Carnot in the Army-list, and were astounded at seeing that the Emperor had, without considering it, placed a chef de bataillon at the head of a crowd of old generals. The service would evidently have suffered from such a state of things; the necessity of remedying it was at once felt, and, in imitation of a certain ecclesiastical personage, who in the same day received the minor orders, the major orders, priesthood, and episcopacy, our colleague, in a few minutes, passed through the various grades of lieutenant-colonel, colonel, brigadier-general, and general of division.

Yes, Gentlemen, Carnot had ambition; but, as he said himself, *it was the ambition of the three hundred Spartans going to defend Thermopylæ!*

The man who, in an all-powerful position, had never thought of making himself the equal of those whose vast operations he was directing, also disdained the gifts of fortune. When he returned to private life, his small patrimony was scarcely intact. How is it, with the most simple tastes, with a strong antipathy for pageantry and show, that Carnot even unintentionally does not reach, if not riches, at least the easy circumstances of those men who, like him, have long held brilliant employments? Some facts will serve as answers.

After the 18th Brumaire, at the moment when Carnot became Minister of War, the pay of the troops, and, what must occasion still more surprise, the pay of the clerks, was fifteen months in arrear. A few weeks elapsed and all was paid up; all, except the salary of the Minister himself!

Pins, was the name given to a sort of gratuity destined in appearance for the wife of any one with whom a farmer, a merchant, or a commissary had concluded a contract, whether public or private. Although pins did not appear in the written conditions, the contracting parties did not therefore regard them as less obligatory; habit, that second nature, had at last come to acknowledge them as legal; the most sensitive consciences satisfied themselves by not fixing their amount.

A horse-dealer, whose offer Carnot had approved, was going, according to custom, to bring him a considerable sum, under the name of pins; it was, I believe, 50,000 francs. The Minister, at first, does not understand. At the Committee of Public Safety, where he had served his apprenticeship, the purveyors took good care not to speak of pins. All is explained at last, and Carnot, far from being angry, receives with a laugh the notes that are presented to him; he receives them with one hand, and gives them back with the other, as a first instalment of the price of the horses that the dealer had agreed to furnish for our cavalry, and demands an immediate receipt.

In the most violent paroxysms of their fury, the factions had the prudence not to attack Carnot as a private man; never did their unhallowed breath try to tarnish the virtues of the son, of the husband, or of the father; as to disinterestedness especially, both friends and enemies were always agreed. I might therefore on this point remain content with the two instances I have given. There is another, however, which it is desirable to rescue from oblivion; the memory of Carnot does not require it, but I have a slight hope that, by being reminded of it, some ministers may feel arrested in their prodigalities, and certain parties from indulging their avarice!

After the 18th Brumaire, the projected operations for the army of reserve imperiously required that Moreau should without delay send one of his divisions to the army of Italy. The direct intervention of the Minister of War did not appear too much to carry so important a negotiation to a successful conclusion. In execution of an order of the Consuls, of the 15th Floreal, year VIII., Carnot, accompanied by six officers of the staff, *two* couriers, and *one* servant, went to Germany. On the route he inspected the troops *échelonnées* between Dijon and Geneva; he then traversed the cantonments of the Rhine, visited the fortresses, arranged with the Commander-in-Chief the plan for the next campaign, and returned to Paris. The Treasury had given him 24,000 francs. On his return, he restored 10,680 francs. He was so fearful that the expenditure of 13,320 francs, (or £550,) for *ten* persons making a long journey should appear too much, that he sent in a detailed report, excusing himself as if he had been prodigal. The following was his letter to the Consuls: "You will have the goodness to remark that you have desired me to give some éclat to my mission; that in the principal places I was obliged, according to your orders, to assume a certain appearance; in short, that it was requisite, from the character of generosity with which you are animated, that I should allow some gratification to my companions in travel and in fatigue!" Be pleased to remember, Gentlemen, that the journey, the éclat, the gratifications amounted altogether to 13,320 francs; do not forget that it was one of the ministers, inspecting armies who was going to decide on the fate of his country, who spoke thus, and you will agree with me, I think, that if the world is improving, it is not in economy.

The Treasury did not know under what form to record the 10,680 francs returned by Carnot; but it was not the first essay on the part of our colleague: by searching back to the epochs when he inspected the Republican armies, as representative of the people, the Clerks of Finance found in their registers the forms they sought, and these occurred as often as Carnot had executed similar missions.

The name of Carnot would still present itself to my mind if, after so many instances furnished by history in all countries, it were yet required to prove that an ardent mind can be allied to cold and reserved manners. Undoubtedly, no one ever had a right to say of him, as D'Alembert said of one of the old secretaries of our Academy: *He is a volcano covered with snow;* but I may be allowed to show at least, that our colleague's conceptions often had a certain something in them that went direct to the heart, touching, moving, electrifying; something, in short, stamped with an indefinable seal, never borne by the works of heartless men, of men whose faculties have no concentration of mind. Two more citations, and my thesis will be proved.

Latour of Auvergne, born of the Turenne family, did

not even express regret at losing his advantageous position through the breaking out of the Revolution ; but when the enemy menaced our frontiers, it was to the frontiers that he was seen to march. Modesty made him decline all promotion ; the old captain obstinately remains a captain. In order not to deprive the country of the eminent services that Monsieur Latour d'Auvergne could render it, Carnot authorizes the representatives of the people to group together all the companies of Grenadiers of the army of the Western Pyrenees, and form a separate corps of them ; never to place a senior officer over them, and to remove with equal care all the captains that were senior to Latour d'Auvergne ; by this arrangement the diffident officer finds himself daily in charge of an important command. The name of *infernal column* given by the Spaniards to this body of troops soon sanctions in a splendid way all that there was of anomalous, of unusual, and strange in the contrivance suggested by Carnot, and carried into effect by the representatives.

Latour d'Auvergne, whom you now know, Gentlemen, as a military man, for the third time quitted his retreat and his beloved learned studies, and asked to serve under Moreau, when Carnot became Minister of War after the 18th Brumaire. Already at that epoch the First Consul would not certainly have approved an arrangement similar to the one that the Conventional representatives adopted in the Pyrenees. Carnot, however, suffered in seeing that the chief of the *infernal column*, he who counted so many dashing services, that the estimable author of the *Gaulish Origins*—must we add, that a correspondent of the Institute, should arrive on the banks of the Rhine as an obscure officer. The title of *First Grenadier of France* strikes his imagination ; Latour d'Auvergne is invested with it by an official act; and from that moment, without quitting his Grenadier epaulettes, he became, in the eyes of the soldiers, the equal if not the superior of all the dignitaries in the army.

The First Grenadier of France was killed by a lance the 27th of June, 1800, at the battle of Neubourg. The army, the whole of France, wept bitterly over this loss. As for Carnot, his deep grief inspired him with an idea that the ancients, otherwise so idolatrous of military glory, might envy us. By an order emanating from Carnot, when the 46th demi-brigade was mustered, the name of Latour d'Auvergne was always called out as the first on the roll. The grenadier placed at the head of the first rank then advanced two steps, and answered in a tone to be heard all along the line—*Died on the field of honour.*

The brief, expressive, solemn homage that a regiment thus daily paid to him who had rendered himself illustrious in its ranks by courage, knowledge, and patriotism, must, I think, continue that excitement which produces heroes. I assert, at all events, that the noble words of Carnot, repeated in the chamber, in the guard-room, under the tent, in the bivouac, had thoroughly preserved the remembrance of Latour d'Auvergne in the memory of our soldiers. "Where are those long files of grenadiers going?" exclaimed the aide-de-camp of Marshal Oudinot, when, in the beginning of Vendémaire, year XIV. (October, 1805), the avant garde of the great army passed through Neubourg. "Why are they swerving from the route laid down for them?" Their silent and grave march awakened curiosity; they are followed, they are observed. The grenadiers were going, Gentlemen, near Oberhausen, thoughtfully to pass their sabres over the rough block of stone that covered the body of *the first Grenadier of France.*

I return thanks, Gentlemen, to M. de Savary, the venerable old man, who, a witness of the touching scene near Oberhausen, has allowed me to draw it from oblivion, and thus to unite in one mutual sentiment, the admirable army of Austerlitz with the admirable armies of the Republic. I am happy also, that names which are dear to you, that the names of two of our old colleagues, that the names of Latour d'Auvergne and of Carnot, happen to occupy so noble a place in this patriotic reminiscence!

Great employments, like great heights, usually occasion a vertigo in the heads of those who reach them suddenly. This man thinks that by pageantry and prodigality he ought to make people forget the years he has passed in mediocrity and constraint. That man becomes disdainful and insolent, harsh and churlish, and thus revenges himself on the unfortunate people who have now to solicit him, for the disdain, the arrogance, the brutality that he had to undergo when he had to solicit them. A crowd of names of individuals suggest themselves to fill up this sketch, in case any one should dispute its fidelity. Do not suppose, however, that by passing over some mushrooms so lightly, I intend to constitute myself the advocate of privilege; I wish to prove, on the contrary, by the example of Carnot, that minds of a certain temperament can resist contagion.

Six months after the coup d'état, on the 18th Fructidor, Carnot is officially accused to the Council of the Five Hundred of having had frequent and intimate communications with Pichegru, at a time when that general, a member of the Legislative Body, soiled his brilliant military reputation by his intrigues. Carnot denies such communications. He proves, besides, that he could not have had secret interviews at his house. He added: "I feel that people will say if it was not at your house it was elsewhere. Well, I declare, that during all the duration of my directorial functions, I have *not gone out twelve times* without being accompanied by my wife, my sisters, or my children!"

It is possible, Gentlemen, that in France, that elsewhere, men in power may have had this simplicity of habits, not to say integrity; but I will acknowledge it, the rumour has not reached me.

I have been speaking to you of the Man; now I will treat of the Minister.

At the battle of Messenheim (1800), near Inspruck, Championnet remarks the temerity, the intrepidity of Colonel Bisson, and demands for him, with the applause of all the army, the epaulettes of a General of Brigade. Weeks elapse, and the commission does not arrive. Bisson grows impatient, goes to Paris, obtains an interview with the Minister, and in his anger, apostrophizes him in a rough manner. "Young man," Carnot calmly replied to him, "it is possible that I may have committed an error; but your improper manners, really, might disincline me to repair it. Go, I will attentively examine your services." "My services! Ah! I know too well that you despise them, you, who from the shelter of your cabinet coolly send us the order to die. Protected from danger, and from the rigour of the seasons, you have already forgotten, and you will continue to forget, that our blood flows, and that we lie on the hard ——." "Colonel, this is too much! For your own interests, our interview must not continue in this tone. Retire! Your address, if you please? Go! you will shortly hear from me."

These last words, pronounced in a solemn tone, unsealed Colonel Bisson's eyes. He runs to a devoted friend, General Bessières, to seek consolation. His friend, on the contrary, gives him to understand that a court-martial will be the inevitable consequence of his folly. In the mean time Bisson hides himself. A faithful servant goes every hour to the hôtel, to learn about the dreaded order for his appearance. The ministerial paquet at last arrives; Bisson, all emotion, tears open the envelop. The paquet, Gentlemen, contains the brevet of General of Brigade, and letters of service!

It is scarcely necessary to add, that the new general flies to Carnot immediately to offer him the homage of his admiration, and of his gratitude, and of his deep repentance. All this proved superfluous, for General Bisson found his orders at the door of the Minister's office. That ardent soul which, notwithstanding all its sincerity of conduct, felt the act somewhat onerous, proved how well he had appreciated the delicate severity of Carnot, and how worthy he was of it, by that very evening publishing the details, which assuredly Plutarch himself would not have disdained.

Of all the qualities that great men can adorn themselves with, diffidence seems the least obligatory; therefore the more credit is given to them for it; and therefore also it leaves the most durable recollections. Who, for example, does not know by heart that letter which Turenne wrote to his wife, a hundred and seventy-nine years ago, on the day of the celebrated battle of the Dunes:

"The enemy came to us; they have been beaten; God be praised. I have worked a little in the course of the day; I wish you good night, and will go to lie down."

Equally with this illustrious general of Louis XIV. did Carnot omit his own participation, both in his private communications and when he wrote to the Convention. I have related to you the part he acted at the battle of Wattignies; well, read the bulletin which that decisive and memorable event inspired him to write, and you will in vain seek a few words to recall the representative of the people; unless, indeed, we are determined to see them in this passage: "The Republicans charged forward with the bayonet, and remained victorious."

But all of you, who knew Carnot, will agree with me, that unless he was pressingly and directly solicited, he would never entertain you with the European events which he had so often directed. Justly jealous of the esteem of France, the old Director, during his exile, answered the diatribes of his accusers in writing. His style on these occasions was lively, poignant, and cut deep; it was evident at each line that it proceeded from an ulcerated heart. Yet the most legitimate irritation never led him beyond the circle that his enemies had traced out. His defence in some parts might resemble an attack; but at bottom, on close examination, it was still a defence. Carnot rejected far from him, the idea of raising a pedestal to himself with the immortal trophies that he had reaped during his Conventional and Directorial career. Modesty, Gentlemen, is a good alloy when it triumphs thus over anger.

In regard to science, the illustrious academician was not less reserved. One would have said, indeed, that he regulated his conduct according to that reflection of the oldest and most ingenious of your interpreters: "When a learned man speaks to instruct other men, and exactly in that line of instruction that they wish to acquire, he does them a favour; but if he speaks only to show off his own learning, they do him a favour in listening."

Modesty, moreover, is not a quality deserving of respect and esteem, except in isolated individuals. Bodies of men, and especially academies, would be guilty of a fault, and would be wanting in a principal duty, if they neglected to adorn themselves in the eyes of the public with the legitimate claims they have earned to the esteem, gratitude, and admiration of the world. The more justly celebrated they are, the stronger is the desire to belong to such institutions, and the more the laborious efforts made to attain this aim turn to the advantage of science, and to the glory of the human mind. This thought has encouraged me, Gentlemen, to unroll to your eyes, in all its details and in its true colours, the very eventful, varied, and stormy life of Carnot. For nearly two centuries the Academy of Sciences conscientiously has preserved the memory of the geometers, the physicists, the astronomers, the naturalists, who have rendered it illustrious. The name of the great citizen who by his genius preserved France from foreign dominion, has appeared to me to deserve being inscribed with some solemnity in this glorious Pantheon.

MALUS.

A BIOGRAPHY PREPARED FOR THE PUBLIC SITTING OF THE ACADEMY OF SCIENCES, 1854; AND READ BY SPECIAL DESIRE OF THAT LEARNED BODY, ON THE 8TH OF JANUARY, 1855.

BIRTH OF MALUS.—HIS LITERARY EDUCATION.—HIS ADMISSION TO THE POLYTECHNIC SCHOOL.

STEPHEN LOUIS MALUS, whose name will be perpetuated by an immortal discovery as long as the physical sciences shall be honoured among men, was born at Paris, on the 23d of July, 1775, his parents being Anne-Louis Malus of Mitry, treasurer of France, and Louisa Charlotte Desbres.

His first studies were principally literary; he acquired a very sound knowledge of the authors who form the glory of Greek and Latin literature. Up to his latest years he continued to be able to recite, without hesitation, long passages of the Iliad, of Anacreon, Horace, and Virgil. Like almost all scholars gifted with some facility of composition, he rashly devoted his youthful talents to productions of a kind really above his powers, and the difficulty of which one of our great poets so energetically characterizes when he calls them, "œuvres du démon." But he carried out his endeavours to an extent beyond what is usual. I have discovered among the papers of Malus, two cantos of an epic poem entitled *Thémelie, or the Foundation of France*, and two complete tragedies; one on the capture of Utica, and the death of Cato; the other recounting the dreadful catastrophes of the family of the Atrides, and entitled *Electra*. The fact that some beautiful verses and some interesting situations occur, would not hinder me from avowing that the youthful author had not as yet discovered his true vocation, were it not that the immense inequality which we observe between the *Hostile Brothers* and the *Andromache*, though both worthy of Racine, shows with what caution we ought to abstain from premature judgment.

Malus pushed forward with equal and distinguished success the study of letters, and of algebra and geometry. He went through the examination for the School of Engineers at Mèzières, in 1793, and was classed the same year as sub-lieutenant in the promotion in which General Bertrand held the first place. But the serious disorders of which the school of Mèzières was the theatre, having caused its suppression, Malus could not profit by his brevet of admission. He enrolled himself as a volunteer in the 15th battalion of Paris, and proceeded to Dunkirk, where he took part in the manual labour of the wheelbarrow, as a common workman in the construction of the field fortifications with which that place was being surrounded. M. Lepère, engineer of roads and bridges, who was directing a part of these constructions, having remarked certain peculiar and unexpected arrangements in the manner in which the soldiers executed the excavations and raised the mounds, was desirous to learn the origin of these practices; they pointed out to him the man who had indicated these as the means best suited to attain the desired end with the least possible fatigue. A few moments' conversation showed the engineer that he had found in the humble labourer of the 15th Battalion of Paris a superior man; and he accordingly sent him to the "Ecole Polytechnique," which had just been founded.

Malus then was one of the first pupils of this celebrated institution. He soon gained the good will of Monge, who became his friend; indeed nothing less than such a warm friendship was necessary to preserve him from the misfortunes he would have incurred from his taking a part in the many political movements by which the capital was then agitated.

On quitting the school, Malus went to Metz, where he was received as a pupil sub-lieutenant of engineers the 20th February, 1796. He was named captain on the 19th June following; and was sent the next year to the army of the Sambre and Meuse, where he took an active and distinguished part in the actions in which that valiant army was engaged.

There has been recently found among the family papers, a small bound book, in which Malus, when captain of engineers, and employed in the army of the East, traced day by day an abridged narrative of all the events of which he had been an eyewitness, or in which he had taken a direct part. These memoranda, which I have read with the greatest interest, and in which our fellow labourer figures chiefly as a military man, seem to me to deserve a detailed analysis. I have resolved to lay it before you, were it only to prove once more, that profound knowledge and a scientific genius did not weaken either the zeal, the constancy, the courage, or the spirit of enterprise, which ought to distinguish an officer of the highest military qualities.

After having read the following details, few would venture to estimate their own services above those which Malus, the man of science, rendered in his sphere.

EGYPTIAN CAMPAIGN.—EXTRACTS FROM THE MEMORANDA OF MALUS.

The events of the war led the Captain of Engineers, Malus, to the right bank of the Rhine. He remained eleven months in garrison in the learned city of Giessen: he was even on the point of contracting a marriage with the eldest daughter of the Chancellor of the university, Professor Koch, when the order came for him to proceed to Toulon, where he was to serve under Caffarelli in the left wing of the army, collected for an expedition of which scarcely any one knew the destination.

The 27th of Floreal,* we find him at Toulon, embarked on board L'Aquilon, a vessel of seventy-four guns, commanded by Thevenard, and making part of the advance guard of the squadron. The 22d Prairial † he took part in the attack, by assault, of the fortress of Malta, the defenders of which, he says, surrendered after having made much noise and done little mischief.

After a short sojourn in Malta, Malus, at the desire of General Desaix, commandant of the division which had arrived at Civita Vecchia, went on board the Courageux, in which that general was embarked. He remarks, "I had in all respects to congratulate myself on this change." The fleet quitted Malta the 3d of Messidor,‡ and we find Malus on the 13th of that month § sailing all night in an undecked sloop in search of the General-in-Chief, to receive his orders as to the point at which the division of Desaix was to disembark.

* May 16. † 10th June, 1798. ‡ June 21. § July 1.

On the 17th * Malus was attached to the advanced guard of the invading army. The 21st,† in the evening, he encamped on the road from Ramanièh. At that time the corps of engineers had neither "material" nor troops. An officer of this service, isolated in the army, was often deprived of the commonest necessaries. We find an instance in the following description, which I quote from the memoranda: "Wanting a picquet to which to attach my horse, I tied him to my leg; I slept, and dreamt peaceably of the pleasures of Europe." On the 25th,‡ he took part in the glorious battle of Chebreys against the Mamelukes. The 2d Thermidor,§ at the battle of the Pyramids, he was in one of the battalions formed in squares on the right wing beside General Desaix.

On the 4th,‖ in the morning, Captain Malus went with a detachment of carbineers into the island of Raouda, reconnoitring the right bank of the Nile to Mekias, and sent over to the left bank the boats which were necessary to enable the army to cross the river. The same evening he accompanied General Dupuis, who was charged with regulating the conditions of the capitulation of Cairo. On the 15th Thermidor,¶ he set out with the advanced guard of the army, which marched against Ibrahim Bey encamped at Belbeys, and took a very active part in the important combats which signalized this expedition; in which many military errors were committed.

Somewhat later, we find Malus accompanying General Regnier in a reconnoitre which had for its object the determination of the exact distance from Salchiéh to the sea. On his return he discovered the remarkable ruin of the ancient city of San, or Thamis. It was during this expedition that he learned the destruction of the

* July 5. † July 9. ‡ July 13. § July 20. ‖ July 22. ¶ August 2.

French fleet in the naval battle of Aboukir; and we read without surprise in the memoranda that he reëntered Cairo fatigued, ill, and a prey to profound grief.

About the period of which we are speaking, General Bonaparte created the Institute of Egypt. Malus was one of its first members.

Some days afterwards, Malus received an order to join General Desaix in Upper Egypt. On his return to Cairo with the division of "the just Sultan," he was charged with the duty of making preparations for the fête of the 4th Vandémiaire,* in the square of Esbékiéh. "This was," he says, "a trifling distraction from the grief which had afflicted me for some time." On the 30th,† and following days, Malus powerfully contributed to repress the insurrection which had arisen in Cairo; having arrested with his own hand, in the heat of the tumult, one of the insurgents, he found in his possession objects which he knew belonged to General Caffarelli, his immediate commander and friend; from these he believed that he had been killed; and it was not till after two days that he learned that Caffarelli had quitted his house before the Turkish revolters had pillaged it.

After the rebellion had been suppressed, Captain Malus commenced the establishment of a fort in the position whence during the insurrection they had cannonaded the grand mosque. The construction of this fort occupied him a long time; it received the name of Dupuis. Afterwards he commanded at the reconnoitring of the communications of the Nile with the lake Menzeleh and with Salchièh. In this expedition the young officer made discoveries of great interest in respect to archæology, and the ancient geography of this part of Egypt.

* September 25. † October 20.

On his return to Cairo, Captain Malus enjoyed some little leisure; by which he profited in order to examine in detail the "Well of Joseph," which he described as a masterpiece of perseverance and skill in construction. He went also to visit the colossal pyramids of Gizeh, in company with a man who might be truly called the colossus of our army from his height and his bravery, General Kléber.

When the army set out on the expedition to Syria, Malus, who was then occupied in reconnoitring the Delta, was attached to the division of General Kléber. We shall not follow him in the difficult route which our brave soldiers had to traverse almost without provisions or drinkable water; the details which we find on this subject in the memoranda only inspire the most painful reflections; we will merely say, that the young officer of engineers took a part with distinction in the siege of El-Harisch. We find him taking by assault, and with great intrepidity, an advanced post situated eighty metres from the place,—commanding in the trenches, and pushing the sap almost up to the foot of the breach, when the enemy offered to capitulate. The young officer denounced in energetic terms the breach of faith of which our generals were guilty in regard to the prisoners, in forcing them to enlist among our soldiers.

Malus relates the march of the army advancing into Syria. It first took the infection of the plague in the town of Gaza, abandoned by the enemy; its divisions arrived at length before Jaffa and invested that town, of which it raised the siege. The operations were conducted in a way which was not conformable to the rules of the science originally laid down by Vauban. Our young officer recounts that the breaching battery, being supported by armed positions on too small a scale, was surprised in the night by a sortie of the troops from the town. The heads of our soldiers carried into Jaffa were paid for by their weight in gold. The head of Malus, however, did not figure in the number of these bloody trophies, for the sole reason that at the moment of the silent invasion of the battery by the Turks he was asleep in one of the angles of the entrenchments. The breach having been opened, and the garrison not having answered to the summons made them, the troops advanced to the assault to the sound of the bands of all the regiments. Here I will no longer abridge, but copy :—

" The enemy was overthrown, discouraged, and retired, after a sharp firing of musquetry from the houses and forts of the city; they kept their ground, however, at some points, and continued their fire for an hour. During this time the soldiers, scattered through all parts, killed men, women, children, old persons, Christians, and Turks ;—every thing that bore the human form was the victim of their fury.

" The tumult of carnage, the broken doors, the houses shaken by the noise of the firing and of arms, the cries of the women, the father and child overthrown one on the other, the violated daughter on the corpse of her mother; the smoke of dead bodies burned in their garments which had been set on fire, the smell of blood, the groans of the wounded, the cries of the conquerors disputing together over the spoils of their expiring prey, infuriated soldiers responding to the cries of despair by exclamations of rage and redoubled blows; lastly, men satiated with blood and gold, falling down in mere weariness on the heaps of corpses ;—such was the spectacle which this unfortunate city presented until night."

This forcible passage of the manuscript of Malus is the faithful picture of what happens in every town taken by storm, even when the assailants belong to the most humane civilized army in the world. When historians know how to place themselves in a more elevated sphere, to free themselves from routine, and to follow in the opinions they express the eternal rules of justice and humanity, while they praise the indomitable courage of soldiers who will brave death in obedience to discipline, they will accord a deeper sympathy to the men who to preserve their nationality consent to expose themselves to scenes of massacre and bloodshed such as those which the narrative of Malus has revealed in all their horrors; their condemnation will be reserved for those who provoke these impious wars, which have no other motive than personal ambition, and the desire for a vain and false glory.

When the army set out for the attack on the town of St. John d'Acre, Malus received an order to remain at Jaffa with General Grezieux. There were left with him only 150 efficient men; the town contained more than 300 wounded and 400 infected with the plague. Malus was charged with the arrangements necessary to be made in the Greek Convent, in order to establish there those suffering with the plague. For ten days successively he passed all his mornings in the infected air of this receptacle of corruption. Thus our celebrated painter Gros might have legitimately placed the portrait of Malus among the figures in that admirable picture for which modern art is indebted to him, in the place of some of those conventionally introduced there, who never really penetrated into the halls then choked up with the dying and dead.

The eleventh day, Malus felt himself infected with the terrible disease which decimated our army. From this moment I will allow him to speak for himself; science may perhaps derive some advantage from the details which I transcribe :—

"A burning fever, and violent pains in the head, forced me to seek repose; a continued dysentery was added; and one by one the symptoms of plague showed themselves. About the same time General Grezieux died. Half of the garrison had already been struck; thirty soldiers fell victims daily; Brinquier, who had taken my place in superintending the hospital, was seized on the fourth day, and died forty-eight hours afterwards. At this period characteristic bubo showed itself on my right groin. I had all along up to this time entertained hope that my disease might not be the plague; the number of days I had lived since the first attack seemed to indicate it; but since the bubo appeared, and the pains at the heart were redoubled, I could no longer feel any doubt; I resigned myself to my fate. I sent to Francisqui, who was with the wounded General Damas, the articles which I wished to leave to my relations and friends. I ought to remark that Francisqui was the sole one of my comrades who had not abandoned me, and who, in order to tranquillize me, had not hesitated to come near me; on the day of his departure he carried his devotion to such an extent as to embrace me, though he was then certain that I was infected.

"Only one man in twelve escaped. St. Simon arrived in Egypt and came to see me; he was then in perfect health, in two days afterwards he was dead. The siege of Acre was protracted, the sick fell back on Jaffa and increased the numbers of the dying; besides this, the plague was in every house of the town where there still were any inhabitants. The refugees of Ramlè, who came to Jaffa to place themselves under our protection, perished nearly to a man. The Convent of the Capuchins, which was placed in quarantine, could not escape the contagion: the greater part of the monks died. All the Frank families perished except two men and one woman.

"I no longer knew a single individual among those now at Jaffa. I had lost successively my friends, my acquaintance, and my servants; there only remained my French servant, who attended me with constancy during my illness, and he died at my side the 24th Germinal.* I was now alone, without strength, without help, without friends; I was so exhausted by the dysentery and the continual suppurations, that my head became extraordinarily weakened; the fever, which redoubled its intensity at night, often made me delirious and agitated me terribly. Two men of the corps of sappers undertook the care of me, and they perished one after the other.

"At length on the 2d Floreal † I was put on board L'Etoile, which was setting sail for Egypt and whose captain had the plague; he died the night of our arrival at Damietta. The sea air produced a sudden effect on me; it seemed to me as if I were relieved from suffocation. After the first day I almost began to feel some wish for food, I was nevertheless very feeble. Contrary winds kept us several days out at sea; this delay produced a very marked amendment in my health; my strength revived, the crust of the bubo fell off; my appetite was restored.

"On the 7th Floreal ‡ we came to anchor before the

* April 12, 1799. † April 21. ‡ April 26.

Bogaz of Damietta; on the 8th * we entered the Nile and the vessel was put under quarantine."

If any one would wish to know how our institutions, when entrusted to persons destitute of humanity, add fresh sufferings to those of natural afflictions, let him continue with us the transcription of Malus's harrowing recital.

"The 10th Germinal † I disembarked and was conducted to the lazaretto of Lesbièh, where were collected those suffering from the plague from Damietta as well as those arrived from Syria. They placed also with me several passengers who had no symptom of the disease, but who in due course took the infection in the lazaretto and died, every one of them. These numerous deaths delayed the period of my enlargement. It was rare that any one got out of this infernal prison who had once had the misfortune to enter it; hardly would they condescend to succour the unhappy persons who came to spend their last hours there. I have often seen them die with rage demanding water of the barbarians who pretended that they did not understand them, or would answer, 'It is not worth while.' Greedy grave-diggers robbed the dying persons before they had yielded their last breath; these unworthy agents of the sanitary commission were the only medical attendants, the only guardians allowed to the sick. Hardly had their victims ceased to live when they carried them over to the opposite shore, where they abandoned them to the dogs and birds of prey. Sometimes they covered them with a little sand; but the wind soon exposed the bodies naked, and the cemetery presented the hideous spectacle of a field of

* April 27.

† Probably a mistake for Floreal, April 30.

battle. One wretched woman, of whom I had taken care because she was absolutely deserted, begged of me the evening of her death to give a piastre to the grave-diggers, that she might be preserved from becoming a prey to the jackals. I fulfilled her wish, and caused them to bury her at the extremity of the plain where the dead were deposited.

"I had been already a month in this abominable abode, when Cazola obtained for me the privilege of being put in quarantine in a separate lodging. My solitude appeared to me delicious, because I had quitted the society of the dying. I succeeded in reëstablishing my health, and in the beginning of Messidor,* I received definitively my liberty, which followed the sacrifice of all my property."

How heartily must we not congratulate ourselves that Malus escaped, in so unhoped-for a way, from the terrible stroke which had mowed down so many victims! If he had fallen under it, the beautiful branch of optical science, of which he planted the first signal after his return to France, perhaps would not have been created, and the admirable progress which the science has made would not have been reckoned among the most striking claims to the admiration of posterity of which the 19th century may boast. Some time after this, Malus was ordered to proceed to Cathièh, where he established himself. The delights of this advanced post, where General Le Clerc commanded, are described *con amore* by him who had just escaped the frightful disease, and the dangers not less dreadful of the lazaretto of Lesbièh.

"We encamped," he says, "in huts whose walls and roofs were composed of palm-leaves interwoven; we

* June 19=Messidor 1.

were lodged like Arabs ; I had close to my cabin a small enclosure containing my horses, camels, and asses ; an aviary full of fowls, geese, and ducks, a pen for my two sheep, another for a boar ; houses for my pigeons, and my goat enjoyed its liberty. It was in a great measure in this society that I passed three months of my sojourn in Egypt which were to me particularly agreeable. A perfect tranquillity, peaceable enjoyments, and waiting for an enemy whom we calculated on conquering, hindered us from wishing for conveniences of which we were deprived."

Malus here does not say all ; at Cathièh he composed a memoir on light, of which we shall have occasion to speak presently. If it should happen that in analyzing this work, we should find therein some results which may, or which ought to be, contested, we may remark that it was composed half a century ago, and that the author was in a position truly exceptional when he was engaged in it.

I find mentioned in the memoranda that in a reconnoissance which he made with a detachment of dromedaries of which he had the command, Malus encountered a caravan, attacked it, dispersed it, and obtained a great number of camels, and a quantity of provisions.

On quitting Cathièh, Malus went to Cairo, where he received from Kléber (October 21, 1799,) the brevet rank of Chief of Battalion, the just recompense of such active services and so much courage displayed by the young captain, ever since the first disembarkation of the French army in Egypt. The commandant Malus having learnt at Cairo that a disembarkation of Turks was preparing near Damietta, hastened thither ; where, when he arrived the 8th Brumaire,* he found the enemy already fortified. The next day but one, after having been in the trenches during the morning, he joined, as a private foot soldier, the troops who charged the Osmanlis with the bayonet, and precipitated them into the sea.

On the 20th Frimaire,† Malus received the command of the position at Lesbièh, where he had destroyed the walls when this fortress was in the hands of the Turks, and which he had rebuilt since it had fallen into the power of the French. On the 22d, ‡ the plague made its appearance at Lesbièh in six different quarters; the commandant, Malus, from his long experience, applied means of preventing its development and propagation; nevertheless it made many victims till the 28th Pluviose.§ On the 29th,‖ the position of Lesbièh was surrendered to the Osmanlis in virtue of the convention of El Harisch. Malus arrived at Cairo the 25th Ventose,¶ and on the 28th ** learned the rupture of the capitulation of El Harisch by Lord Keith. The same day, at two o'clock in the afternoon, appeared the proclamation of Kléber, which ended with these celebrated and prophetic words: "The army will respond to this disloyal proceeding, and to the demand to lay down their arms, by new victories." The army was in fact on its march on the next day to fight the forces of the Grand Vizier. Malus, attached to the division of General Friant, personally took part in the immortal battle of Heliopolis, when 11,000 men triumphed over more than 60,000.

The day after the victory a particular circumstance which I find related in the memoranda, had some unfortunate consequences. "On the 30th,†† at two o'clock in

* October 29.
† December 10.
‡ December 12.
§ February 26, 1800.
‖ February 27.
¶ March 15.
** March 18.
†† March 20.

the morning," Malus says, "the army commenced its march for Belbeys, where we reckoned on finding the Turkish army collected. I went with the division of Friant. After an hour's march I suspected that we were losing our way in the desert. As the night was very dark we had lost the ordinary tracks. I represented the matter to the general, who listened to me for a moment, but other persons brought forward opposite opinions with so much assurance, that the march was continued. One hour and a half afterwards, we were taking a direction exactly towards the point whence we had started. This I perceived from the position of the pole star, which we had at starting behind us. This time I was listened to, and I led back the division on the right route. This mistake nevertheless caused us much delay, and the other divisions were obliged to wait for us at one league distance from Belbeys."

We see on what little circumstances the great events of war often depend. If there had been in the division of Friant only an ordinary small compass of a few millimetres in diameter, like those which are hung among the trinkets to watches, or even if self-conceited officers had not obtained a preference for their opinions over that of Malus, the divisions of our army would have been reunited much sooner; and that of the Grand Vizier would have experienced near Belbeys very considerable losses.

Malus, now attached to the division of General Regnier, took part in the expedition which, after several serious affairs, drove back the Ottoman army across the desert. Afterwards he returned to Cairo, then in a state of revolt excited by the Mamelukes, who, on the day of the battle of Heliopolis, fell back on the great city. We see at once the nature of the service of an officer of engineers in such an attack as that on Cairo, where he was obliged, in order to take the barricades, to turn them by passing through the interior of the houses. After the complete surrender of Cairo, Malus was quartered at Gizeh, when on the 25th Prairial,* General Kléber was assassinated in his garden at Cairo by a Turk arrived from Syria.

We will here terminate the long extract from the memoranda of Malus. It would be too painful to us to follow the well-founded, but very bitter criticisms which he directs against General Ménou. A single trait will suffice to show his opinion of the former Commander-in-Chief of the army of the East. "Kléber," says Malus, "was assassinated on the 24th Prairial; some days afterwards General Ménou, in attacking the honour of the deceased General Kléber, has assassinated him over again."

In going over the memoranda, which, amid the chances of war, might very probably fall into the hands of indiscreet persons, friends or enemies, I remarked that Malus indicates very exactly the date at which he received letters from his father, his uncle, &c. As to letters from Giessen (and we easily guess whose hand wrote them) he gives no indication or trace. I notice this extreme delicacy for the instruction of ill-informed, or malevolent persons, who believe sentiments of the kind referred to incompatible with geometrical studies.

MARRIAGE OF MALUS.—HIS MILITARY CAREER.

Malus quitted Egypt and made the voyage on board The Castor, an English transport ship, according to the

* June 13.

arrangement made between General Ménou, Commander-in-Chief of our army, and the hostile generals. He arrived at Marseilles the 1st October, 1801, and was immediately put into quarantine. After the pestiferous scenes of Jaffa, of Damietta, and Lesbièh, he must have found the lazaretto in which he was now confined a place of luxury. As soon as he was set at liberty he repaired to Paris. After a short visit to his relations, bound by his sentiments even more than by his promise, he hastened to Giessen, where he once more joined Mademoiselle Wilhelmine Louise Koch, affianced to him for four years, and was married to her. This union completed his happiness; we shall soon have to relate the rare proof of devotion which Madame Malus gave the husband of her choice during the afflicting illness which took him from her and from the sciences.

The subsequent military career of Malus may be stated in a few lines. In 1802–3 he was employed at Lille. We find him in 1804 at Antwerp, planning measures, according to the orders of Napoleon, for completing the naval establishment of the city, and extending its lines of fortification. In this elaborate work, the account of which is preserved in the depôt of fortifications, accompanied by eleven sheets of drawings, the author treats analytically, but without neglecting the arithmetical applications, two questions of mechanics, which, under the circumstances and in that locality, possess a great importance, viz: 1. The amount which ought to be deducted for the weight of men marching in a tread-wheel, to move the inclined twisted pipes, or Archimedean hydraulic screws, used in draining: 2. The employment, for the same purpose, of the force of wind, acting on wind-mills having horizontal sails disposed in such a way as to turn always in the same direction. In 1805, Malus was attached to the Army of the North. In 1806–7–8, he was sub-director of the fortifications of Strasbourg. In this capacity he presided over the reconstruction of the fortifications of Kehl, and made some very judicious remarks on the form of the revetments,* and applied an exact analysis to the determination of their thickness. In 1809 he was recalled to Paris. He became major of engineers in 1810. The archives of the Committee of Arms prove that the inspectors-general often consulted him with much advantage on the merit of works submitted to them.

MEMOIR ON LIGHT.—COMPOSED IN EGYPT.

We have henceforth to occupy ourselves only with the life of Malus as a physicist and member of the Academy; without departure from this view, I may say a few words on the optical memoir which he composed in the hut at Lesbièh.

The author announces clearly, in the first part of the MS. memoir which I have before me, the object which he proposes; this is to prove that light is not a simple substance; that its constituent principles are caloric and oxygen, in a particular state of combination. To establish this theory, he cites numerous facts furnished by chemistry, which prove that he was perfectly initiated, not only in the general principles, but even in the details of this science. It must be observed, however, that all the deductions of Malus, even the most plausible at the present day, can be subverted by a single word; it suffices to cite, in contradiction to all the phenomena

* The masonry encasing and supporting the earthworks in a fortification.

which our friend alleges, the instance of the light which is engendered in a vacuum, by the aid of the voltaic current, passed through simple substances, such as carbon, platinum, &c.

In the second part of the memoir Malus seeks to establish that the different natures of various lights only differ from each other in the greater or less proportion of caloric which they contain. The red light would thus be the most heating, the violet the least so, which agrees with experiment. According to a singular opinion professed by the author, all rays, if possessing a certain high *intensity*, ought to produce the sensation of whiteness.*

The third part of the work is devoted to mechanical consequences which result by analysis from the suppositions explained in the first two sections. It may suffice to say, that the author finds, like all the partisans of the system of emission, that the velocity of light ought to be greater in water than in air: every one therefore will see how superfluous it would be now to go into a discussion of the details of such a subject.

* The "singular" opinion here ascribed to Malus is perhaps not altogether without foundation, at least in some cases. It is certain that while the prismatic spectrum of the white light of the clouds present a clear *yellow* and *green* portion, that same portion, when the direct rays of the sun are substituted, appears to the eye intensely brilliant and *white*. And it is far from certain that in some other experiments, which have been the occasion of some little controversy and where the *colour* of certain parts of the spectrum has appeared to undergo a change, the *intensity* of the light reaching the eye may not be concerned. In fact, the *sensation* of colour is one so entirely dependent on unknown physiological causes, that we can hardly venture to predict what the result may be on different individual eyes, though all the optical conditions may be precisely the same. It may not be altogether without a bearing on this subject, to remark the extremely contradictory statements made by different observers as to the *colour* of intensely brilliant meteors.—*Translator*.

The memoir of which I am speaking was destined for the Institute of Egypt. I find in fact, in a letter from Malus to Lancret, the following passage :—

"I send you, my dear Lancret, the work of which I have already spoken : mark out for me those things in it which any one might call repetitions of what has been already said, or which are useless ; if, after this expurgation, it should be reduced to zero, we will put it aside, and there will be no more question about it."

It is just to remark, after the critique from which I could not abstain when I considered that my task was not that of a panegyrist but of a biographer aiming at the truth, that the third part of the memoir was written before the publication of the fourth volume of the *Mécanique Céleste*, in which the same subject is treated with the greatest care. I would add that no army in the world ever before counted in its ranks an officer who occupied himself in the spare hours of advanced posts with researches so complete and so profound. The truth of this remark is not affected by the recollection which it brings up of the expedition of Alexander. It is true, men of science, at the recommendation of Aristotle, then accompanied the great general : but their mission was solely to collect the scientific achievements of the conquered nations, and not to make advances in the sciences by their own labours. This difference, altogether in favour of the French army, deserves, I think, to be here noticed.*

I see by a letter of Lancret, of the 14th Vendémiaire,†

* If this comparison were worth carrying out, the author might have added that the men of science in Alexander's expedition were not *officers of the army* charged at the same time with onerous and hazardous duties, but leisurely investigators, having no other occupation.—*Translator.*

† October 5, 1800.

an. IX., that Malus was occupied theoretically with that most important meteorological question, the distribution of heat in different climates. I have never been able to find what has become of this work.

TREATISE ON ANALYTICAL OPTICS.

On the 20th April, 1807, Malus presented to the first class of the Institute, a treatise on analytical optics, in which he treats of rays of light by geometry of three dimensions.

The choice of academicians to whose examination the work was entrusted, sufficiently indicates the reputation which the author had already acquired. These commissioners were Lagrange, Laplace, Monge, and Lacroix. The report of this distinguished commission was presented by Lacroix, and bears date the 19th October, 1807.

The author of the memoir examines the nature and relative position of the surfaces formed by straight lines successively intersecting one another according to given laws. After having deduced from his researches some general theorems, of a very remarkable kind, he proceeds to make an application of them to the case of rays of light proceeding in similar directions, either by reflexion or by refraction. He thus generalizes the theory of plane caustics, formerly broached by Tschirnhausen. Among the curious results which he deduces from his formulas, we will merely quote the following :—

"Reflexion and refraction furnish sometimes optical images which are erect in one of their dimensions and inverted in the other."

The report, for which I will not presume to substitute my personal opinion, concludes in these terms :—

"To apply thus, without any limitation on its generality, calculation to phenomena;—to deduce, from a single consideration of a very general kind, all the solutions which before were only obtained from particular considerations,—is truly to write a treatise on analytical optics, which, concentrating the whole science in a single point of view, cannot but contribute to the extension of its domain."

The Academy decided (which is the highest degree of approbation it can bestow) that the memoir of Malus should be printed in the *Recueil des Savants Etrangers.**

MEMOIR ON THE REFRACTIVE POWER OF OPAQUE BODIES.

On the 16th November, 1807, Malus presented to the Academy a memoir in which he treats a point of optics of great importance, a question, in fact, involving no less

* Malus's analytical theory contained in his *Traité d' Optique*, is prefixed to his prize memoir on Double Refraction, Paris, 1810.

The ordinary deviations by reflexion or refraction which rays undergo on impinging on given surfaces, may be investigated in all the simpler cases by means of elementary geometrical constructions, leading to the theory of foci, caustics, &c. But more general investigations of the same kind have been pursued by considering the algebraic equations of rays undergoing such deviations. This higher generalization leads to, and includes, the same results. An excellent discussion of the subject treated in this point of view will be found in Dr. Lloyd's *Treatise on Light and Vision.* It is a still higher generalization of this kind which was followed out by Malus. The reader who is desirous of seeing a condensed abstract of the leading mathematical principles involved, is referred to a brief but luminous summary drawn up by the Rev. A. Neate, M. A., and inserted in Professor Powell's *Elementary Treatise on Optics*, p. 71, Oxford, 1833. But the entire subject has been treated by a far higher analysis with extreme generality, and by a new and powerful principle of his own, by Sir W. R. Hamilton, in his essay on the *Theory of Systems of Rays.* Mem. of R. Irish Academy, vols. xv. and xvi., and Supplement, vol. xviii.—*Translator.*

than the grounds for a decision between the claims of the two rival theories of light.

The celebrated physicist Wollaston, some years before, had proposed a method by means of which to deduce the refractive power of all substances whether transparent or opaque. This method rests on the determination of the angle under which these substances applied immediately in contact with one of the surfaces of a prism of glass, through which we look at them, begin to cease to be visible.

Now according to the theory of reflexion* expounded

* To render what follows intelligible, many readers may find it perhaps desirable if we here explain, very briefly, the view of *ordinary reflexion* and *refraction* of light as explained respectively by the *emission* and the *wave* theories.

On the former a molecule of light resembles an elastic body, which if projected obliquely against a hard plane surface, by the principles of mechanics rebounds at *an angle equal to* that at which it impinged.

In refraction the investigation is more difficult: a molecule of light is here supposed to enter, projected with great velocity, among the molecules of the refracting transparent medium which are at such relative distances as to allow it freely to pass among them; but at its first entry among them it is of course *attracted* by them; it then becomes a problem of dynamics, requiring the aid of the higher mathematics, to determine what will be the path which it will pursue under their influence. In general it is clear, that under these united attractions urging it on, its velocity will be *accelerated:* but to go into the complete solution, would be beyond the limits of a note. It was fully investigated by Newton (*Principia*, lib. i. sect. xiv. prop. 94), where he demonstrates that on these principles the deviation of the refracted ray will follow the law that the *sines* of the angles of incidence and refraction are in a *constant ratio.*

Similar investigations have been pursued by Laplace, more especially with regard to atmospherical refraction, the atmosphere being supposed to consist of strata of different densities. (*Méc. Céleste*, vol. iv. liv. x. ch. i. 2, 3.)

On the *wave* hypothesis, the explanation admits of a very simple kind of illustration.

in the 10th book of the *Mécanique Céleste,* and founded on the corpuscular hypothesis, the formulas would be different for opaque and for transparent bodies. It is on

A set of waves propagated circularly from any source, when they get to a considerable distance, may be regarded as proceeding in parallel planes. In all cases, the portions of circles or spheres which are their true form have a common tangent which marks what is called the "front" of the wave.

But whenever waves encounter any kind of obstacle, or *enter any new medium,* then, from and round each point of such encounter, a new set of spherical waves begins to spread. In *denser* media these new waves spread *more slowly* than in *rarer*, but when the obstacle is still surrounded by the same medium, then the velocity is unaltered.

On these principles the ordinary laws of reflexion and refraction are proved on the theory of waves.

In reflexion, if parallel waves u u' follow at equal intervals λ, u im-

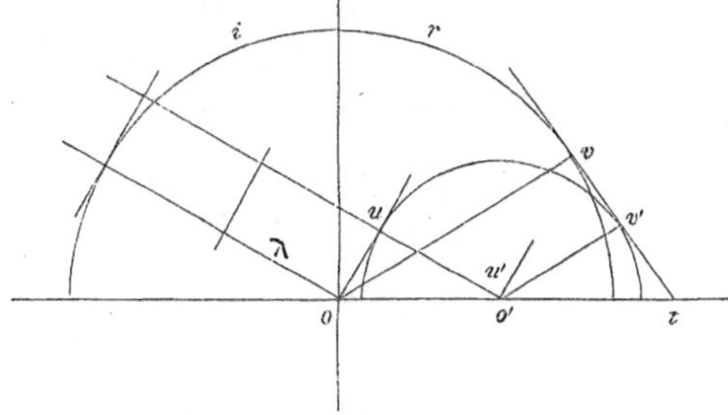

pinging on the surface at o, will cause a new circular wave to spread backwards from that point as a centre; when the next wave u' impinges at o', it will do the same, and so on in succession. But when the wave from o' has spread to a radius $=\lambda$, that from o will have spread to a radius $=2\lambda$, and so on. Hence to these contemporaneous circular waves drawing a common tangent $v\ v'\ t$ this will be the front of the reflected waves, and the radii to the points of contact $o\ v$, $o'\ v'$, will give the *inclination* of the *reflected* rays, which is easily seen to be *equal* to that of the *incident*, since $o'\ v'=o'\ u=\lambda$, and $o\ v=2o'\ v$, whence $o\ o'=o'\ t$, and the triangles upon these equal bases being right-angled, the angle $v\ t\ o=u\ o\ o'$, or the angle of *incidence*, is equal to that of *reflexion.*

this point then, they would say, that Wollaston was deceived. The object which Malus proposed in his memoir was to submit this point to a decisive experimental test. He chose a substance, beeswax, whose refractive power could be measured in the transparent state, and in the opaque state by the method of Wollaston. He applied to the angles of disappearance corresponding to these two conditions, and sufficiently different one from the other, the formulas of the *Mécanique Céleste*, and he found there would result refractive powers perfectly identical. This

For refraction; by an analogous construction, the circles which

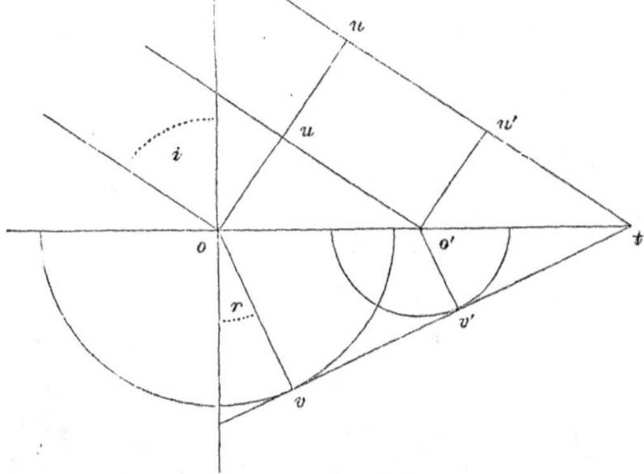

spread in the denser medium are smaller than those in the first, the radii being *diminished* in the ratio of the *velocities* or inversely as the densities. Thus when the new wave originating at o' has spread to v', that from o will have spread to *double* the same radius at v. The common tangent or front of the refracted waves will be inclined at an angle $o\,t\,v$, which is easily determined by drawing the parallel through t of the incident light, whence we have (i and r being the angles of incidence and refraction) $u\,t = o\,t$ sin. i, and $o\,v = o\,t$ sin. r; but $o\,v$ and $u\,t$ being the radii of waves in the two media, are in the constant ratio of the densities $=\mu$; hence sin. $i = \mu$ sin. r, which is the experimental law of refraction.

identity of the refractive powers of wax, when transparent and when opaque, which seemed to be a necessary result, appeared both to the author, to Laplace, and to all the

The law of refraction may also be more briefly deduced thus: taking the fronts of the incident and refracted rays perpendicular to their

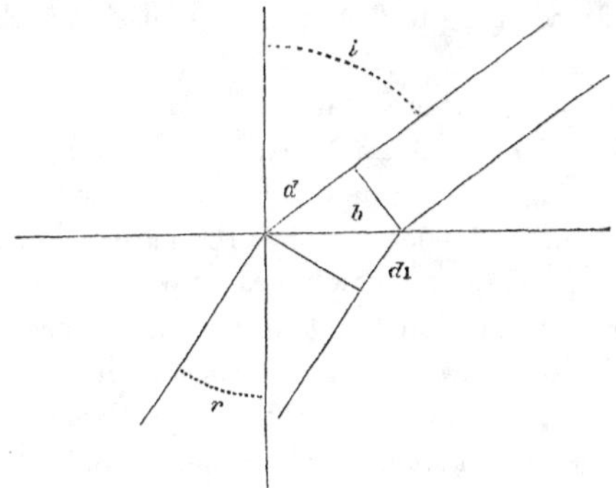

directions, their inclinations will be determined by the relative velocities with which those fronts advance; and while the incident front has advanced through a space d, that of the refracted will have advanced through d_1 proportional to their velocities; or,

$$\frac{d}{d_1} = \frac{v}{v_1} = \mu.$$

But geometrically for any breadth,

$$d = b \sin. i \qquad d_1 = b \sin. r,$$

Hence,

$$\mu = \frac{\sin. i}{\sin. r},$$

which is the law of refraction.

This method, though in a less concise form, is given by Mr. Power (*On Absorption of Rays, &c., Philos. Trans.* 1854, part i.,) who nevertheless calls in question the principle of the assumption that the *front* of the rays is strictly perpendicular to their direction, and proposes a more general view: from which, without any assumption as to the nature or law of refraction, he shows that the formula of the sines is directly deducible from his analysis. Objections, however, have been raised against his reasoning.—*Translator.*

mathematicians and physicists of the Emission School in Europe, to afford a mathematical proof of the truth of the emission theory. It is assuredly a singular thing that there should be this perfect identity of refractive powers calculated from angles of disappearance differing from each other, and according to formulas very dissimilar between themselves.

But what proof was there that the refractive powers ought to be identical? Ought we to suppose that the change from the solid to the fluid state in any substance would be without influence on its refractive power? Might we not cite cases in which heat modifies the refractive power of bodies independently of their density? Again, were the temperature of the wax and its density well ascertained at the moment of the experiment such as Malus was obliged to make it? Besides, would it be strange to suppose that within those limits where the action of bodies on light operates, there are no substances truly opaque!

Now that the system of emission is overthrown without hope of restoration, I endeavour to recall all the circumstances by which Malus might possibly have been misled. But, for my own part, I feel sure that I do not deceive myself in affirming that the memoir of which we are speaking offers a new proof of the mathematical spirit and experimental talent which Malus possessed in so high a degree. We ought only to regret that the conclusions in the report were so explicit that they represented the atomic theory of light as completely established; and that such a decision, emanating from individuals so competent as Laplace, Haüy, and Gay-Lussac, may perhaps have contributed to alienate our illustrious associate from that experimental path which

Fresnel a few years afterwards showed to be so astonishingly fruitful in results.*

* In the remarks here made by Arago on Malus's investigation of the refractive powers of solid and liquid wax, there appears some little obscurity of statement, and a degree of importance attached to the result as decisive between the rival theories, which it does not appear to deserve.

Perhaps for the general reader a few words explanatory of the method may be necessary, in order to see the general bearing of the case.

When a ray passes out of a denser medium m into a rarer n, the angle of refraction r will be greater than that of incidence i, according to the well-known law of the sines, which here becomes $\sin r = \mu \sin i$. But μ being constant for the same two substances, there is a certain limit to i when $\sin r = 1$ or $r = 90°$ or $\sin i = \frac{1}{\mu}$ that is, the refracted ray coincides with the bounding surface of the media, or it ceases to be refracted: and if i exceed this value, $\sin r$ would be greater than unity, which is impossible, *or the ray cannot emerge* from the denser medium, but must remain wholly within it. This alone, however, does not prove that it will be reflected. Experiment, however, shows that it is, and the precise angle i at which this begins to take place, or when $\sin i = \frac{1}{\mu}$ for any *pair* of media, can be easily and accurately determined; thus μ is found for that *pair* of substances, but μ is the compound ratio of the separate refractive powers of each out of vacuum or air; if, therefore, one of these is known, the other is deduced.

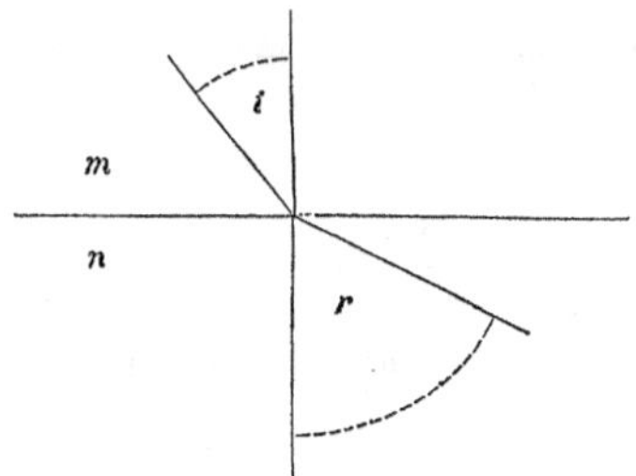

On this principle Dr. Wollaston's method was founded (*Phil. Trans.*

1802). Any substance *n*, of less refractive power than glass in optical contact with the base of a glass prism *m*, can be seen by an eye

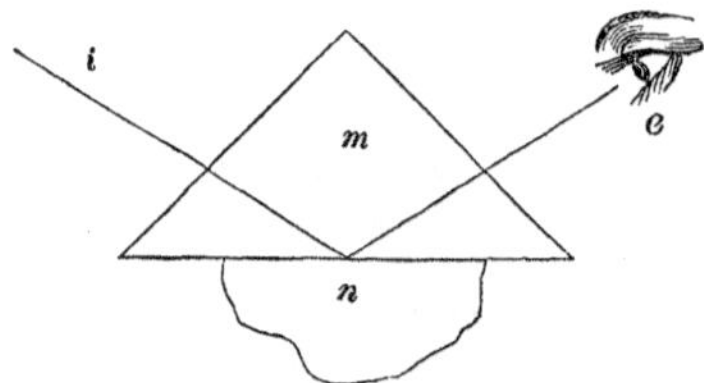

at *e* at any incidence *within* the limit just mentioned, or while the ray *i* entering the other side of the prism and impinging on its base, is incapable of being refracted out at the base, and therefore reflected from within; but as soon as this limit is exceeded, or the ray is refracted out at the base, then *n* ceases to be visible at *e*. The exact incidence or "critical angle" at which this takes place, is measured by an appropriate apparatus, and the refractive index for *n* deduced, that of the prism being known, a series of substances being applied in succession, whether transparent or opaque, Dr. Wollaston in this way determined their refractive indices. As the different primary rays have indices a little differing, and which are greatest for red light, Dr. Young remarked that the *limit* thus found applies in strictness to the *extreme red ray*.

In this way Dr. Wollaston found the refractive indices as follows:—

White wax,	boiling - - -	1.542
Ditto	cold - - - -	1.535

In the same way Malus found

Wax at 14° Reaum. (=63° Fahr.) - -		1.5123
Ditto	melting - - -	1.4503
Ditto	boiling - - -	1.4416

(These numbers are all lower than the former, probably from a different sort of wax being used.)

Dr. Wollaston, in applying the simple calculation above indicated to the observed angles, did not question the very natural assumption, that the same formulas would apply to the observed angles equally, whether the substance was opaque or transparent, solid or fluid.

Laplace, in a theoretical investigation founded on certain considerations derived from the molecular theory, framed his formulas on the assumption that the conditions were different for opaque and for transparent bodies, and even for the same substances in the two states respectively. The question at issue was the truth of this assumption, though it must be confessed that little appears in the tenth book

MALUS GAINS THE PRIZE PROPOSED BY THE ACADEMY FOR A MATHEMATICAL THEORY OF DOUBLE REFRACTION.

On the 4th January, 1808, the Academy proposed, as the subject for a prize in physical science to be decided in 1810, the following question:—

"To give a mathematical theory, confirmed by experiment, of the double refraction which light undergoes in passing through different crystallized bodies."

The memoir of Malus received the prize. Doubtless fearing lest he should be forestalled by some of the competitors, in the discovery of the singular properties of light which he had observed, this eminent physicist communicated the most essential parts of his researches to the Academy on the 12th December, 1808, without waiting for the period at which, according to the programme, the competition was to be closed. It is then to the end of the year 1808 that the immortal discoveries belong of which I proceed immediately to give you an analysis. The commission appointed to judge of the competitors was composed of Lagrange, Haüy, Gay-Lussac,

of the *Méc. Céleste* by which this conclusion can be considered as established.

Malus observed by Wollaston's method the *angles* at which the disappearance took place in wax, solid and in fusion. These *angles* were different; and calculated in the usual way, the *indices* of refraction resulted different also (as seen in the above tabular view).

The same observed *angles*, however, calculated by Laplace's formula gave the resulting *index* the *same* in both cases.

Now Laplace, Malus, and the emissionists, considered the identity of refractive power thus resulting to be a *necessary* truth—why so, we do not see; it is obviously, at best, a mere consequence of the *assumption* made at the first. The result is no proof of its truth, and decides nothing either way. Arago's laboured remarks therefore seem superfluous.—*Translator.*

and Biot. The report was presented by Lagrange, and thus nothing was wanting duly to signalize the important discovery of Malus.

DISCOVERY OF POLARIZATION BY REFLEXION.

We must go back to Erasmus Bartholimus to find the first observations relative to the existence of double refraction in Iceland spar, also called calc spar, or rhomboidal carbonate of lime. Huyghens had occupied himself with the study of these phenomena, and pointed out a geometrical construction of a very simple and elegant kind by which we can determine, in all directions and at all incidences, the position of the extraordinary ray relative to the ray properly called the ordinary ray, whose position is determined by the well-known law of the sines, made known by Descartes. Huyghens arrived at the discovery of this construction by means of an ellipsoid, which, as he tells his readers, he derived from considerations borrowed from the theory of waves.

The reporter of the Academy on Malus's memoir of the 12th December, 1808, entitled *Memoir on a Property of Light reflected by transparent Bodies*, who was no other than Laplace, wished that Huyghens had been contented to have given his law as the result of experience only. But I may be permitted to ask, Is not the hatred of theory carried too far when it leads to the suggestion of dissimulation or the want of sincerity?

Newton contended for substituting other rules instead of that of Huyghens; but these have not been found conformable to facts.

Among modern observers, Wollaston was the first who established the truth of the principles laid down by the Dutch philosopher. To make this verification he availed himself of the ingenious method by which he found the index of refraction by means of total reflexion. It appears that in 1808 these verifications had not appeared sufficient to the physicists of the Academy of Sciences, since they proposed the question as the subject of a prize for experimenters. However this may have been, Malus translated the construction of Huyghens into analytical formulas: he compared the deviation of the extraordinary rays deduced from these formulas with the numbers resulting from very accurate observations, and the accordance was in all cases very perfect. Thus the geometrical conception of Huyghens was found to be completely established, although originally the author was led to it by theoretical views.

A ray of light divides itself into two rays which are of exactly the same intensity whatever be the position of the crystal which it traverses, and in which the division into two is produced. But the case is different when the rays pass out of one crystal and are received into, and analyzed by, a second crystal exactly similar. If this second crystal is situated relatively to the first in such a way that the corresponding faces are respectively parallel to each other, the ordinary ray in traversing it only undergoes the ordinary refraction, and the extraordinary ray also remains exclusively an extraordinary ray. The natural light then in traversing the first crystal has thus changed its nature. In fact, if, in becoming double, it had preserved its original properties, the ordinary ray and the extraordinary would *each* have been divided into two rays in traversing the second crystal. At emergence from the second crystal we should have had four images instead of two. The first idea which occurs to the mind would be that the natural light is composed of parts which are susceptible, some of them undergoing the ordinary, some the extraordinary, refraction, and an equal number of each. But this hypothesis is radically subverted by a very simple experiment.

If we cause the second crystal to turn through one fourth of a revolution round itself, retaining the parallelism of its upper and under surfaces to those of the first, the ordinary ray will now become extraordinary, and the extraordinary will now undergo only the ordinary refraction.*

* The subject of double refraction, of which the most characteristic results are here stated by the author, is one which is rarely made intelligible to a general reader by a mere cursory description, and without going into some detail of the successive changes which result on receiving the two rays emitted from one crystal of calc spar on to another placed in successively varied positions with respect to the first. Perhaps few points are however easier to exhibit experimentally—which affords by far the readiest way of familiarizing ourselves with the whole phenomenon and its laws. It is only necessary to procure two moderately clear rhombs of calc spar, and attach to the side of one of them a card containing a small hole at the centre. It is then easy to look through the two crystals at the light admitted through the small hole; and keeping the two crystals with their surfaces in contact, the one next the eye can be turned round so that its angles point in different directions with respect to those of the other. For this purpose, by far the most convenient arrangement is to fix the two crystals in small tubes (such as card pill-boxes), which can turn one in the other: and if the crystals, and consequently the hole, be small (for the images not to overlap), it is very convenient to magnify the images by a small lens fixed in the tube next the eye, so that the object to be viewed in focus is the small hole at the farthest surface of the second crystal. The series of changes are these: setting out from a position in which the two rhombs are similarly situated, (as if parts of one larger crystal,) there are two images well separated. These are represented at B in the figure (the two at A being drawn for comparison when only one rhomb is used). Now, making one

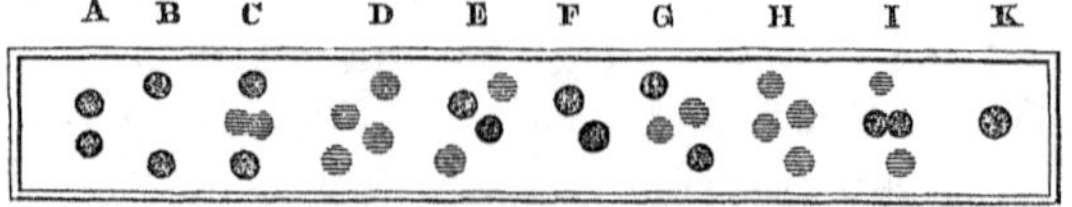

Thus, then, the two rays on emerging from the first crystal, instead of being changed in their nature, are exactly alike; it suffices, to show them undistinguishable from each other, to make one of these rays turn round the line of its own direction through 90°. Thus we are brought by the phenomena of double refraction to distinguish in rays of light *different sides* endowed with different properties. We are brought by observation to acknowledge that the extraordinary ray emerging from a

rhomb revolve continuously, we have *four* images (as at C) unequally bright by pairs: at 45° four *equally* bright (D), the other pair now become faint (E), until at 90° they are reduced to two, (F). The same changes are repeated at G and H; when at 135° the four are equally bright, till, after two become faint at I, we arrive at 180°, where, as at K, the two brighter coalesce into one. The same changes then take place in reverse order; four images at 225°, two at 270°, four at 315°, and lastly two at 360°.

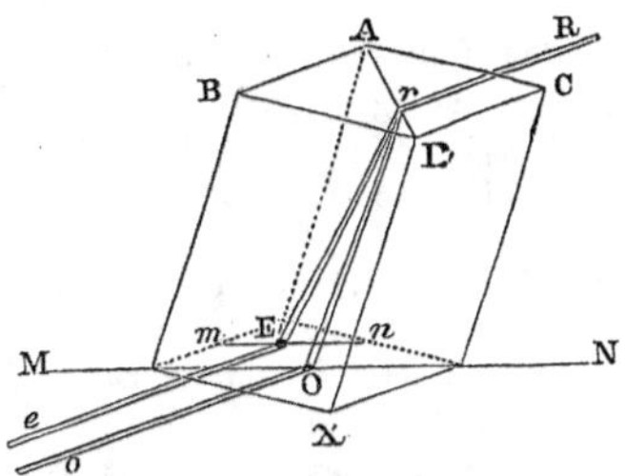

To give any idea of the analysis of these phenomena, it is necessary in the first instance to observe accurately the form of the crystal, and obtain a distinct idea of the terms the *axis* and the *principal section* of the crystals, which will be understood at once by the aid of the annexed diagram; where taking the *short* diagonal of two of the opposite faces of the crystal, as A D, the plane passing through it A D X, is the *principal section*, and the diagonal of that plane A X, the *axis* of the crystal. The double refraction of a ray R is represented by its division into two rays, O the ordinary, and E the extraordinary.

Whatever theory we adopt as to the nature of light, the phenomena can only be explained by supposing a section of each of the rays

crystal of Iceland spar, has the properties of an ordinary ray if we only make it turn round itself through a quarter of a revolution.

within the crystal to be of an *elongated* form; it may be represented by a short straight line, as O and E in the annexed figure (1.): if the

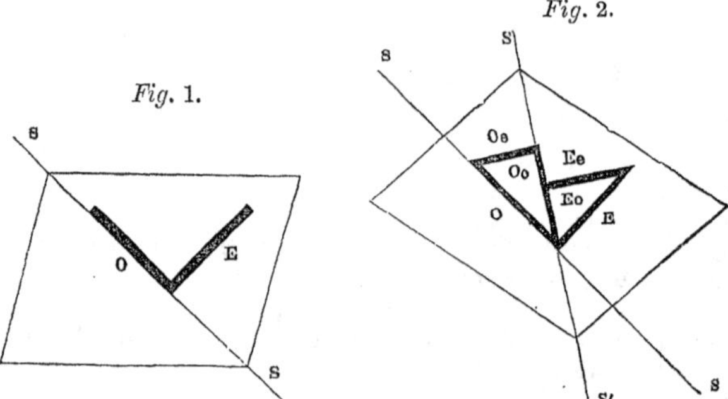

rhomb represent a section of the crystal looking down perpendicularly upon it, and supposing the light to fall on it in the same perpendicular line, S S will be the projection of its principal section, and the short lines O and E will be the projections of the sections of the ordinary and extraordinary rays.

Now let us conceive this first crystal to retain its position, and its principal section S S to remain parallel to itself, as in *fig.* 2, and a second crystal placed upon it, having its principal section S' S' inclined at any angle to the former; then supposing the sections O and E to remain as before, relatively to S S, that is one parallel, and the other perpendicular to it, when those rays enter the second crystal, the effect is that they can only pass through it in such portions as are either parallel or perpendicular to its principal section S' S'. It becomes then simply a case of *resolution of motions*, represented by the lines O, E, and it seems nearly impossible to imagine this without associating it with vibrations. At all events, the only way of conceiving the matter is to admit that in some way O is simply resolved into two components at right angles; one in the plane S' S', the other perpendicular to it, which are represented by O_o and O_e. In like manner E is resolved into E_o, parallel to S' S', and E_e perpendicular to it. According to the inclination given to S' S', relative to S S, the

If we call to mind that rays of light are so immensely attenuated that myriads of them can pass through the eye of a needle without mutual disturbance, reflecting minds will recognize how much there is most admirable and almost incomprehensible in the fact which we have just cited, the discovery of which is also due to Huyghens. The two pencils of rays which, after emergence from the crystal of Iceland spar, have sides endued with different properties, are called rays "polarized" in contradistinction to rays of natural light, possessing the same property all round their circumference, since they separate into two beams of the same intensity in whichever direction their *sides* may lie with respect to the form of the crystal with which they are analyzed. I have mentioned what ought to be the position of a second crystal, so that the ordinary and extraordinary rays emerging from the first crystal may preserve respectively the same denominations. In the intermediate positions of the second crystal, the rays, whether ordinary or extraordinary, coming from the first, in general divide themselves each into two, but the intensities of the two portions are ordinarily very different.

changes in magnitude in these resolved parts will give the relative brightness of the images.

Rays whose sections are represented as in the figure, are said to be polarized in the planes of O and E respectively; but it was long a disputed question whether the *vibrations* of which they consist, according to the wave theory, are actually performed *in* those planes, or perpendicular to them; the latter has now been shown to be the fact.

It need hardly be added that this can be considered only as a very general and popular kind of illustration; and for the more exact statement of the laws of these changes, especially with regard to the relative *distances* of the several images, or differences of ordinary and extraordinary refraction, recourse must be had to more profound mathematical investigations. See especially Herschel on *Light*, art. 785, *et seq.*—*Translator.*

Such was the state of our knowledge on this delicate and singular branch of optics, when, one day, in his house in the Rue d'Enfer, Malus happened to examine through a doubly refracting crystal, the rays of the sun reflected by the glass panes of the windows of the Luxembourg Palace. Instead of the two bright images which he expected to see, he perceived only one,—the ordinary, or the extraordinary, according to the position which the crystal occupied before his eye. This singular phenomenon struck him much; he tried to explain it by supposing some particular modifications which the solar light might undergo in traversing the atmosphere. But when night came, he caused the light of a taper to fall on the surface of water, at an angle of 36°, and found, by the test of a double refracting crystal, that the light reflected from the water was also polarized, just as if it had emerged from a crystal of calc spar. The same experiment made with a glass reflector at the incidence of about 35°, gave the same result. From that moment it was thus proved that double refraction is not the sole means of polarizing light, or of making it lose the property of dividing itself constantly into two pencils on traversing calc spar. Reflexion at the surface of transparent bodies—a phenomenon occurring every instant, and as ancient as the world—possessed the same property, without being hitherto suspected by any one. Malus, however, did not stop here; he caused an ordinary and an extraordinary ray from calc spar to fall simultaneously on the surface of water, and observed that at the incidence of 36° these two rays acted in a very different manner.

When the ordinary ray underwent a partial reflexion, the extraordinary ray was not reflected at all,—that is, traversed the liquid undiminished. If the position of the crystal was such, relatively to the plane in which the reflexion took place, that the extraordinary ray was partially reflected, then it was the ordinary ray which was entirely transmitted.

The phenomena of reflexion become thus a means of distinguishing from each other rays polarized in opposite directions. On the evening which followed the chance observation of the sun's light, reflected from the windows of the Luxembourg, Malus created one of the most remarkable branches of modern optics, and acquired the title which no one will ever contest to an immortal renown.

I should exceed the limits prescribed me, if I were here to analyze all the observations which our colleague made, in tracing the course of the direct and reflected rays in which the phenomena of polarization were developed. But I cannot omit, in order to prepare the reader for understanding the curious facts with which Malus enriched the science in 1811, to give the definition of a term which I shall have occasion to employ, that of a ray "partially polarized."

A ray of *natural* light always gives two images of the same intensity, whatever may be the position of the face of the crystal which it traverses, relatively to this ray. A ray *completely* polarized, only gives one image in two particular positions of the face of the crystal. A ray *partially* polarized, possesses in some sort properties intermediate to those of the natural and the completely polarized ray. Like the natural ray, it gives always two images; and as with the polarized ray, these two images have variable intensities, according to the position of the analyzer. Rays reflected from water or from glass, at angles greater or less than that of complete polarization, are partially polarized, and in a greater degree, as their inclination to the reflecting surface approaches nearer to 35° or 36° respectively.

Malus conceived that rays reflected from *metals* are not polarized even partially; but this was a slight error which was soon after rectified.

After his first researches, Malus believed that reflexion from certain transparent and opaque substances, besides double refraction, was the *sole* means of polarizing light. About the end of the year 1809, his views on this subject underwent a great extension; he, in fact, recognized, experimentally, that light which has passed through a plate of glass, shows at certain inclinations evident traces of partial polarization; and that if we form a pile of glasses, the natural ray which traverses them emerges completely polarized.

He did not fail to remark, that the polarization of the ray, in this case, was the opposite to that with which the *reflected* ray under the same circumstances was affected; so that if the latter were identified with the ordinary ray, emerging from a crystal placed in a given position, the former, *i. e.* the ray passing through the pile of glass plates, would be similar to the extraordinary ray of the same crystal.

It does not enter into our plan to point out either the detailed and very curious consequences which Malus deduced from his experiments, or the further improvements they have received. I shall content myself by here saying that whenever we find a substance which alone, at the angle of complete polarization, reflects one half of the incident light, the ray transmitted through a single plate will also be completely, instead of partially, polarized. We have no longer need, in order to obtain this complete polarization by refraction, to resort to a pile of glasses as Malus did; a single plate will suffice.*

After the experiments of Huyghens on the double refraction of Iceland spar and of rock crystal,† mineralogists recognized that there exists in nature a great num-

* The statement which Arago here gives as to the *complete* polarization of a ray by transmission through a single plate, is a result of the theoretical investigations of Fresnel; being in fact only a particular case of one of his general formulas which include the whole theory of polarization, both complete and partial.

According to Fresnel's principle, *common* light is *equivalent* to a combination of two rays of *equal intensity*, *polarized* in planes at right angles to each other. At reflexion each component gives a reflected and a refracted ray, which, again, are in planes at right angles to each other; but in these rays in the *reflected* pencil it follows, from Fresnel's formulas, that the portion polarized in the plane of incidence, will always be of *greater intensity* than the other, and the excess will show itself in the *partially* polarized character of the reflected ray at all incidences; and in the *refracted* ray there will in like manner always be an excess polarized in the plane at right angles to that of incidence. This excess changes with the incidence. At the angle of complete polarization the *whole* of the reflected ray is polarized, but as this amounts to one half the incident ray, the remaining half which is transmitted is also wholly polarized in the rectangular plane.—*Translator.*

† As the discovery of the very small double refractive power of rock crystal has been sometimes ascribed to later experimenters, it may be interesting to give the passage in which Huyghens describes his own observations of it.

He remarks, that his theory seems more probable "from certain phenomena which I have observed in *ordinary crystal which grows in a hexagonal form*, and which, in consequence of this regularity, seems also to be composed of particles of a certain figure, and regularly disposed. This crystal has a double refraction, as well as Iceland spar, though less evident. In cutting it into prisms by different sections, I remarked that in all, looking through them at the flame of a candle, or the leaden divisions of a casement, they appeared double, though with images very little separated; whence I saw the reason why this body, though so very transparent, is useless for telescopes when they are of any great length." *Traité sur la Lumière*, ch. v. § 20.—*Translator.*

ber of crystals endowed with double refraction; but when a crystal was proposed for examination, there was no way of determining whether it could be classed among this description of crystals, until after it had been cut into a prism, and trial made whether the image of a very narrow body, such as the point of a needle, would be double, seen through the two inclined surfaces, whether artificial or natural. But in 1811 a member of the Academy* showed that it was possible to decide such questions, without being restricted to the proof, often very difficult, of doubling the image. He proved thus the existence of double refraction in the thinnest plates of mica, which could in no way have been subjected to the former mode of examination. Malus generalized the results thus obtained by his friend, in a memoir entitled, *On the Axis of Refraction of Crystals and Organized Substances*, read to the Academy August 19, 1811.

LETTER FROM YOUNG TO MALUS.

On the 22d of March, 1811, Dr. T. Young wrote to Malus, in terms of great courtesy, to inform him that the

* Arago here alludes to his own discovery of the polarized tints displayed by any plate of a doubly refracting crystal when interposed between the polarizing and the analyzing parts of the apparatus. By this means the eye recognizes at once, by the appearance of colour, the existence of double refraction in that crystal plate which might be far too minute in the deviation of images it would give to be detected by the nicest observation; as well as the existence of polarization in any light examined by this test. It was thus that Arago detected polarization in the light of comets, proving that they shine by reflexion.

The same principle might be applied, to distinguish *on inspection* a small *fixed star* from an *asteroid*, and thus probably enable astronomers rapidly to discover more of those bodies, were it not that all known forms of polarizing apparatus necessarily involve so great a loss of light, that the method would probably be inapplicable to such faint objects.—*Translator*.

Council of the Royal Society of London had awarded to him the Rumford Medal.

So little was the progress which had been made in England in these new theories, that Young requested Malus to assure him whether a ray polarized by reflexion from glass, was really not reflected by a second glass suitably placed, as Malus had announced. In the opinion of the learned Secretary of the Royal Society, the rays which after a first reflexion were incapable of reflexion at a second surface ought to be absorbed or rendered inert.

Again we read in this same letter: "Your experiments demonstrate the *insufficiency* of a theory (that of interferences) which I had adopted, but they do not prove its *falsity*."

Malus, who was a declared and immovable partisan of the theory of emission, accepted with great joy the declaration of Young on the insufficiency of the doctrine of interferences. He always held out the opinion of the celebrated Secretary of the Royal Society to those who entreated him to examine, with his superior genius, the hypothesis in favour of which such men as Huyghens and Euler stood so openly committed. He did not remark that Young, in admitting the *insufficiency* of that theory in 1811, had the caution to add that nothing up to that time, even after the discovery of polarization, had proved its *falsity*.*

* It may illustrate further the want of due appreciation of the value of Malus's discovery on its first announcement, if, besides the letter of Young here quoted, we refer to several other passages in his correspondence, from which it appears how entirely the discovery of polarization was regarded as something if not quite at variance with the theory of waves, yet as wholly incapable of representation by its principles.

Young, himself, went so far as to predict that it was a problem

INVENTION OF THE REPEATING GONIOMETER.

Physical theories and experimental methods have a mutual reaction on each other. The former cannot be

which "would probably long remain to mortify the vanity of an ambitious philosophy, completely unresolved by any theory."

Again, in a review of Malus's paper (in 1811), he considers it "conclusive with respect to the *insufficiency* of the undulatory theory in its present state, for explaining all the phenomena of light." And again, in a letter to Sir David Brewster, five years later, he expresses himself thus: "With respect to my fundamental hypotheses respecting the nature of light (*i. e.* the wave theory), I become less and less fond of dwelling on them, as I learn more and more facts like those which M. Malus discovers; because, *though they may not be incompatible with those facts, they certainly give no assistance in explaining them.*"[1] Even Malus himself was at first of opinion that the phenomena of polarization were equally irreconcilable with both the undulatory and molecular theories; an opinion which he distinctly expressed in a letter[2] to Young.

Somewhat later, however, we find Young beginning to entertain a more satisfactory view of the case, as appears by the following passage from a letter addressed by him to Arago in 1817: "I have been reflecting upon the *possibility* of giving an *imperfect* explanation of the affection of light which constitutes polarization, without departing from the genuine doctrine of undulations. It is a principle of this theory that all undulations are simply propagated through homogeneous mediums in concentric spherical surfaces, like the undulations of sound, consisting simply of the direct and retrograde motions of their particles in the direction of the radius, with their concomitant condensations and rarefactions. And yet it is possible to explain in this theory a *transverse vibration*, propagated also in the direction of the radius, and with equal velocity; the motions of the particles bearing a certain constant direction with respect to that radius; and this is polarization."[3]

Now that the idea of transverse vibrations has become familiarized, it seems to present little difficulty; yet it was at first opposed to the prepossessions even of the most zealous undulationists. Fresnel long

[1] Dean Peacock's Life of Young, p. 379.

[2] Works, vol. i. p. 248, note.

[3] Life, p. 390.

brought to perfection without at the same time inducing a corresponding amelioration in the latter. In proportion as the crystallographic ideas of Haüy acquired more exactness, it was found necessary to employ, for the measurement of the angles of the crystals, methods of increasing precision.

Wollaston supplied this want by the invention of the reflective goniometer which bears his name.* Malus

hesitated fully to adopt the idea, after it had occurred to him as the only mode of representing polarization, on the ground of being unable to reconcile it with mechanical notions; and this more precisely as to the notion of *transverse* vibrations *alone* being produced, which constituted this theory in all its simplicity; whereas Young had (as we have just seen) believed both these and *longitudinal* vibrations to coexist. To establish *this* point, he expressly says, was the main difficulty which embarrassed him.[1]—*Translator*.

* The essential principle of the reflective goniometer of Wollaston is extremely simple, and consists in this: a piece of crystal or any

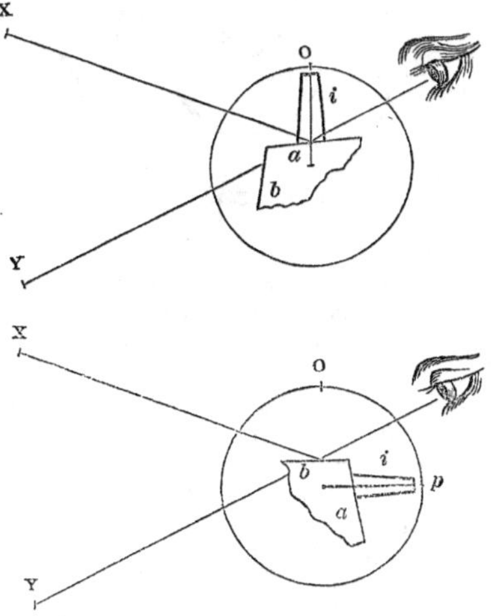

1 Ann. de Chimie, 1831, tom. xvii. p. 184.

added to the perfection of the English instrument by giving it the principle of *repetition.** He desired thus to

other object having two plane surfaces *a* and *b*, capable of reflecting light, is fixed at the centre of a graduated circle, to its index *i*. It is first brought into such a position that the image of an object X, by reflexion from the surface *a*, is seen by the eye coincident with another object Y, seen directly; the index marking 0. It is then turned round till the same thing is observed with the surface *b*, when the index marks *p;* the arc O *p* measures the inclination of the two surfaces *a b*, since the surface *b* now occupies the same position with respect to the circle which *a* did before.—*Translator*.

* The principle of "*repetition*" may be thus briefly stated. To *any*

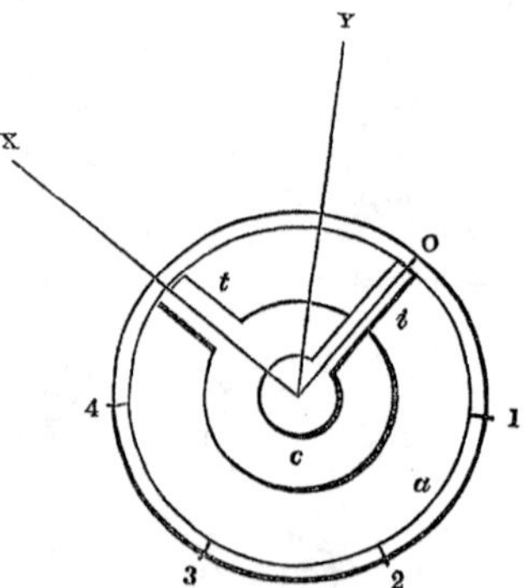

graduated circular instrument intended for measuring the *angular* distance of two objects X Y, there is added an inner circle *c*, moving about the same centre, to which is fixed the part *t*, which (by whatever means) fixes the position of the object; while an index *i* can be either fixed to the inner *c*, or to the outer circle *a*, by clamping, or can move independently. First, the index *i* being clamped to *c*, then pointing to 0, while *t* is directed to the object X; the part *t* is then turned to Y, while *i* moves over an arc O 1, equal to that between X and Y, and points to 1. Secondly, *i* is clamped to *a* at 1, and unclamped from *c;* *t* is moved back on X; *i* is unclamped from *a*, and clamped to *c;* and *t* moving with *i* is directed to Y; *i* consequently comes to 2, passing over an equal arc. Thirdly, the same operation is repeated, and *i* comes to 3, and so on for as many times as may be desired. The arc read off in each instance will, from the errors of

be able to compensate the errors of division by successive readings off, and to render the observer independent of the inaccuracies which the artist might have committed in dividing the circles. Unfortunately natural crystals, on which it is possible to use with any advantage the method of repetition, are by no means common. But the method preserves all its theoretical value when it is the object, in optical researches, to measure the angles of prisms formed by truly worked and perfectly polished planes. At the same time it is but just to observe that the idea of employing the reflexion of light for the measurement of angles, is due to the celebrated physicist Lambert.

MALUS A CANDIDATE FOR THE ACADEMY OF SCIENCES. —SITUATIONS WHICH HE FILLED.—HIS DEATH.

The more than ordinary labours of Malus, of which I have just given a rapid analysis, obtained for him the most sincere testimonials of esteem and admiration from men of science of all countries. He was named a member of the Society of Arcueil, which was composed of a small number of men of science assembling under the auspices of Laplace and Berthollet.*

A place in the Section of Physics of the Institute having become vacant in 1810 by the death of Montgolfier, Malus was naturally one of the candidates who presented themselves to fill up the place of the illustrious physicist.

graduation, be different. As *any* number of repetitions may be taken, we may have a mean result accurate to any extent desired.—*Translator.*

* The members of the Society of Arcueil were—Laplace, C. L. Berthollet, Biot, Gay-Lussac, Humboldt, Thénard, De Candolle, Collet-Descoutils, A. B. Berthollet, Malus, Arago, Berard, Chaptal, Dulong, Poisson.

Among the candidates there was conspicuous an engineer of roads and bridges, who had also borne a part in the Egyptian expedition, and whose connections with the academicians were numerous and of old date. Every one, therefore, foresaw that the place would be vigorously contested. On the day of election, August 13, 1810, one of Malus's friends undertook to bring him the news of the result the moment it was known. But by an unfortunate combination of circumstances the scrutiny was not opened till a later time than usual. Malus obtained 31 votes, his opponent 22. The friend of Malus, just alluded to, did not lose a moment in going to him to announce the happy result. But the usual hour at which the news ought to have reached him having long passed, the great physicist believed himself to have been defeated, and abandoned himself, in spite of all the consolations which his wife afforded him, to the deepest despondency. Thus the intrepid soldier of the army of Sambre and Meuse,—he who had seen the near approach of death at the combat of Chebreys, at the battle of the Pyramids, on the day of the revolt of Cairo, in the immortal day of Heliopolis,—the officer who at Jaffa and Damietta had sustained the attacks of the plague with such firmness of mind,—allowed himself to yield and sink under the supposed want of success in an election of the Academy! Let us preserve and value these recollections! Who will venture to maintain the uselessness of such institutions when he sees the author of one of the greatest discoveries of modern times attach such a price to the title of Academician? Who does not perceive with what emulation young experimentalists ought to be animated, when the society in which they aspire to take their place, constantly anxious to repel from itself all suspicion of party influence, holds itself in the first position in public esteem by taking the greatest care always to recruit its ranks solely from among those who are most worthy.

Malus had become major, a rank corresponding with that of lieutenant-colonel, December 5, 1810. The government had often entrusted him with the mission to classify in their order of merit the officers of artillery and engineers at their departure from the Practical School of Metz. He became afterwards examiner of the pupils of the Ecole Polytechnique for descriptive geometry, and the sciences dependent on it.

On the 14th Vendémiaire an IX.* Malus wrote from Benisouf to his friend Lancret: "I live here like a hermit; I pass whole days without speaking a word." It appeared that our friend often abandoned himself to his taste for silence. The pupils of the Ecole Polytechnique and the Ecole d'Application, related that in going over their exercises he contented himself by pointing out with his finger the parts on which he required explanations, without saying a word. This mode of asking, which contrasted so singularly with that of some other examiners, his contemporaries, not a little astonished them. But they did not the less do complete justice to the enlightened patience, the intelligence, and the perfect honesty which characterized all the decisions made by Malus at the close of his examinations. Malus filled, *ad interim*, in 1811, the functions of Director of Studies at the Ecole Polytechnique. There were only wanting some regimental formalities to entrust to him definitively this important employment.

The companion of his choice whom he went to seek at Giessen after the expedition to Egypt, threw over his

* October 5, 1800.

existence an unspeakable happiness. The most celebrated academies of Europe were envious to secure him as an associate. He was loved, honoured, and esteemed by all who knew him. He might look forward to fresh and brilliant discoveries of which his genius gave promise. He possessed, in a word, after the warlike labours of his youth, all that could attach him to life. It was at this juncture that, to the loss of his connections, of his friends, of the sciences, and the national glory, life failed him.

A consumption, of which he felt the first symptoms about the middle of 1811, made rapid and alarming progress, perhaps from some seeds of the plague which still lurked in his debilitated constitution.

Our colleague did not believe himself fatally attacked; for on the evening before his death, he exacted from one of his friends a promise to accompany him in the course of the week to Montmorency, whither he wished to retire for a short time to breathe the country air. But I can cite a still more demonstrative proof, if possible, of the illusion under which he laboured till the last. Returned from Egypt with the full persuasion that consumption is contagious, and above all that it follows attacks of the plague, he nevertheless allowed Madame Malus, with his head reposing against hers, to watch his least motions, and constantly to be surrounded with the atmosphere which he had breathed.

To the last this admirable woman could not believe in the misfortune which threatened her; and when the illustrious savant breathed his last, it was needful almost to use violence to detach her from the inanimate body of her husband. She survived him only a few months. Malus was only thirty-seven years of age when the Academy lost him.

CHARACTER OF MALUS.—MAXIMS AND PRECEPTS.—SUSCEPTIBILITY OF MALUS ON QUESTIONS OF SCIENTIFIC PRIORITY.

Our colleague was of a middle height and size. In spite of his reserved and cold manners, he had a friendly heart. An excellent son, a tender and irreproachable husband, a devoted friend,—he has left behind him, in the minds of all who knew him, the reputation, so much to be envied, of a truly good man. His conduct, always beyond reproach even in the most difficult conjunctures, was not merely dictated by an instinctive sense of right. In the leisure of his bivouacs in Egypt he had put down on scattered papers the thoughts and maxims on which he considered that his conduct ought to be modelled. I will here cite some of them which would not disgrace, I think, the most celebrated collections published by any of our philosophers.

"All the actions of life ought to tend towards the perfection of the soul and to social harmony."

"Hope is a source of happiness which is not to be neglected."

"I will found my enjoyments on the affections of the heart, the visions of the imagination, and the spectacle of nature."

"We must exercise patience, as the virtue most absolutely necessary for happiness in our moral existence."

"Mediocrity is a desirable condition of life, since it requires little expense."

"A great part of life often depends on circumstances. There are good things of which we must take advantage as they may occur;—as we enjoy the spring of the year; the brightness of a fine day; or the odour of a rose."

"As we cannot give children the idea of good, we ought to give them the habit of it."

"Even when we stifle reason, conscience comes as a *corps de reserve* to oppose a barrier to irregularity."

"I do not like men who weigh their own good deeds."

I find also in the papers from which the preceding forms a very short extract, a thought expressed in the following terms :—

"One becomes the slave of any man, if injustice on his part can offend and grieve us."

This last precept is full of wisdom ; but did the author himself always strictly conform to it? On questions of scientific priority has he not sometimes, to use his own expression, become the slave of his opponents? See and judge for yourselves.

Malus suspected a member of the Institute of Egypt of having wished to invade his rights on the occasion of an analytical calculation being communicated to that learned body. He was so preoccupied with this idea that in a letter addressed to his colleague he omitted to write before his signature, "I am, with consideration, your humble servant." The meaning of this suppression of a customary form of politeness is indicated in positive terms in a letter which I have before me from the officer of engineers to his friend Lancret.

A great geometer conceived the idea of a means of reconciling the phenomena of double refraction with the principle of "least action," and published on this subject a note which every one may read in our scientific journals.

Malus was convinced that he had himself first conceived the possibility of this investigation, and that he had spoken of it publicly before the publication of that note. He did not content himself with giving publicity to his first ideas without making any mention of the note from the pen of so justly celebrated a writer; but, in spite of his accustomed reserve, he expressed himself on this subject on every occasion with a vehemence of which he would not have been supposed capable.

I will cite a third example: An academician believed he had a right to contest with Malus the priority in an important discovery with respect to polarization. Malus was then at Metz; his letters bear witness, in terms which I know not how to repeat, to his extreme irritation. It appeared to him that the pretensions of his opponent were not well founded in fact, and also that justice enjoined that he should have been allowed reasonable time to explore the first beds of a mine the discovery of which belonged incontestably to him. I ask, nevertheless, whether the susceptibility of Malus can be altogether blamed? Those who defend with so much reason the rights of property as the corner-stone of modern civilization cannot be astonished to see our colleague attach himself with so much ardour to the defence of what is the first and most incontestable kind of property,—that which consists in the works of the intellect. Is it moreover quite certain, when the illustrious physicist showed himself so sensitive on the subject of the fruits of his labours and his genius, that he was not looking forward to one of these solemn meetings where the claims of men of science to the remembrance of mankind are enumerated and appreciated before an enlightened and impartial public,—a judge from whom there is no appeal? Would it then be strange that, seeing himself in imagination before this formidable tribunal, he had dreamed of coming there furnished with the greatest possible number of discoveries uncontested and incontestable? and that under the pressure of these preoccupations he had forgotten for an instant an abstract maxim of philosophy? However this may have been, the integrity and perfect honour of Malus will never be called in question.

In the collection of thoughts from which I have just given extracts, I read:—

"There are very few men, who, when they die, leave behind them any traces of their existence."

I hazard little in asserting that Malus will be reckoned among these privileged few. His name will go down to the most distant posterity, coupled with one of those great discoveries which, independently of their individual merit, have opened a vast career to the investigations of science. The immortal name of Malus will remain ever inseparable from that of *polarization*, under which all the most curious, the most fertile, the most brilliant phenomena of modern optics are grouped.

FRESNEL.

PRELIMINARY NOTICE.

THE Biography of Fresnel, the first which I had to read, as Perpetual Secretary, at a public meeting of the Academy, gave rise to incidents which several historians of our Revolution of 1830 reported incorrectly. I thus feel myself bound to give the true version of the facts. On arriving at the Academy, July the 26th, 1830, I read in the *Moniteur* the famous ordinances.* I understood in an instant all the political consequences which these acts would bring in their train; I considered them as a national misfortune, and I at once resolved to take no part in the literary solemnity for which we had been convoked. I announced my resolution in these lines, which were to be substituted for the prepared *éloge* :—

"Gentlemen,—If you have read the *Moniteur* your thoughts must doubtless be impressed with a deep sadness, and you will not feel astonished that, for my part, I have not sufficient calmness of mind to be able to take part in this ceremony."

I committed the fault of communicating this resolution to several of my colleagues. From that moment difficul-

* In allusion to the abrogation of the Charter by the ministers of Charles X.

ties arose on all sides. "If you execute your project," they said to me, "the Institute will be abolished; now, have you, the youngest member of the Academy, any right to provoke such a catastrophe?" And to support this remark, they pointed out to me several savants whose sole livelihood lay in their appointment as members of the Institute. These observations, strongly represented, shook my determination. The strife nevertheless became hotter; I could consent to read Fresnel's *éloge*, but I obstinately refused to cut out the passages which just before had appeared to be irreproachable, on the necessity to comply with the charter strictly, if it was not wished to open again the career of revolutions. Cuvier, from friendship for me, and also from interest in the Academy, was especially eager to obtain these suppressions. I communicated this circumstance to Villemain, who, without perceiving that the great naturalist was within hearing, exclaimed: "That is signal cowardice." From thence quarrels and personalities arose, of which I should feel scruples in depositing the remembrance here. The result, at the time of this lamentable circumstance, was, that the passages in question were preserved in the reading, and became the object, on the part of the public, of enthusiastic applause, which did not appear to be merited either by the matter or the form. I must own that I was much surprised when, on coming out of the meeting, the Duke of Ragusa whispered to me, "God grant that I may not have to go to-morrow to seek for you at Vincennes."

This Biography was read at the Public Meeting of the Academy of Sciences on the 26th of July, 1830.

Gentlemen,—"There are men who may be succeeded, but whom no one can replace." These words of one of the most honoured writers of our time, so often reproduced as the conventional formula on occasions like the present, are to-day in my mouth the faithful expression of what I feel. How could I, indeed, without the deepest emotion, now occupy before this tribunal a place which has been so worthily filled, during eight years, by the illustrious geometer whose unexpected death has been a source of no less regret to friendship, than to science and to letters.

It is not here, Gentlemen, for the first time that this sincere avowal of my well-founded diffidence has been heard. Nearly all the members of the Academy have in turn been the confidants of my scruples, and their encouraging kindness had scarcely succeeded in surmounting them. Devoted for a long time past to purely scientific researches, entirely destitute of the *literary* claims, which up to this moment had appeared indispensable in the difficult functions which were confided to me, I could only possess in the eyes of the Academy the slight merit of continued zeal, of unlimited devotion to its interests, of an ardent desire manifested on all occasions to see the renown which it had acquired enlarge, if that were possible, and extend itself in all quarters. The void which M. Fourier has left among us (as I was the first to acknowledge, and I acknowledged it without reserve) will be especially felt in these solemn meetings; it is then that you will recall to mind that language in which the most rigorous precision was so happily allied with elegance and with grace. Also I could not but persuade myself that the indulgence of the Academy presaged in some degree that with which the public would deign to honour me; otherwise could I have dared to make an inexperienced voice heard here, after the eloquent interpreter whom we have just lost, and by the side of him whom we have the happiness still to possess?

I hasten, moreover, to explain that this *éloge* departs from the ordinary form. I shall even ask the favour of its being looked upon as simply a scientific memoir, in which, taking occasion from the labours of our late associate, I have the opportunity of examining the progress which has been made in our times in several of the most important branches of optics. At an epoch when the courses of lectures at the *Collége de France*, of the *Faculté de Paris*, of the *Jardin du Roi* are attracting so great a concourse of auditors, it has occurred to me that the Academy of Sciences might directly address itself to the public (that friend of our studies, showing its good will by so numerous an attendance at our meetings) on some of the various questions with which we are specially occupied. At the same time this is but a simple attempt of my own on which I should wish to be enlightened; the critic will find me docile. I hope, however, that the satisfaction of becoming initiated in a few minutes into the most curious discoveries of one century, may appear a sufficient compensation for the inevitable tediousness which so many minute details must cause.

For my own part, the indulgence on which I count will not prevent my making every effort to render myself clear. Fontenelle, on a similar occasion, asked of his auditory (I quote his own expression) "the same attention which they would necessarily give to the romance of the Princess of Clèves if they wished closely to follow the plot, and to know the whole beauty of it." I am aware that I should not be right in demanding so little; but, on the other hand, I have the advantage of speaking before an assembly familiarized with deep study, and from which one may confidently claim a degree of attention which Fontenelle himself, at the commencement of the eighteenth century, would have found it difficult to gain from the frivolous assembly he was addressing.

INFANCY OF FRESNEL.—HIS ENTRANCE INTO THE POLYTECHNIC SCHOOL AND INTO THE CORPS OF BRIDGES AND HIGHWAYS.—HIS DEPOSITION FOR HAVING GONE TO JOIN THE ROYAL ARMY AT PALUD.

Augustine John Fresnel was born the 10th of May, 1788, at Broglie, near Bernay, in that part of the ancient province of Normandy which now forms the department of Eure. His father was an architect, and in this quality had been entrusted by the military engineer with the construction of the Fort of Querqueville, at one of the extremities of the harbour of Cherbourg; but the revolutionary storm having forced him to abandon this work, he retired with all his family to a moderate property which he owned near Caen, at Matthieu, a little village which already was not without some notoriety, being the birthplace of the poet John Marot, father of the celebrated Clement. Madame Fresnel, whose family name (Mérimée) was also to become one day dear to literature and the arts, was endowed with the most happy qualities of heart and mind; the solid and varied instruction which she had received in her youth enabled her to assist actively, during eight consecutive years, in the efforts which her husband made for the education of their four children. The progress of the eldest son was brilliant and rapid. Augustine, on the contrary advanced extremely slowly in his studies ; at eight years of age he could scarcely read. This want of success might be attributable to the very delicate condition of the young scholar, and to the precautions which it rendered necessary ; but it will be still better understood when it is known that Fresnel never had any taste for the study of languages ; that he always set very little value on the exercises which address themselves solely to the memory ; that his own, which was moreover very rebellious generally, refused almost absolutely to retain words from the moment that they were detached from a clear argument and displaced in arrangement : I must also own, without hesitation, that those whose predictions concerning the future of a child are founded on the precise estimate of the first places which he obtained at the college, in theme or in translation, would never have imagined that Augustine Fresnel would become one of the most distinguished savants of our epoch. As to his young comrades, they had, on the contrary, judged with that sagacity which rarely deceives them ; they called him "the genius." This pompous title was unanimously accorded him on account of the experimental researches (I may be allowed this expression, it is but just) to which he devoted himself at the age of nine years, whether for determining the relative length and bore which give the greatest power to the little elderwood popguns which children use in their play, or in determining which are the woods, dry or green, which are best to use in making bows, under the double consideration of elasticity and strength. The physicist of nine years old had, indeed, executed this little work with so much success, that the toys, hitherto very inoffensive, had become dangerous arms, which he had the honour of seeing proscribed by an express resolution of the assembled parents of all the combatants.

In 1801, Fresnel, aged thirteen, quitted the paternal hearth, and went to Caen with his elder brother. The central school of this town, where the instruction has always been creditable, presented then a *réunion* of professors of the rarest merit. The excellent lessons in mathematics from M. Quenot, the course of general grammar and logic from the Abbé de la Rivière, eminently contributed to develop in the young pupil that sagacity, that rectitude of mind, which guided him afterwards so happily in the apparently inextricable labyrinth of natural phenomena which he succeeded in clearing. The communication of knowledge is, of all the benefits which we receive in our youth, that of which a generous heart preserves the deepest remembrance. Hence the gratitude which Fresnel had felt towards his worthy professors at Caen was always lively and respectful. The central schools themselves always occupied a large share of his recollections; and I have some reason to believe that many reminiscences of these ancient institutions would have been found in a plan of study which he wished to publish.

Fresnel entered the Polytechnic School at the age of sixteen and a half, where his eldest brother had preceded him one year before. His health was at that time extremely weak, and gave reason to fear that he would be unable to support the fatigue of so rough a noviciate; but that feeble body enclosed the most vigorous soul, and in all things the firm will to succeed is already half the success; moreover, the dexterity of Fresnel in the graphic arts was nearly unequalled, and on this ground he could fully compete with the cleverest of his comrades, even whilst imposing upon him far less work in a day. When Fresnel went through the course at the Polytechnic School, a savant, whose zeal age has not cooled,—whom the Academy of Sciences has the happiness to number amongst its most active and most assiduous members, and whom, as he is listening to me, I will only designate by the simple title of the chief of living geometers,—fulfilled the duties of examiner. In the course of the year 1804, he proposed to the pupils, as a subject of competition, a geometrical question. Several solved it; but the solution of Fresnel particularly struck the attention of our colleague; for superior men enjoy the happy privilege of discovering, even from slight indications, the talents which will shine brightly. M. Legendre (his name escapes from my lips) complimented the young prize-man publicly. Proofs of encouragement coming from so high a quarter revealed to Fresnel, perhaps for the first time, the secret of his own merit, and conquered an excessive feeling of mistrust, which with him produced the most vexatious results, because it prevented him from attempting new paths.

On leaving the Polytechnic School, Fresnel passed into the department of the "ponts et chaussées." When he had obtained the rank of *ingénieur ordinaire*, he was sent into the department of the Vendée, where the government, desirous to efface the traces of our deplorable civil discord, raised up all that war had thrown down, opened communications destined to give life to the country, and laid the foundations of a new town. Every *pupil*, whatever may be the career he is about to enter upon, awaits with the most eager impatience the instant at which he may give up that title. To him, in four-and-twenty hours, the appearance of the world becomes completely changed; he has hitherto received instruction; he is going to create it. His future seems, moreover, to promise him all that a century may have offered in the way of brilliant occurrences to some few individuals favoured by fate.

Few engineers, for example, receive their diplomas without believing themselves from this moment called (like new "Riquets") either to join the ocean to the Mediterranean by a great canal which will carry merchantmen even to the centre of a kingdom, or to trace on the slope of the Alps the winding and bold road whose summit is lost amidst eternal snow, but which the traveller nevertheless will face even in the depth of winter. One has conceived the hope of ornamenting the capital with one of those light, and at the same time steady bridges, where the bold chisel of a David may some day come to animate the marble; another, remodelling the gigantic works of Cherbourg, arrests tempests at the entrance of roadsteads, provides useful harbours for merchantmen, associates himself finally with the glory of the national squadrons by furnishing them with new means of attack and defence. The less ambitious have dreamt of improving the course of the principal rivers, and rendering their waters deeper and less rapid by means of embankments; of checking those moving mountains which, under the name of sandhills, gradually invade rich countries and transform them into sterile deserts.

I will not venture to affirm that, notwithstanding the extreme moderation of his desires, Fresnel entirely escaped these happy dreams of youth. At all events the sequel was unexpected. To level small portions of road; to seek, in the countries placed under his superintendence, for beds of flint; to preside over the extraction of the materials; to see to their deposition on the road, or in the wheel ruts; to execute, here and there, a bridge over the irrigation drains; to reëstablish some metres of bank which the torrent has carried away in its progress; to exercise principally an active surveillance over the contractors; to verify their accounts; to estimate scrupulously their works,—such were the duties, very useful, though not very lofty, not very scientific, which Fresnel had to fulfil during from eight to nine years in Vendêe, in Drôme, and in Ille et Vilaine. How heavily must a mind of such power have been affected, when he compared the use which he might have made of those hours which pass away so quickly, with the way in which they were being spent! But with Fresnel conscientiousness was always the foremost part of his character, and he constantly performed his duties as an engineer with the most rigorous scrupulousness. The mission to defend the revenues of the state, to obtain for them the best employment possible, appeared to his eyes in the light of a question of honour. The functionary, whatever might be his rank, who submitted to him an ambiguous account, became at once the object of his profound contempt. Fresnel could not comprehend the conduct to which persons, in other respects very estimable, believe themselves bound sometimes by an *esprit de corps*. All fraternity ceased for him, notwithstanding the similarity of title and uniform, as soon as any one lost a probity free of suspicion. Under such circumstances the habitual gentleness of his manners disappeared, and gave place to a sternness, I will even say a roughness, which in this age of concessions drew upon him numerous vexations.

The purely speculative opinions of a studious man concerning the political organization of society, must generally be of too little interest to the public to render their mention necessary; but the influence which they exercised on the career of Fresnel will not allow me to be silent upon them.

Fresnel, like so many good men, associated himself deeply in 1814 with the hopes to which the return of the Bourbon family gave rise. The charter of 1814, executed without retrospective effect, appeared to him to contain all the germs of a wise liberty. He saw in it the aurora of a political regeneration which would, without a check, extend itself from France over all Europe. His patriotic spirit was excited with the idea that our beautiful country was about to exercise such a pacific influence over the good of nations. If, during the Imperial dynasty, the great events of Austerlitz, of Jena, of Friedland, had not strongly excited his imagination, it was solely because they appeared to him destined to perpetuate that despotism under which France at that time bent. The disembarkment at Cannes, in 1815, appeared to him an attack on civilization; and thus, without being hindered by the disordered state of his health, he was anxious to go and join one of the detachments of the royal army of the south. Fresnel flattered himself with the hope of meeting only with men of his own disposition, if I may judge from the painful impression which he experienced at his first interview with the general under whose orders he went to place himself. Touched by the invalid appearance of the new soldier, the general testified his surprise that in such a condition he should expose himself to the fatigues and dangers of a civil war. "Your superiors, Sir," said he, "have enjoined on you this expedition." "No, general," he replied, "I have taken no advice but my own." "I pray you tell me without reserve, has any one threatened you with not paying your appointments?" "No such threat has been made; my appointments have been regularly paid." "Very well; I ought, between ourselves, to warn you that you can here reckon only on what may be got by chance." "I have reckoned my own resources; I neither hope nor desire any other recompense. I present myself to you to fulfil my duty." "I admire you, Sir; it is thus that every good servant of the royal cause ought to think and act; I participate in your honourable sentiments; you may reckon on my good will."

That good will, in fact, did not fail; and the questions which at first had been painful to Fresnel, showed solely that his questioner, less a novice in the ways of the world, knew by experience that a popular gathering, under whatever colour it may show itself, includes more than a few individuals who under high pretensions conceal personal interests.

Fresnel returned to Nyons, his usual residence, almost dying. The news of the events of the Palud had preceded him. The populace (we know what this term signifies in the south) offered him a thousand insults. A few days afterwards an imperial commissary declared his deprivation of his office, and placed him under the surveillance of the police. Far be it from me to extenuate the odious nature of such a transaction. I ought, however, to say that it was executed without needless rigour, and that Fresnel obtained permission to go to Paris; that he lived there without being disturbed; that he was able to renew his acquaintance with his old fellow students, and to prepare for those scientific researches which he designed to pursue in the retreat where his younger years had been passed. At this time Fresnel had but a very confused idea of the brilliant discoveries, which, in the early years of the present century, entirely changed the aspect of optical science.

FRESNEL'S FIRST SCIENTIFIC PAPERS.

The first memoir on science which Fresnel drew up, dates from this same year, 1814. It was an essay whose object was to rectify the explanation, considered as imperfect, of the phenomenon of the aberration of the light of the stars hitherto generally followed in elementary works. Both geometry and physical science equally bore out this new administration; but, unfortunately, it too closely resembled that already given by Bradley himself and by Clairault. I say unfortunately, because, if we should suppose that such coincidences are pleasing to the self-love of a *débutant*, or stimulate his zeal, it would be a mistake. On the other hand, an author may support with philosophy, I admit, the unpleasant fact of having uselessly employed his powers for years in the search after a truth already long since established; he may give up, with the best grace, the flattering hope of seeing his name associated with some brilliant discovery; but might he not feel much more disquieted when there was ground to fear, that from mere ignorance of the existence of prior researches, of which no one dreamed, he might stand charged with plagiarism? when he might apprehend that an irreproachable character was no safeguard against such imputations? The public, notwithstanding the most express denials, will always believe that an author knows all that he might be supposed to know; and the right with which it is invested, to treat with implacable severity those who knowingly borrow from the labours of their predecessors, is the origin of more than one act of injustice. Thus, Lagrange has recounted that in his youth he experienced just such a profound mortification, on finding, by accident, in the works of Leibnitz, an analytical formula which he had completely forgotten, and of which he had spoken to the Academy of Turin as a discovery of his own. From that day he had nearly renounced altogether the study of mathematics. The demonstration of aberration was a matter of too little importance to inspire Fresnel with a similar discouragement; and besides, he had not printed it; but this circumstance rendered him extremely timid; and subsequently he never published any memoir without assuring himself by the testimony of some of his friends, to whom the academical collections were more familiar, that he had not, according to a popular proverb which he habitually adopted, "broken through open doors." *

* It is much to be regretted that this early production of Fresnel should not have been preserved—more especially when we recollect that the theoretical explanation of the aberration of light, though apparently well given by Clairault and others, was for a long time by no means clearly apprehended, and far from being exempt from all necessity for further elucidation. In proof of this it may suffice to allude to the fact that, on the occasion of the transit of Venus in 1769, two eminent astronomers, Bliss and Hornsby, calculated the effect of aberration as *accelerating* the phases of the transit, while Professor Winthrop, of Cambridge, U. S., argued that it ought to be that of *retarding* them. Other discrepancies of opinion in past times might also be cited; but the most striking fact has been the controversy in which the whole subject has been involved in our times, arising out of the somewhat startling ideas proposed by Professor Challis, and so largely discussed by that eminent mathematician and

The first experimental researches of Fresnel do not date earlier than the beginning of 1815; but setting out from this epoch, memoirs succeeded to memoirs, discoveries to discoveries, with a rapidity of which the history of science offers few examples. On the 28th of December, 1814, Fresnel wrote from Nyons, "I do not know what is meant by the polarization of light; beg my uncle, M. A. Mérimée, to send me the best works from which I may obtain information on this subject." Eight months had scarcely elapsed, when highly skilful researches placed him among the most celebrated physicists of our era. In 1819 he carried off the prize proposed by the Academy on the difficult question of diffraction. In 1823 he became a member of that body by an unanimity of suffrages,—a kind of success extremely rare, since it implies not only merit of the highest order, but also, on the part of all the competitors, a frank and explicit avowal of inferiority. In 1825 the Royal Society of London admitted him a foreign associate; and, lastly, two years later, the same body adjudged to him the Rumford Medal. This homage from one of the most illustrious scientific bodies in Europe,—this judgment, pronounced among a rival people, by the countrymen of Newton, in favour of an experimenter who attached little value to his discoveries, except as subverting a system of which that great genius was the defender,—appears to me to possess all the characters of a decree which posterity will confirm. I hope, then, it will be permitted me to appeal to this decree, if in spite of all my desire

Professor Stokes. (See *Philos. Mag.* 1845–6.) We merely allude to these points in order to show how interesting it would have been to have become acquainted with the view taken of such a subject by a mind so eminently *anticipative* as that of Fresnel.—*Translator.*

to confine myself to the strict boundaries of truth, and the consciousness which I have of never having transgressed them, it should happen that this *éloge* should be accused of some exaggeration. Though I must avow it would be a reproach for which I should feel little as the friend of Fresnel, if it were incumbent on me to repel it, it would be solely in the capacity of the organ of the Academy: the office which I this day fill, in the name of my colleagues, ought to be marked by a precision and severity as great as that of the exact sciences with which it is concerned.

REFRACTION.

The labours of Fresnel almost exclusively relate to optics. In order to avoid tedious repetitions, I shall classify them, without regard to the order of dates, in such a way as to collect in a single group all those which relate to analogous subjects. The first which will engage my attention are the phenomena of *refraction.*

A straight rod partly immersed in water appears bent or broken; the rays by which we see the part immersed must, therefore, have changed their route or have been *broken* themselves, in passing out of the water into the air. It was till lately supposed that to this one observation we were to restrict the entire knowledge of the ancients on the subject of refraction. But in exhuming from the dust of libraries, where so many treasures are yet concealed, a manuscript of the optics of Ptolemy, it has been found that the School of Alexandria had not confined itself to establishing the mere fact of refraction; for this work includes from all incidences, numerical determinations, tolerably exact, of the deviations of the rays, whether they pass out of air into water or into glass, or whether they enter glass on passing out of water. As to the mathematical law of these deviations, which the Arabian Alhasen, the Pole Vitellio, Kepler, and other physicists had sought in vain, it is to Descartes that we owe its announcement: I say Descartes, and Descartes* alone; for if the later claims put forth by

* In thus strongly claiming for Descartes the discovery of the law of refraction which English writers ascribe to Willebrod Snell, Arago might be supposed actuated by a feeling of national pride, which not, unfrequently, perhaps, influenced him on questions of this kind. The strong expression with which he concludes the sentence, seems, however, to point to a more philosophical motive, and to refer the claim of Descartes to considerations derived from the connection of the law of refraction with his theories. However this may be, it may be well briefly to recapitulate the facts of the case. The ancients, especially Ptolemy, had amassed many measured results. Alhasen (A.D. 1100) stated the general principle that refraction in a denser medium causes the ray to deviate nearer to the perpendicular. Vitellio collected a number of measured results in different media at different angles of incidence; among which Kepler attempted, with his usual ardour, to endeavour to deduce some general numerical relation. He, however, could proceed no further than this—that while the *angle of incidence* is but small, it is in a *constant ratio* (dependent on the nature of the medium) to that of *refraction;* but that, as we deviate more from the perpendicular, the rule becomes less accurate, and soon fails.

Willebrod Snell, in 1621, investigated and established, by comparison of numerical results, a general geometrical mode of representing the case, which, expressed in modern terms, is the true law of refraction (or $\sin i = \mu \sin r$), a constant ratio between the *sines*, not the angles, where i and r are the angles of incidence and refraction, and μ the constant or refractive index. And the relation observed by Kepler, which is true so long as the angle is small enough to be nearly proportional in its sine, is thus extended and generalized. Snell died in 1626 without having printed his discovery; but it had been shown in MS. to many persons, especially to Huyghens, who fully perceived its value and importance. And it is on his authority that the discovery was properly assigned to Snell by Montucla, Bossut, and other writers. Huyghens, however, did not *publish* any account of the matter till it appeared in his *Dioptrica*, which was printed after his death in 1700.

Huyghens in favour of his fellow countryman Snell be accepted, we must give up the pretence of writing the history of science.

A mathematical law has more importance than an ordinary discovery, for it is itself a source of discoveries. From it simple analytical transformations point out to observers a multitude of results more or less hidden, of which they would with difficulty have become aware; but such results cannot be accepted without reservation, so long as the truth of the primary law rests *solely* on measurements. It is necessary for science that this law should acquire that character of demonstration which mere experiments alone, however precise, cannot confer, by being traceable upwards to the first principles of matter.

Descartes then attempted to establish his law of refraction by considerations purely mathematical; perhaps it was thus also that he discovered it? Fermat combated the demonstration of his rival, and replaced it by a method more rigorous, but which had the serious fault

Vossius states that, among others, the contents of Snell's MS. were shown to Descartes.

That philosopher, however, in a manner very usual with him, commences treating the subject on entirely original grounds; and, in the course of a purely theoretical speculation deduces the same law of refraction as a consequence of his *à priori* principles (*Dioptrica*, 1637, ch. ii. § 9), without making the slightest allusion to Snell. Hence the discovery of the law has been assigned to him, especially by French writers. It is to be observed, however, that he in no way attempts to found his deduction on any comparison of experimental results. Thus, even admitting that Descartes is entitled to the establishment of the law as a *theoretical* deduction, he clearly has no claim to the experimental verification of it, which is by far the most material point; and the more so as his theory is based on the assumption, now proved to be false, that light is *accelerated* in passing through the denser medium.—*Translator.*

of being dependent on a metaphysical principle of which he did not show the necessary truth.* Huyghens ar-

* The theoretical principles here glanced at, are those connected with speculations on one of the most curious points presented by the theory of light; which, perhaps, it may be desirable briefly to explain. Ptolemy had shown that when light is reflected from any surface, the law of reflexion, or equality of angles, is precisely that which causes light to pass from any one point in its course, before incidence to any other in its reflected course, by the *shortest* path and in the *least* time, its velocity being uniform and equal before and after reflexion.

Fermat extended the same principle, called the "principle of least time," to the case of *refraction* according to the law of sines, provided we suppose the velocity *diminished* in the denser medium: that is, he showed that *the sum of the times*, or of the *spaces* DIVIDED *by the velocities*, is a minimum.

Huyghens, adopting the theory of waves, deduced from it the law of the sines; and as, in conformity with that theory, the velocity must be *diminished* in the denser medium, on this theory the principle of "least time" applies to the case of refraction, and that of reflexion also easily follows as a particular case.

On the other hand, on the *molecular theory*, the law of refraction is deduced on the principle of attraction, which the molecules undergo in the medium, and it is a necessary consequence that the velocity must be *increased* in the denser medium. Maupertuis, on these principles, attempted an analogous investigation; but here it was necessary to adopt, not the principle of "least time," but that of "least action," or that the sum of *the* PRODUCTS *of the spaces and velocities* is a minimum; and, on this view, the law of the sines equally results as that which fulfils the condition.

This refers to ordinary refraction: when the same inquiry was extended to double refraction, or to the extraordinary ray, more complex considerations were introduced. This subject is fully discussed by Dr. Young in his Life of Fermat. (*Works*, ed. Peacock, vol. ii. p. 584.) The same principle was the basis of Laplace's investigation of double refraction, of which ("Sur la Loi de la Réfraction Extraordinaire, &c.," *Journal de Physique*, 1809) Dr. Young produced his well-known refutation in the *Quarterly Review* for the same year.

In the case of ordinary refraction, the investigation is very simple. As it is not clearly stated, as far as we are aware, in any elementary treatise, it may be satisfactory to some readers to have it briefly put before them.

Let any lengths, respectively, of the incident and refracted rays be

rived at the result, setting out from the ideas he had adopted of the nature of light. And, lastly, Newton de-

$l\ l'$, described with the velocities $v\ v'$, which are in a constant ratio to each other; and in times which will be $\frac{l}{v}\ \frac{l'}{v'}$. Then, on the principle of "least time," the condition is,

$$\frac{l}{v}+\frac{l_{\prime}}{v_{\prime}}=\text{minimum};$$

or, differentiating and multiplying by $v\ v'$,

$$v'\,d\,l+v\,d\,l'=0\ \ldots\ .\ (1).$$

Then if x be the surface of the medium, taking equal increments $d\,x$ on each side of the point of incidence, and dropping perpendiculars

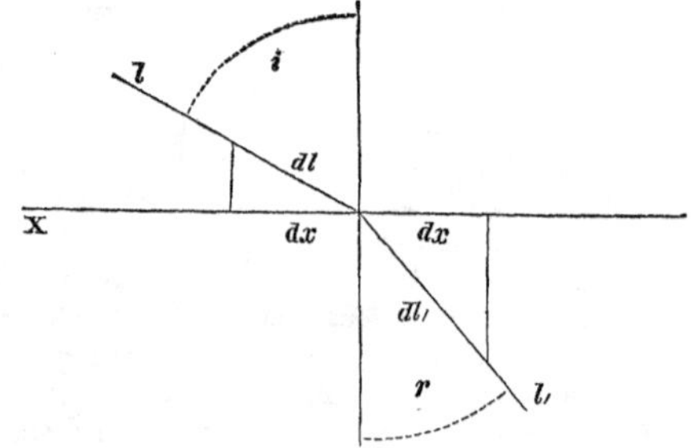

to give corresponding increments $d\,l\ d\,l'$, i and r being the angles of incidence and refraction, we have geometrically

$$d\,l=\frac{\sin i}{dx}d\,l'=\frac{-\sin r}{dx}\ \ldots\ .\ (2);$$

and substituting in (1) it becomes

$$v'\sin i-v\sin r=0,$$

or

$$\sin i=\frac{v}{v'}\sin r.$$

But, as i is necessarily greater than r, it follows that the v must be greater than v': or the law of the sines fulfils the condition of "least time" on the wave theory.

On the other hand, the principle of "least action" requires, instead of equation (1), that we have

$$l\,v+l'\,v'=\text{minimum},$$

or

$$v\,d\,l+v'\,d\,l'=0:$$

whence, by precisely the same process, there results

$$\sin i=\frac{v'}{v}\sin r;$$

duced it from the principle of attraction, because that law

which can only agree with observation provided v' be greater than v, or the velocity be *increased* in the refracting medium, which agrees with the molecular theory.

On either supposition, if $v = v'$, and sin r positive, the case becomes that of *reflexion*, and we have $i = r$, which is the law of reflexion, whence Ptolemy's conclusion is manifest as a particular case of the general theory. The case of reflexion is, in fact, nothing more than a geometrical problem.

Let two points I R, be given without a given straight line X X′, and let O be the point in that line at which straight lines drawn from I

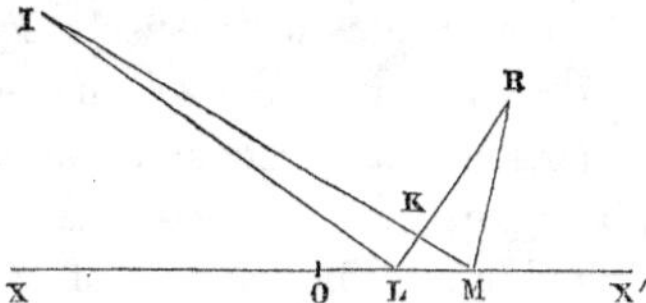

and R make equal angles with X X′. Then taking any other pairs of lines I L, L R, and I M, M R, terminating in the same points and meeting X X′ in L and in M, they will each form unequal angles with X X′; R L X′ greater than I L X, and R M X′ greater than I M X. Let I M and L R intersect in K.

Then we have the angle R L M greater than I L X, which is greater than the opposite and interior I M L; and therefore in the triangle K L M, K M is greater than K L.

In the limit, when M approaches L, we have ultimately I K=I L, and K R=M R; whence I L+L K+K R is less than I K+K M+M R, or the pair of lines nearest to O are together less than the more remote. The same reasoning will apply to all pairs of lines on either side of O; therefore the lines meeting at O are a minimum.

It is an extension of this principle which forms the basis of the investigations of Sir W. R. Hamilton. Observing that in some parallel instances the action is, in fact, not a case of minimum, but of maximum, he has adopted the more generic term, "stationary action;" and upon this has based his fundamental idea of the "characteristic function," by the aid of which his profound analytical system, applicable equally in questions of optics and dynamics, is constructed. For an admirable exposition of the general principle the student should consult Sir W. R. Hamilton's paper on "The Paths of Light and of the Planets" in the *Dublin University Review*, Oct. 1833.—*Translator*.

occupied the attention of the greatest geometers of the seventeenth century.

The question had arrived at this point, when a traveller, returning from Iceland, brought to Copenhagen some beautiful crystals from the Bay of Roërford. Their great thickness and remarkable transparency rendered them particularly proper for experiments on refraction. Bartholinus (1669), to whom they were sent, took care to subject them to different trials ; but what was his astonishment when he perceived that the light divided itself into two distinct beams of precisely equal intensities,—when he recognized, in one word, that seen through the Iceland spar (which has been since found in many other localities, being nothing but carbonate of lime) all objects appear double ! The theory of refraction, so many times recast, had now need of a new examination. At all events it was incomplete, for it spoke only of one ray, and two were here seen. Besides, the direction and the magnitude of the deviation of the two rays changed, apparently in the most capricious manner, when we passed from one face of a crystal to another, or when on one face the direction of the incident ray varied.*

Huyghens surmounted all these difficulties ; a general law was found to comprehend in its announcement all the lesser details of the phenomena ; but this law, in spite of its simplicity and elegance, was misconstrued. Hypotheses had been for so many ages useless or faithless guides ; they had been so long considered as constituting the whole of physics, that, at the epoch of which I speak, experimenters had on this point arrived at a sort of reaction ; and in such reactions, even in science, it is rare to be

* See above, note, p. 150.

able to keep a just mean. Huyghens had given his law as the result of an hypothesis; men rejected it therefore without examination. The measures on which it was founded could not redeem it from what was thought vicious in its origin. Newton himself took part among its opponents; and from this moment the progress of optics was arrested for more than a century. Since that period, the numerous experiments and measures of two of the most celebrated members of this Academy, Wollaston and Malus, have replaced the law of Huyghens in the rank to which it is entitled.*

* Newton had rejected Huyghens's law, and substituted one founded on measures of his own. In 1788 Haüy repeated the measurements, and showed that Huyghens's rule was far more accurate than Newton's. In 1802 Wollaston repeated similar observations by his new method, in ignorance of Huyghens's law; but found them well represented when that law was pointed out to him—probably by Dr. Young, as the circumstance is stated by him in an article in the *Quarterly Review*, Nov. 1809, p. 338.

Some idea may be given of the simple geometrical construction determining the direction of the extraordinary ray which results from Huyghens's theory, as follows: Supposing portions of the concentric sphere and spheroid within the crystal, whose axis a coincides with the axis of revolution of the spheroid; and conceiving a second spherical surface concentric, and of greater radius, as that which would have been the wave surface if the velocity had remained undimin-

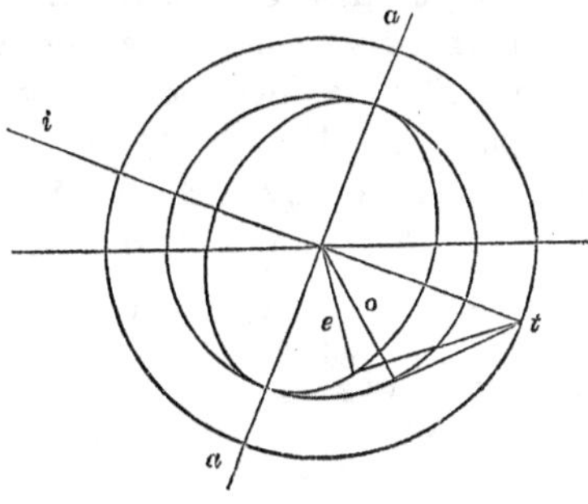

During the long discussions which took place among physicists on the mathematical law according to which double refraction is produced in Iceland spar, the existence of the second ray was generally considered as an anomaly affecting half the incident light; the other half, it was said, obeyed the old law of refraction laid down by Descartes: the carbonate of lime, in its crystallized state, then, enjoys certain particular properties, but without losing those which all ordinary transparent media possess. All this was exact in the instance of the Iceland spar, and it seemed as if it might without hazard be asserted generally; but in fact those who maintained this deceived themselves. There are crystals in which the principle of ordinary refraction is not verified; and in which the two rays into which the incident light divides itself *both* undergo anomalous refractions, where the law of Descartes does not indicate the course of either ray.

When Fresnel for the first time published this unexpected result, he had as yet verified it only by the aid of an indirect method, remarkable for the strange circumstance that the refraction of the rays was deduced from experiments in which no refraction took place. Thus our colleague found more than one incredulous reader. The singularity of the discovery, perhaps, demanded some hesitation: perhaps also in the eyes of some persons, it had the fault, like the law of Huyghens, of being the fruit of an hypothesis. However it may have been, Fresnel met the difficulty boldly. By showing that in a parallelopiped of topaz, formed of two prisms of the same

ished; then from the extremity *t* of the incident ray *i* as if produced to meet this sphere, drawing tangent planes to the sphere and spheroid respectively, the points of contact will give the position of the ordinary and extraordinary rays *o* and *e*. See Peacock's *Life of Young*, p. 373.—*Translator*.

angle, opposed, no ray passes between the opposite and parallel faces without undergoing deviation, he rendered all objections vain.*

* The paradoxical mention of proofs of refraction, where no refraction takes place, may need a brief explanation.

Fresnel's experiment, here referred to, was performed by means of the simple interference of two rays produced by reflexion from plane mirrors very little inclined from the same plane, or by transmission through a very obtuse-angled prism. If, in the path (as explained in a subsequent note) of each of the two interfering rays, plates of glass of exactly the same thickness are interposed, the position of the stripes remains unaltered; but if the plates be cut from a *biaxial* crystal in different directions with respect to its axis, but still of exactly the same thickness, even if we employ those rays which correspond to the *ordinary* rays in Iceland spar, there will be a displacement of the stripes, showing a difference of velocity or refraction, in these rays, on the principle hereafter explained, (see note *infra.*)

The more direct experiment alluded to consists in this: Fresnel cut two prisms in different directions from the same crystal of topaz, which, being cemented together with their axes in one line, were ground together to exactly the same angle, and the whole achromatized by another opposed prism. On looking through the two prisms thus fixed side by side at a line of light, that line was seen to be broken at the junction, indicating different refractions in the two.

The law of Huyghens, or the construction of the sphere and spheroid, was found to hold good not only in Iceland spar, but in many other doubly refracting crystals. But these were all characterized by possessing only *one* axis or line along which there was no double refraction, and which, by the aid of polarized light, is easily detected as forming the centre of the rings.

Sir D. Brewster, in examining a vast variety of crystals, discovered a class in which there was not *one* such axis, but *two*, and in which the rings consequently assumed new and more complex forms, being either arranged in two separate sets if the axes were distant, or in coalescing curves if they were close.

For biaxial crystals Huyghens's law will not apply. The incident ray is divided into two; but neither of them follows the law of the sines represented by the sphere in his construction. One of the rays is, indeed, usually less subject to deviation than the other, and thus, for convenience, is still often called the ordinary ray; but both are, in strictness, *extraordinary* rays.

Those physicists (I could here cite the names of some of the most celebrated) who have sought to include in a

Hence the necessity for a more comprehensive theory. As Huyghens had constructed such a theory by means of an independent sphere and spheroid, Fresnel not only generalized the construction by a method giving two curved surfaces of higher forms, but he did what Huyghens's method did not effect, even in the simple case which he considered,—he showed also a *necessary connection* between the two surfaces; they were in fact *not two*, but portions of one surface—parts of the geometrical representation of the same algebraic equation, or, in the language of mathematicians, "a curve surface of two sheets." Thus Fresnel's theory showed not only the laws by which each ray was refracted, but also why there must be *two* rays.

Of this more generalized mathematical investigation, the greater part of the steps were omitted by Fresnel in his memoir, as being of too complicated and tedious a nature for the patience of his readers; he presents only the conclusions, which are derived from certain suppositions with respect to the elasticity of the ether, as being different in different directions within the crystal, and ultimately lead to an algebraic equation, representing a curved surface of the fourth order, consisting of two sheets or portions, as the general form assumed by the waves, but which in certain cases, as in calc spar, is reducible to the simpler form of the sphere and spheroid of Huyghens.

For a connected view of these investigations the reader is referred to Professor Powell's *Treatise on the Undulatory Theory, &c.* page 48. London, 1841.

The mathematical investigation has since called forth much elucidation, especially in supplying the suppressed processes of Fresnel, in which the analysis of Mr. A. Smith, as well as those of Sir J. Lubbock, Professor Sylvester, Sir W. R. Hamilton, and others, have been eminently successful; while the last-named mathematician pointed out the very curious consequence that this surface, mathematically speaking, presents, at the extremities of the axis, *conoidal cusps*,—that is, depressions of a pointed funnel shape,—which, physically interpreted, would show that a ray passing along that direction ought to emerge no longer a *single* ray, but spread out in a *conical surface* whose surface would not be a *point* of light, but a *ring* with a dark central space. This extraordinary prediction, so wholly unlike any thing hitherto imagined, was, however, fully verified by the observations of Dr. Lloyd on a crystal of aragonite; the phenomenon being known by the name of "*conical* refraction."—*Translator.*

single rule all the possible cases of double refraction, were thus misled, for they all admitted, as a fact of which no one could doubt, that for half the light, for the rays called "ordinary rays," the deviation ought to be the same at the same incidence in whatever direction the plane of incidence cut the crystal. The true law of these complicated phenomena—the law which includes, as particular cases, the laws of Descartes and of Huyghens—is due to Fresnel. This discovery required in an eminently high degree the union of a talent for experiment with the genius of invention.

I freely admit that the phenomena of double refraction recently analyzed by Fresnel, and the laws which connect them, are not exempt from a certain complexity. This is indeed a subject of regret—almost, I might say, of lamentation—among some idle minds, who would wish to reduce every science to those superficial notions of which they might make themselves masters by a few hours' work. But does not every one see that with such ideas the sciences would not make any progress; that to neglect such phenomena because one feeble intellect may experience some trouble in grasping them, would be to be false to our vocation, and that thus we should often allow the most important discoveries to pass by us.

Thus astronomy, while limited to a knowledge of the constellations, and to some insignificant remarks on the risings and settings of the stars, was within the capacity of minds of any class: but could we then call it a science? From that time till after the most colossal labour which one man ever went through,—Kepler had substituted elliptic motions not uniform, for the circular and regular motions which, according to the ancients, prevailed in the planets,—his contemporaries might with equal right have complained of complexity. But again, some time after, in the hands of Newton, these motions, complex in appearance, became the basis of the greatest discoveries of modern times, of a principle as simple as it is fertile; they served to prove that every planet is governed in its elliptic course by a simple force, by an attraction emanating from the sun.

Those observers again, who, in their turn refining upon Kepler, showed that simple elliptic motions would not suffice to represent the true paths of the planets, did not *simplify* the science. But besides that the derangement (known under the name of perturbations) would not the less have existed if, in the dislike of all complexity, we had obstinately determined to shut our eyes to them, I ought to say, that in studying them with care we have been conducted, among many other important results, to the means of comparing the *masses* of the different bodies of which our solar system is composed; and that if at the present day we know, for example, that it requires not less than 350,000 times the globe of the earth to form a weight equal to that of the sun, we owe it to the observation of those very small inequalities, which those would certainly have neglected, who at all risks would admit nothing but *simple* phenomena.

Without extending these remarks farther, I may then admit that optics would be a more easy science, more at the command of the generality of men, more susceptible of demonstration in public lectures, before the extension of it which has been made in our times. But this extension is a real source of riches; it has given occasion for the most curious applications; it has thence afforded those indications of impossibilities in certain theories of light, which may claim to rank among discoveries; for in the search after causes, we are often reduced to proceed by the method of exclusion, and in this point of view, there is no experiment which is without use; we cannot multiply them too much. That universal genius, Voltaire, who often took pleasure in concealing a profound meaning under a burlesque form, compared a theory to a mouse, which passes, he said, through nine holes, but is caught in the tenth. It is in multiplying indefinitely the number of these holes, or to speak in a manner less trivial, the number of tests which a theory ought to satisfy, that astronomy is placed in the rank which it occupies in the estimation of men, and that it has become the first of the sciences. It is in following the same route that we shall be able in like manner to give to other branches of science the character of evidence which they yet want in some respects. In every science of observation we must distinguish the facts, the laws which connect them, and the causes. Often the difficulties of the subject arrest experimenters after the first step; hardly ever do they allow them to pass freely to the third. The progress which Fresnel made in the two former respects, in the study of double refraction, by natural consequence, led him to inquire on what so singular a phenomenon depended. And here again he obtained striking success. But pressed for time, I can only make known the most prominent of his results.

When Huyghens published his *Traité de la Lumière*, there were only known two crystals possessing double refraction,—carbonate of lime and quartz. At present it would be far shorter to enumerate those which have not this property, than those which have it. Formerly, it was necessary that a substance should distinctly show double images, to allow us to assimilate it with Iceland spar. Whenever the separation of the two rays was so small as to escape detection by the eye, the observer remained in doubt and did not venture to pronounce it doubly refractive. Now, however, by the aid of a method which a member of the Academy has pointed out,* the existence of double refraction manifests itself by characteristics quite independent of the separation of the two images. No substance, however thin it may be, possessed of this property, can escape this new mode of examination. But, if it were certain that double refraction could not exist without our perceiving the very manifest phenomena on which this method is founded, it would not appear equally incontestable that it ought necessarily to accompany them; and a doubt in regard to this might seem the more natural since the author of this method has himself found certain plates of glass which, without separating the images in a perceptible degree, yet give birth to all the phenomena in question: —since a distinguished philosopher of Berlin, M. Seebeck, afterwards proved that all glass rapidly cooled enjoyed the same property;—and since, lastly, a very able experimenter of Edinburgh produced the same

* The author here alludes to his own discovery of the *polarized colours*, made also quite independently by Brewster about the same time. These tints are now familiar to most persons by means of the little instrument called the polariscope. By placing a plate of selenite, mica, &c., far too thin to exhibit any separation of images, in polarized light, and viewing it through an analyzer, these brilliant tints convey distinct evidence of the existence of that property, since they are shown *theoretically* to depend solely upon its *existence*, however insensibly small its *amount* may be. It therefore seems important for the verification of theory, to show independently its existence in any substances which exhibit the tints. Glass ordinarily possesses no such power; but plates of *unannealed* glass exhibit the tints. Hence the importance of the experiments mentioned to show its existence directly.—*Translator*.

phenomena by compressing pieces of glass with great force in certain directions. To show that a piece of ordinary glass, thus modified by cooling or compression, always really separates the light into two rays,—and to render this separation incontestably evident, was the important problem which Fresnel proposed to himself, and which he resolved in his usual happy manner.

By placing in the same line, and in a frame of iron carrying powerful screws ingeniously arranged, a number of prisms of glass, which by these screws were subjected to very powerful pressure, Fresnel caused a manifest double refraction to appear. In an optical point of view this assemblage of pieces of common glass became a true Iceland crystal; but here the separation of the images, and all the other properties which flow from it, resulted exclusively from the action of the compressing screws. Now this action, carefully analyzed, ought only to produce one effect, a close approach to each other of the molecules of the glass in the direction of the pressure; while, in the direction perpendicular to this, the molecules preserve their original distances. Can we then doubt, after this remarkable experiment, that an analogous arrangement of the molecules produced during the act of crystallization was thus the general cause of the double refraction in carbonate of lime, quartz, and all minerals of the same kind. If we consider with attention the ingenious apparatus, by the aid of which Fresnel, in thus giving an artificial double refraction to ordinary glass, has caused so great a step to be made in the science, we are struck with the great amount of aid which the spirit of invention borrows, whether from the knowledge of the arts, or from that manual dexterity which has been so well described by Franklin when he required of experimenters to be able to saw with a file, and to file with a saw.

Want of time will not permit me to refer here to other various labours of our colleague equally relative to the refraction of light, and of which I do not exaggerate the importance in saying that they would alone suffice to establish a reputation equal to that of many physicists of the first eminence. I hasten to pass on to an optical theory not less interesting, and altogether of modern date; which is designated by the name of the theory of "Interferences." It will furnish me with new occasions to render apparent the astonishing perspicuity of Fresnel's mind, and the inexhaustible resources of his inventive genius.

INTERFERENCES.

The very name of "interference" has as yet hardly emerged beyond the precincts of scientific societies, and yet I know not whether any branch of human knowledge presents phenomena more varied, more curious, more strange. Let us endeavour to disengage the capital fact which pervades this whole theory of the technical language in which it is commonly enveloped, and we may hope it will before long be admitted that it deserves in a high degree to attract public attention.

I will suppose that a ray of the sun's light falls directly on any screen, as for instance on a sheet of fine white paper. The part of the paper on which the ray falls will of course be brightly illuminated; but it might seem incredible if we assert that it depends on the experimenter to render this spot perfectly dark without stopping the ray or touching the paper.

What then is the magical process which allows us to

transform at pleasure light into darkness, day into night? The *process* will excite more surprise than even the *result.* It consists in directing upon the paper, but by a route very slightly different, a second ray of light, which, taken by itself, would also have brilliantly illuminated it. The two rays in mixing together, it might be expected, would produce a yet more brilliant illumination; no doubt, it would seem, could exist on this point; but in point of fact, under certain conditions, they entirely destroy each other, and we find ourselves to have created darkness by adding one portion of light to another.

A new fact requires a new term; this phenomenon, in which two rays in mixing together destroy each other, either wholly or partially, is termed "*an interference.*"

Grimaldi had long ago (before 1665) formed some notion of the action which one beam of light may exercise upon another; but in the experiment which he cites this action was but obscurely manifested; and, besides this, the *conditions* which were essential to its production had not been pointed out, and thus no other experimenter followed up the inquiry.

In searching after the cause of the iridescent colours with which soap bubbles shine so brilliantly, Hooke believed that they were the result of interferences; he even very ingeniously pointed out some of the circumstances which cause their production; but it was a theory destitute of actual proofs. And as Newton, who knew of this theory, did not deign even once in his great work to discuss it critically, it remained more than a century in oblivion.*

* The silence of Newton as to Hooke's attempt at explaining the colours of films by the wave theory may, we conceive, be fully ex-

The complete experimental demonstration of the fact of interferences will always be the principal title of Dr. Thomas Young to the recognition of posterity. The researches of this illustrious physicist (whose recent loss the sciences have to deplore) had already led to the general principles which I do not think I ought here to abstain from announcing, although the genius of Fresnel seized upon them, extended them, and showed their great fertility.*

plained from the extremely vague nature of that explanation; it, in fact, amounted to no more than a general notion that some such periodical action might be occasioned by a concurrence of waves or pulses. It did not amount to a theory; it had no reference to measures of the phenomenon, and indicated nothing like a law. At the time Hooke does not appear to have been aware of the composition of white light, and thus all accurate analysis of the phenomenon was out of the question. Newton pursued the subject on professedly experimental grounds *alone;* it was not his plan to enter on any theoretical considerations; he, therefore, could not be expected to refer to Hooke's, which must necessarily have seemed to him wholly gratuitous, and even visionary.—*Translator.*

* Young's investigations of diffraction was rather general, and *qualitative*, though the demonstration as to the nature of the effect was perfectly conclusive; but the later researches of Fresnel carried out the subject to a *quantitative* determination. This being made to include the combined effect of an infinite number of interferences acting at every point, involved the use of the higher calculus; and the result was established by means of integrations giving the intensity of light at all parts of the screen or image. This remark applies not merely to the particular case of diffraction, but to that of thin plates, and other analogous cases, in which the principle of interference is applied. This analytical extension constituted one of the most characteristic excellences of Fresnel's researches. In an experimental point of view, Fresnel's researches are characterized by scarcely less improvements. The most material modifications he introduced were those of (1.) viewing the image of the stripes directly by an eye lens, instead of throwing them on a screen;—(2.) discarding any interposition of an opaque body, and causing two rays simply to act on each other, by causing the sun's light diverging from a minute aperture or

Two rays cannot destroy each other unless they have a common origin; that is to say, unless they both emanate from the same particle of an incandescent body. The rays from one side of the sun's disk do not interfere with those from the other side, or from the centre.

Among the thousands of rays of different tints and refrangibilities of which white light is composed, those only are capable of interference which possess colours and refrangibilities identically the same; thus, in whatever manner we take them, a red ray will never destroy a green ray.

With respect to rays of the same origin and the same colour, they are constantly mixed and superposed without influencing each other; they produce effects represented by the sum of their intensities,—if at the moment of their crossing each other they have gone through routes perfectly equal in length.

An interference can alone take place when the routes through which the rays have passed are unequal; but it

the focus of a small lens, to be divided into two streams, either by reflection from two mirrors very little inclined to each other, or trans-

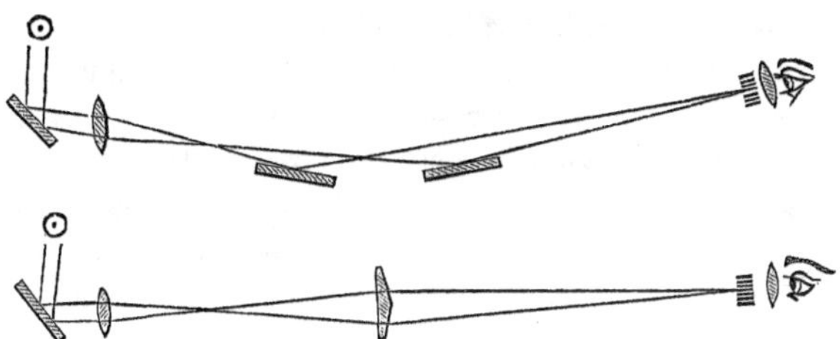

mission through a very obtuse angled prism. Here the interference stripes are seen by the eye-glass in the middle of the mixed light in the greatest purity and intensity of alternation of brightness and darkness.—*Translator.*

is not every inequality of this kind which will necessarily produce a destruction of light; such difference may, on the contrary cause the rays to reinfore each other.

But when we know what is the *least* difference of route gone through, at which the rays may be superposed *without influencing each other*, we then obtain all the other differences of route which give the same result in a very simple manner; for it suffices to take the double, the triple, the quadruple, &c., i. e. *every* whole multiple, of the first number to give them.

If we have noted in like manner the least difference of route which produces *complete destruction* of the two rays, every *odd* whole multiple of this first number will also be the indication of a like destruction.

As for differences of route which are not numerically comprised either in the first or in the second of the above series, they correspond only to *partial* destructions of the light, or mere weakening of its intensity.

These series of numbers, by aid of which we can tell whether two rays at the moment of intersection ought to interfere or merely to combine without influencing each other, have not the same values for the differently coloured rays; the smallest values belong to the violet rays, the greatest to the red, and the intermediate values to the intermediate rays. It results, that if two white rays cross at a certain point, it may be possible that in the infinite series of differently coloured rays of which that light is composed, the red, for example, alone may be destroyed and disappear, and thus the point of concourse may appear green, as being the white light deprived of its red component.

Interference, then, which in homogeneous light produces only changes in intensity, will manifest itself when we operate with white light in phenomena of coloration. In the course of such singular results we may, perhaps, be curious to find the numerical value of these differences of route, so often mentioned, and which place two rays in the conditions either of accordance or complete destruction. I will mention, then, that for red light we pass from the one of these conditions to the other when we make the difference of route amount to three ten thousandths of a millimètre.*

* The numerical values of the differences of route, as Arago expresses it, or the connection of the wave lengths for different rays with the intervals between the stripes is easily investigated; and the latter being readily susceptible of accurate micrometrical measurement, the former may be deduced. Let two rays be inclined at a very small angle $2\,\theta$. Then the crossings of the waves will give rise to a set of bright and dark points at $+$, o, &c., according as like or unlike portions meet. Let c be the interval between two successive bright points and λ the wave lengths. Then we have obviously the relation —

$$c = \frac{\lambda}{2} \cot \theta$$

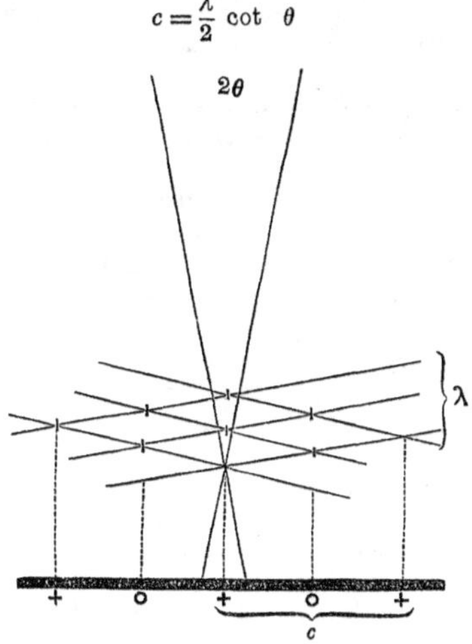

In order that the difference of route alone may determine whether two rays of the same origin and the same colour shall reinforce or destroy each other, it is necessary that both should be traversing *the same medium*, solid, liquid, or gaseous. If it be not thus, we must then also take into account (as a member of the Academy*

and similarly for successive values of c, measured from the central point, involving successive multiples of λ; and if a plate of glass whose refraction index is μ, be interposed in the path of one of the rays, whose thickness is t, the difference of retardation will be equivalent to a difference of route expressed by

$$d = t(\mu - 1)$$

and this being substituted for the particular multiple of λ, which expresses the difference of routes in the first formula, gives for the displacement

$$c = t(\mu - 1)\frac{\cot \theta}{2}$$

It may be added that the values of the wave lengths determined by this method from the observed widths of the stripes, or by others of an analogous kind, give results exactly accordant with those long ago assigned by Newton for the length of the "fits" derived from his measures of the diameters of the coloured rings, and by which, from the known curvatures of the lenses, he determined the thickness of the films, and thence the lengths of the "fits."—*Translator.*

* The retardation of one of the rays, and consequent shifting of the stripes, is here alluded to, which was the discovery of Arago; being in the first instance exhibited by the total disappearance of the stripes, as must be the case if the plate of glass have more than almost an infinitesimal thickness. The fact was first announced as a sort of paradox, that as Young had found the stripes entirely disappear by interposing an opaque screen on *one* side only, so Arago produced the same effect with a perfectly transparent screen. In order to explain this effect, let us conceive the simple case of two rays of white light, made to interfere as in Fresnel's experiment.

The slightest consideration will show that, at the middle point of the mixture of light, two concurring rays, of whatever primitive colour or wave length, have gone through precisely the same length of route; and thus the central stripe and its immediate neighbour on each side, are absolutely white and black, and perfectly defined; but in proportion as we recede from this point on either side, the differ-

has proved by incontestable experiments) the thickness and the refractive power of the body through which the

ences of route of the concurring rays become necessarily greater. But white light is a compound of primary coloured rays of different wave lengths. Hence all the interference stripes, except the exactly central ones, are formed by the concurrence of rays having gone through more or less different lengths of route, and consequently with a want of exact concurrence for the different primary rays, which will be greater, as we recede more from the central point; in other words, the stripes towards each side become more and more coloured, and superimposed, till beyond certain limits the stripes disappear, and the whole mixed light is sensibly white.

Now, if owing to any cause one of the two interfering rays were *retarded* in its course behind the other, the two rays would not concur under the same conditions of equal route, as before, at the central point, but it would not be until at some distance *towards the side* on which the retardation took place, that they would be, as it were, placed on equal terms to make up for the retardation in the one by greater length of route in the other; the central point of the stripes, and therefore the whole system with it, would thus be *shifted* towards that side. This may be more clearly illustrated as follows: Let

Fig. 1. *Fig.* 2.

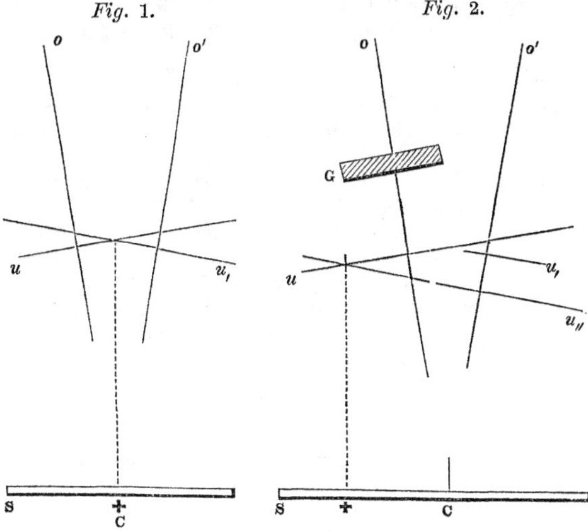

rays respectively pass. By making the thickness of such media vary gradually, the rays which traverse them may still destroy or reinforce each other, just as if they had traversed routes perfectly equal.

It hardly ever happens that any part of space receives *direct* light alone ; a hundred rays from the same origin arrive at that point after reflections or refractions more or less oblique. Now, after what has been said, we may

two rays oo' interfere, as in *fig.* 1, arriving simultaneously by an equal number of undulations respectively, at u and u', and thus giving rise to a light stripe at the centre of the screen s, which corresponds to the point of concurrence for equal routes, or when the differences for the different colours are insensible. But now, as in *fig.* 2, let the ray o be intercepted by a glass screen G, by which its undulations are retarded. When o' has, as before, arrived at $u_{,}$, o will be at u, several undulations behind it: and the point of concurrence of u with $u_{,}$, will not be the same for different colours, and the central stripe, or point of concurrence for equal *equivalent* routes, will be that with some after wave $u_{,,}$ or will be at + at some distance from C towards G, or the whole body of stripes will be shifted towards the side on which G is placed.

This was accordingly exactly what Arago found to take place when he placed in the path of the light on one side a *transparent* screen. The process by which it is effected is most clearly seen by intercepting the two rays with two plates of glass of exactly the same thickness; and causing one of them to incline very slightly, so that the ray on that side passes through a slightly greater *effective* thickness, or is a very little retarded; the stripes are then seen to shift towards that side, until on increasing the inclination, they disappear altogether.

So delicate are the indications afforded by this experiment, and so perfect the accordance between the *degree of shifting* of the fringes, and the *refractive power* of the intercepting medium, that Arago and Fresnel saw the advantage of employing it for the *inverse* problem of determining the most minute differences of *refractive power*, especially those of gases and vapours, for which no other method could be made sufficiently sensible. To demonstrate *at once* the *fact*, and the *law* that this retardation is exactly in proportion to the refractive power of the glass, the translator long ago adopted a simple modification of this experiment, for an account of which the reader is referred to the *Philos. Mag.*, January, 1832.—*Translator.*

conceive to how many phenomena these repeated crossings of light may give rise; and how superfluous it would have been to seek the reason of them as long as the laws of interference were unknown. Let us only remark that nothing as yet has indicated whether these laws be equally applicable when, before the rays mix, they have received that modification of which I have already spoken, and which is designated by the name of *polarization.*

This question was important; it formed the object of a difficult investigation, which Fresnel undertook in conjunction with one of his friends (Arago). The example which they have set in publishing their researches, of distinguishing which portion each of them contributed, if not with respect to the material execution of the different experiments, at least to the invention of them, deserves, I think, to be followed. For associations of this kind often produce mischief, because the public persisting, often through blind caprice, in not treating the parties concerned on a footing of perfect equality, may improperly excite the self-love of an author;—perhaps of all human passions that which requires the most control.

Let us look at the results of the researches in question, as, without reference to the important *consequences* which have been deduced from them, they deserve to be stated, were it only on account of their intrinsic singularity.

Two rays which are made to change directly from the state of common light to that of rays polarized in the same direction, preserve, after having received that modification, the property of interfering as before; they reinforce or destroy each other as ordinary rays do, and under the same conditions. Two rays which change directly from the natural state to that of rays polarized at right angles to each other, lose altogether the property of interfering; let them be modified afterwards as to the routes they pursue in a thousand ways, or as to the nature and thicknesses of the media they traverse; or even more, let them be brought back by suitable reflexions to the condition of parallel polarization; nothing of this kind can give them again the property of being able to destroy each other.

But if two rays already polarized in directions at right angles to each other, and which in consequence cannot act one on the other, have then received *parallel* polarization, in passing out of their natural state, it will suffice, in order that they again acquire the power of interference, to cause them to resume the kind of polarization which they originally possessed.*

* The question as to the nature and modifications of the vibrations whose aggregate in their different stages, or phases, constitutes a wave, may require a word or two of illustration.

In the first instance, in the conception of waves, those who pursued such a theory generally adopted the idea that the æthereal molecules oscillated backwards and forwards *in the line* of the ray; they could not admit the idea of their oscillating in any other direction. Yet, oscillations in any direction occurring in regular succession, might constitute a wave.

The difficulty, when more fully examined, had reference to the determination on admitted dynamical principles of the mode in which the force propagating the ray and acting in its direction could give rise to *lateral disturbance.* Yet it is easy to admit, as a rough illustration, the case of a rope fastened at one end and agitated at the other by the hand; when we can easily cause a series of waves to run along it; but the particles of the rope really retain their original distances from the hand, and merely move up and down in directions *transverse* to its length. In a somewhat similar way, the æthereal molecules are, according to this theory, made to vibrate, or as Fresnel afterwards graphically expressed it, to "tremble laterally."

At length, Young began to entertain the idea that the molecules

It is impossible not to feel astonishment, when we for the first time learn that two rays of light can mutually

might oscillate in parallel directions *transverse* to the direction of the ray; though he thought that the longitudinal vibrations might exist also. But he long hesitated to adopt such an idea, regarding it as inexplicable on any dynamical principles. Fresnel independently started the same idea of transverse vibrations, alone; but he was equally reluctant to propose it, on the ground of a similar mechanical difficulty; yet he distinctly acknowledged Young's priority in the announcement of the general idea. "M. Young," he says, "more bold in his conjectures and less confiding in the views of geometers, published it before me, though perhaps he thought of it after me." And on the same point, Dr. Whewell mentions from personal information, that "Arago was wont to relate that when he and Fresnel had obtained their joint experimental results of the non-interference of oppositely polarized pencils, and that when Fresnel had pointed out that transverse vibrations were the only possible translation of this fact into the undulatory theory, he himself protested that he had not the courage to publish such a conception; and, accordingly, the second part of the memoir was published in Fresnel's name alone. What renders this more remarkable is, that it occurred when Arago had in his possession the very letter of Young (1818), in which he proposed the same suggestion."—*Hist. of Inductive Sciences*, ii. 418.

Fresnel deduced transverse vibrations on dynamical grounds which had been open to some degree of question. But the nature of the relation between the partial differential equation which he gives, and the wave function which is the solution of it, clearly involves no necessary restriction of the direction of vibration. That equation is of the same general form as that given by Euler, as referring to sound. Such an equation suffices for light considered as homogeneous. It expresses generally the relation of particles in motion, such that if the time and the position of the particles be increased by corresponding changes, the form of the function will be unaltered, or the motions recur periodically, which constitutes the essential idea of a wave. Its form is generally

$$\frac{d^2u}{dt^2} = -c\,\frac{d^2u}{dx^2}$$

where t is the time, x, the distance along a given axis, and u, the displacement corresponding to the time, t; c, a constant. The solution of this equation is easily seen to be the wave function.

$$u = \sin\,(nt - kx)$$

destroy each other, that darkness may result from the superposition of two portions of light. But when this

Since, if we take the partial differentials in respect to t and to x,

$$\frac{du}{dt} = n \cos (nt - kx) \qquad \frac{du}{dx} = k \cos (nt - kx)$$

$$\frac{d^2u}{dt^2} = - n^2u \qquad \frac{d^2n}{dx^2} = - k^2u$$

Whence,

$$\frac{d^2u}{dt^2} = - \frac{n^2}{k^2}\frac{d^2u}{dx^2}$$

And since that wave-function goes through all its changes while t, increases to $\frac{2\pi}{n}$ and the velocity $v = \frac{n}{k}$ the time of the undulation

$$\tau = \frac{2\pi}{n} \text{ and } v = \frac{\lambda}{\tau} = \frac{\lambda n}{2\pi}$$

Whence,

$$n = \frac{2\pi v}{\lambda} \text{ and } k = \frac{2\pi}{\lambda}$$

Or the formula becomes (adopting an arbitrary coefficient, a, for the amplitude of vibration which is wholly independent of the other quantities)

$$u = a \sin \frac{2\pi}{\lambda} (vt - x).$$

Here it is to be observed, all depends on the coefficient $\frac{n}{k}$ being *constant*. To obtain a similar equation with a *variable* velocity or refraction is the object of the researches of M. Cauchy.

The more extended views of M. Cauchy have led to the deduction of analogous, but more complex, equations, exhibiting resulting expressions for the displacement, in three rectangular directions; besides including in the analysis a coefficient which expresses the variable relation of the velocity which gives the theoretical explanation of unequal refrangibility. These forms thus include the deduction of transverse vibrations, as a direct consequence of the first assumptions, as to the constitution of an æthereal medium. But, with reference to light, considered as homogeneous, the conditions admit of great simplification; which is best shown in that form of the investigation which was pursued by Sir J. Lubbock (*Philos. Mag.* Nov. 1837), where, if the fourth powers of the disturbed distances of the molecules are neglected, the equations are at once reduced to the form above.

The object of M. Cauchy's researches here alluded to was to ex-property of the rays has been once established, is it not still more extraordinary that we can deprive them of it?

plain the unequal refrangibility of light. To give some general notion of the nature of the subject, we may here briefly observe, that in the explanation of refraction before given, [Life of Malus, note,] it is clear that as the inclination of the common tangent to the contemporaneous circular waves determines the refraction, this depends on the diminution of the wave length within the denser medium; and if this inclination be determined for a ray of any given wave length, then for another whose wave length within the medium is different, and in a given ratio to the former, the radii of the contemporaneous waves will be in the same ratio as the former, or their difference from the former will be in the same ratio, consequently the common tangent of these second circles will not be parallel to the first, but inclined at a different angle: or the angle of refraction will be different. Thus if for any particular primary ray the wave length within the medium be $\lambda_{\prime} = \frac{\lambda}{\mu_{\prime}}$ that of the incident ray being λ and μ the index for that ray, $\lambda = b \sin i$.

then $$\lambda_{\prime} = b \sin r = \frac{\lambda}{\mu_{\prime}}$$

or in other words, the refraction will be different from each primary ray. But $\mu_{\prime}$ and $\lambda_{\prime}$ do not follow any simple ratio. The more complex expression on which that relation depends, is the result of M. Cauchy's theory, viz:—

$$\frac{1}{\mu^2} = \text{P} - \frac{1}{\lambda^2}\text{Q} + \frac{1}{\lambda^4}\text{R} - \&c.$$

[See Professor Powell's Treatise on the Undulatory Theory, sect. vi.]

Experimentally, the transverse vibrations receive their main support from the analysis of the coloured tints, developed in polarized light by the interposition of plates of crystal (such as those of mica, selenite, &c.), when examined by an analyzer.

Young ascribed these colours generally to *interference;* but both Fresnel and Arago pointed out that this explanation was incomplete. Why did it only take place in *polarized* light, and even then not until the analyzer had been applied? These questions could not be answered till another law had been discovered; as it soon after was, by the joint labours of those two philosophers.

It was clear that in polarization all the vibrations were performed *in one and the same plane,* in whatever direction they might be exe-

that a given ray loses it momentarily, and that another given ray, on the contrary, is deprived of it for ever? The theory of interferences, considered in this point of view, seems more like the reveries of a disordered brain, than the exact, inevitable consequence of numberless experiments, clear of all possible objection. And fur-

cuted. But it was not until after lengthened investigation that the two philosophers just named succeeded in establishing *experimentally* the important law (obvious as it now seems,) that "*polarized rays can only interfere when they are polarized in the same plane.*" If they were polarized in rectangular planes (for example), no interference could result, were all other conditions ever so perfectly fulfilled. Now, this could only be explained on the supposition of the vibrations being performed in planes *transverse* to the ray. Granting that in a ray polarized in *one* plane all the vibrations take place in *one* plane, (whether *in* the *same* plane or perpendicular to it,) it is then readily seen that when the vibrations of two rays are at *right angles to each other*, there can be no mutual destruction, or mutual coöperation. It is only when they are in the *same* plane that this can occur.

This principle was at length found to supply the explanation of the polarized tints. Every ray of the light (P) originally polarized in one

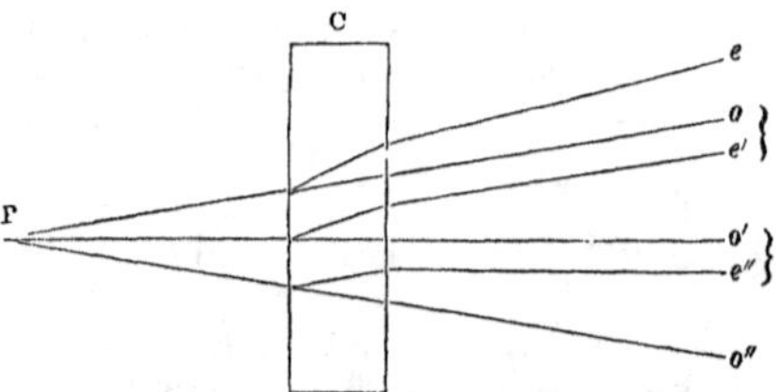

plane, in traversing the crystal plate (C) was divided into two; an ordinary (*o*) and an extraordinary (*e*); all those of the one kind, *o*, *o′*, *o″*, &c. being polarized in one plane, and all of the other, *e*, *e′*, *e″*, &c., in a plane at right angles to the last. But in each ray *o*, and *e*, diverge from each other by a very small angle. The whole pencil also diverges at a small angle from P; thus, the only rays which can *coincide* in direction, will be a ray *o*, of one set, with a ray *e′* of the next; —*o′*, with *e″*, &c. &c., and as these are unequally retarded in different degrees according to their inclination, they would be in a condition to give interference, were it not that being polarized in *places*

ther, it is not only on account of its singularity that this theory ought to command the attention of the physicist; Fresnel found it the key to all the beautiful phenomena of colours, which are produced in plates of crystal possessing double refraction; he analyzed them in all their details; he determined their most hidden laws; he proved that they were only particular cases of interferences. He thus overturned from their base many scientific romances to which these phenomena had given birth, and which had secured more than one proselyte, whether by their striking nature or the distinguished merit of their authors. In a word, here, as in every branch of science which is advancing towards perfection, the facts have seemed complicated only because we examined them at too near a distance and with too microscopic a view; but at the same time, by a more enlarged conception, their causes have been found to be more simple than we might have expected.

POLARIZATION.

Although I am aware at what point we risk tiring even the most kindly disposed audience when we speak long

at right angles to each other they could not. It only required then the action of the analyzer (A) to resolve each vibration again into

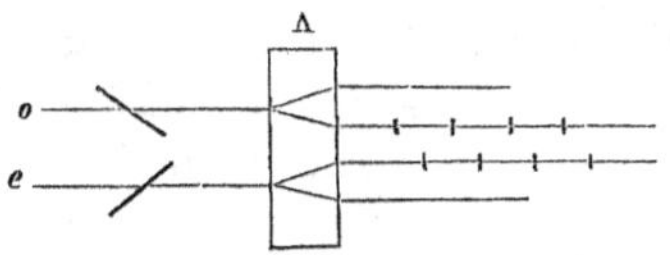

two, at right angles, of which two sets in a plane perpendicular to that of analyzation are suppressed; and two in that plane transmitted; and which, consequently, being in parallel planes, are able to give interference, and produce the observed coloured tints.

on the same subject, I find myself still carried back, by the nature of Fresnel's labours, to the subject of double refraction: but, this time, instead of occupying myself with the manner in which the rays divide in passing through certain crystals, I will examine the permanent modifications which they receive: I will present, in one word, the principal features of the new branch of optics which bears the name of *polarization of light.*

Every ray of light falling even perpendicularly on any surface, natural or artificial, of the transparent crystals of carbonate of lime, called also calc spar, or Iceland spar, is divided into two. One portion passes through the crystal without deviation, which we call the ordinary ray; the other undergoes a sensible refraction, and for that reason has very justly the name of the extraordinary ray. Both the ordinary and extraordinary ray lie in one plane perpendicular to the face of the crystal. The consideration of this plane is important, for it is this which determines the direction which the extraordinary ray will take; and in consequence a special name has been given to it, "*the principal section.*"

These points being premised, I will suppose, to fix the ideas, that a particular crystal of calc spar has its principal section directed north and south. Below this, and at any distance, we will place another similar crystal turned similarly; that is, so that its principal section shall also lie in the meridian. What will result from this disposition, if light traverse the whole system? A single ray impinges on the first crystal but it emerges in two rays: each of these again seems as if it should undergo a double refraction in the second crystal; and thence we might expect four emergent rays. Yet this does not happen. The rays emanating from the first crystal are not divided again by the second. The ordinary ray remains an ordinary ray, and the extraordinary undergoes solely an extraordinary refraction. Thus, in traversing the first crystal, the luminous rays have changed their nature; they have lost one of their former characteristics, that of constantly undergoing double refraction in traversing Iceland crystal.*

It is necessary that we should fully bear in mind what rays of light are, and then, perhaps, we shall admit that an experiment, by the aid of which they change their original properties in so manifest a way, deserves to be known even by those to whom science is merely an object of curiosity.

The idea which in the first instance presents itself to the mind, when we wish to explain this singular result of which I have just given an account, consists in supposing that in every ray there might exist two distinct species of molecules: that the one species must always undergo the ordinary refraction; the other, the extraordinary alone. But a very simple experiment upsets this hypothesis entirely. In fact, when the principal section of the second crystal, instead of being directed north and south as above supposed, is pointed east and west, the ray which was the ordinary ray in the first crystal, becomes the extraordinary in the second; and reciprocally.

What, then, is there different in reality between the two experiments which give results so dissimilar? There is one circumstance, very simple, and full of import at first sight: it is, that at first the principal section of the second crystal cuts the rays coming from the first through their north and south sides, and in the second case, through their east and west sides.

* For illustration of this subject, see note to the Life of Malus.

There must be then, in each of these rays, north and south sides in some way different from their east and west sides. And further, the north and south sides of the ordinary ray ought to have precisely the same properties as the east and west sides of the extraordinary ray; so that if this last ray make a quarter of a circuit about the line of its length it will be impossible to distinguish one from the other. The rays of light are so subtle that thousands of millions of these rays can pass simultaneously through the eye of a needle without interfering: yet we find ourselves obliged to take into account the idea of their *sides*, and to recognize, on their *opposite sides, dissimilar properties.*

When speaking of a *magnet*, natural or artificial physicists affirm it to have *poles.* They mean only that certain points on its surface are found endowed with certain properties which are not found, or at least only show themselves feebly, at any other points. We have, then, equal reason to say the same thing of the ordinary and extraordinary rays of light which proceed from the division of the beam which passes through Iceland spar; and in contradistinction to the natural rays in which all points appear alike, we may rightly call them *polarized rays.*

In order, however, that we may not extend beyond its proper limits the analogy of a polarized ray and a magnet, it is important to remark well that *in the ray,* the *poles diametrically opposite* appear to possess exactly the *same* properties; whilst the *dissimilar* poles are situated on sides of the ray whose positions are *at right angles* to each other.

The lines resembling diameters, which join the *similar* poles, in every ray deserve particular attention. Whenever, in two distinct rays, these lines are parallel, we say that the rays are polarized in the same plane. There is, consequently, no need to add that two rays polarized at right angles to each other must have their similar poles in two directions perpendicular the one to the other.

The two rays, the ordinary and the extraordinary for example, given by any crystal are always polarized at right angles to each other.

All that I have just said of polarization of light was recognized by Huyghens and Newton before the end of the 17th century; and never, certainly, had a more curious subject for research been offered to the meditations of experimenters. Nevertheless, we must pass over an interval of a century after that period before we find, I do not say any fresh discoveries, but even any more researches for the object of carrying out this branch of optics.

The history of all sciences presents a multitude of singular incidents of a similar kind. In the progress of each science there occur periodically certain epochs when, after great efforts, men usually suppose themselves to have arrived at a limit in their advance. Then experimenters are in general timid; they fancy themselves chargeable with a want of modesty, with a sort of profanation, if they dare to lay an indiscreet hand on the barriers which their illustrious predecessors have erected; and thus they generally content themselves with perfecting the numerical elements, or filling up some deficiencies, bestowing on the inquiry a labour often arduous, and which yet scarcely attracts any notice from the world.

In a word, the experiments of Huyghens had clearly established the fact that double refraction modifies the original properties of light in such a manner that, after having once undergone this modification, the rays remain single, or again subdivide into two, according to the direction in which they fall upon a second crystal presented to them. But do these modifications show a relation exclusively to double refraction? do all their other properties remain uninfluenced?

It was from the labours of one of our most distinguished colleagues (like Fresnel, early snatched away from the sciences of which he was the hope) that we have been enabled to answer these important questions. Malus discovered, in fact, that, in the act of reflexion, polarized rays are differently affected from common rays: the latter, as every one knows, are partially reflected when they fall even on transparent bodies, whatever may be the angle of incidence, and whatever the position of the reflecting surface with respect to the *sides* of the ray. When, on the contrary, the case is one of polarized light, there is always one situation of the reflecting surface, relatively to the poles, or sides, in which all reflexion disappears if in this situation the reflexion take at a particular incidence, which is different for each reflecting surface, according to the nature of the substance of which it is formed.

If, after this curious observation, double refraction ceased to be the *only* means of distinguishing polarized from common light, at least it seemed to be the only way by which rays of light could become polarized. But soon a new experiment of Malus taught the scientific world, to its great surprise, that there existed other methods, far less abstruse, for producing this modification. The most simple phenomenon of optics, the reflexion of light from a transparent mirror, is a powerful means of producing polarization. Light, which is reflected at the surface of water at an angle of 37°, or from the surface of glass at an inclination of 35° 25′, is as completely polarized as the two rays, ordinary and extraordinary, proceeding from a crystal of Iceland spar.

The reflexion of light long ago occupied observers in the age of Plato and of Euclid: since that epoch it had been the object of thousands of experiments, of hundreds of theoretical speculations; the law according to which it proceeds serves as the basis of a great number of instruments, ancient and modern. Among the multitude of enlightened minds, of men of genius, of skilful artists, who, during more than 2300 years, have been occupied with this phenomenon, no one ever aimed at any other object than the means of making the rays divide, or of causing them to diverge or converge; no one ever imagined that reflected light ought not to possess all the same properties as the incident light, or that a change of path would be the cause of a change of nature. Generations of observers thus succeeded each other during several thousands of years, every day touching closely on the most beautiful discoveries without actually making them.

Malus, as I have already explained, gave a means of polarizing light different from that which Huyghens had formerly announced. But the polarizations produced by the two methods were identically the same. The reflected rays and those which proceed out of an Iceland crystal possess exactly the same properties. Since that time a member of this Academy (Arago) has discovered a kind of polarization* entirely distinct, and which mani-

* It may be necessary for some readers to explain that, in this somewhat paradoxical mode of speaking, the author is referring to his own discovery of the polarized tints; and his meaning is simply that if, in polarized light, there be placed a thin film, *e. g.*, of selenite or mica, and it be viewed through a doubly refracting crystal as an analyzer,

fests itself in a different way from that of difference of intensity. The rays subjected to it, for example, always give two images in traversing calc spar; but these images are each entirely tinted with a bright and uniform colour. Thus, though the incident light may be white, the ordinary ray may be entirely red, orange, yellow, green, blue, or violet, according to the direction in which the principal section of the crystal cuts the ray: and as to the extraordinary ray, it will not suffice to say that it never resembles the ordinary; we must say that it differs from it as widely as possible; that if the one, for example, is coloured *red*, the other shows a bright *green*, and so on for the rest of the prismatic tints.

When this new kind of polarized rays are reflected from a transparent mirror, we perceive other phenomena not less curious. Let us conceive, in fact, to fix the ideas, that one of these rays be vertical, and that it fall on a reflector of pure glass at an angle of about 35°, this mirror may be on the right side of the ray: and the inclination remaining constant, it may be turned to its left, before it, or behind it, or in any intermediate position. We may remember that the incident ray was white; then, in any of these positions of the glass reflector, the ray will not have this colour: it will be now red, now orange, yellow, green, blue, indigo, violet, according to the *side* on which the glass presents itself to the incident ray; it is, in fact, precisely in this order that the tints succeed one another,

both the images will be coloured, and their tints complementary. The originally polarized light is divided again into two oppositely polarized pencils in passing through the film, or as Professor J. Forbes has termed it, DI*polarized;* others had termed it DE*polarized.* This is what Arago here calls a new and entirely distinct kind of polarization; though the term is, perhaps, not very happily applied. This is what was explained at large in a previous note.

as we gradually make the mirror go through all possible changes of position. Here there are not only four poles placed in two rectangular directions, which we must admit in the constitution of the ray, but we see that there are thousands ; that every point in the circumference round the ray has a special character ; that every face which it presents produces in the reflexion a particular tint. This strange *dislocation* of the natural ray (I may be allowed this word, since it exactly expresses the fact) thus affords the means of *decomposing* white light by means of *reflexion.* The colours, it must be avowed, have not all the homogeneity of those which Newton obtained by the prism ; but also the object from which they originate does not undergo any *distortion,* as in prismatic refraction : and in a multitude of researches this is a point of material importance.

To discover whether a ray has received the polarization of Huyghens and Malus, or that of which I have just spoken, and which we call *chromatic polarization,* it suffices as we have seen, to make it undergo double refraction : but from the fact that a ray in traversing a crystal of Iceland spar always gives two images of white light and of equal intensity, it will not follow that it is formed originally of common light : this is again the discovery of Fresnel.* It is he who first pointed out

* The author would have expressed his meaning more clearly to general apprehension if he had said, that natural or unpolarized white light, on traversing Iceland spar, gives two white images in all positions: an ordinarily polarized ray does not; but there is a kind of light which gives always two images, and yet is not unpolarized: this is the *circularly* polarized light, discovered by Fresnel. One test which distinguishes it from common light is, that *on interposing* a crystallized plate of selenite, mica, &c., before receiving the light on

that a ray may have the same properties round all points of its circumference, and yet not be common light. To show by a single example that these two species of light comport themselves differently, and ought not to be confounded, I will observe that, in undergoing double refraction, a natural ray after traversing a plate of crystal gives two *white* images, while under the same conditions the ray of Fresnel is decomposed into two beams, each *brilliantly coloured.*

This new modification, which, having no reference to the different *sides* of a ray, has been designated *circular polarization,* can be impressed upon rays ordinarily polarized, by making them undergo two successive *total reflexions* from the internal surfaces of a piece of glass suitably formed.* The pleasure of having his name associated with a new kind of polarization hitherto unsuspected, would probably have sufficed for the vanity of an ordinary experimenter, and his researches would not have extended beyond that point. But Fresnel was actuated by more elevated sentiments; in his eyes nothing seemed to have been done while any thing remained to do. He sought, therefore, if there were not

the double refracting crystal, the two images in the former case will be always white, in the later coloured.

* In the instance mentioned, Fresnel showed, by a remarkable instance of theoretical prediction, that a ray polarized at 45° to the plane of incidence, and *twice* reflected internally from glass, will emerge in the condition of two rays polarized in planes at right angles, and one retarded by one fourth of a wave-length behind the other; these being superimposed will, by mathematical consequence, give rise to vibrations, no longer plane, but performed in circles; or in ellipses, if the retardation be any other fraction of a wave-length. Such a piece of glass is called Fresnel's Rhomb. The course of the ray will be apparent by inspection of the annexed diagram, which needs no further explanation.

other means by which to produce circular polarization; and, as usual, a remarkable discovery was the reward of these efforts. This discovery may be announced in two words; there is a *particular kind of double refraction* which communicates to rays *circular* polarization, as the double refraction of Iceland spar communicates the com-

The mechanical conception of two rectilinear vibrations at right

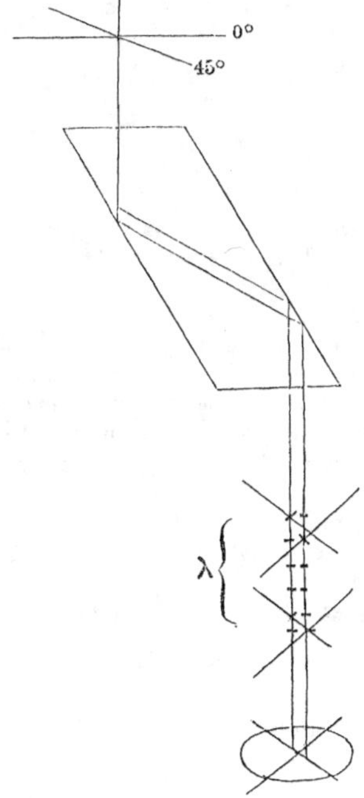

angles compounded, giving an elliptical or circular vibration, may be illustrated by a very simple contrivance, which may be described as follows:—

On any convenient support, there projects an arm terminating in

mon polarization of Huyghens. This special double refraction, results not from the nature of the crystal, but

two branches, on which, by the pivots G G′, a small frame swings. In

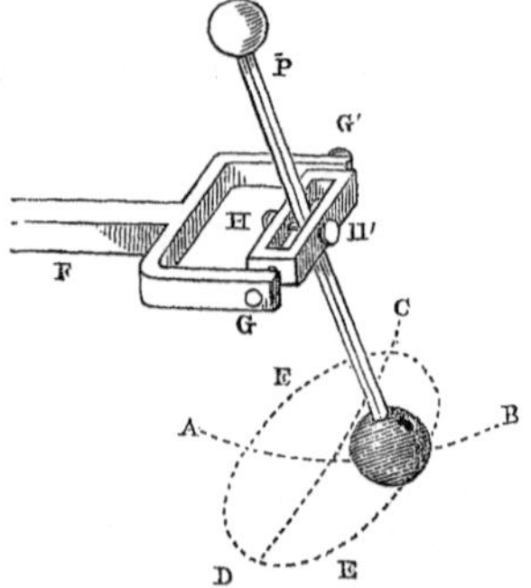

this frame, by the pivots H H′, whose axis is at right angles to G G′, a pendulum P vibrates. (The upper end is light, and carries a white ball or disk, carried up to such a height as to be conspicuous for lecture illustrations.)

Now, by the pivots H H′ the pendulum can only vibrate in the plane of C D, and by the pivots G G′ it can only vibrate in the plane of A B at right angles to C D. If now motion be given it in one of these planes, and at an *instant after* in the other, the result will be a revolution in the ellipse E E′, which will be a circle if the interval be exactly one fourth of a vibration.

Or mathematically thus:—

Let the waves in planes at right angles, with a difference of retardation d, be expressed by

$$z = a \sin (nt - kx) \qquad y = \beta \sin (nt - kx + d)$$

Hence, $\frac{z}{a} = \sin (nt - kx)$ and $\sqrt{1 - \frac{z^2}{a^2}} = \cos (nt - kx)$,

or expanding y and substituting

$$y = \beta \left(\frac{z}{a} \cos d + \sqrt{1 - \frac{z^2}{a^2}} \sin d \right).$$

Whence transposing and squaring

$$\frac{y^2}{\beta^2} + \frac{z^2}{a^2} - \frac{yz}{a\beta} \cos d = \sin^2 d$$

The equation to an *ellipse:* which becomes a circle if $a = \beta$ and $d = 90°$.—*Translator.*

from certain sections of it which Fresnel pointed out. The properties of rays circularly polarized also led our colleague to new and very curious means of producing coloured polarization.*

* The author must be supposed here to allude to that remarkable instance of circular polarization which is produced by transmitting a plane polarized ray along the axis of quartz or rock crystal, and which depends, as he says, not on the *nature* of the crystal, but on the *section* of it, that is to say, on the *thickness:* the effect continually *changing* as slices are cut from the crystal perpendicular to its axis of increasing *thickness.* This statement is somewhat remarkable, as he here unequivocally ascribes the discovery to *Fresnel,* which has been usually by English writers ascribed to *himself.*

The term "rotatory" polarization has been since appropriated to describe this phenomenon. Yet the student must be careful to distinguish the application of this term from that of "circular" polarization. The light is in fact circularly polarized: but the effect called "rotation" is quite distinct from the "circularity." It may be desirable to add a brief explanation. Let a ray, R, polarized in a

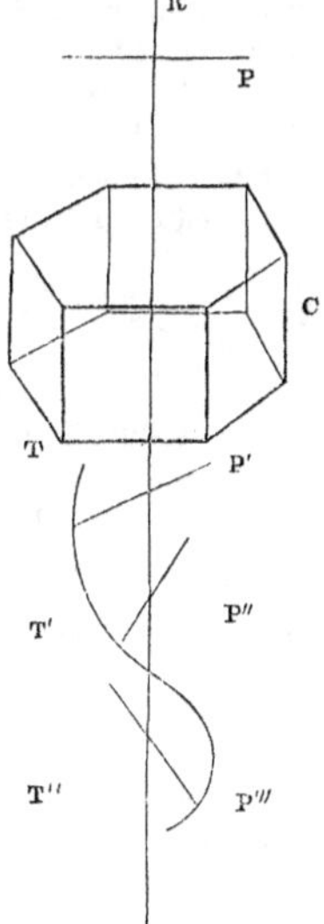

In all times and all countries, we find morose dispositions, who, though ready enough to proclaim the glories of the dead, do not treat their contemporaries with any thing like the same favour. As soon as a discovery is announced, they deny its truth: they contest its novelty, and pretend to detect it in some passage of an ancient writer, obscure and forgotten; or, lastly, they maintain that it was only the result of chance.

I do not know whether the men of our age are better than their predecessors: but certainly no doubt has been raised either as to the accuracy, or the novelty, or the importance of the discoveries of which I have just given an account. As to the effect of chance, the blindest envy

plane P, pass along the axis of rock crystal C, of the thickness T: it emerges polarized in a new plane P′, inclined to P, by a certain angle. If the crystal were of a greater thickness T′, the plane would be turned still further into the position P″, at T′ into P‴, and so on. Thus the successive planes of polarization formed a *twisted surface* like a cork-screw staircase. In some crystals this twisting takes place towards the right, in others towards the left. The change of plane is also different for each of the different primary coloured rays. Thus examined by an analyzer, the transmitted ray always presents a succession of colours.

Sir J. Herschel showed that the right or left handed character of the polarization agreed with the like inclination of the small facets of the complete crystal round the summit. Biot and Seebeck discovered the same property to exist in certain liquids such as oil of turpentine, and even in some vapours.

The phenomenon is explained theoretically by supposing two rays, each circularly polarized in opposite directions, traversing the axis together, but with unequal velocities. In this case it is shown mechanically that the resultant of such vibrations will be a plane vibration in a continually changing direction, proportional to the retardation which one of the rays has undergone, behind the other, in traversing successive thicknesses. This was the discovery of Fresnel. For rays deviating a little from the direction of the axis, Mr. Airy showed that a similar theory would apply with *elliptically* polarized light.

could not dare to appeal to it, so complicated, so minute, and so directly designed for the purpose proposed were the experimental means employed by Fresnel in the study of circular polarization. Perhaps it may be proper to observe that the greater part of them were suggested by theoretical ideas; for without that, most of the experiments of our colleague offer combinations, of which, so to speak, it would seem impossible that any one would have thought. If, in writing the history of the sciences, it is just to put in their full light the discoveries of those who have cultivated them with distinction, it is important also, —it seems to me right,—though freely stating the truth, yet not to put it in such a light as might render it a source of discouragement to any who might be engaged in the same pursuits.

PRINCIPAL CHARACTERISTICS OF THE SYSTEM OF EMISSION AND OF THAT OF WAVES.—GROUNDS ON WHICH FRESNEL WAS LED TO REJECT UNRESERVEDLY THE SYSTEM OF EMISSION.

After having studied with so much care the properties of luminous rays, it was natural to inquire *of what light consists?* This scientific question, one of the grandest, without contradiction, on which men have ever occupied themselves, has given occasion for the most animated discussion. Fresnel took an active part in it. I will therefore endeavour to point out precisely the nature of the question, and give a concise analysis of the experiments to which it has given rise.

The senses of hearing and smell enable us to discover the existence of bodies at a distance by totally different means. Every odorous substance undergoes a species of evaporation: minute particles are sent off from it incessantly, they mix with the air, which becomes a vehicle for them, and diffuses them in every direction. A grain of musk, whose subtle emanations penetrate through all parts of a vast surrounding circuit loses its power from day to day; it ends by being entirely dissipated and totally disappearing.

It is not the same with a sounding body. Every one knows that a distant bell, whose sound strikes faintly on our ear, nevertheless does not send to us a single molecule of metal; that it can resound without interruption for successive centuries without losing any of its weight. When the clapper strikes it, its sides vibrate, they undergo an oscillatory motion which communicates itself immediately to the neighbouring portions of the air, and thence by degrees to the whole atmosphere. These atmospheric vibrations constitute sound.

Our organs, whatever may be their nature, cannot be put in relation with distant bodies, except in one or the other of these two ways: thus either the sun emits incessantly, as odorous bodies do, material particles from all points of his surface with a velocity of 77,000 leagues in a second, and these are minute solar fragments which by penetrating into the eye produce vision;—*or* else that luminary, in this respect like a bell, excites simply an undulatory movement in a medium extremely elastic, filling all space, and these vibrations proceed to agitate our retinas as the sonorous undulations affect the membrane of the tympanum.

Of these two explanations of the phenomena of light, one is called the theory of emission, the other is known under the name of the system of waves.* We find long

* To assist the general conception of the mode of propagation of waves by transverse vibrations, perhaps it may be desirable to refer

ago traces of the former in the writings of Empedocles. Among the moderns I can cite among its adherents, Kepler, Newton, and Laplace. The system of waves does not reckon less illustrious partisans; Aristotle, Descartes, Hooke, Huyghens, Euler, adopted it. Such names on either side render a choice difficult, if in a matter of sci-

the reader to a very simple machine, represented in the annexed figure contrived by the translator, which exhibits a set of white balls, repre-

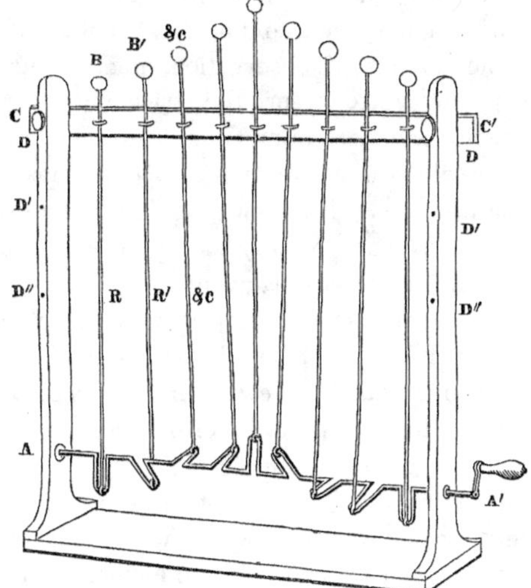

senting the molecules of ether: these are attached to rods, which are moved on turning the handle by cranks at their lower end, so arranged that each ball is in succession raised or lowered nearly in a straight line; so that they follow each other in the form of a wave. When the bar supporting the rings through which the rods pass, is lowered, the balls no longer move up and down in straight lines, but describe each a kind of oval curve, which becomes more rounded the lower the bar is placed. In the former case the machine represents a wave with plain vibrations, in the latter, with elliptic or circular vibrations.

ence the most illustrious names could be authorities capable of determining the point.

If, however, it astonish us to see men of such great genius thus divided, I would say that in their times the question in dispute *could not be resolved;* that the necessary experiments were wanting; and that then the two different theories of light were not logical deductions from facts, but, if I may so express myself, simple matters of persuasion; and that, in a word, the gift of infallibility is not granted even to the most skilful, if they transgress the bounds of observation, and, abandoning themselves to conjecture, desert the strict and sure path by which science advances in our age on reasonable principles, and by which it has been enabled to make such incontestable progress. Before we review the great inroads which have been recently made on the theory of emission, it will be perhaps convenient to cast a glance over the vigorous attacks of which it was the object, in the writings of Euler, of Franklin, and others; and to show that the partisans of Newton might then, without looking forward too much, have considered the solution as adjourned for a long period. The effects which a cannon ball can produce depend so directly on its mass and its velocity jointly, that we can, without altering them, change at pleasure one of these elements, provided we make the others change in an inverse ratio. Thus a ball of two kilogrammes may overthrow a wall; a ball of one kilogramme will also overthrow it, provided we impress on it a velocity double of the former. If the weight of the ball were reduced to $\frac{1}{10}$th or $\frac{1}{100}$th of its original amount, to produce the same effect we must give a velocity ten times or one hundred times as great. Now we know that the velocity of a cannon ball is the 640,000th of that of light; if the weight of a luminous molecule were the 640,000th part of that of the cannon ball, it would in like manner overthrow a wall.

These deductions are certain: but let us look at the facts. A luminous molecule not only cannot overthrow a wall, but it even penetrates into an organ so delicate as the eye without occasioning the least pain, without even producing any sensible dynamic effect. We can say more: in experiments undertaken with the view of rendering sensible the impulsions of light, physicists have not been content to use an isolated agent, they have brought to act simultaneously the immense quantity of light which can be condensed at the focus of a large lens; they have not opposed to the shock of the rays very resisting objects, but bodies so delicately suspended that a breath could derange them enormously; they have operated for example, on the extremity of a very light lever suspended horizontally by a spider's thread. The sole obstacle to the rotatory movement of such an apparatus would be the force of reaction, which the thread would acquire in twisting. But this force might be considered as nothing, since from its nature it always increases rapidly with the degree of torsion; and, in this instance, one of the observers whose experiments I am analyzing, found no perceptible force of this kind, after having had the patience to give the thread 14,000 turns, by turning the lever round on its centre. It is then well established that, in spite of their excessive velocity, myriads of luminous rays acting simultaneously produce no perceptible force. But we should be going beyond the legitimate consequences which this interesting experiment authorizes, if we concluded that a ray is not composed of material elements endowed with a rapid motion of translation.

We may, indeed, fairly deduce from the absence of all rotation in the lever suspended by the spider's thread, under the action of an enormous quantity of light, that the elementary particles of the luminous rays have not dimensions comparable to the millionth part of the finest molecules possessing any weight. But as there is nothing to show any absurdity in supposing them a million, or a myriad, times less than this, this kind of experiment and argument (the first idea of which is due to Franklin) cannot furnish any decisive conclusion.

Among the objections which Euler has presented in his works against the theory of emission, I will point out two, on which he has particularly insisted, and which seem to him irresistible. "If the sun," (said this great geometer,) "continually darts out particles of his own substance in every direction, and with enormous velocity, he must end by exhausting himself: and during the many ages which elapsed since the historical period, some diminution ought already to have become sensible."

But is it not evident that this diminution depends on the magnitude of the particulars? Now there is nothing to hinder our supposing them of such small diameters that, after millions of years' continual emission, the mass of the sun should not be sensibly altered. And, besides, there is no accurate observation to prove that this luminary does not waste, or that its diameter is really as great as it was even in the time of Hipparchus.

No one is ignorant of the fact, that millions of rays can penetrate together into a dark room through a pin-hole, and there form distinct images of external objects. In crossing each other in that minute space, the material elements of which we suppose this multitude of rays to consist ought, nevertheless, to encounter and clash against each other with great violence, to change each other's directions in a thousand ways, and to mingle together without any order. This difficulty is no doubt specious, but it does not appear insurmountable.

The chance that two molecules setting out from the same hole should encounter each other, depends both on the absolute diameter of the molecules, and on the intervals which separate them. We might then by suitably diminishing the diameters reduce the chances of encounter to nothing. But we have here also in the intervals of the molecules another element, which alone would in a great degree lead to the same conclusion. In fact every sensation of light lasts for a certain time; the luminous object which has darted its rays into the eye still remains visible (as experiment has proved) at least for an hundredth of a second after the object has disappeared. Now, in an hundredth of a second, light has gone through 770 leagues. Thus the luminous molecules which form each ray may be at 770 leagues interval from one another, and nevertheless produce a continuous sensation of light. With such distances what becomes of the repeated clashings spoken of by Euler, and which in any circumstances ought to put a stop to the regular propagation of the rays? It is almost humiliating to see a geometer of so rare a genius believe himself authorized by such futile objections to call the system of emission a mistake of Newton,—a gross error,—the belief of which, he says, can only be accounted for by recollecting the remark of Cicero, "There is nothing so absurd but that it has been maintained by some philosopher." *

* It has been too common a practice, both with the advocates and the opponents of the wave theory, to rest its defence or its refutation

However, the system of emission has few partisans; but it is not under the blows dealt by Euler that it has

on single points; to uphold a solitary experimental fact as decisive one way or the other. A single favourable fact will not prove the theory; and, on the other hand, the only real conclusion in cases where a single fact appears to stand out as an objection is, that (granting the fact incapable of being otherwise interpreted) the theory requires remodelling; and that some undue assumption has crept into it. Such reconstruction has always been the process by which it has been successively found to adapt itself to new phenomena, even when at first sight they appeared most opposed to it. But even were it otherwise, the theory is one which is not to be staked on single facts; it rests its claim (in the first instance) in being that which *connects* by a common principle, and *thus explains the greatest number* of facts. Many of the old theories, as of inflexion, attractions, &c., each explained a certain small number of facts; but the real argument against them was, that they did not explain each other. Every new partial explanation of the wave theory, on the contrary, not only explains a certain class of facts, but connects these with some other class similarly explained. Newton had proposed one idea (that of fits of easy reflexion and transmission) to account for the alternations in the colours of thin plates; another totally unconnected theory of inflexion, or bending in and out in passing the edge of a body, to explain the phenomena of diffraction: a third idea of polarity, for double refraction; besides other occasional references to waves, or even a combination of vibrations with molecular emission in some cases; but all *unconnected with, and independent of, each other*, and each confessedly a mere *arbitrary* assumption, not pretending to stand on any other ground than that it explained in a certain way the particular phenomenon in relation to which it was adduced.

On the undulatory view, on the contrary, every subordinate law successively established, and every class of phenomena explained, has become directly *connected* with all the others. Every part is in intimate relation with every other part, and the progressive improvement and enlargement of the theory has regularly kept pace with the advance of experimental discovery; every new modification, as it were, has grown out of the simple principles at first laid down by a natural sequence, without any new hypothesis, or forced and arbitrary changes. It is a theory of which an eminent philosopher, by no means unduly biased in its favour, and at a time when it had by no means reached its present point of perfection, emphatically said, "It

fallen. Insurmountable objections have been found in various phenomena of whose very existence that philosopher was necessarily ignorant. This great advance in the science belongs to the physicists of our own day, and is due in a great measure to the labours of Fresnel. This consideration alone obliges me to point them out in detail, even if the interest of the question did not oblige me to do so.

If light is a wave, the rays of different colours, similar in that respect to the sounds employed in music, are composed of vibrations unequally rapid; and the red, green, blue, and violet rays, are transmitted through the ethereal spaces, as are all the notes of the gamut through the air, with velocities exactly equal.

If light be an emanation, the rays of different colours are formed of molecules necessarily different, either as to their nature, or their mass, and which besides are endowed with different velocities.

An attentive inspection of the borders of the shadows produced by the satellites of Jupiter in their passage across the luminous disk of the planet, and better still, the observations on changeable stars, have proved that all the rays of light move equally fast. Thus a characteristic feature of the system of waves is found verified.

In each of the two systems of light* the original

is a series of felicities; and if not true, eminently deserves to be true." And the increasing proof which it continues to receive by its readiness in meeting nearly every new experimental case as it arises, augments in the same proportion our conviction that it will sooner or later be equally successful in the solution of those few phenomena, which still appear to stand out as exceptional instances to its application.—*Translator.*

* When the author affirms that *in each of the two* theories, (dans l'un et dans l'autre des deux systèmes,) the original velocity of a ray determines its refraction, there seems to be a certain degree of con-

velocity of a ray determines the refraction which it must undergo when it falls obliquely on the surface of a trans-

fusion, which it is difficult to explain. The assertion is clear, and the whole subsequent argument agrees with that assertion, *in regard to the emission theory.* Here, undoubtedly, the original velocity with which a ray enters a new medium, when it is acted upon by the attractions of a number of surrounding particles, will essentially determine the velocity with which it will continue to move under the influence of these attractions, and the path it will take. But *on the wave theory* there appears nothing obviously and antecedently to show what will be the case.

The author proceeds, *as if continuing the last topic*, to quite another point, viz: the experimental fact that light from the most different sources, both terrestrial and celestial, moves with precisely the same velocity *through air or* vacuum. He argues that this is a "mathematical consequence" of the wave theory; *because*, in the parallel case of sound, tones produced by the most different instruments are propagated through the air with the same rapidity. It is certainly a close analogy, but hardly a "mathematical consequence." The remark which follows as to the consequence of molecular theory, in rendering light from different sources unequally rapid in its flight from their differences of attractive power, presents, no doubt, a formidable difficulty to that theory, as being in contradiction to the experimental result just mentioned.

But when in reference to his own beautiful experiment on observing the refractions of light when its velocity is respectively increased and diminished by the whole velocity of the earth, he adds, "such rays ought to be unequally refracted," I can only understand the meaning by referring to the mention made of the *emission* theory in the next line, and supposing *that* theory alone to be intended. *On that theory*, it is true, such rays *ought to be* unequally refracted.

Observation, however, gives a perfect equality of refraction in the two cases, and thus far completely contradicts the idea of molecular attractions. And when he adds, that the only way in which this contradiction could be reconciled with emission, would be by inventing the subsidiary gratuitous hypothesis that the stars emit an infinite number of rays, endowed with all possible velocities, and that only those of a certain velocity can affect our organs with the sense of vision, this would obviously only be to add "cycle on epicycle," "to save appearances," and would afford no real explanation. On the other hand, with respect to the undulatory theory, it does not appear

parent body. If this velocity increase, the refraction will be less, and, reciprocally, a diminution of velocity

that it would, on any obvious *à priori* grounds, enable us to predict the result of such an experiment one way or the other. There is indeed involved the difficult and complex consideration of the propagation of vibrations through æther, while the earth and transparent media upon it are moving through that æther; a problem which exercised the ingenuity of Fresnel, and which, after a long investigation, he decided by concluding that the effects would be exactly the same as if the earth were at rest. This, however, may be still regarded as one of those points connected with what is the most difficult part of the wave theory, viz: the primary conception of æther and its properties.

But apart from this consideration, and looking only to the abstract problem of light (suppose emitted on the surface of the earth) falling on a refracting body with *different velocities*, there is nothing apparently *in theory* to determine whether the refraction will be affected, or in what way, by this difference.

On the undulatory principle, it is true, *velocity* is intimately connected with *refraction; retardation* and *refraction* being coextensive and almost equivalent terms; but it must be borne in mind that it is *not absolute* but *relative* velocity which is thus connected with refraction. It is the *relative* retardation in the denser medium, whatever the *absolute* velocity may be, which causes refraction. If in theory it were shown that the ratio would be constant for all velocities, it would give a constant refraction for the medium. But this is the very point in question; and there appears nothing antecedently to show, on any distinct theory of the nature of æther or of waves, that the relative velocities must necessarily be in a constant ratio. There is, however, nothing in any conception of waves *at variance* with the idea; and it must be admitted as in itself a rational and probable supposition, fairly admissible in the first instance to ground any reasoning upon. When therefore the *fact* was established by Arago's experiment, while it completely subverted what was a *necessary* consequence of the *emission* theory, it offered no contradiction to the undulatory; but the proposition it established being one already *probable*, and *consistent* with that theory, was now to be recognized as an essential part of it. Yet the result of Arago's experiment has been represented by some able writers as of a very startling and unexpected nature, and, at first sight, equally perplexing on either hypothesis.

will manifest itself by an increasing deviation. Refraction thus becomes a sure means of comparing the velocities of all sorts of rays. In following out this research with experimental means so precise that they would mark differences of one fifty-thousandth part of the whole amount in question, we have been able to ascertain that the light of all the heavenly bodies,—of our fires, of tapers, and lamps, (with double currents of air,) and even more, the feeble rays emitted by glow-worms, all go through 77,000 leagues in a second, as well as the burning light of the sun.

It is easy to conceive in what way this result is a mathematical consequence of the *system of waves*, if we only remark that all the notes of the musical scale are propagated with equal rapidity through the air, whether they originate from the voice of a singer, from the metallic string of a piano, the catgut of a violin, the glass surface of an harmonica, or the metallic sides of the great pipe of an organ. Now, there is no reason why the *luminous notes* (if I may be pardoned the expression) should proceed differently in æther. *On the hypothesis of emission* the explanation is not so simple. If light is composed of material elements, it would find itself sub-

The undulatory view of refraction depends entirely on the assumption that the velocity must be diminished in the denser medium; but as the refraction is proved to be constant for all velocities, this *diminished* velocity must be always *in a constant ratio* to the *original* velocity. This is the condition to which our conception of æther must conform. As to the *fact* of a *retardation*, that has been directly proved by another beautiful experiment devised by Arago, but carried out by the experimental skill of Foucault, on the principle of Wheatstone's revolving mirror, which, if it received one of two rays at the smallest interval of time *after* another, would reflect it in a *different direction*. Thus the existence of any *retardation* in one of the rays would be manifested.

ject to universal attraction; it would with difficulty be darted out from an incandescent body, because the attraction of that body will tend to carry it back again; hence a gradual diminution of its original velocity must undoubtedly take place; it is only necessary to inquire whether observation can enable us to discover it. It would be a simple question of calculation how, in making some suppositions with respect to the physical constitution of certain fixed stars in respect to their size and density, which do not appear extravagant, we find that they may, by their attractive force, annihilate altogether the velocity of emission of luminous molecules; that after having proceeded to a given distance, these molecules, which had so far separated themselves from the body, must return thither by a retrograde movement. Thus, certain stars might be as luminous as the sun, to the distance of 40,000,000 leagues, for example, and beyond that be altogether dark; that distance being the exact limit beyond which none of their rays could pass. If we change considerably the volumes and densities which give these results; if we assume for stars of the first magnitude such dimensions as no astronomer would refuse to consider as probable, they will no longer present such strange phenomena, they will no longer be dazzling at this distance, and completely dark at a little farther distance; but the velocity of their light will *change* with the distance; and if two such stars are at very different distances from the earth, their rays will arrive at our eyes with *dissimilar velocities.* Is it not then a formidable objection against the theory of emission, that there should be this perfect equality of velocity in all cases, which all observations testify?

There exist very simple means for altering to a notable extent, if not the absolute, yet the relative velocity of a ray; it is to make observations on it when, in the annual course of the earth, its motion is directed *towards* the star from which the ray proceeds, and again when it is diametrically in the opposite direction. In the former case, it is as if the velocity of the ray was *increased* by the whole of that of our globe; in the second, the numerical difference has the same amount, but the velocity is *diminished.* Now no one is ignorant that the velocity of the earth's revolution is quite *comparable* with that of light; being in fact about a ten-thousandth part of it. And again; to observe a star, towards which the earth is moving, and then one from which it is receding, is to operate upon rays whose velocities differ from each other by one five-thousandth part. Such rays ought to be unequally refracted; the theory of emission furnishes the means of expressing in numbers the amount of the inequality; and we may easily see that it will far exceed the small errors of observation. Now precise measures have completely negatived such calculation; the rays proceeding from all stars, in *whatever region* they are situated, *undergo precisely the same refraction.*

The disagreement between this theory and experience, could not be more manifest, and from that moment the system of emission seemed to be overturned from its very foundations. Nevertheless, this definitive sentence has been suspended by the aid of a supposition which I can explain in two words;—it consists in admitting that incandescent bodies emit rays with all sorts of velocities, but that a special and determined velocity is necessary to make them rays of light. If a ten-thousandth part of increase or diminution in their velocity takes away from rays their luminous properties, the observed equality of deviation is the necessary consequence of this supposition, since in the multitude of rays which strike on the eye, whether it is apparently towards or receding from the stars, it will perceive, in either case, those only whose molecules have the same relative velocity; but this hypothesis, it cannot be denied, deprives the system of emission of the simplicity which constitutes its main recommendation. The clashing of molecules on which Euler so much insisted, would then become the inevitable consequence of their inequality of velocity, and would entail on the propagation of the rays disturbances to which observation does not show them to be subject.

Light exercises a striking action on certain bodies; it rapidly changes their colour. Nitrate of silver, as is well known, possesses for example this power in a high degree. It suffices to expose it for a few seconds to the diffuse light of a cloudy sky for it to lose its original whiteness, and to become of a bluish black. In the rays of the sun it changes almost instantaneously. Chemists have believed that they could see in this discoloration a phenomenon analogous to that they produce every day. According to them the light would be a true "reagent," which in being added to the constituent principles of the compound on which it acts, sometimes modifies its original properties; sometimes also the luminous matter only determines by its action the disengagement of one or more elements of the body on which it strikes.

These explanations, although based on specious analogies, do not seem to be admissible, since it has been shown that, in interfering, the luminous rays also lose the chemical properties with which they are endowed. How can we conceive, in fact, that the matter of two rays can combine with a given substance if each ray strike it singly, while on the contrary no such combination can take place when these same rays strike it together, after having pursued (for this condition is necessary) routes differing from one another by quantities comprised within a certain regular series of numbers ?

In geometry, in order to demonstrate the inaccuracy of a proposition, we follow it out to all its consequences until there results something which is completely absurd. Ought we not to class in this category a chemical action which is generated, or which disappears, according to the length of route which the reagent has gone through ?

Natural phenomena ordinarily present themselves under very complicated forms, and the true merit of the experimenter consists in disengaging them from a multitude of accessory circumstances which hinder us from at once seizing their laws.

If, for example, we had not observed the shadows of bodies except in the open air, if we had never illuminated these bodies by light proceeding from extremely small luminous points, no one would have guessed how many curious subjects of research are offered by a phenomenon so common. But place in the middle of a dark room, and in a beam of homogeneous light, diverging either from a minute hole, or from the focus of a glass lens, any opaque body whatever, and its shadow will show itself marked by a series of contiguous stripes, alternately bright, and completely dark. Substitute white light for the homogeneous beam, and similar stripes vividly coloured will appear to occupy the place of the former.

Grimaldi first perceived these singular affections of light, to which he gave the name of diffraction. Newton afterwards made them the subject of a special investigation; he thought he saw here the manifest proofs of an intense attractive and repulsive action, which bodies exercise on rays passing close to them. This action, supposing it real, could only be explained by admitting the materiality of light. The phenomena of diffraction, then, deserves in an eminent degree to fix the attention of physicists. Many in fact studied it, but by very inexact methods; Fresnel finally gave to this class of observations a perfection unhoped for, in showing that in order to see these diffracted bands, it is not necessary to receive them on a screen, as Newton and all the other experimenters had done hitherto;—that they are found distinctly in space, where we can follow them with all the resources which result from the employment of the astronomical micrometer, with a high magnifying power.

According to the precise observations of Fresnel, by the aid of these new modes of observation, if we still wish to attribute the effects of diffraction to attractive or repulsive forces acting on material elements, we must admit that these actions are totally independent of the nature or density of the bodies employed, for a spider's thread and a wire of platinum produce bands exactly the same; the masses have no more influence, since the back and the edge of a razor produce the same effect. We find ourselves inevitably brought to this conclusion, that a body acts on the rays passing near its surface with so much the less energy as the rays come from a greater distance, since, if on placing the luminous point at the distance of a centimetre, the angular deviation is 12, it will not amount quite to 4 in similar circumstances with light coming from ten times the distance.

These various results, especially the last, are impossible to reconcile with any idea of an attraction. The experiments of Fresnel destroy entirely all the arguments which had been relied on in the phenomena of diffraction to establish the materiality of light.

The important branch of optics which treats of the intensity of reflected light, transmitted and absorbed by bodies, which is designated by the name of photometry, is but in its infancy; it at present consists of nothing more than isolated results, whose exactness may be open to much question. General mathematical laws are wholly wanting. Some attempts made a few years ago have, however, led to a very simple rule which, for every kind of transparent media, connects the angles of the first and second surface at which the reflexions are equal.*

* The measures of intensity of light here alluded to are those of M. Poisson; which, however, were in a great degree anticipated by Dr. Young [Chromatics, *Encycl. Brit.*], though Poisson calls his reasoning indirect, an opinion in which Sir J. Herschel says he cannot concur. Poisson takes the case of perpendicular incidence, and adopts the hypothesis of the vibrations being *coincident* with the *direction of the ray;* he thus obtains expressions for the relative intensities of the incident, reflected, and transmitted rays; and thence, again, of the ray reflected at the second surface. These result in terms of the index of refraction. Arago applied this principle (as far as any photometrical measurements can be relied on) for the intensity of light reflected from Mercury to determine its refractive index. The formula of Young is derived from the analogy of the motion communicated from a portion of æther in one medium, to that in a different state of density in another, with that of the impact of unequal elastic bodies, and *without any assumption* as to the *direction* of the vibrations; the same principle on which the formulas of Fresnel are deduced in Mr. Airy's Tract, (Art. 128.) See Sir J. Herschel on Light, Art. 592; and Lloyd's Lectures on the Wave Theory, p. 31.

Mathematically, Young's formula is deduced in this way. If m and m' be the masses of two elastic bodies, m impinging on m' at rest, by the principles of mechanics (the velocity of m being unity) it is well known that after impact m retains a velocity

In the system of *emission* these two angles have *no necessary dependence;* the *contrary* is the case if the luminous rays are sets of *waves*, and the relation which, in setting out from this hypothesis, one of our most distinguished colleagues has deduced from his scientific analysis is precisely that which experience has furnished. Such an accordance between calculation and observation ought at the present day to take its place among the most forcible arguments which we can produce on which to support the system of vibrations.

$$v' = \left(\frac{m - m'}{m + m'}\right) \qquad (1.)$$

and m' receives a velocity

$$v' = \left(\frac{2\,m}{m + m'}\right) \qquad (2.)$$

It is also *assumed* that this analogy may be applied to a mass of æther (m) in vibration outside the reflecting surface, and communicating its vibrations partly to another mass (m') at rest within the medium; these masses are dependent on and partly retaining it in reflexion. Dependent on the densities, in two contiguous media, and the inclination of the ray.

At a *perpendicular* incidence the two masses are simply proportional to the densities or of the refractive powers; or $\frac{m}{m'} = \frac{1}{\mu}$; hence in this case the velocity of the incident ray being taken as unity, that of the reflected ray will be $\left(\frac{\mu - 1}{\mu + 1}\right)$ and according to the principle of *vis viva* the *intensity* will be proportional to the *square* of this quantity. This is, however, only a particular case of the general formulas discovered by Fresnel, and applying universally to intensities of reflected light at all incidences. The demonstration of these formulas involves some difficulties which Fresnel did not clear up, but which he, with marvellous sagacity, got over by suppositions somewhat of an empirical and hypothetical kind.[1] To express the masses of the corresponding vibrating portions of æther in the two adjacent media, we take lengths l and l' of the incident and refracted rays inversely pro-

[1] See Mr. Airy's Tract of the Undulatory Theory. Art. 128, *et seq.*

The interferences of rays have occupied so great a space in this biography that I cannot dispense with

portional to their refractions or retardations, or inversely as the densities, that is, as sin r; sin i; and drawing parallels to them, the

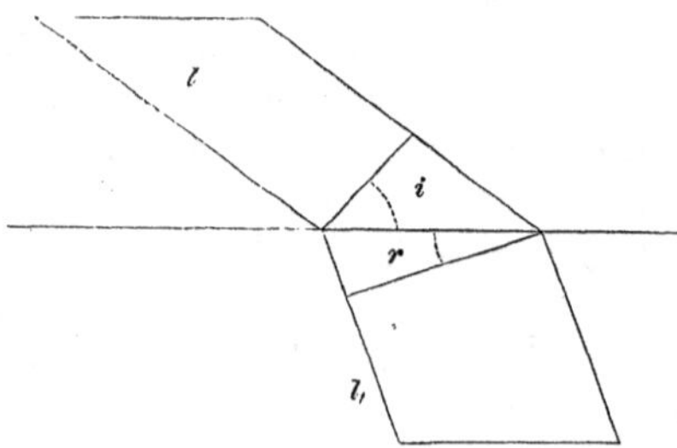

breadths of the parallelograms on the same base are easily seen to be in the ratio of cos i; cos r, and thus the ratio of the simultaneously vibrating masses is,

$$\frac{m}{m_{\prime}} = \frac{\sin r \cos i}{\sin i \cos r}$$

Hence Fresnel deduced for vibrations *parallel* to the plane of incidence the ratio of the amplitudes, that of the incident ray being unity,

$$\text{reflected } k^{\prime} = \frac{\sin 2i - \sin 2r}{\sin 2i + \sin 2r} = \frac{\tan(i-r)}{\tan(i+r)} \qquad (3.)$$

$$\text{refracted } k_{\prime} = \frac{4 \sin r \cos i}{\sin 2i + \sin 2r} = \left(1 - \frac{\tan(i-r)}{\tan(i+r)}\right) \frac{\cos i.}{\cos r.} \qquad (4.)$$

For vibrations *perpendicular* to the plane of incidence he found,

$$h^{\prime} = \frac{-\sin(i-r)}{\sin(i+r)} \qquad (5.)$$

$$k_{\prime} = \frac{2 \sin r \cos i}{\sin(i+r)} \qquad (6.)$$

As to the mode of deducing these formulas, considerable discussion has arisen, and the question cannot be regarded as yet settled.

On merely geometrical grounds, the *directions* of the incident reflected and refracted rays are seen to form a triangle, whose angles are $(i+r)$, $(i-r)$, and $\pi - 2i$), and their sines being as the opposite sides $h\ h^{\prime}\ h_{\prime}$ we have, considering h for the incident ray as unity, pointing out how they are connected with the two theories of light; how in the theory of emission I do not

values very much resembling the last yet differing from them; viz:—

$$h' = \frac{\sin (i - r)}{\sin. (i + r)} \quad (7.) \qquad h_{\prime} = \frac{\sin 2\, i}{\sin (i + r)} \quad (8.)$$

If we draw lines perpendicular to the directions of these rays, they

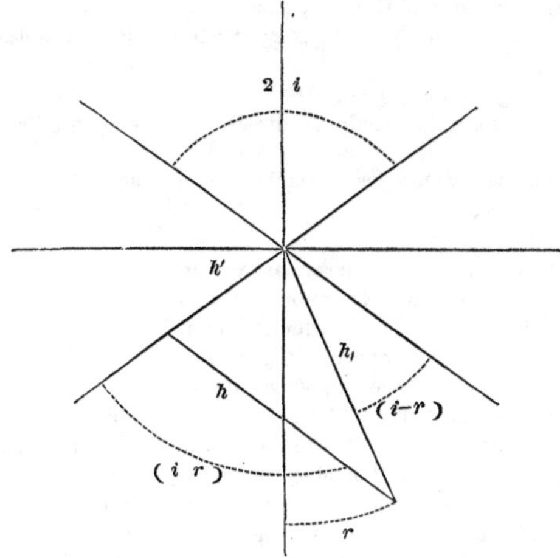

will also form a similar triangle, among whose sides the same relations will subsist. Hence, Professor Maccullagh inferred that these would represent the directions of the *vibrations in the plane of incidence;* and as the lengths or amplitudes of these vibrations are unknown, but are dependent upon, as they are the measures of,—the vibratory forces acting,—so if one of the sides of the triangle be assumed to represent the magnitude of the incident vibration, the others will represent those of the reflected and refracted rays, they being the mechanical components of which the former is the resultant.

On this construction, and by assuming the hypothesis of equal density within and without the medium, he deduced the above formulas (7.) (8.) for vibrations *parallel* to the plane of incidence, and others *resembling* (3.) and (4.) for vibrations *perpendicular* to that

hesitate to say, if we admit no dependence between the motions of the different luminous molecules (and I know

plane, thus differing essentially from the former. See Professor Maccullagh's paper "On the Laws of Crystalline Refraction," Transactions of the Irish Academy, vol. xviii.; and Dr. Lloyd's Lectures on the Wave Theory, part ii. p. 30. The whole subject has been fully discussed by the Translator in three papers in the Philosophical Magazine for July, August, and October, 1856.

The demonstration in either case is grounded on the assumption of the law of *vis viva;* viz:

$$m\,(h^2 - h'^2) = m_{\prime}\,h_{\prime}^{2}.$$

And Fresnel's formulas would be directly deduced *if* we had also the relations

$h + h' = h_{\prime}$ for vibrations perpendicular to the plane of incidence,

and $h - h' = h_{\prime}\dfrac{\cos r}{\cos i}$ . . . . parallel to the plane of incidence.

The difficulty is, that these formulas are not *both* deducible from the principle of equivalent vibrations as laid down by Professor Maccullagh. Another mode of deduction, on a different assumption, is pointed out in the Philosophical Magazine for Oct. 1855, by means of the geometrical construction above given.

The theory of Fresnel, it will be easily seen, is equivalent to the assertion that "the plane of vibration is *perpendicular* to the plane of polarization," whereas in that of Maccullagh they are *coincident.*

Several classes of experiments have been now shown to necessitate the adoption of the former view: for an account of which the reader is referred to the Philosophical Magazine for Aug. 1856, before cited.

To proceed to the *applications* of these formulas: we may consider common light as consisting of two portions of equal intensity, polarized at right angles to each other. If the intensity of the incident light be 1, that of each of these components will be $\frac{1}{2}$. At reflexion each component gives a reflected and a refracted ray polarized respectively at right angles. In the reflected ray the intensity of the portion polarized in the plane of incidence (I) will be $= \frac{1}{2}\,h'^2$. That in the plane perpendicular to (K) will be $= \frac{1}{2}\,k'^2$, and it is easily seen, from the nature of the fractions, that of these quantities the first will always be the greater; and thus in their sum or the total intensity there will be an *excess* of light polarized in the *plane of incidence*, or the light is at all incidences partially polarized in the plane of incidence. The difference of the two expressions gives the quantity of light so polarized.

not what dependence we can establish between isolated projectiles), the fact, and above all the laws, of inter-

In the refracted ray the intensities of the residuary portions respectively will be

$$\tfrac{1}{2}(1-h'^2) \text{ in I}$$
$$\tfrac{1}{2}(1+k'^2) \text{ in K.}$$

Here the second is always the greater: and the refracted ray contains an *excess* of light polarized *perpendicularly to the plane of incidence.* The difference or quantity of light polarized is *the same* as in the reflected ray. Hence the light will be completely polarized at any incidence for which either of the expressions (3.) or (5.) vanishes. No value of i will make (5.) vanish, since we can never have $i=r$. But the expression (3.) becomes $=0$ when $i+r=90^{\circ}$. In this case *the light is completely polarized in the plane of incidence.* But in this case we have also

$$\cos i = \sin r = \frac{\sin i}{\mu} \text{ or } \tan i = \mu,$$

which is Brewster's law; also if $i+r > 90^{0}$ we have $-\tan(i+r)$.

Also at this incidence $\frac{1}{2}$ the incident light is reflected, wholly polarized in I; $\frac{1}{2}$ is also transmitted wholly polarized in K. *This is the case referred to by Arago in the text.* From (5.) also another remarkable inference follows: if the reflexion be internal, or the ray be incident on the second surface of a dense medium, we have r greater than i, or

$$+\frac{\sin(i-r)}{\sin(i+r)};$$

that is, the *phase* of the reflected vibration is changed by 180° equivalent to a difference of $\frac{\lambda}{2}$ in route, from what it would be in reflexion at the first surface at the same incidence. *This explains the supposed assumption of the half undulation in Newton's rings.*

Again: if a polarized ray be incident on a reflecting surface with its plane of vibrations inclined to the plane of incidence (I), at an angle (a), its vibration (h) may be resolved into two, one in the plane (I), and one perpendicular to it (K), in the ratio of sin a and cos a, or after reflexion we shall have for the respective amplitudes (5.) and (3.)

$$k' \sin a, \text{ and } h' \cos a.$$

These by composition will give a resultant ray polarized in a plane (P), inclined to (I) by angle (β), and we have from the formulas (5.) and (3.)

$$\tan\beta = -\tan a \frac{\cos(i+r)}{\cos(i-r)}$$

ference appear wholly inexplicable. I will add besides, that none of the partisans of the system of emission

This formula exhibits remarkable changes at successive incidences: at incidences *less* than that of complete polarization, the new plane of polarization (as indicated by the sign of the tangent) deviates on the side of the plane *opposite* to that of polarization (P) — at (I,) incidences *greater*, it deviates on the *same* side as P; results which *agree exactly with numerous and accurate observations of Fresnel, Arago, and Brewster.*

We have also the following results of this last formula:

While a has any finite value, when $i = 0$, $\beta = a$, or the plane of polarization is unchanged.

When $(i + r) = 90°$, $\beta = 0$, or at the angle of complete polarization P coincides with I.

When $i = 90°$, $\beta = a$ again, or P has its original position.

If $a = 0$, $h' \sin a = 0$, and if at the same time $(i + r) = 90°$, then $k' = 0$, or we also see that *at the polarizing angle an incident ray polarized in* I *will cease to give any reflected ray;* which agrees with the observation originally made by Malus.

From the same formulas another more curious inference was made by Fresnel as follows: In passing out of a denser into a rarer medium, in general it is well known if $i = 90°$, $\sin i = \frac{1}{\mu}$.

Consequently a ray making this incidence internally on the bounding surface will not be refracted out; and at incidences more oblique is experimentally found to be totally reflected internally: theoretically, the conversation of *vis viva* would require that the whole vibratory force, since none of it is expended on refraction, must be occupied in communicating vibrations internally, which can only produce internal waves or internal total reflexion.

Now at the critical incidence, in the formulas for h' and k', $\sin (i - r) = \cos i$, $\sin (i + r) = \sin i$ and $\tan (i - r) = \cot i \tan (i + r) = \tan i'$; whence $h' = 1$ and $k = 1$, which accords with total reflexion.

At incidences greater than this the values become *imaginary;* and by introducing into them empirically certain terms[1] multiplied by $\sqrt{-1}$ Fresnel obtained in such cases an expression of the form,

$$(\cos \theta + \sqrt{-1} \sin \theta) \sin \frac{2\pi}{\lambda} (vt - x)$$

[1] See Airy's Tract, Art. 153.

have attempted in any published work to remove the difficulty, and it is not to be supposed that they had despised it.

And by the analogy of certain geometrical cases where the multiplication by $\sqrt{-1}$ indicates a line differing in angular position by 90°, he hazarded the inference that such an interpretation might hold good here, and that this expression would be equivalent to one of the form,

$$\cos\theta\sin\frac{2\pi}{\lambda}(vt-x)+\sin\theta\sin\frac{2\pi}{\lambda}(vt-x+90^\circ)$$

which is trigonometrically the same as

$$\sin\left(\frac{2\pi}{\lambda}(vt-x)+\theta\right)$$

This applying to the component in the plane of incidence, a similar expression would apply to that perpendicular to it,

$$\text{or }\sin\left(\frac{2\pi}{\lambda}(vt-x)+\theta'\right)$$

The difference of these expressions, or the relative retardation of the two sets of waves, will be $\theta-\theta'=\delta$.

In general, δ having any value, and the plane of polarization being inclined at an angle a to the plane of incidence on the rhomb, the components are,

$$y=\sin a\sin\frac{2\pi}{\lambda}(vt-x+\delta) \quad (1.)$$

$$z=\cos a\sin\frac{2\pi}{\lambda}(vt-x) \quad (2.)$$

This then is precisely the same case as that considered in a former note; and exactly in the same way we obtain,

$$\frac{y^2}{\sin^2 a}+\frac{z^2}{\cos^2 a}-\frac{2yz\cos\delta}{\cos a\sin a}=\sin^2\delta.$$

The general equation to an *ellipse*. If $\delta=90^\circ$, the semi-axes are $\sin a$ and $\cos a$, parallel and perpendicular to the plane of incidence. If $a=45^\circ$ and δ variable, it is still an ellipse. If $a=45^\circ$ and $\delta=90^\circ$, it becomes a circle. *Thus a ray polarized at an angle a, with the plane of incidence, after two internal reflexions in glass, emerges elliptically or circularly polarized, according to the above condition.*

From the empirical terms before mentioned, Fresnel derived expressions from which he calculated that for crown glass, where $\mu=1{\cdot}51$, an internal incidence $i=54^\circ\ 37'$ would give $\delta=45^\circ$. Thus experimentally cutting a rhomb of such glass at that angle, so that the ray polarized at 45° to the plane of incidence, entering one face

As to the system of waves, the interferences are so natural a deduction from it, that we have some reason to be astonished that experimenters should have discovered them before theory had indicated them. To convince ourselves of this, it suffices to remark that a wave, in propagating itself through an elastic medium, communicates to the molecules of which it is composed an oscillatory motion, in virtue of which they displace themselves successively in two opposite directions: this being understood, it is evident that a series of waves will destroy completely the effect of another series, if at every point in the fluid the motion in one direction which the first wave produces alone, shall coincide with the motion in the opposite direction which would result from the sole action of the other wave. The molecules solicited at the same time by equal forces diametrically opposed, will then remain at rest, for as long a period as they would have freely oscillated if under the action of one wave alone. Motion has destroyed motion; now motion is light.

I will not push further this enumeration, because we can already judge on how many points the antagonists of the emission theory have been successful in their attacks. Experiments so numerous, so varied, so delicate, as those I have referred to, do not alone testify all the importance which the question seems to them to possess; they must

perpendicularly, might be reflected internally at that angle, and, passing to the opposite side, be reflected again internally at the same angle; after two reflexions it would emerge, consisting of two pencils polarized at right angles to each other, and having a difference of phase $\delta = 90°$, and would thus possess a circular polarization; or if the inclination was any other than 45° and δ differing from 90, the polarization would be elliptic of different degrees; all which conclusions are fully verified by experiments as before noticed.

be regarded further as a striking mark of respect towards the great man whose name, so to speak, has been identified with the theory which they think ought to be rejected. As to the theory of waves, the Newtonians have not done it the honour to discuss it with the same detail; it has seemed to them that a single objection was sufficient to annihilate it; and this objection they have drawn from the manner in which sound is propagated in air. If light, they say, is a vibration like the vibrations of sound, it will be transmitted in all directions; just as we hear the sound of a distant bell when we are separated from it by a screen which conceals it from our eyes, in the same way we ought to perceive the light of the sun behind every kind of opaque body. Such are the terms to which we must reduce the difficulty, for analogy does not permit us to say that light ought to extend itself behind screens without losing some of its intensity; since sound itself, as every one knows, does not penetrate obstacles without being enfeebled in a sensible degree. Thus, in speaking of the extension of light into the geometrical shadow of a body as an insurmountable difficulty, Newton and his adherents certainly did not suspect the answer which it would bring with it; yet this answer is direct and simple. You maintain that the luminous vibrations ought to extend into the shadow,—*they do so.* You say that in the system of waves, the shadow of an opaque body can never be completely dark,—*it never is so.* It includes a number of rays which give rise to a multitude of curious phenomena, of which you may have some knowledge, since Grimaldi perceived them in part so long ago as before 1633.* Fresnel,—and here is incon-

* Among the earliest difficulties which seemed to attend the conception of the wave theory, was the consideration, which appeared so

testably one of the most important of his discoveries,—has shown how and under what circumstances this diver-

unanswerable, that on this principle there ought to be no *darkness;* light ought to spread equally into the shadow, and we ought to see round a corner.

It was the fertile principle of interference which was to supply the answer, as indeed had been long before hinted generally by Huyghens. The waves diverging from the *different parts* of a luminous source of any *sensible* magnitude interfere with and neutralize each other, except in the main direction, when alone they exactly concur; —a principle called "the mutual destruction of secondary waves." Young dwelt much at first on this objection; and afterwards, in a letter to Arago, he renews a similar expression of the difficulties he felt in another point of view: "If light has so great a tendency to diverge into the path of neighbouring rays, and to interfere with them, as Huyghens supposed, I do not see how it escapes being totally extinguished in a very short space, even in the most transparent medium."—Peacock's Life, p. 140. But the principle just adverted to shows that the middle portion of the light coming from a point of any physical magnitude is not subject to those mutual interferences, and does not diverge, but is perpetually reinforced by the supply of fresh waves incessantly propagated from the original source. In these explanations Young at length expressed his full concurrence in a letter to Fresnel. The actual divergence of light into a shadow is demonstrated by the existence of the internal stripes. This, however, is an effect only produced to a very limited extent; and the general law of the "mutual destruction of secondary waves" in ordinary cases applies to produce the effect of destroying all apparent lateral divergence. There are, however, some cases where this cause operates less extensively (such, at least, would seem to be the case, and is the view upheld by some mathematicians); at all events, under certain conditions, the divergence is rendered very much more conspicuous, and reaches to a far greater distance from the edge. This appears to have been the case in a remarkable experiment, mentioned both by Newton and Hooke, and probably observed by each independently, but described, especially by Newton, in somewhat obscure terms (see Optics, book iii. part i. obs. 5, (Ed. 1721,) but more precisely by Hooke: see Posthumous Works, pp. 186 and 190, and plate 11, fig. 8, p. 155, Ed. 1705). Hooke ascribes it to a "deflexion of light differing both from reflexion and refraction, and seeming to depend on the unequal density of the constituent parts of the ray," &c. Newton enters on

gence of light takes place: he has further shown that in a complete wave which is freely propagated, the rays are

no theoretical considerations whatever, but mentions it only among those unfinished inquiries which, as he says, he had left imperfect and was unable to carry out.

Both the fact, and all questions relating to it, seem to have been overlooked until, in reference to a somewhat similar case, M. Babinet supposed that under particular conditions the mutual interference of the secondary waves might be interrupted by stopping one of the interfering portions of light, and thus the other portion be rendered effective, and consequently diverging rays made visible. The author of this note, in relation to what appears a closely allied, if not identical phenomenon, the formation of a corona or ring of light round the dark disk of the moon in a total eclipse of the sun, tried some analogous experiments, and rendered the same kind of effect conspicuous and easy to be studied by an arrangement of this kind:—

The rays of the sun ⊙ are transmitted by reflexion from an inclined mirror (*m*) through a small hole (*h*) in a shutter, and in the diverging beam is placed an opaque circular disk (*d*) which intercepts the rays at a point where they have an area *considerably less* than its own diameter. From the edge of (*d*) rays are seen to diverge into its shadow and cross at successive points along the axis; they are thus rendered

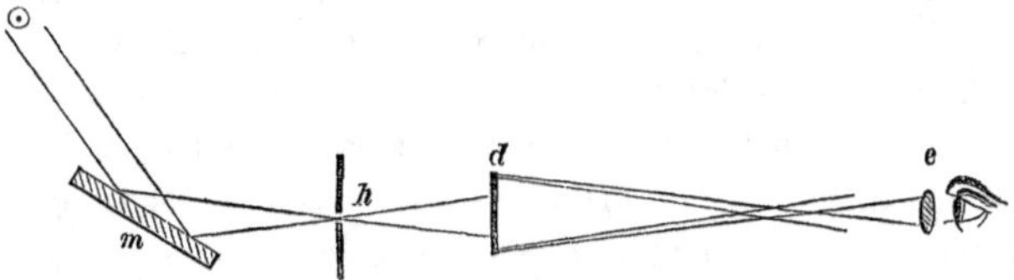

visible by means of a small eye lens at (*e*) which presents the appearance of the shadow of the circular disk, having a multitude of rays converging inwards from its edge to its centre, where they form a point or small circle of great relative brightness. If, on the other hand, the disk (*d*) under the same conditions be viewed *directly* by the eye, without the lens, its shadow is seen relatively and uniformly dark, but surrounded by a bright luminous ring on its outside. The same appearance of the ring is also presented if, instead of the solar rays, we use the light of a flame placed at the principal focus of a lens inserted in a screen so as to send out a beam of parallel pencils intercepted in like manner by the disk. In this case, however, the con-only sensible in the directions which, prolonged, terminate in the luminous points, although in each of its successive positions the different parts of the primitive wave are in fact themselves the centres of disturbance, whence emanate new waves in all directions; but these oblique or secondary waves interfere with each other, and destroy each other entirely. There remain then only the normal waves; and thus the rectilinear propagation of light finds an explanation in the system of vibrations.

When the original wave is not entire, when it is broken or intercepted by the presence of an opaque body, the result of the interferences (which in this case play an important part) is not so simple to explain: the rays which go off obliquely from all parts of the wave not intercepted, do not necessarily destroy each other. In one part they conspire with the normal ray, and produce a brilliant light; in another these same rays destroy each other, and all light disappears. From the point where a ray is broken, its propagation is effected thenceforward according to special laws; the light which falls upon a screen is no longer uniform: it necessarily is composed of alternate stripes of brightness and darkness regularly placed. If the opaque intercepting body is not very large, the oblique waves which cross each other within

verging rays cannot be seen. This apparently paradoxical effect has been supposed by some not sufficiently explained on M. Babinet's principle. The reader will find some observations on the subject, and its applications in the author's two papers in the Memoirs of the Royal Astronomical Society, vol. xvi., on Luminous Rings round Shadows, and in vol. xviii., on Irradiation. Some further remarks also will be found in his paper on Lord Brougham's Experiments, Phil. Mag. July, 1852.—*Translator.*

its shadow produce, by their reciprocal action, stripes analogous to the former, but differently distributed.

I perceive that, without intending it, in following the theoretical speculations of Fresnel, I have mentioned the principal features of those curious phenomena of diffraction, which I have before cited under another point of view, to which Newton devoted one entire book of his *Optics*. Newton believed that he could not give any explanation of these phenomena (so difficult did they seem to him), except by admitting that a ray of light cannot pass close to a body without there undergoing a sinuous movement like that of an eel. In the explanations of Fresnel this strange supposition is superfluous.

The opaque body which seems to be the original cause of the diffracted bands does not act at all on the rays, either by attraction or by repulsion ; it simply intercepts a part of the principal wave. It stops in the ratio of their breadth a great number of oblique rays, which, but for this interruption, would have gone into certain parts of space to mix with other rays, and to interfere more or less with them.

Thus it is no longer surprising that, as observation has proved, the resulting effect is independent of the nature and mass of the body. The periods of maximum and minimum of the light, as well without as within the shadow, are directly deducible from the theory of Fresnel with a degree of precision of which hitherto, perhaps, no branch of physical science had afforded so striking an example. Thus, whatever reserve it may be prudent to impose on ourselves when we run the risk of speaking of the labours of our successors, I would almost venture to affirm that, with regard to diffraction, they will add nothing essential to the discoveries with which Fresnel has enriched the science. Theories are, in general, only methods, more or less happy, of linking together a certain number of facts *already known*. But when all the *new consequences* which we can deduce from them are found to agree with experience, they claim a higher importance. This kind of success has not been wanting to Fresnel. His formulas of diffraction include, by implication, a very strange result, which he had not perceived. One of our colleagues*—I shall have no need to mention his name, if I say that he has been placed long since among the greatest geometers of this age, as well by a multitude of important labours in pure analysis, as by the most happy applications to the system of the world, and to physics,—perceived at a glance the consequence of which I have spoken; he showed that, in admitting the formulas of Fresnel, the centre of the shadow of an opaque and circular screen ought to be as bright as if the screen did not exist. This consequence, apparently so paradoxical, was subjected to trial by direct experiment, and observation has perfectly confirmed the result of calculation.

In the long and difficult discussion to which the nature of light has given birth, and of which I have just traced the history, the task of the physicists has been nearly fulfilled; as to that of the mathematicians, it unhappily still offers some deficiencies to be filled up. I would venture then, if I had the right, to adjure that great geometer to whom optical science owes the important result just mentioned, to try whether the half empirical formulas by which Fresnel has attempted to express the intensities of light reflected under all angles and for all kinds of surfaces, may not be found deducible also from the general equations of motion of elastic fluids. It remains,

* Poisson.

above all, to explain how the different undulations can undergo unequal deviations at the bounding surfaces of transparent bodies.

LIGHT-HOUSES.

In an academy of sciences, if it properly appreciate its functions, the author of a discovery is never exposed to the discouraging question so often addressed to him in the world, of *cui bono?* Here every one comprehends that the animal life ought not to be the sole occupation of man; that the cultivation of his intellect,—that an attentive study of this infinite variety of animated beings, and inert matter, with which he is surrounded, forms the most beautiful portion of his destined pursuits.

But besides, even if we were desirous to find nothing in the sciences but the means of facilitating the reproduction of substances for food,—of weaving with more or less economy and perfection the different fabrics which serve for clothing,—of constructing with elegance and solidity the convenient habitations in which we escape the vicissitudes of the seasons,—of extracting from the bowels of the earth so many metals and combustible matter, which are necessary for the arts of life,—of annihilating a hundred material obstacles which oppose themselves to the intercommunication of inhabitants of the same continent, of the same kingdom, even of the same city,—of extracting and preparing the medicaments proper for combating the numerous disorders with which our organs are incessantly threatened,—the question of *cui bono?* will be found completely announced. Natural phenomena have innumerable points of connection with each other, often hidden, the discovery of which one age bequeathes to another. At the moment when these relations are discovered, important applications rise up, as if by enchantment, out of experiments which, until then, would seem likely to remain for ever among the number of abstract speculations. A fact which no direct utility had as yet recommended to the attention of the public becomes, perhaps, the step on which a man of genius supports himself to climb up to those primary truths which change the whole face of science, whether for creation of some economical moving power, which all manufacturing arts will henceforth adopt, and of which not the least merit is that of delivering thousands of operatives from overwhelming toils which assimilated them with the brutes, ruined their health, and brought them to a premature death. If to fortify these reflections examples may be thought necessary, I should feel no other embarrassment than that of too wide a choice. But here there is no necessity to enter on such details; for to all the theoretical researches already mentioned, Fresnel has added an important labour, having an immediate practical application, which will certainly place his name among those of the benefactors of the human race. This work, every one knows, had for its object the improvement of *light-houses*. I will proceed to trace the outline of its progress, and shall thus have finished the sketch which I proposed to offer you of the brilliant scientific career of our late colleague.

Persons unacquainted with nautical matters are usually seized with a sort of fear when the vessel which carries them, at a distance from continents or islands, has no other witness of its progress than the stars and the waves. A view of any coast the most barren, the most rocky, the most inhospitable, dissipates, as if by enchantment, those undefined fears which their absolutely isolated position had inspired, while, to the experienced navigator, it is near the land alone that the dangers are seen to commence.

Such danger occurs in ports into which no prudent sailor would enter without a pilot; it occurs where, even with this help, no one would risk attempting to penetrate at night; we easily see, then, how indispensable it is, if we would avoid irreparable accidents, that after sunset signals of flame, easily visible, should indicate on all sides the proximity of land. It is necessary moreover that every ship should perceive the signal far enough off for it to find, in evolutions often sufficiently difficult, the means of keeping itself at some distance from the shore until the moment when day shall appear. It is not less desirable that the different lights which we kindle along a certain extent of coast should not be confounded with each other; and that at first sight of these hospitable signals the navigator, who by an unfavourable sky has been for some days deprived of the means of directing his course, should know, for example, on returning from America, whether he is about to enter the Gironde, the Loire, or the harbour of Brest.

On account of the roundness of the earth, the range of a light-house depends on its height. In this respect men have always obtained without difficulty the range which the wants of navigation demanded: it was a simple question of expense; every one knows, for instance, that the great edifice with which the famous architect Sostrates of Cnidus adorned the harbour of Alexandria, nearly three hundred years before our era, and most of the light-houses constructed by the Romans, were of considerably greater height than the most celebrated modern towers. But in an optical point of view, these light-houses were but little remarkable; the feeble rays which proceeded from fires of wood or of coal, lighted in the open air on their summits, could never penetrate the thick vapours which in all climates obscure the lower regions of the atmosphere.

Nevertheless, as to the intensity of light, the modern light-houses were but little superior to the ancient. The first important amelioration which they received, dates from the double-current lamp of Argand; that admirable invention which would be much better appreciated, if, while our museums include works of the period of the decline of art in a purely historical point of view, the repositories of industrial science presented successively to public inspection the various means of illumination, so dull, so bad, so ill-suited, so nauseous, which were employed only fifty years ago, by the side of those elegant lamps whose pure and brilliant light rivals that of a summer day.

Four or five Argand lamps united, would give without doubt as much light as the large fires which the Romans used with so much trouble, on the lofty towers of Alexandria of Puzzuoli, or of Ravenna; but in combining these lamps with reflecting mirrors, their natural effects may be prodigiously increased. The principle of this last invention ought to arrest our attention for an instant, because it will enable us rightly to appreciate the value of Fresnel's labour.

The light of a burning body expands uniformly in all directions,—one part falls on the ground, and is lost; another portion ascends, and is dissipated in space; the sailor whose route we wish to enlighten, profits only by those rays which are emitted horizontally, or nearly so, from the lamp across the sea; all the rays, even those which are horizontal, directed towards the land, have only been produced to be entirely wasted.

This horizontal beam of rays not only forms a very small part of the total light; it has also the serious inconvenience of diminishing in intensity as it diverges, and of not extending itself to a distance without being sensibly enfeebled. To destroy this unfortunate loss of light,—to profit by *all* the light which the lamp emits,—was the twofold problem which remained to be resolved in order to extend the range, and thus the utility, of light-houses. Concave metallic mirrors, called *parabolic reflectors*, have furnished a satisfactory solution.

When the lamp is placed at the focus of such a mirror, all the rays which emanate from it are brought, by the reflexion they undergo against its sides, into a common direction; their original divergence is destroyed; they form, as they issue from the apparatus, a cylinder of light parallel to the axis of the mirror. This beam is transmitted to the greatest distances with the same brightness, except that the atmosphere absorbs a small part of it.

Before proceeding further, let us stop to observe that this construction is not without an inconvenience. We thus indeed easily bring to bear on the horizon of the sea a multitude of rays which would otherwise have been lost on the ground, in space above, or on the side towards the land; and we overcome the divergence of those rays which would naturally be directed towards the navigator. But the cylinder of reflected rays can have no greater breadth than that of the mirror; the space which it illuminates has precisely the same breadth at all distances; unless indeed we employed many similar mirrors, pointed different ways, and even then the horizon would include many large spaces completely dark, in which the pilot would perceive no signal. This great evil is overcome by giving, by means of clockwork, an uniform motion of rotation to the reflector. The luminous beam issuing from this mirror is then successively directed to all points of the horizon; every ship sees the light at one instant appear, and at another disappear; and if in a great length of coast, as for example from Brest to Bayonne, there do not exist any two light-houses with the same period of rotation, all the signals are, so to speak, individualized. According to the interval which elapses between two appearances or two eclipses of the light, the navigator always knows what point of the coast is in view; he finds himself no longer liable to mistake the light-house for a planet or star of the first magnitude near to it rising or setting, or even for those accidental fires, kindled on the coast by fishermen, woodcutters, or charcoal burners,—fatal mistakes which have often been the cause of deplorable shipwrecks.

A transparent lens brings to parallelism all the luminous rays which traverse it, whatever might be their original degree of divergence, provided the point from which the rays diverge be coincident with that point belonging to the lens which we call its focus. Glass lenses, then, may be substituted for mirrors, and in fact a light-house with lenses has been long ago executed in England under the idea, at first sight very plausible, that it would be much more brilliant than light-houses with reflectors. Yet it was found in practice that mirrors, notwithstanding the gross loss of light which they produce at their surface in the act of reflexion, direct to the horizon a more intense beam of light. Lenses were therefore abandoned.

The unknown author of this abortive attempt proceeded

at hazard. In occupying himself with the same problem, Fresnel, with his habitual penetration, perceived at the first glance where the difficulty lay. He saw that the lenticular light-houses could only become superior to those with reflectors, by increasing considerably the intensity of the flame which supplied the illumination; or by giving to the lenses enormous dimensions which seemed to surpass all that any ordinary work could accomplish. He observed also that the lenses must have a very short focal length; that, in making them according to the usual forms, they had too great a thickness, too small a transparency; and that their weights were considerable, and pressed too much on the machinery for making them rotate, so as speedily to bring on its destruction.

To avoid this excessive thickness of the ordinary lenses, their enormous weight, and want of transparency, which were its consequences, they were replaced by others of a peculiar form, which Buffon had imagined for another purpose, and which he called *lenses by steps.* (*Lentilles à échelons.*)* It is possible at the present day to con-

* The nature of these lenses *à échelons* will be understood at once from the annexed sketch, where this construction is represented in front view and in section. The effect of one continuous lens is made

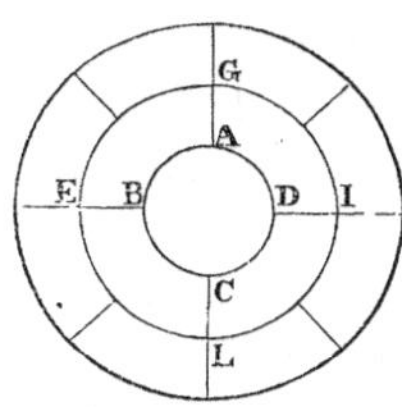

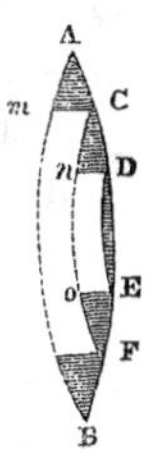

up by a combination of separate pieces, instead of one large lens as indicated by the dotted outline.—See Brewster's *Optics.* Cab. Cyclop. p. 322.

struct the largest lenses of this kind, although we do not yet know how to fabricate thick masses of glass free from defects. It suffices to compose them of a number of distinct small pieces; a plan proposed by Condorcet.

I can here affirm that, at the moment when the idea of these lenses "by steps" occurred to the mind of Fresnel, he had not the least knowledge of the previous projects of Buffon and Condorcet. But assertions of this kind are interesting only to the author in regard to his own claims, they have no value for the public. In its eyes there is not,—I will say more, there ought not to be more than one inventor,—he who first makes public the discovery. After so large a concession, it may at least be allowed me to remark that in 1820 there did not exist a single lens of this construction in the physical cabinets, and that besides, up to that time, lenses had only been regarded as the means of producing great effects of *heat;* that it was Fresnel who created methods to construct them with exactness and economy; that it was he, and he alone, who even imagined the application of them to *light-houses.* This application, however (as I have just pointed out), could never have led to any useful result if it had not been combined with suitable modifications of the lamp; if the illuminating power of flame had not been greatly augmented. This important part of the system required special studies, numerous and delicate experiments. Fresnel and one of his friends (Arago) devoted themselves to the inquiry with ardour; and their common labour led to the construction of a lamp with many concentric wicks, whose brilliancy was twenty-five times that of the best lamps, with only a double current.

In the glass lenses imagined by Fresnel, each lens sent successively to all parts of the horizon a light equivalent to that of 3,000 or 4,000 Argand lamps united; that is, eight times that produced by the beautiful silvered parabolic reflectors of which our neighbours make use; it is also equivalent to the light which we should obtain by uniting in one the third part of the total quantity of the gas-lights which illuminate the streets, the shops, and the theatres of Paris. Such a result does not seem devoid of importance, if we remark that it is obtained with a single lamp. In perceiving such powerful effects, the Government took care to authorize Fresnel to cause to be constructed one of his instruments, and selected the lofty Tower of Cordouan, at the mouth of the Gironde, as the point where it should be placed. The new light-house was at length constructed in the month of July, 1823.

The light-house of Fresnel has since had for judges, during seven consecutive years, the multitude of mariners of all countries who frequent the Gulf of Gascony. It was also studied assiduously at the place by skilful engineers, who came expressly from the north of Scotland with a special mission from the British Government. I shall here be the interpreter of the opinions both of the one and the other, when I affirm that France, since there the important invention of revolving lights had its origin, possesses, thanks to the labours of our scientific colleague, the most beautiful light-houses in the world. It is always glorious to march at the head of the sciences; but we experience above all a lively satisfaction in claiming the first rank for our country, when the question relates to one of those happy applications in which all nations are called upon to take an equal part, and of which humanity will never have occasion to complain.

There exist at present on the ocean and on the Mediterranean twelve light-houses, more or less powerful, constructed on the principles of Fresnel. To complete the general system of lighting our coasts, thirty new light-houses appear still necessary. Every thing induces us to hope that these important works will be promptly executed, and that we shall deviate in the least possible degree from the happy direction given to this branch of the public service by our colleague. Routine and prejudice will here be without power, since the parties interested who are the true judges, the mariners of all nations, have unanimously proclaimed the superiority of the new system. No one can allege pretexts of economy, for to produce equal effect, the lenticular light-houses do not require so much oil as those of the old construction; are of a much less expensive kind to keep up, and procure definitively to the state an annual economy of about half a million. This beautiful invention, then, ought to prosper at least, if since the death of Fresnel it did not fall into the hands of those persons, strangers to the subject, who think themselves fit for all employments, although, under different states of public affairs, they have had no other places of study than the antechambers of ministers. Candidates, if I am rightly informed, were not wanting; but happily, this time, intrigue yielded to merit, and the chief superintendence of the light-houses was intrusted to the younger brother of Fresnel, like himself a former pupil of the Ecole Polytechnique, like himself an engineer of the "ponts et chausées,"—skilful, zealous, and conscientious.

Under his inspection, the construction and the disposition of great lenses "in steps" has received important improvements, and the public will not have to fear that any negligence will deprive these beautiful instruments of any part of their power. Such inheritances of national glory will surely never be allowed to suffer neglect.

LIFE AND CHARACTER OF FRESNEL.—HIS DEATH.

The numerous discoveries which I have just described were all made in the short interval between 1815 and 1826, without occasioning any neglect of the duties confided to Fresnel, either as engineer of the pavements of Paris, or as secretary of the commission of light-houses. But our colleague, at the same time, entirely withdrew from the temptations to idleness, which abound more in Paris than any other city, and which those who yield themselves to them call the duties of society, in order to appease their consciences, and to explain to themselves how their time is so ill employed. A life in the study, a life altogether intellectual, however, was but ill suited to the frail constitution of Fresnel. However, the anxious cares of his estimable family were abundantly bestowed on him;—the thoroughly contented disposition of this simple-minded man, than whom no one ever better deserved the title, reacted powerfully in preserving his health;—and lastly, his extreme temperance led to the hope that he might be long spared to the sciences.

The emoluments of the two offices held by Fresnel, that of engineer and academician, would have amply sufficed for his moderate desires, if the craving for scientific research had not been with him a second nature. The construction and purchase of those delicate instruments, without which, at the present day, we cannot produce any thing exact in physics, absorbed every year a considerable part of his fortune. He, therefore, was anxious to create new resources. The situation, so very moderately remunerated, of temporary examiner of the pupils at the Ecole Polytechnique offered itself; Fresnel obtained it; but his friends were not slow to perceive that he had presumed too much on the powers of his constitution; that the ardour with which he fulfilled his new duties and the anxieties he felt,—in fact unduly exaggerated,—in classing the candidates in the order of merit, seriously affected his health, already so precarious; and yet, how could they advise a resignation, of which the inevitable result would be the abandonment of many glorious labours? Under these circumstances, one of the most desirable scientific offices, among all those of which the government has the disposal, that of examiner of the pupils in navigation, became vacant. This office requires only moderate labour. The annual journey which it involves was, in the eyes of his medical advisers, a reason why it should be more desirable that Fresnel should obtain it. He determined, therefore, to become a candidate; as every one would believe, there is no impropriety in asking for an employment, for which long studies peculiarly qualify a person, and which he could conscientiously fulfil. Literary men suppose that after undertaking toilsome labours they can, without reproach, aspire to the enjoyment in their old age of that independence which the most inconsiderable artisan in Paris is sure of obtaining one day, however slight may be his labours or inferior his rank. No one has ever maintained that there is not both propriety and advantage in every case in choosing the most worthy. The glory which such men as Lagrange, Laplace, Legendre, reflected on the board of longitude and on the Academy, seemed to associate itself with the eminent services which, under other other titles, these illustrious geometers had rendered to the Ecole Polytechnique. In the public courses, the pupils claim that the professors should be earnest, lucid, and methodical; but it is no concern of theirs to inquire whether other audiences in other establishments receive instruction from the same men. The sciences will not appear an idle superfluity; and we may admit that Papin, in inventing the steam-engine; Pascal, in pointing out the principle of the hydraulic press; Lebon, in imagining lighting by gas; Berthollet, in inventing bleaching by chlorine; Leblanc in teaching us to extract from sea-water the soda which formerly had to be imported at high prices; have nobly paid to society the debt of science.

If we ought to believe some persons, whose intentions I would rather commend than their enlightenment, I should have to enumerate a long series of prejudices, and should have to defend the author of so many beautiful discoveries, the originator of a new system of light-houses, the man of science whose name navigators will eternally bless, from the charge of having desired, by the union of two offices, to procure for himself an annual life-income of 12,000 francs, of which the greatest part would certainly have been devoted to the expenses of new researches. The defence of our colleague would, without doubt, be an easy task; but I may omit it; Fresnel did not obtain the employment he sought, and that from causes which I would willingly pass over in silence, if they were not such as to give me occasion for showing that men of letters,—whose character there have recently been attempts to dishonour, by representing them as harpies rushing without rule or moderation to prey upon the public purse,—know well how to renounce nobly the most desirable offices, even those which they might claim as a sacred debt, as soon as their dignity would become compromised.

I have already mentioned how much the duties of examiner at the Ecole Polytechnique endangered the health of Fresnel; how desirable it became that his wish for a less laborious situation should be attained. The incontestable superiority of his scientific claims, the withdrawal of all competitors, the behaviour of one of our honourable colleagues, one of the first geometers of the age; and lastly, the active conduct of M. Becquey, who, on every occasion, treated Fresnel with the kindness of a father, had smoothed over many obstacles. The minister on whose decision the appointment depended had himself, during his youth, been occupied with the study of the sciences in a distinguished degree; he had even kept up the taste for them; he desired to see our colleague, and from that moment his nomination seemed sure; for the reserved manner of Fresnel, the sweetness of his character, the unaffected modesty of his language, conciliated instantly the goodwill even of those who did not understand his works; but, alas, in the train of civil discords, to how many mistakes are we not exposed, if we proceed to judge of that which will be from that which ought to be. How many little circumstances, paltry interests, heterogeneous elements, come in and mix themselves with affairs the most simple, and prevail over rights the most incontestable. For my own part, I cannot say on what occasion the Minister of the Interior, addressing himself to the royalist volunteer of the Drôme, put the following question, clearly intimating that his nomination depended on the answer he gave: "Sir, are you truly on our side?" "If I understand rightly, Monseigneur, I should answer that there exists no one more devoted than myself to the august family of our kings, and to the wise institutions which France owes to it." "All this, sir, is too vague; we shall understand one another better by using plain terms. If you were a deputy, by the side of which member would you sit?" "Monseigneur," replied Fresnel, without hesitation, "by the side of Camille Jordan, if I were worthy." "Many thanks for your frankness," replied the minister. The next day an unknown individual was named examiner of the marine.

Fresnel received this repulse without a word of complaint. In his mind, the personal question was entirely effaced in comparison with the pain he felt in seeing, after thirty years of debates and troubles, political passions still so little subdued. When a minister, whose private qualities might claim the homage of good men of all parties, considered himself obliged to ask a scientific examiner, not for proofs of incorruptibility, of zeal, or of knowledge, but for an assurance that, if by chance he should ever happen to become a deputy, he would not determine to sit at the side of Camille Jordan, a good citizen could not but fear that our political future was not to be exempt from storms.

The body of instructors of the Ecole Polytechnique, under all régimens, has suffered little from political influences. There the examiner and the professor must daily discharge their duties in person; there, under the eyes of a nursery of skilful hearers, and in some slight degree inclined to malice, inaccurate refinements, false calculations, bad experiments in chemistry or physics would in vain seek refuge under the shelter of the opinions of the day. Fresnel might then hope that, notwithstanding his recent profession of faith, they would not deprive him of the place of temporary examiner. Besides, this office is extremely laborious, and experience has sufficiently shown, that sinecures are the places sought after with more especial ardour. Fresnel then continued his former functions: but at the close of the examination of 1824, an attack of hemoptysis forced him to retire from his labours, and caused the most serious alarm to his friends. From this moment our unfortunate colleague was obliged to abandon every scientific research which required close attention, and to devote solely to the business of the light-houses the few moments of relief which his malady left him. The most tender and marked attentions soon became powerless against the rapid progress of the disease. It was then resolved to try the effects of country air; alas! but a too evident indication of the little hope entertained by the skilful physician in whom Fresnel confided. However, not to distress his family, our unfortunate colleague affected to entertain hope, and at the beginning of June, 1827, he was removed to Ville d'Avray. There he saw the approach of death with the calmness and resignation of a man whose whole conduct had been without reproach. A young engineer of high distinction, M. Duleau, found, in the lively friendship which united him to our colleague, an irresistible impulse to take part in the melancholy kind offices of which he was the object; and he also established himself at Ville d'Avray. M. Duleau was the first who informed us how little Fresnel was under any delusion as to his condition. "I could have wished," he exclaimed sometimes (when the presence of a mother and a brother, who were agitated by poignant disquietude, did not impose upon him a reserve which his tender feelings for them would not infringe), "I could have wished to live longer, because I perceive that there are in the inexhaustible range of science, a great number of questions of public utility, of which, perhaps, I might have had the happiness of finding the solution." Fresnel was still in the country when the Royal Society of London charged me with the office of presenting to him the Rumford Medal. His powers, then almost exhausted, scarcely permitted him to cast a glance of his eye over this testimony, so rarely bestowed, of the estimation of that illustrious society. All his thoughts were directed towards his approaching end: all were concentrated on that object. "I thank you," he said to me, in a feeble voice, "for having undertaken this mission. I guess how much it must have cost you, for you have perceived, is it not so? that the most beautiful crown is worth little when it is only to be deposited on the tomb of a friend!"

Alas! these melancholy anticipations were not long in being accomplished. Eight days more had hardly elapsed when our country lost one of its most virtuous citizens; the Academy one of its most illustrious members; and the scientific world, a genius of the highest order.

Newton, on learning the premature death of Cotes, a young geometer whose first labours had led to great expectations, pronounced those words, so simple, so expressive, that the history of science has treasured them up: "If Cotes had lived we should have known something!" From the mouth of Newton this short eulogy might pass without comment; it belongs to genius to pronounce such sentences, and we shall always believe its word. For myself, Gentlemen, devoid of all such authority I have felt myself bound laboriously to go through so many details, not to affirm, but to prove to you, that we know some things although Fresnel lived so short a time.

THOMAS YOUNG.

A BIOGRAPHY READ AT A PUBLIC SITTING OF THE ACADEMY OF SCIENCES THE 26TH OF NOVEMBER, 1832.

GENTLEMEN,—It seems as if death, who is incessantly thinning our ranks, directed his stroke with a fatal predilection, against that class of our body so limited in number, our foreign associates. In a short space of time the Academy has lost from the list of its members, Herschel, whose bold ideas on the structure of the universe have acquired every year more of probability; Piazzi, who on the first day of the present century presented our solar system with a new planet; Watt, who, if not the inventor of the steam-engine, the inventor having been a Frenchman,* was at least the creator of so many admirable contrivances, by the aid of which the little instrument of Papin has become the most ingenious, the most useful, the most powerful means of applying industry;

* This is not the place to enter on the controversy respecting the invention of the steam-engine. It may, however, be remarked, that we may be well content to allow it to remain a question of *degree.* Every tea-kettle is a steam-engine. A very slight and obvious contrivance will enable steam to raise a piston. Let any one define what they mean precisely by the term steam-engine, and the question of priority of invention will be easily settled.—*Translator.*

Volta, who has been immortalized by his electric pile; Davy, equally celebrated for the decomposition of the alkalies and for the invaluable safety lamp of the miner; Wollaston, whom the English called the pope, because he never proved fallible in any of his numerous experiments, or of his subtile theoretical speculations; Jenner, lastly, whose discovery I have no need to extol in the presence of fathers of families. To pay to such of its distinguished ornaments the legitimate tribute of the regret, of the admiration, and the gratitude of all men devoted to study, is one of the principal duties which the Academy imposes on those whom it invests with the responsible honour of speaking in its name in these solemn meetings. To pay this grand debt with the least possible delay, seems an obligation not less imperative. Gentlemen, the native academician always leaves behind him, among the colleagues with whom he has been united by the election of the Academy, many confidants of his secret thoughts, of the origin and course of his researches, of the vicissitudes which he has gone through. The foreign associate on the contrary resides far away from us; he rarely joins in our meetings; we know nothing of his life, his habits, his character, unless from the reports of travellers. When several years have passed over such fugitive documents, if we still find any traces of them, we cannot reckon on their accuracy. Literary intelligence which has not found a record in print is a sort of coin, the circulation of which alters at the same time the impression, the weight, and the inscription.

These reflections tend to show why the names of such men as Herschel, Davy, or Volta ought to be mentioned in our assemblies before those of many celebrated academicians whom death has snatched from our more immediate circle. Moreover, I hope that after what I shall be able to adduce, even in a few minutes, no one will be able to deny that the man of universal science whose life I am about to describe, and whose labours I shall analyze, has some real claims to preference.

BIRTH OF YOUNG.—HIS CHILDHOOD.—FIRST ENTRANCE ON HIS SCIENTIFIC CAREER.

Thomas Young was born at Milverton in the county of Somerset, June 13, 1773, of parents who belonged to the Society of Friends. He passed his earliest years at the house of his maternal grandfather, Mr. Robert Davies, of Minehead, whom the active business of commerce had not been able to divert from the cultivation of classical literature. Young could read fluently at the age of two years. His memory was extraordinary. In the intervals of his attendance at the house of a village schoolmistress in the neighbourhood of Minehead, at four years old, he had learned by heart a number of English authors, and even several Latin poems, which he could repeat from beginning to end, although he did not understand a word of the language. The example of Young, like many others of celebrity recorded by biographers, may then contribute to keep up the common prepossession of so many good fathers of families, who see in certain lessons according as they may be recited without faults, on the one hand, or are badly learnt on the other, infallible indications of an eternal mediocrity in the one case, or the beginning of a glorious career in the other. It would indeed be far from our object if these historical notices should tend to strengthen such prejudices. Thus, without wishing to weaken the vivid and pure emotions which every year the distribution of prizes excites, we may remind some, in order that they may not abandon themselves to dreams which they will not realize, and others, in order to fortify them against discouragement, that Picus de Mirandola, the phœnix of learners of all ages and countries, became in mature age an insignificant writer; that Newton—that powerful intellect of whom Voltaire, in some well known lines, asks the angels whether they are not jealous,—the great Newton, we observe, made but indifferent progress in the classes of his school; that study had for him no attractions; that the first time he felt the wish to labour it was merely to take the place of a turbulent school-fellow, who, by reason of his rank in the school was seated on a form above him and annoyed him by kicks; that at the age of twenty-two he was a candidate for a fellowship at Cambridge, and was beaten by one Robert Uvedale, whose name but for this circumstance, would have remained to this day perfectly unknown; that Fontenelle, lastly, was more ingenious than exact when he applied to Newton the words of Lucan, "It is not given to men to see the Nile feeble and at its source."

At the age of six years, Young entered under a teacher at Bristol,* whose mediocrity was a fortunate circumstance for him. This, Gentlemen, is no paradox; the pupil, not being able to accommodate himself to the slow and limited steps which his master took, became his own instructor. It is thus that those brilliant qualities developed themselves which too much aid would certainly have enervated.

* The master, whose name was King, at first kept school at Stapleton, and thence removed to Townend, both near Bristol. Young's acquaintance with the surveyor commenced after he quitted that school. See Peacock's *Life*, p. 5.—*Translator*.

Young was only eight years of age, when chance, whose influence in the events of man's life is more considerable than our vanity often allows us to admit, took him from studies exclusively literary, and revealed his real vocation. A surveyor of much merit in the neighbourhood took a great fancy for him; he took him out into the country sometimes on holidays, and permitted him to amuse himself with his instruments of surveying and natural philosophy. The operations, by whose aid the young scholar saw the distances and elevations of inaccessible objects determined, powerfully struck his imagination. But soon several chapters of a mathematical dictionary made all that seemed mysterious in the matter disappear. From this moment, in his Sunday excursions, the quadrant took the place of the kite. In the evening, by way of amusement, the engineering novice calculated the heights measured in the morning.

From the age of nine to fourteen, Young went to a school at Compton in Dorsetshire, kept by Mr. Thomson, whose memory he always cherished. During these five years all the pupils of the school were occupied exclusively, according to the practice of English Schools, in a minute study of the principal writers of Greece and Rome.* Young continually maintained his place at the head of his class: and yet he learned at the same time French, Italian, Hebrew, Persian, and Arabic: French and Italian, from the chance object of satisfying the curiosity of a schoolfellow who possessed some works

* It would appear from Young's own account, that a far more liberal system was really pursued in this school. Also, the praises of the usher, Josiah Jeffery, should never be omitted, who initiated Young at leisure hours into a variety of experimental and practical subjects, which contributed materially to his future success. See Peacock's *Life*, p. 6.—*Translator*.

printed at Paris, of which he was desirous to know the contents:—Hebrew, in order to read the Old Testament in the original: Persian and Arabic, with the view of deciding a question started at table, whether there were as marked differences between the Oriental languages as between those of Europe?

I perceive the necessity of mentioning that I write from authentic documents, before I add that during what might appear so fabulous a progress in languages, Young, during his walks at Compton, was seized with a violent passion for botany: and that being destitute of the means of magnifying objects of which naturalists make use when they wish to examine the delicate parts of plants, he undertook to construct a microscope himself, without any other guide than a description of the instrument in a work by Benjamin Martin: that to arrive at this difficult result it was necessary to acquire some skill in the art of turning: that the algebraic formulas of the optician having presented to him symbols of which he had no idea (those of *fluxions*), he was for a moment in great perplexity; but not being willing at last to give up the enlargement of his pistils and stamens, he found it more simple to learn the differential calculus, in order to comprehend the unlucky formula, than to send to the neighbouring town to buy a microscope. The ardent activity of the juvenile Young had led him to exertions beyond the strength of his constitution. At the age of fourteen his health was sadly altered. Various indications excited fears of a disease of the lungs; but these menacing symptoms at length yielded to the prescriptions of art, and the anxious cares of which this malady made him the object on the part of all his relations.

It is rare among our neighbours on the other side of

the Channel * that a rich person, entrusting his son to the care of a private instructor, does not seek for him a fellow-pupil of the same age among those who have been remarkable for their success. It was in this capacity that Young became, in 1787, the fellow-pupil of the grandson of Mr. David Barclay, of Youngsbury, in Hertfordshire. On the day of his first appearance there, Mr. Barclay, who doubtless felt the right of showing himself somewhat exacting with a scholar of fourteen years of age, gave him several phrases to copy, with the view of ascertaining his skill in penmanship. Young, perhaps somewhat humiliated by this kind of trial, demanded, in order to satisfy him, permission to retire to another room; this absence being prolonged beyond the time which the transcription would have required, Mr. Barclay began to joke on the want of dexterity he must evince, when at length he reëntered the room. The copy was remarkably beautiful; no writing-master could have executed it better: as to the delay, there was no longer any need to speak of it, for "the little quaker," † as Mr. Barclay called him, had not been content to transcribe the English phrases set him; he had also translated them into nine different languages.

The preceptor, or as they call him on the other side of the Channel, the *tutor*, who had to direct the two scholars at Youngsbury was a young man of much distinction, at that time entirely occupied in perfecting himself in the knowledge of the ancient languages; he was the future

* The reader will of course make due allowance in this and many other passages for the ideas of a foreigner as to English habits. The anecdote of Young's penmanship which follows, is differently given by Dr. Peacock, p. 12.—*Translator.*

† This seems improbable, as Mr. Barclay's family were of the same sect.—*Translator.*

author * of the Calligraphia Græca. He was not long, however, in perceiving the immense superiority of one of his pupils, and he recognized, with praiseworthy modesty, that in their common studies the true *tutor* was not always he who bore that title. At this period Young drew up, continually referring to the original sources, a detailed analysis of the numerous systems of philosophy which were professed in the different schools of Greece.† His friends spoke of this work with the most lively admiration. I know not whether the public is destined ever to see it. At all events it was not without influence on the life of its author, for in giving himself up to an attentive and minute examination of the singularities (to use a mild term) with which the conceptions of the Greek philosophers teemed, Young perceived the attachment which he retained to the principles of the sect in which he was born became weakened. However, he did not separate entirely from it till some years afterwards, during his sojourn in Edinburgh.

The little studious colony at Youngsbury quitted the country during some months in the winter to reside in London. During one of these excursions Young met with a teacher worthy of him. He was initiated into chemistry by Dr. Higgins, ‡ whose name I can the less dispense with mentioning since, in spite of his earnest and frequent remonstrances, there was an obstinate disinclination to acknowledge the share which legitimately belonged to him in the establishment of the theory of

* Mr. Hodgkin.

† This work is not mentioned by Dr. Peacock.—*Translator*.

‡ The share borne by Dr. Higgins in the suggestion or discovery of the atomic theory has been variously estimated. For an apparently perfectly fair view of the case, the reader is referred to Dr. Daubeny's *Atomic Theory*, p. 33.—*Translator*.

definite proportions, one of the most valuable discoveries of modern chemistry.

Dr. Brocklesby, the maternal uncle of Young, one of the most popular physicians in London at the time, justly confident of the distinguished success of the young scholar, communicated occasionally his productions to men of science and literature, and to men of the world, whose approbation might have greatly flattered his vanity. Young thus found himself at an early period in personal relation with those celebrated men Burke and Wyndham, of the House of Commons, and the Duke of Richmond. The last nobleman, then Master of the Ordnance, offered him the place of private secretary. The two other statesmen, although they wished him also to follow a career connected with the public administration, yet advised him first to go through a course of law at Cambridge.* With such powerful patrons Young might reckon on one of those lucrative offices which persons in power are not slow to bestow on those who will spare them all study and application, and daily furnish them with the means of shining at the court, the council, the senate, without compromising their vanity by committing any indiscretion. Young happily had a consciousness of his powers; he perceived in himself the germ of those brilliant discoveries which have since adorned his name: he preferred the laborious, but independent, career of the man of letters, to the golden chains which they exhibited so temptingly to his eyes. Honour be to him for such a determination! May his example serve as a lesson to so many young men whom

* "Mr. Wyndham advised him not to accept the appointment, and recommended him rather to proceed to Cambridge, and study the law." Peacock's *Life*, p. 45.—*Translator.*

political ambition diverts from a more noble vocation, to transform themselves into mere officials; but who might learn, like Young, to turn their eyes to the future, and not sacrifice to the futile and transitory satisfaction of being surrounded by persons soliciting favours, the solid testimonies of esteem and gratitude which the public rarely fails to offer to intellectual labours of a high order; and if it happen in the illusions of inexperience, that they should think too heavy a sacrifice imposed on them, we would ask them to take a lesson of ambition from the mouth of a great captain whose ambition knew no bounds; to meditate on the words which the First Consul, the victor of Marengo, addressed to one of our most honoured colleagues (M. Lemercier) on the day when he, quite in accordance with his character, had just refused a place then of great importance, that of Councillor of State:—

"I understand, Sir, you love literature, and you wish to belong altogether to it. I have nothing to oppose to this resolution. Yes! I, myself, if I had not become a General-in-chief, and the instrument of the fate of a great nation, do you think I would have gone through the offices and the salons, to put myself in dependence on whoever might happen to be in power in the position of minister or ambassador? No! no! I would have taken to the exact sciences. I would have made my way in the path of Galileo and Newton: and, since I have succeeded constantly in my great enterprises, truly I should have been equally distinguished by my scientific labours. I should have left behind me the remembrance of great discoveries. No other kind of glory would have tempted my ambition."

Young made choice of the profession of medicine, in

which he hoped to find fortune and independence. His medical studies were commenced in London under Baillie and Cruikshank; he continued them at Edinburgh, where at that time Drs. Black, Munro, and Gregory were in the height of their celebrity. It was only at Göttingen, in the following year (1795), that he took the degree of Doctor.* Before going through this form, so empty, yet always so imperatively exacted, Young, hardly beyond the period of youth, had become known to the scientific world by a note relative to the gum ladanum; by the controversy which he sustained against Dr. Beddoes on the subject of Crawford's theory of heat; by a memoir on the habits of spiders, and the theory of Fabricius, the whole enriched with erudite researches; and lastly, by an inquiry on which I will enlarge on account of its great merit, the unusual favour with which it was received at its first production, and the neglect into which it has since fallen.

The Royal Society of London enjoys throughout the whole kingdom a vast and deserved consideration. The Philosophical Transactions which it publishes have been for more than a century and a half the glorious archives in which British genius holds it an honour to deposit its titles to the recognition of posterity. The wish to see his name inscribed in the list of fellow-labourers in this truly national collection, beside the names of Newton, Bradley, Priestley, and Cavendish has always been

* The author has omitted that, in 1797, Young entered as a fellow-commoner at Emmanuel College, Cambridge; and in due time graduated there regularly in medicine; a step at that time necessary for his admission to the College of Physicians, in order to enable him to practise as a physician in London. See Peacock's *Life*, p. 115. In the university he was familiarly known by the name of "Phenomenon Young."—*Translator*.

among the students of the celebrated universities of Cambridge, Oxford, Edinburgh, and Dublin,* the most anxious as well as legitimate object of emulation. Here is always the highest point of ambition of the man of science; he does not aspire to it unless on occasion of some capital investigation; and the first attempts of his youth come before the public by a channel better suited to their importance, by the aid of one of those numerous periodicals which, among our neighbours, have contributed so much to the progress of human knowledge. Such is the ordinary course; such consequently ought *not* to have been the course followed by Young; at the age of twenty he addressed a paper to the Royal Society. The council, composed of the most eminent men of the Society, honoured this paper with their suffrage, and it soon after appeared in the Philosophical Transactions. The author treated in it of the subject of vision.

THEORY OF VISION.

The problem was any thing but new. Plato and his disciples, four centuries before our era, were occupied with it; but at the present day their conceptions can hardly be cited but to justify the celebrated and little flattering sentence of Cicero: "There is nothing so absurd that it has not been said by some of the philosophers."

After passing over an interval of 2000 years, we must from Greece transport ourselves to Italy, if we would find any ideas on the wonderful subject of vision which merit the remembrance of the historian. Where, without hav-

* And, it might be added, probably to a far more numerous class not of those bodies.—*Translator*.

ing ever, like the philosopher of Egina, proudly closed their school against all who were not geometers, careful experimenters marked out the sole route by which it is permitted to man to arrive without false steps at the conquest of unknown regions of truth; there Maurolycus and Porta proclaimed to their contemporaries that the problem of discovering *what is* presents sufficient difficulties to render it at least somewhat presumptuous to cast ourselves upon *the world of intelligences* to search after *what ought to be;* there these two celebrated fellow countrymen of Archimedes commenced the explanation of the functions of the different media of which the eye is composed; and showed themselves contented, as were at a later period Galileo and Newton, not to ascend above those kinds of knowledge which are capable of being elaborated or corrected by the aid of our senses, and which had been stigmatized under the porticos of the Academy by the contemptuous epithet of *simple opinion.* Such is always human weakness that, after having followed with a rare success the principal deviations which light undergoes in passing through the cornea and the crystalline, Maurolycus and Porta, when very near attaining their object, stopped short, as if before an insurmountable difficulty, when it was objected to their theory that objects ought to appear in an inverted position if the images formed in the eye are themselves inverted. The adventurous spirit of Kepler, on the contrary, did not remain embarrassed. It was from psychology that the attack originated; it was equally from psychology—clear, precise, and mathematical—that he overthrew the objection. Under the powerful hand of this great man, the eye became, definitively, the simple optical apparatus known by the name of the *camera obscura;* the retina is the ground of the picture, the crystalline replaces the glass lens.*

This assimilation, generally adopted since Kepler's time, remains open only to one difficulty; the *camera obscura,* like an ordinary telescope, requires to be brought to *a proper focus* according to the distance of objects. When objects are near it is indispensable to increase the distance of the picture from the lens; a contrary movement becomes necessary as they become more distant. To preserve to the images all the distinctness which is desirable, without changing the position of the surface which receives them, is therefore impossible: at least, always supposing the curvature of the lens to remain invariable; that it cannot increase when we look at near objects, or diminish for distant objects.

* The author seems to have left this illustration incomplete. Kepler's suggestion of the identity of the eye with the camera obscura, after all, does not touch the difficulty of the *inversion* of the image. Nor has it been considered as completely cleared up even till much later times. The solution which, it is believed, is now most generally assented to is this. It is a law of our constitution, dependent on some physiological principle unknown, that we refer impressions on the retina to objects existing, or believed to exist, in the rectilinear direction *from which* the impression comes to the retina. Consequently, as rays cross at the pupil, an impression arriving at (r) in the direction

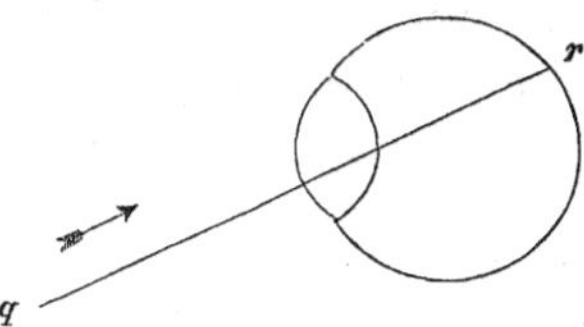

of the arrow, will convey the idea of an object existing at (q); in other words, a ray falling on the *upper* part of the retina suggests an object lying *below*, or an *inverted* image suggests an *erect* object.

Among the different modes of obtaining distinct images, nature has assuredly made a choice, since man *can* see with great distinctness at *very different* distances. The question thus put has afforded a wide subject of remark and discussion to physicists, and great names have figured in the debate.

Kepler and Descartes held that the whole ball of the eye is susceptible of being elongated and flattened.

Porterfield and Zinn contended that the crystalline lens was movable; and that it could place itself nearer to, or further from the retina, as might be needed.

Jurin and Musschenbroeck believed in a change in the curvature of the cornea.

Sauvages and Bourdelot supposed also that a change in curvature took place, but only in the crystalline lens. Such is also the system of Young. Two memoirs which our colleague successively submitted to the Royal Society of London include the complete development of his views.

In the first of these, the question is treated almost entirely in an anatomical point of view. Young there demonstrates by the aid of direct observations of a very delicate kind, that the crystalline is endowed with a fibrous or muscular constitution, admirably adapted to all sorts of changes of form. This discovery overthrew the only solid objection which had, till then, opposed the hypothesis of Sauvages and Bourdelot.

That hypothesis had no sooner been announced than it had been attacked by Hunter.

Thus this celebrated anatomist aided the cause of the young experimenter by the attention drawn to the subject, while his labours were as yet unpublished, and not even communicated to any one. However, this point of the discussion soon lost its importance. The learned

Leuwenhoeck, armed with his powerful microscopes, traced out, and gave figures of, the muscular fibres in all their ramifications in the crystalline of a fish. To awaken the attention of the scientific world, tired with these long debates, nothing less was necessary than the high renown of two new members of the Royal Society who entered the lists: one, a celebrated anatomist, the other the most eminent instrument-maker of whom England could boast. These jointly presented to the Royal Society a memoir, the fruit of their combined labours, intended to establish the complete unalterability of the form of the crystalline. The scientific world was not prepared to admit that Sir Everard Home and Ramsden together, could possibly make inaccurate experiments, or be deceived in micrometical measurements. Young himself could not believe it; and in consequence he did not hesitate publicly to renounce his theory.

This readiness to own himself vanquished, so rare in a young man of twenty-five, and especially on the occasion of a first publication, was in this instance an act of modesty without example. Young, however, had really nothing to retract. In 1800, after having withdrawn his former disavowal, our colleague developed anew the theory of the change of form of the crystalline in a memoir against which, from that time, no serious objection has been brought.

Nothing could be more simple than his line of argument; nothing more ingenious than his experiments. Young, in the first instance, got rid of the hypothesis of a change of curvature *in the cornea* by the aid of microscopic observations, which were of a kind to render the most minute variations appreciable. We can say more; he placed the eye in special conditions where changes of curvature in the cornea would have been without effect; he plunged the eye in water, and proved that there was still the same faculty of seeing at different distances perfectly preserved. The second of three possible suppositions, that of an alteration in the dimensions of the whole organ, was again overthrown by a multitude of objections and of experiments which it was difficult to resist.

The problem thus seemed finally settled. Who does not see, in fact, that if, of three only possible solutions, two are put out of the question, the third is necessarily established; that if the radius of curvature of the *cornea* and the longitudinal *diameter of the whole eye* are invariable, it must follow that the form of the crystalline is invariable? Young, however, did not stop there; he proved directly, by the minute phenomena of the changes in the images, that the crystalline really changes its curvature; he invented, or at least, gave perfection to, an instrument susceptible of being employed even by the least intelligent persons, and those least accustomed to delicate experiments; and, armed with this new means of investigation, he assured himself that those individuals in whose eyes the crystalline has been removed in the operation for cataract, did not enjoy the faculty of seeing equally distinctly *at all distances.**

* This instrument, called an "Optometer," was originally proposed by Dr. Porterfield, and consists of a simple and ingenious contrivance for ascertaining the focal length of the eye, which varies so greatly in different individuals, and often in two eyes of the same person, and in the same eye under different conditions. Dr. Young greatly improved upon the original construction. It will be found described in the *Lectures on Natural Philosophy*, vol. ii. p. 576. The principle of it consists in measuring accurately the distance of an object from the eye at which perfectly distinct vision is obtained, and which is determined when the object, seen through *two* small apertures close to the eye, presents only a single image, while in other positions it shows two images.—*Translator*.

We might fairly be astonished that this admirable theory of vision, this combination so well framed when the most ingenious reasonings and experiments lent each other mutual support, did not occupy that distinguished rank in the science of the country which it deserved. But to explain this anomaly, must we necessarily recur to a sort of fatality? Was Young then really, as he sometimes described himself with vexation, a new Cassandra, proclaiming incessantly important truths which his ungrateful contemporaries refused to receive? We should be less poetical, but more true, it seems to me, if we remarked that the discoveries of Young were not known to the majority of those who would have been able to appreciate them. The physiologists did not read his able memoir, because in it he presumes upon more mathematical knowledge than is usually attained in that branch.

The physicists neglected it in their turn, because in oral lectures, or printed works, the public demands little more at the present day than superficial notions, which an ordinary mind can penetrate without difficulty. In all this, whatever our distinguished colleague may have believed, we perceive nothing out of the ordinary course. Like all those who sound the greatest depths of science, he was misunderstood by the multitude; but the applauses of some of the select few ought to have recompensed him. In such a question we ought not to *count* the suffrages;—it is more wise to *weigh* them.*

* Arago, in assigning the probable causes of the neglect of Young's speculations, seems to fall short of his usual point and perspicuity. It might be true that his memoir was neglected by physiologists because it was mathematical, and by parity of reason it might have been neglected by physicists and mathematicians as being physiological. But it is surely no reason to say that it was neglected by physicists *because*

INTERFERENCES.

The most beautiful discovery of Young, that which will render his name imperishable, was suggested to him by an object in appearance very trivial; by those soap bub-

the public are superficial, &c. Young may have been, in most of his speculations, too profound for the many; but this particular instance of the structure of the eye and theory of vision is, perhaps, of all his researches, that which can be the least open to this charge. The subject is not itself abstruse: it is one easily understood by every educated person, without mathematical attainments; and the point at issue was a simple question of fact requiring no profound physiological knowledge to appreciate, whether the crystalline has or has not a muscular structure capable of changing its convexity. The real state of the case seems to be very satisfactorially explained by Dean Peacock (p. 36, *et seq.*), from whose account, as well as from what has been since written, it appears, after all that has been done both by Dr. Young and others, that there is even at the present day considerable difference of opinion on the subject.

Perhaps the most comprehensive survey of the whole subject which recent investigation has produced will be found in the paper of Professor J. D. Forbes in the *Edin. Transactions*, vol. xvi. part I. 1845. After giving a summary view of preceding researches, and adverting to the prevalent opinion among men of science, that the true explanation yet remains to be discovered (most anatomists denying as a fact the existence of the *muscular* structure which Young conceived he had proved), Professor Forbes proposes, as his own view of the cause, the consideration of the remarkable *variation in density* of the crystalline towards its central part; coats of different density being disposed in different layers, may be acted on by the pressure of the humours of the eye when the external action of the muscles compresses them, and thus increase the curvature of the lens, when the eye is directed to a near object, the whole consistence especially in the outer parts being of a gelatinous or compressible nature, and the central part more solid and more convex. Thus uniform pressure on the outer parts would tend to make the outer parts conform more nearly to the more convex interior nucleus.

It may be added that many physiologists are of opinion that, after all, there does not exist a sufficient compressive action on the ball of the eye to produce the effect supposed.—*Translator.*

bles so brilliantly coloured, so light, which when just blown out of a pipe become the sport of every imperceptible current of air. Before so enlightened an audience, it would without doubt be superfluous to remark that the difficulty of producing a phenomenon, its variety, its utility to the arts, are not the necessary indications of its importance in a scientific point of view. I have, therefore, to connect with a child's sport the discovery which I proceed to analyze, with the certainty that its credit will not suffer from its origin. At any rate I shall have no need to recall the apple, which, dropping from its stalk and falling unexpectedly at the feet of Newton, developed the ideas of that great man respecting the simple and comprehensive laws which regulate the celestial motions; nor the frog and the touch of the bistoury, to which physical science has recently been indebted for the marvellous pile of Volta. Without referring in particular to soap bubbles, I will suppose that a physicist has taken for the subject of experiment some distilled water, that is to say, a liquid, which in its state of purity never shows any more than some very slight shade of colour, blue or green, hardly sensible, and that only when the light traverses great thicknesses. I would next ask what we should think of his veracity if he were to announce to us, without further explanation, that to this water, so limpid, he could at pleasure communicate the most resplendent colours; that he knew how to make it violet, blue, green; then yellow like the peel of citron, or red of a scarlet tint, without affecting its purity, without mixing with it any foreign substance, without changing the proportions of its constituent gaseous elements. Would not the public regard our physicist as unworthy of all belief, especially when, after such strange assertions, he should add, that to produce colour in water, it suffices to reduce it to the state of a thin film; that "thin" is, so to speak, the synonym of "coloured;" that the passage of each tint into one the most different from it is the necessary consequence of a simple variation of the thickness of the liquid film; that this variation, for instance, in passing from red to green, is not the thousandth part of the thickness of a hair! Yet these incredible propositions are only the necessary consequences deduced from the accidental observation of the colours presented by soap bubbles, and even by extremely thin films of all sorts of substances.

To comprehend how such phenomena have, during more than 2000 years, daily met the eyes of philosophers without exciting their attention, we have need to recollect to how few persons nature imparts the valuable faculty of being astonished to any purpose.

Boyle was the first to penetrate into this rich mine. He confined himself, however, to the minute description of the varied circumstances which gave rise to these iridescent colours. Hooke, his fellow-labourer, went further. He believed that he had discovered the cause of this kind of colours in the coincidences of the rays, or to speak in his own language, in the mutual action on each other of the *waves* reflected by the two surfaces of the thin film. This was, we may admit, a suggestion characteristic of genius; but it could not be made use of at an epoch when the compound nature of white light was not as yet understood.

Newton made the colours of thin films a favourite object of study. He devoted to them an entire book of his celebrated treatise the "Optics." He established the laws of their formation by an admirably connected chain of experiments, which no one has since surpassed in excellence. In illuminating with homogeneous light the very regularly formed series of bands of which Hooke had already made mention, and which originated round the point of contact of two lenses pressed closely together, he proved that for each species of simple colour there exists, in thin films of every substance, a series of thicknesses gradually increasing, at each of which no light is reflected from the film. This result was of capital importance; it included the key to all these phenomena.

Newton was less happy in the theoretical views which these remarkable observations suggested to him. To say, with him, that the luminous ray which is reflected is "in a fit of easy reflexion,"—to say that the ray which passes through the film entire, is "in a fit of easy transmission,"—what is it but to announce, in obscure terms, merely the same fact which the experiment with the two lenses has already taught us? *

* In regard to the theory of the "fits," the author here seems to represent Newton's view, as in fact mere tautology; while in other places he is supposed to have indulged in a visionary theory on the subject. Newton, however, expressly says, "what kind of action or disposition this is;—whether it consist in a circulating or vibrating motion of the ray, or of the medium, or something else, I do not here inquire." (*Optics*, p. 255, ed. 1721.)

The fact is, Newton in his optical researches expressed the same avowed and systematic dislike to indulging in *any* gratuitous theories as in his other inquiries. "Hypotheses non fingo" was his motto in these as well as other researches. In adopting the idea of "fits of easy reflexion and transmission," we are of opinion that he did not violate that maxim, and that it was in fact the only legitimate first expression of the conclusion which the facts warranted. At certain points *no light appeared;* it was the legitimate inference, in the then state of knowledge, *that none was reflected.* But light was clearly under the same circumstances *transmitted;* at a distance a little greater along the ray, an opposite effect was witnessed; and so on.

The theory of Thomas Young is not amenable to this criticism. Here there is no longer admitted any peculiar kind of "fits" as primordial properties of the rays. The thin film is here assimilated in all respects to any thicker reflector of the same substance. If at certain points in its surface no light is visible, Young did not conclude that therefore its reflexion had ceased; he supposed that, in the special directions of those points, the rays reflected by the second surface proceeded to meet with those reflected from the first surface, and completely destroyed them. This conflict of the rays is what the author designated by the term "*interference*," which has since become so famous.

Observe then here the most singular of hypotheses! We must certainly feel surprised at finding night in full sunshine, at points where the rays of that luminary arrive freely; but who would have imagined that we should thence come to suppose that darkness could be engendered by adding light to light!

A physicist is truly eminent when he is able to announce any result which, to such an extent, clashes with all received ideas; but he ought, without delay, to support his views by demonstrative proofs, under the penalty of being assimilated to those Oriental writers whose fantastic reveries charmed the thousand and one nights of the Sultan Schahriar.

It was nothing more than the strict inference that at those points successively *something occurred* in the course of the ray which disposed it for, or induced, reflexion in the one case, and non-reflexion in the other; accompanied in the latter case by the like tendency to transmission. These apparent "fits" must be still acknowledged as *phenomena;* the *mechanism* by which they are produced is, however, now known to be nothing inherent in the light, no essential property recurring, but the simple periodicity of conspiring or counteracting wave-action.—*Translator*.

Young had not this degree of prudence. He showed at once that his theory would agree with the phenomena, but without going beyond mere possibility. When at a later period he arrived at real proofs of it, the public had other prepossessions, which he was not able to overcome. However, the experiment, whence our colleague deduced so memorable a discovery, could not excite the shadow of a doubt.*

* In the retrospective glance which the author thus gives over the progress of discovery previous to the period at which Dr. Young first entered on the field, what we have chiefly to observe is, that up to that date nothing like a *connected view* of the physical character of this wonderful agent had been attained; a few isolated speculations had indeed been put forth respecting a theory of emitted molecules on the one hand, and of waves in an ethereal medium on the other; and a few experimental facts bearing on the choice between such hypotheses had been ascertained.

The several distinct phenomena of common reflexion and refraction, of double refraction, of inflexion or diffraction, and of the coloured rings, did not seem to be connected by any *common* principle; nor, even, separately considered, could it be said that they were very satisfactorily explained. It was now the peculiar distinction of Young to perceive, and to establish in the most incontestable manner, a great principle of the simplest kind, which at once rendered the wave hypothesis applicable to the two last-named classes of facts, and thus directly connected them with the former.

It is not always that we are enabled to trace the first rise and progress of the idea of a great discovery in the inventor's mind. We cannot forbear from here noticing, that Dr. Young has left on record the progress of the first suggestions which occurred to him on the subject of interference. The first view which presented itself was that of the *analogies* furnished by *sound*, which, as is well known, is conveyed by means of waves propagated in air. And in the case of two sounds differing a very little from the same pitch, produced at the same time, we have, not a continuous sound, but *beats*, that is, alternations of sound and silence; the waves in the one case conspiring with and reinforcing each other, in the other counteracting, neutralizing, and destroying each other.

But in more special reference to light, Dr. Young's account of the origin of his ideas is so clear and striking that we must give it in his

Two rays, proceeding from the same source by slightly unequal routes, crossed one another at a cer-

own words: "It was in May, 1801, that I discovered by reflecting on the beautiful experiments of Newton, a law which appears to me to account for a greater variety of interesting phenomena than any other optical principle that has yet been made known. I shall endeavour to explain this law by a comparison: Suppose a number of equal waves of water to move upon the surface of a stagnant lake, with a certain constant velocity, and to enter a narrow channel leading out of the lake;—suppose, then, another similar cause to have excited another equal series of waves, which arrive at the same channel with the same velocity, and at the same time with the first. Neither series of waves will destroy the other, but their effects will be combined; if they enter the channel in such a manner that the elevations of the one series coincide with those of the other, they must together produce a series of greater joint elevations; but if the elevations of one series are so situated as to correspond to the depressions of the other, they must exactly fill up those depressions, and the surface of the water must remain smooth; at least, I can discover no alternative, either from theory or from experiment. Now, I maintain that similar effects take place whenever two portions of light are thus mixed; and this I call the general law of the interference of light." [1]—*Translator.*

For the sake of many readers, it may not be superfluous or useless here briefly to illustrate the application of these theoretical ideas. We have only to imagine in like manner, in the case of the rays of light, two sets of waves propagated through an ethereal medium and coinciding in direction, when it will be easily apparent that just as in the case of the supposed canal, they may have their waves either conspiring or counteracting, and consequently giving a point of brightness or darkness accordingly.

Thus, a coincidence in the periods, or an interval of an integer number of entire wave-lengths, would cause the two systems of waves to conspire and reinforce each other; a difference of periods of half a wave-length, or any odd number of half wave-lengths, would cause the two systems to counteract or neutralize each other. Thus, according to the thickness, there would be a point of darkness or of brightness for each primary ray, and the succession of tints would be perfectly explained.

This would directly apply to the *thin films.* A ray impinging would be partly reflected at the first surface of the thin film, partly entering

[1] Works, vol. i. p. 202.

tain point in space. At this point was placed a sheet of white paper. Each ray, taken by itself, made the paper

it would be reflected internally at its second surface, and emerge coinciding in *direction* with the first, but retarded behind it from the thickness traversed in its *undulations* either by a whole, or half undulation, or some multiples of these,—thus giving either a point of brightness or one of darkness accordingly; or by some intermediate fraction, giving an intermediate shade. And this would go on alternately at successively greater thicknesses of the film, giving a succession of such points or bands.

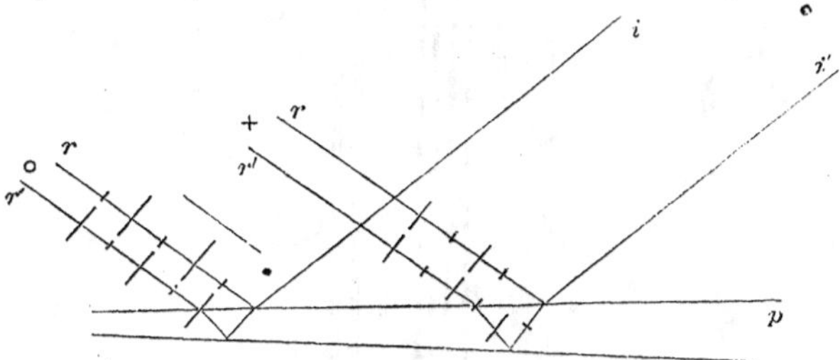

Thus at two successive thicknesses of the plate (p), the incident rays falling on it in parallel directions, i i, are reflected partially from the first surface, r r, and partially from the second, r' r'. According to the difference of thickness traversed, these may be in accordance giving a point of brightness as at +, or in discordance giving a point of darkness as at ∘.

If two rays or sets of waves, instead of being exactly superimposed be supposed to *meet* inclined at a very acute angle, in a somewhat similar way they would, at a series of points, alternately conspire or clash with each other, thus giving rise to a series of bright and dark points, the assemblage of which will produce bands or stripes on a screen intercepting the rays. Now as to actual experimental cases, it was in the application of this latter theoretical idea that the invention of Dr. Young was peculiarly displayed. The former case was that alone which seems to have occurred to Hooke in reference to the colours of thin plates, and even this was in his mind but a very indefinite conception; nor did it seem at first sight readily comparable with such cases as the diffraction fringes, or still less with the internal bands of a shadow observed by Grimaldi. If Hooke had imagined any theoretical views of this kind, it was probably confined to the

more bright at that point, but when the two rays united and arrived at that point together, all brightness disappeared; complete night succeeded to day.

one case of the thin films; Young's great merit was the comprehensiveness of his principle; and in following out the investigation, he proceeded at once to such a generalization as evinced that comprehensiveness and connected immediately those classes of phenomena apparently so different in character,—the thin films, the internal bands, and the external fringes. When, as in Grimaldi's experiment

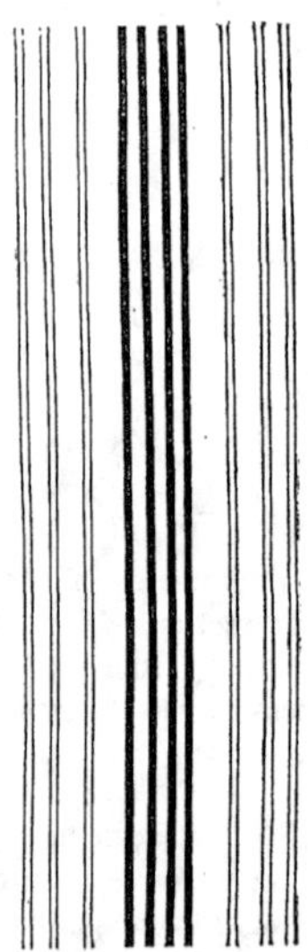

(since called the phenomena of diffraction), a narrow slip of card was placed in a very narrow beam of solar light, dark and bright stripes parallel to the sides internally marked the whole shadow longitudinally, while the external fringes appeared on the outside at each edge. The general appearance of the shadow of a long narrow body with parallel sides in a beam of solar light issuing from a minute hole in a shutter, or, what is better, the focus of a small lens collecting the rays to a point, is that of a shadow marked with longitudinal stripes and externally bordered by parallel fringes or bands of light slightly coloured, as seen in the annexed figure.

Two rays do not always annihilate each other completely at their point of intersection. Sometimes we

To *exhibit these* appearances ordinarily requires the sun's light. But the translator has found a very simple method of exhibiting these phenomena on a minute scale by candle light, by merely placing a fine wire across one surface of a lens of short focus, and looking through it at light admitted through a narrow slit parallel to the wire, or even the flame of a candle at a considerable distance.

Next, as to the theoretical explanation, an inspection of the accompanying diagram will perhaps help to convey an idea of the manner in which the several sets of waves are formed and interfere in the case now supposed.

Young conceived the beam of light as a series of waves propagated onward, till, on reaching the card, they were broken up into two new sets of waves spreading in circles round each edge as a new centre, while part of the original set continued to pass on at each side. On the principle just mentioned these would *interfere* with the new portions on the outside; and the two new portions would *interfere* with

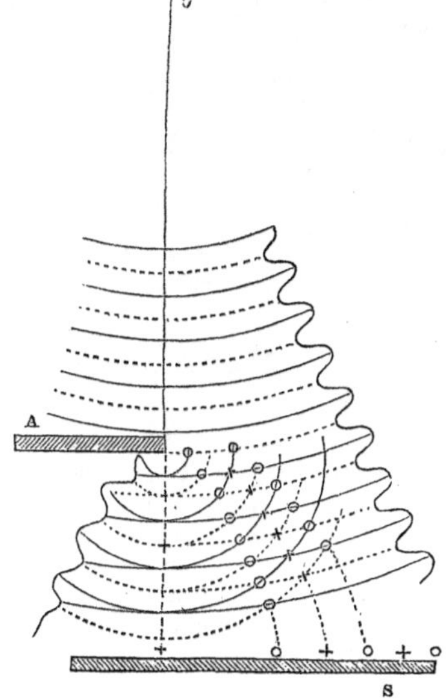

observe only a partial weakening of intensity, sometimes, on the other hand, the rays conspire and increase the illumination. Every thing depends on the difference in the length of route which they have gone through, and

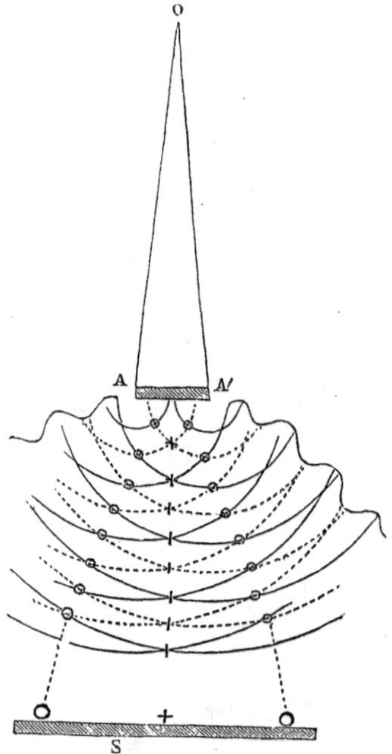

each other in the inside of the shadow; in either case giving stripes or bands. To complete the proof, when an opaque screen was placed so as to intercept the rays on one side, though abundance of light was present on the other, yet all the internal bands immediately disappeared; demonstrating that the effect was due solely to the *concurrence* of the light from *both* sides. The bands produced by light admitted through narrow apertures, and numerous other phenomena of the same kind, may receive a general and popular explanation in the same way.—*Translator.*

that, according to very simple laws, the discovery of which in any age would suffice to immortalize a physicist.

The differences of route which produce these conflicts between the rays, accompanied by their entire mutual destruction, have not the same numerical value for the differently coloured primary rays. When two white rays cross, it is then possible that one of their chief constituent parts, the red, for example, may alone be in the condition fit for mutual destruction. But white, deprived of its red, becomes green! Thus interference of light manifests itself in the phenomena of coloration. Thus the different elementary colours are placed in evidence without any prism to separate them. We should, however, remark that there does not exist a single point in space where a thousand rays of the same origin do not proceed to cross one another after reflexions more or less oblique, and we shall perceive at a glance the whole extent of the unexplored region which interferences open to the investigations of experimenters.

When Young published this theory, many phenomena of periodical colours had been already offered to the notice of observers; and we should add, had resisted all attempts at explanation. Among the number we might instance the coloured rings which are formed by reflexion, not on thin films, but on mirrors of thick glass slightly concave; the irridescent bands of different breadths with which the shadows of bodies are bordered on the outside, and in some instances covered within, which Grimaldi first noticed, and which afterwards uselessly exercised the genius of Newton, and of which the completion of the theory was reserved for Fresnel; the bows coloured red and green, which are perceived in greater or less number immediately under the innermost of the prismatic bands of the rainbow,* and which seemed so completely inexplicable, that the writers of elementary books on physics had given up making mention of them; and lastly, the "coronas," or broad coloured circles with varying diameters, which often appear surrounding the sun and moon.

If I call to mind how many persons do not appreciate scientific theories, except in proportion to the immediate applications which they may offer, I cannot terminate this enumeration of the phenomena which characterize the several series of more or less numerous periodical colours, without mentioning the rings, so remarkable by their regularity of form and purity of tint with which every brilliant light appears surrounded, when we look at it through a mass of fine molecules or filaments of equal dimensions. These rings, in fact, suggested to Young the idea of an instrument, extremely simple, which he called an "eriometer," and with which we can measure without difficulty the dimensions of the most minute bodies. The eriometer, as yet so little known to observers, has an immense advantage over the microscope in giving at a single glance the *mean magnitude* of millions of particles which are contained in the field of view. It possesses, moreover, the singular property of remaining *silent* when the particles differ much in magnitude among themselves, or, in other words, when the question of determining their dimensions has no real meaning.

Young applied his eriometer to the measurement of the globules of blood in different classes of animals,—to

* This explanation has been recently controverted by Professor Potter.—*Philos. Mag.* May, 1855.

that of powders furnished by different species of vegetables, of the fineness of different kinds of fur used in the manufacture of different fabrics, from that of the beaver, the most valuable of all, down to that of the common sheep of the Sussex breed, which stands at the other extremity of the scale, and is composed of filaments four times and a half thicker than that of the beaver.

Before the researches of Young, the numerous phenomena of colours* which I have just pointed out were not only inexplicable, but nothing had been found to connect them with each other. Newton, who was long engaged on the subject, had not perceived any connection between the rings in thin films and the bands of diffraction. Young reduced these two kinds of coloured bands alike to the law of interference. At a later period, when the coloured phenomena of polarization had been discovered, he observed, in certain measures of the thicknesses at which they occurred, some remarkable numerical analogies, which made it very reasonable to expect that sooner or later this singular kind of polarization would be found connected with his doctrine. He had in this instance, however, we must admit, a very wide hiatus to fill up. The knowledge of some important properties of light, then completely unknown, would have been necessary to permit him to conceive the whole singularity of the effects which in certain crystals, cut in certain directions, double

* Every one may have remarked the threads of a spider's web occasionally exhibiting brilliant colours in the sunshine. The same thing is seen in fine scratches on the surface of polished metal, produced in a more regular way, by the fine engraved parallel grooves in Barton's buttons. The colours of mother-of-pearl are of the same kind; all these colours Dr. Young showed were due to *interference* of the portions of light reflected from the sides of the narrow transparent thread or groove.—*Translator.*

refraction produces by the destruction of light resulting from the interference of rays; but it is to Young that the honour belongs of having opened the way; it was he who was the first to decypher these hieroglyphics of optics.*

* It has been well observed that simplicity is not always a fruit of the first growth, and accordingly some of the earliest of Young's researches were complicated by unnecessary conditions. Thus, to exhibit the effect of *two* rays interfering, he at first not unnaturally transmitted the narrow beam of light through *two* small apertures near together. In point of fact, though the real effect is here seen, it is mixed up with others of a more complex kind. The narrow apertures each exhibited coloured fringes, in addition to the interference stripes seen between them. The coloured fringes of *apertures* (unless very wide) are distinct from those formed by one external edge of an opaque body; the light from *each side* conspires to the effect in a somewhat complex manner. If the aperture be otherwise than long with parallel sides, the phenomenon becomes still more complex, and the calculation difficult; few such cases have ever yet been solved, and some such cases have been dwelt upon as formidable objections to the theory; they are simply cases to which the formula, from its mathematical difficulties, has not *yet* been extended.

In all these cases of diffraction an *opaque* body was used, and it might still be suspected that *some action of the edge* of that body might be concerned in the result. Numerous experiments of Maraldi, Dutour, Biot, and others, were directed to the investigation of this point. Biot showed that an *opaque* body was not necessary, inasmuch as the edge of a plate *of glass*, or even the bounding line of two faces of a glass cut at a slight inclination to each other, gave the same fringes; indeed, Newton also had noticed something of the kind. Haldat varied the conditions of the edge in every conceivable way, whether of form or nature, by the influence of magnetism, galvanism, electricity, or temperature from freezing to a red heat, without producing the slightest difference in the fringes; a result which it would be impossible to conceive compatible with any idea of an atmosphere of attraction or repulsion surrounding the edge.

Again, though we have given the explanation of the *external* fringes in its simple and correct form, yet both Young and Fresnel failed in the first instance to see it in that light, both believing that the *reflexion* of a portion of rays from the *edge* of the opaque body was *mainly* concerned in producing the interference. Subsequent experiments showed

EGYPTIAN HIEROGLYPHICS.—HISTORY OF THE FIRST EXACT INTERPRETATION GIVEN OF THEM.

The word hieroglyphic, regarded not metaphysically, but in its natural acceptation, carries us into a field which

that even in cases where that edge reflects any sensible amount of light, its influence on the diffracted fringes is quite inappreciable. In fact, Young, in a letter to Fresnel, in returning thanks for a copy of a later memoir in which he had shown this supposition to be unnecessary, also concurs in abandoning it. It did but complicate and injure the beauty of the result.[1] And every doubt must have disappeared in the minds of those who compared the minute arithmetical accuracy with which the places of the fringes, as computed from the simple theory in the investigations of Fresnel, agreed with those actually determined by the nicest micrometical measurements.

In enumerating the discoveries of Young in the first establishment of the wave theory, it is somewhat singular that Arago (whether from accident or design) should have overlooked one investigation which must be regarded as among the most important. The great support which the emission theory received in recent times was that derived from Laplace's memoir on the law of double refraction (1809), in which, on the principle of "least action," as maintained by Maupertuis and applied to the idea of luminous molecules, he explained the observed laws of ordinary and extraordinary refraction in Iceland spar. This investigation exercised a powerful influence in favor of the molecular theory over the minds of the men of science in France who bowed implicitly to the authority of Laplace. But the memoir of Laplace was the subject of a very powerful attack on the part of Dr. Young, carried on in an article in the Quarterly Review, November, 1809, in which he disputed the mechanical and mathematical grounds of Laplace's theory, and showed that the same laws of double refraction could be far more easily deduced from the undulatory hypothesis. Next to the discovery of interference, this refutation of the strongest point of the emission theory cannot but be regarded as one of the most material in the development and establishment of the undulatory view.

To the statement of these various cases of interference it should be added that when the tints of polarized light were discovered, Young in 1814, applied to the phenomena the *general* consideration of *inter-*

[1] Young's Works, i. 393.

has been long the theatre of numerous and animated debates. I have hesitated whether to risk offending the feelings which this question has excited. The secretary of an Academy occupied exclusively with the exact sciences, might indeed, without impropriety, remit this philological subject to other more competent judges. I also feared, I will avow, to find myself in disagreement on several important points with the illustrious man of science whose labours it has been so delightful for me to analyze, without having to add a word of criticism from my pen. All these scruples, however, vanish when I reflect that the interpretation of hieroglyphics has been one of the most beautiful discoveries of our age; that Young himself has mixed up my name with discussions relating to it; that to examine whether France can pretend to this new title to glory, is to enhance the importance of the task confided to me at this moment, and to perform the duty of a good citizen. I am aware that some may find narrowness in these sentiments. I am not ignorant that the cosmopolitan spirit has its good side; but with what name shall I stigmatize it, if, when all neighbouring

ference, that is to say, he showed that owing to the differing obliquities of the paths of the rays within the crystal they would be unequally retarded in their passage, and would consequently emerge in conditions, with regard to length of route, respectively of accordance or discordance at corresponding distances round the centre line or axis of the crystal, and thus might give rise to coloured rings. Arago, however, soon noticed that the explanation was incomplete; the main point in fact remained to be accounted for, viz: why we see no colours till the *analyzer* is applied, and why even the previous polarization is necessary to the result. It was not until about two years afterwards that Arago and Fresnel jointly succeeded in discovering a new law, which not only furnished the complete solution of the polarized rings, but at length cleared away all the difficulties which from the first had surrounded the idea of polarization itself. For an account of this see memoir of Fresnel.—*Translator*.

nations enumerate with triumph the discoveries of their sons, it should hinder me from seeking, even in the present circle, among those colleagues whose modesty I would not hurt, the proof that France is not degenerate; that she also adds every year her glorious contingent to the vast deposit of human knowledge.*

I approach, then, the question of Egyptian writing, and I do so free from all prejudice, with the firm wish of being just; with the lively desire to conciliate the rival pretensions of two men of science whose premature death has been to all Europe a legitimate subject of regret. Lastly, I shall not in this discussion on hieroglyphics transgress the bounds imposed on me; happy if those who listen to me, and whose indulgence I ask, may find that I have known how to escape the influence of a subject whose obscurity is proverbial.

Men have imagined two systems of writing entirely distinct. One is that employed by the Chinese, which is the system of hieroglyphics; the other, at present in use among all other nations, bears the name of the alphabetical or phonetic system.

The Chinese have no letters properly so called: the characters which they use in writing are strictly hiero-

* In bringing out a part of this chapter on Egyptian Hieroglyphics in the Annuaire for 1836, Arago has added: "The first exact interpretation which has been given of Egyptian hieroglyphics will certainly take its place among the most beautiful discoveries of the age. Besides, after the animated debates to which it has given birth, every one would desire to know whether France can *conscientiously* pretend to this new title to glory. Thus the importance of the question, and the national self-love properly understood, unite in encouraging me to publish the result of a minute examination to which I have devoted myself. Can I, then, be blind to the danger which there always is in attempting difficult subjects in matters which we have not made the special subject of our studies?"

glyphics; they do not represent *sounds* or articulations, but *ideas*. Thus a house is represented by a unique and special character, which does not change even when the Chinese have come to çall a house, in their spoken language, by a name totally different from that which they formerly pronounced. Does this result appear surprising? Imagine the case of our cyphers, which are also hieroglyphics; the idea of one added to itself seven times is expressed everywhere in France, in England, in Spain, &c., by the aid of two circles placed vertically one over the other, and touching in one point; but in looking at this hieroglyphic sign (8) the Frenchman pronounces "huit," the Englishman "eight," the Spaniard "ocho." No one is ignorant that it is the same with compound numbers. Thus, to speak briefly, if the Chinese idiographic signs were generally adopted, as the Arabic numerals are, every one would read in his own language the works which they presented to him, without the need of knowing a single word of the language spoken by the authors who have written them.

It is not so with alphabetical writing:—

> "He who first taught us the ingenious art
> To paint our words, and speak them to our eyes,"

having made the capital remark that all words of a spoken language, even the most rich, are compounded of a very limited number of elementary articulate sounds, invented artificial *signs* or letters to the number of twenty-four or thirty to represent them. By the aid of these signs differently combined he could write every word which struck his ear even without knowing the meaning of it.

The Chinese or hieroglyphic writing seems to be the infancy of the art. It is not always, as has been sometimes said, that to learn to read it, even in China, occupies the whole life of a studious Mandarin. Rémusat (whose name I cannot mention without recalling one of the most heavy losses which literature has lately sustained) has established, both by his own experience and by the fact of the excellent scholars he has formed every year by his lectures, that we may learn Chinese like any other language. It is not true, as was once imagined, that the characters are appropriated solely to the expression of common ideas; several pages of the romance of Yu-kiao-li, or the Two Cousins, will suffice to show that the most subtle abstractions, the quintessence of refinements, are not beyond the range of the Chinese writing. The chief fault of this mode of writing is, that it gives no means of expressing new names. A letter from Canton might have told at Pekin, that on the 14th of June, 1800, a great and memorable battle saved France from great peril; but it would not have been able to express in these purely hieroglyphic characters that this glorious event took place near the village of Marengo, or that the victorious general was called Bonaparte. A people among whom the communication of proper names, from one place to another, could only take place by means of special messengers, would be, as we see, only in the first rudiments of civilization. These preliminary remarks are not useless. The question of priority, which the graphic methods of Egypt have called forth, thus come to be easy to explain and to comprehend. As we proceed, in fact, we find in the hieroglyphics of the ancient people of the Pharaohs, all the artifices of which the Chinese make use at the present day.

Many passages of Herodotus, of Diodorus Siculus, of Clement of Alexandria, have taught us that the Egyptians had two or three different sorts of writing, and that in one of these, at least, symbolic characters, or the representatives of ideas, played a principal part. Horapollon has even preserved to us the signification of a certain number of these characters. Thus we know that the *hawk* designated *the soul;* the *ibis*, the *heart;* the *dove* (which might seem strange), a *violent man;* the *flute*, an *alien;* the number *six*, *pleasure;* a *frog*, an *imprudent man;* the *ant*, *wisdom;* a *running knot*, *love*, &c.

The signs thus preserved by Horapollon form only a very small part of the eight or nine hundred characters which have been found in the ancient inscriptions. The moderns, Kircher among others, have endeavoured to enlarge the number. Their efforts have not given any useful result, unless it be so to show to what errors even the best instructed men expose themselves when, in the search after facts, they abandon themselves without restraint to imagination. In the want of data, the interpretation of the Egyptian writings appeared for a long time, to all sound minds, a problem completely incapable of solution; when in 1799, M. Boussard, an engineer officer, discovered in the excavations which he was making near Rosetta, a large stone covered with inscriptions in three kinds of characters quite distinct.

One of the series of characters was Greek. This, in spite of some mutilations, made clearly known that the authors of the monument had ordained that the same inscription should be traced in three different sorts of characters, viz: in the sacred characters or Egyptian hieroglyphics, in the local or vulgar characters, and in Greek. Thus, by an unexpected good fortune, the philologists found themselves in possession of a Greek text, having also before them its translation into the Egyptian language, or at least a transcription in two sorts of characters, anciently in use on the banks of the Nile.

This Rosetta stone, since so celebrated, and which M. Boussard presented to the Institute of Cairo, was taken from that body at the period when the French army evacuated Egypt. It was preserved, however, in the British Museum, where it figured, as Thomas Young said, as a monument of British valour. Putting valour out of the question, the celebrated philosopher might have added, without too much partiality, that this invaluable trilingual monument thus bears some witness to the advanced views which guided all the details of the memorable expedition into Egypt, as also to the indefatigable zeal of the distinguished savants whose labours, often carried on under the fire of the forts, have added so much to the glory of their country. The importance of the Rosetta stone struck them, in fact, so forcibly, that in order not to abandon this precious treasure to the adventurous chances of a sea voyage, they earnestly applied themselves, from the first, to reproduce it, by copies, by impressions taken in the way of printings from engravings, by moulds in plaster or sulphur. We must add that antiquaries of all countries became first acquainted with the Rosetta stone from the designs given by the French savants.

One of the most illustrious members of the Institute, M. Silvestre de Sacy, entered first in 1802 on the career which the trilingual inscription opened to the investigations of philologists. He only occupied himself on the Egyptian text in common characters. He there discovered the groups which represent the different proper names, and their phonetic nature. Thus in one of two inscriptions, at least, the Egyptians had the signs of sounds, or true letters. This important result found no opponents after a Swedish man of science, M. Akerblad, in completing the labours of our fellow-countryman, had assigned, with a probability bordering on certainty, the phonetic value of each of the different characters employed in the transcription of the proper names which the Greek text disclosed.

There remained, all along, the purely hieroglyphic part of the inscription, or what was supposed such; this remained untouched; no one had ventured to attempt to decypher it.

It is here that we find Young declaring, as if by a species of inspiration, that in the multitude of sculptured signs on the stone representing either entire animals, or fantastic forms, or again instruments, products of art, or geometrical forms, those of these signs which were found inclosed in elliptic borders, corresponded to the proper names in the Greek inscription; in particular to the name of Ptolemy, the only one which in the hieroglyphic inscription remains uninjured. Immediately afterwards Young said that in the special case of the border or scroll, the signs included represented no longer ideas, but sounds. In a word, he sought by a minute and refined analysis to assign an individual hieroglyphic to each of the sounds which the ear receives in the name of Ptolemy in the Rosetta stone, and in that of Berenice, in another monument.

Thus we see, unless I mistake, in the researches of Young on the graphic systems of the Egyptians, the three culminating points. No one, it is said, had perceived them, or at least had pointed them out, before the English philosopher. This opinion, although generally admitted, appears to me open to dispute. It is, in fact, certain that in 1766 M. de Guignes, in a printed memoir, had indicated that the *scrolls* in Egyptian inscriptions included all the proper names. Every one might also see in the same work the arguments on which the learned orientalist relied to establish the opinion which he had embraced on the constant phonetic character of the Egyptian hieroglyphics. Young then has the priority on this point alone: to him belongs the first attempt which had been made to decompose in letters the groups of the scrolls, to give a phonetic value to the hieroglyphics which composed in the stone of Rosetta the name of Ptolemy.

In this research, as we might expect, Young furnished new proofs of his immense penetration; but misled by a false system, his efforts had not a full success. Thus sometimes he attributes to the hieroglyphic characters a value simply alphabetical, further on he gives them a value which is syllabic or disyllabic, without being struck by what must seem so strange in this mixture of different characters. The fragment of an alphabet published by Young includes then something both of truth and falsehood; but the false so much abounds that it would be impossible to apply the value of the letters which compose it to any other reading than that of the two proper names from which it was derived. The word *impossible* is so rarely met with in the scientific career of Young, that I must hasten to justify it. I will say then that after the composition of his alphabet Young himself believed that he saw in the scroll of an Egyptian monument the name of "*Arsinoe*," where his celebrated competitor had since shown with irresistible evidence the word "*autocrator;*" that he believed he had found "*euergetes*" in a group where we ought to read "*Cæsar*."

The labors of Champollion, as to the discovery of the phonetic value of hieroglyphics, are clear, distinct, and cannot involve any doubt. Each sign is equivalent to a single vowel or consonant. Its value is not arbitrary: every phonetic hieroglyphic is the image of a physical object whose name in the Egyptian language commences with the vowel or the consonant which it is wished to represent.*

The alphabet of Champollion, once modelled from the Stone of Rosetta and two or three other monuments, enables us to read inscriptions entirely different; for example, the name of Cleopatra on the obelisk of Philoë, long ago transported into England, and where Dr. Young, armed with his alphabet, could discover nothing. On the temple of Karnac, Champollion read twice the name of Alexander: on the Zodiac of Denderah, the title of a Roman emperor; on the grand edifice above which it is placed, the names and surnames of the emperors Augus-

* This will become clear to every one, if we seek, by following the Egyptian system, to compose hieroglyphics in the French language. A may be represented by (agneau) a lamb; (aigle) an eagle; an ass, anemone, artichoke, &c. B by a balance, a whale (baleine); a boat, &c. C by cabana (badger); cheval (horse); cat, cedar, &c. E by épée (a sword), elephant, epagneul (spaniel), &c. Abbé then would be written in French hieroglyphics by putting any of the following figures in succession:—a lamb, a balance, a whale, an elephant. Or an eagle, a boat, a sword, &c.

This kind of writing has some analogy, as we see, with the rebus in which confectioners wrap their bonbons. Thus we see at what stage these Egyptian priests were of whom antiquity has so much boasted, but who, we must say, have taught us so little.

M. Champollion calls *homophones* all those signs which, representing the same sound or the same articulation, can be substituted indifferently for each other. In the actual state of the Egyptian alphabet I perceive six or seven homophone signs for A, and more than twelve for the Greek sigma.—*Arago.*

tus, Tiberius, Claudius, Nero, Domitian, &c. Thus, to speak briefly, we find, on one hand, the lively discussion, to which the age of these monuments had given rise, completely terminated; on the other, we observe it established beyond question that under the Roman dominion hieroglyphics were still in full use on the banks of the Nile.

The alphabet which had given such unhoped for results, whether applied to the great Obelisks at Karnac, or to other monuments which are also recognized as being of the age of the Pharaohs, presents to us the names of many other kings of this ancient race; the names of Egyptian deities; we can say more, substantives, adjectives, and verbs of the Coptic language: Young was then deceived when he regarded the phonetic hieroglyphics as a modern invention; when he advanced that they had served solely for the transcription of proper names foreign to Egypt. M. de Guignes, and above all, M. Etienne Quatremère, established, on the contrary, a real fact and one of great importance,—that the reading of the inscriptions of the Pharaohs is corroborated by irresistible proofs, while they show that the existing Coptic language was that of the ancient subjects of Sesostris.

We now know the facts; I may then confine myself to confirm, by a few short observations, the consequences which appear to me to result from them.

Discussions of priority, even under the dominion of national prejudices, will have become embittered if they can be reduced to fixed rules, but in certain cases the first idea is every thing; in others, the details offer the chief difficulties; sometimes the merit seems to consist less in the conception of a theory than in its demonstration. We then infer how much the choice of a particular point of view must depend on arbitrary conditions; and, lastly, how much influence it will have on the definitive conclusion. To escape from these embarrassments I have sought an example in which the parts respectively played by two rival claimants for an invention may be assimilated to those of Champollion and Young, and which has, on the other hand, united all opinions. This example, I believe, I have found in *the Interferences*, even leaving out of the question, as regards the subject of the hieroglyphics, the quotations from the memoir of M. de Guignes. It is as follows:—

Hooke in fact had announced before Dr. Young that luminous rays interfered, just as the latter had asserted before Champollion that the Egyptian hieroglyphics are sometimes phonetic. Hooke did not prove directly his hypothesis; the proof of the phonetic values assigned by Young to different hieroglyphics could only rest on readings which had not as yet been made and which could not then be made.

From want of knowing the composition of white light, Hooke had not an exact idea of the nature of interferences, as Young on his part deceived himself by an imagined syllabic or dissyllabic value of hieroglyphics.

Young, by unanimous consent, is regarded as the author of the theory of interferences. Thence, by a parity of reasoning which seems to me inevitable, Champollion ought to be regarded as the author of the discovery of hieroglyphics.

I regret not to have sooner thought of this comparison. If in his lifetime Young had been placed in the alternative of being the originator of the doctrine of interferences, leaving the hieroglyphics to Champollion, or to keep the hieroglyphics, giving up to Hooke the ingenious optical theory, I do not doubt he would have felt obliged to recognize the claims of our illustrious fellow-countryman. At all events there would have remained with him, what no one could have contested, the right to appear in the history of the memorable discovery of the interpretation of hieroglyphics in the same relative position as that in which Kepler, Borelli, Hooke, and Wren appeared in the History of Universal Gravitation.

NOTE.

We have here put before our readers the literal version of Arago's statement respecting the claims of Young in regard to the discovery of the principle of interpreting the Egyptian hieroglyphics. Arago's representations have been, as is well known, greatly called in question. And though he throughout speaks in a tone of marked courtesy and candour towards Young, yet it is clear that he espouses the cause of Champollion with an ardour which many, in this country, believe has, in some degree, blinded him to the truth of the case.

At any rate, in the vivid and highly coloured sketch here presented by M. Arago, the reader may need some caution in discriminating the fair share of merit which may be claimed by the respective parties engaged in the inquiry. The author's national partialities may very naturally have had some influence in biassing his judgment. It is impossible here to enter on details of controversy. But both as to the actual amount and accuracy of Dr. Young's investigations and the relative claims of M. Champollion, the reader may find it desirable to refer to the extended discussion of the subject given in Dr. Peacock's *Life of Young*. Without the pretension, or, indeed, the possibility, of adequately going into this question within the limits of such a commentary as can be here given, we shall content ourselves with pointing out to the notice of our readers a few of those passages in that work in which Dr. Young's claims are so powerfully vindicated. The conclusions turn on such a variety of points of details that it would be wholly impracticable to attempt any analysis of them in this place. But the result tends to assign a considerably larger share of credit in the discovery to Dr. Young than Arago seems disposed to allow him. Dr. Peacock's able and elaborate work is doubtless in the hands of all those who take any interest in a question so important to the advance of philological and ethnological science as well as to general literature. Yet a slight sketch of the chief points referred to may not be useless.

We may first mention that Dr. Young's article "Egypt" in the *Supplement to the Encyclopedia Britannica*, published in 1819, contains the most comprehensive survey of his labours and conclusions on the subject of hieroglyphic literature up to that date. It does not profess to go into those minutiæ of critical detail, for which reference must be made to his numerous other writings on the subject. But as a general and popular view it will always be consulted with advantage. Nevertheless, the reader must always bear in mind that, in the statements thus given, much had to be revised, or even reversed, from the improved disclosures of his later researches.

Dr. Peacock has alluded but briefly to the views of Arago, and towards the conclusion of the chapter, sums up the representation of the case as given in the éloge, remarking only that the whole of his previous statements constitute the refutation of it.

The following extract will show the main claims of Young, insisted on by his biographer.

"It was Dr. Young who first determined, and by no easy process, that the 'rings'* on the Rosetta stone contained the name of Ptolemy. It was Dr. Young who determined that the semicircle and oval, found at the end of the second ring,

* Certain portions of the hieroglyphical characters are found surrounded by a ring or enclosure called by the French "Cartouches."

in connection with the former, was expressive of the feminine gender; and it was Dr. Young who had not only first suggested that the characters in the ring of Ptolemy were phonetic, but had determined, with one very unimportant inaccuracy, the values of four of those which were common to the name of Cleopatra, which were required to be analyzed. All the principles involved in the discovery of an alphabet of phonetic hieroglyphics were not only distinctly laid down, but fully exemplified by him; and it only required the further identification of one or two royal names with the rings, which expressed them in hieroglyphics, to extend the alphabet already known sufficiently to bring even names which were not already identified under its operation."

Dr. Peacock states that Champollion and Young, while engaged simultaneously in the prosecution of the researches connected with these points, in some instances had opportunities of personal communication with each other. But Champollion enjoyed especial advantages from circumstances which placed some of the papyri in his possession; and thus enabled him to take precedence in the publication of results, while his competitor, if he had enjoyed the same facilities, would, no doubt, have been equally competent to perceive the force of the new evidence thus adduced, and equally ready to make use of it, even if setting aside some of his early inferences and conjectures.

Dr. Peacock, after reflecting with much severity on Champollion, expresses his regret to find so eminent a writer as Chevalier Bunsen, whose remarks are quoted before, (p. 311,) "supporting, by the weight of his authority, some of the grossest of these misrepresentations" (p. 337).

Dr. Young displayed singular modesty and forbearance in his controversy with Champollion, treating him throughout with all the respect due to his acknowledged eminence; and while mildly reproaching him with omitting to give him the due credit for his own share in the research, yet in no way insinuating that any discreditable motive led to the omission.

Dr. Peacock, however, thinks a far more stringent tone of

criticism might have been fairly applied; he takes up the cause of Young with a less scrupulous zeal; and though with perfect good temper, yet with deeply damaging force of argument and statement of facts, exposes the very unjustifiable nature of Champollion's assumptions, and vindicates the claims of Young to his fair and important share in these discoveries.

He dwells on the tone of assumption in which Champollion presents himself to his readers as in exclusive possession of a province of which he had long since been the sole conqueror, and regards every question raised as to his exclusive rights as an unjustifiable attack to be resented and repelled; while he studiously suppresses the *dates* of the successive stages of the discovery, and thus attacks Young on the assertions made on imperfect knowledge in the earlier stages of his investigations, with the aid of all his own accumulated information acquired subsequently; a proceeding the iniquity of which needs only stating to stand exposed.

As instances of this, it is mentioned that Young, in 1816, on the strength of comparatively imperfect information then acquired, made some representations respecting the enchorial characters in the Rosetta inscription, and their relation to those employed in the funereal rolls. These Champollion criticizes and exposes without reserve, from the more full knowledge he had obtained in 1824; entirely passing over Young's own *later* statement on the same subject, correcting his former views, and from which even Dr. Peacock considers Champollion himself probably derived a large portion of his own knowledge of the subject!

Dr. Peacock has collected, in one point of view, Champollion's main assertions as representing the state of the case. But he has shown that some of the propositions dwelt upon were, in point of fact, *never maintained* by Dr. Young; and it was chiefly by his later researches, that the erroneous impressions at first entertained, respecting the points to which they relate, had been corrected, and their true nature established.

In 1821, Champollion denied altogether the existence of an alphabetic element among the hieroglyphics. But in the following year he adopted the whole of Young's principles, and applied them with one modification only. The analogy of certain marks in the Chinese hieroglyphics, to signify proper names, the principle that the phonetic power of the symbol is derived from the initial letter or syllable of the name of the object which it represents in the Egyptian language, are among the chief of those which he borrows without acknowledgment, or claims without regard to their prior announcement by Young. "It would be difficult," says Dr. Peacock, "to point out in the history of literature a more flagrant example of disingenuous suppression of the real facts bearing on an important discovery.—*Translator.*

MISCELLANEOUS WORKS OF DR. YOUNG.

The limits prescribed do not permit me even to quote the mere titles of all the numerous writings which Dr. Young published. Nevertheless, the public reading of so rich a catalogue would certainly have sufficed to establish the celebrity of our colleague. Who would not imagine in fact that he had before him the register of the labours of several academies, and not those of a single individual, on hearing, for instance, the following list of titles :—

Memoir on the Establishments where Iron is wrought.
Essays on Music and Painting.
Remarks on the Habits of Spiders and the Theory of Fabricius.
On the Stability of the Arches of Bridges.
On the Atmosphere of the Moon.
Description of a new Species of Opercularia.
Mathematical theory of Epicycloidal Curves.
Restoration and Translation of different Greek Inscriptions.
On the means of strengthening the Construction of Ships of the Line.

On the play of the Heart and of the Arteries in the phenomena of circulation.

Theory of Tides.

On the Diseases of the Chest.

On the Friction of the Axes of Machines.

On the Yellow Fever.

On the Calculation of Eclipses.

Essays on Grammar, &c.*

CHARACTER OF YOUNG.—HIS POSITION AS A PHYSICIAN.—HIS ENGAGEMENT ON THE NAUTICAL ALMANAC.—HIS DEATH.

Labours so numerous and varied seem as if they must have required the laborious and retired life of that class of men of science, which, to say the truth, is beginning to disappear, who from their earliest youth separate themselves from their companions to shut themselves up completely in their studies. Thomas Young was, on the contrary, what is usually called a man of the world. He constantly frequented the best society in London. The graces of his wit, the elegance of his manners, were amply sufficient to make him remarkable. But when we figure to ourselves those numerous assemblies in which fifty different subjects in turn are skimmed over in a few minutes, we may conceive what value would be attached to one who was a true living library, from whom every one could find, at the moment, an exact, precise, substantial answer on all kinds of questions which they could propose to him. Young was much occupied with the fine arts. Many of his memoirs testify the profound

* This list, it should be borne in mind, is intended by the author merely as a specimen of the vast catalogue which might be made of Young's writings; the reader will find ample details as to his innumerable productions in Peacock's *Life*.—*Translator*.

knowledge which he had happily acquired of the theory of music. He carried out also to a great extent the talent of executing it; and I believe it is certain that of all known instruments, even including the Scottish bagpipe, only one or two could be named on which he could not play. His taste for painting developed itself during a visit which he paid to Germany. There the magnificent collection of Dresden absorbed his attention entirely; for he aspired not solely to the easy credit of connecting together, without mistake, the name of such or such an artist with such or such a painting; the defects and the characteristic qualities of the greatest masters, their frequent changes of manner, the material objects which they introduced into their works, the modifications which those objects and the colours underwent in progress of time, among other points, occupied him in succession. Young, in one word, studied painting in Saxony, as he had before studied languages in his own country, and as he afterwards studied the sciences. Every thing, in fact, was a subject of meditation and research. The university contemporaries of the illustrious physicist recalled a laughable instance of this trait of his mind. They related that entering his room one day, when for the first time he had taken a lesson in dancing the minuet, at Edinburgh, they found him occupied in tracing out minutely with the rule and compasses, the route gone through by the two dancers, and the different improvements of which these figures seemed to him susceptible.

Young borrowed with happy effect, from the sect of the Friends, to which he then belonged, the opinion that the intellectual faculties of children differ originally from each other much less than is commonly supposed. "Any man can do what any other man has done," became his favourite maxim. And further, never did he personally himself recoil before trials of any kind to which he wished to subject his system. The first time he mounted a horse, in company with the grandson of Mr. Barclay, the horseman who preceded them leapt a high fence. Young wished to imitate him, but he fell at ten paces. He remounted without saying a word, made a second attempt, was again unseated, but this time was not thrown further than on to the horse's neck, to which he clung. At the third trial the young learner, as his favourite motto taught, succeeded in executing what another had done before him.* This experiment need not have been referred to here, but that it had been repeated at Edinburgh, and afterwards at Gottingen, and carried out to a further extent beyond what might seem credible. In one of these two cities Young soon afterwards entered into a trial of skill with a celebrated rope-dancer, in the other, (and in each case the result of a challenge,) he acquired the art of executing feats on horseback with remarkable skill, even in the midst of consummate artistes, whose feats of agility attract every evening such numerous crowds to the circus of Franconi. Thus, those who are fond of drawing contrasts may, on the one side, represent to themselves the timid Newton,† never riding in a carriage, so much did the fear of being upset preoccupy him, without holding to both the doors with extended arms, and, on the other, his distinguished

* This anecdote seems at variance with what is stated on the authority of a Cambridge contemporary of Young in Dr. Peacock's *Life* (p. 119), that he only once there attempted to follow the hounds, when a severe fall prevented any further exhibitions of the kind.—*Translator.*

† This practice has been described as that of Newton, but the motive assigned by Arago is novel.

rival galloping on the backs of two horses with all the confidence of an equestrian by profession.

In England, a physician, if he does not wish to lose the confidence of the public, ought to abstain from occupying himself with any scientific or literary research which may be thought foreign to the art of curing diseases. Young for a long time did homage to this prejudice. His writings appeared under an anonymous veil. This veil, it is true, was very transparent. Two consecutive letters of a certain Latin motto served successively in regular order as the signature to each memoir. But Young communicated the three Latin words to all his friends both in his own country and abroad, without enjoining secrecy on any one.

Besides, who could be ignorant that the distinguished author of the theory of interferences was the Foreign Secretary of the Royal Society of London; that he gave, in the Theatre of the Royal Institution, a course of lectures on mathematical physics; that, associated with Sir H. Davy, he published a journal of the sciences, &c.? and moreover, we must say that his anonymous disguise was not rigorously observed even in his smaller memoirs, and on important occasions, when, for instance, in 1807, the two volumes in quarto appeared of eight hundred or nine hundred pages each, in which all branches of natural philosophy were treated in a manner so new and profound, the self-love of the author made him forget the interests of the physician, and the name of Young in large letters replaced the two small Italics whose series was then terminated, and which would have figured in a rather ridiculous manner in the title-page of this colossal work.

Young had not then, as a physician, either in London

or at Worthing, where he passed the sea-bathing season, any extended practice. The public found him, in fact, too scientific. We must also avow that his public lectures on medicine, those, for instance, which he delivered at St. George's Hospital, were generally but ill-attended. It has been said, to explain this, that his lectures were too dry, too full of matter, and that they were beyond the apprehension of ordinary understandings. But might not the want of success be rather ascribed to the freedom, not very common, with which Young pointed out the inextricable difficulties which encounter us at every step in the study of the numerous disorders of our frail machine?

Would any one expect at Paris, and especially in an age when every one seeks to attain his end quickly and without labour, that a professor of the faculty would retain many auditors if he were to commence with these words, which I borrow literally from Dr. Young:—

"No study is so complicated as that of medicine; it exceeds the limits of human intelligence. Those physicians who precipitately go on without trying to comprehend what they observe, are often just as much advanced as those who give themselves up to generalizations hastily made on observations in regard to which all analogy is at fault." And if the Professor, continuing in the same style, should add, "In the lottery of medicine the chances of the possessor of ten tickets must evidently be greater than those of the possessor of five," —when they believed themselves engaged in a lottery, would those of his auditors whom the first phrase had not driven away, be at all disposed to make any great efforts to procure for themselves more tickets, or, to explain the meaning of our Professor—the greatest amount of knowledge possible?

In spite of his knowledge, perhaps even from the very cause that it was so extensive, Young was totally wanting in confidence at the bedside of the patient. Then the mischievous effects which might eventually result from the action of the medicine even the most clearly called for presented themselves in a mass to his mind; seemed to counterbalance the favourable chances which might attend the use of them; and thus threw him into a state of indecision, no doubt very natural, yet on which the public will always put an unfavourable construction.

The same timidity showed itself in all the works of Young which treated on medical subjects.* This man, so eminently remarkable for the boldness of his scientific conceptions, gives here no more than a bare enumeration of facts. He seems hardly convinced of the soundness of his thesis, either when he attacks the celebrated Dr. Radcliffe, whose whole secret in the most brilliant and successful practice was, as he has himself said, to employ remedies exactly the reverse of the usual way: or when he combats Dr. Brown, who found himself, as he says, in the disagreeable necessity of recognizing, and that in accordance with the official documents of an hospital attended by the most eminent physicians, that, on the average, fevers left to their natural course are neither

* This timidity in medical speculation is entirely borne out by the tenor of Young's intellectual character as exhibited in such forcible lineaments in the portrait presented to us by Dr. Peacock. His mind was essentially cast in a matter of fact positive, demonstrative mould; hence all subjects of abstract or doubtful inquiry, in which probabilities alone could be estimated, or when the conclusions were to be the result of moral discrimination, were utterly unsuited to him. His medical character has been viewed, however, in a much higher light by Dr. Peacock, who has sought to combat the unfavourable impressions here advanced. See especially p. 213 and p. 222.—*Translator*.

more severe nor of longer duration than those treated by the best methods.

In 1818, Young, having been named Secretary to the Board of Longitude, abandoned entirely the practice of medicine to give himself up to the close superintendence of the celebrated periodical work known under the name of the *Nautical Almanac*. From this date the *Journal of the Royal Institution* gave every quarter his numerous dissertations on the most important problems of navigation and astronomy. A volume entitled *Illustration of the Mécanique Céleste of Laplace*, a scientific discussion on the tides, amply attested that Young did not consider the employment he had accepted as a sinecure. This employment became nevertheless to him a source of unceasing disgust. The *Nautical Almanac* had always been from its commencement a work exclusively destined to the service of the navy. Some persons demanded that it ought to be made, besides, a complete astronomical ephemeris. The Board of Longitude, whether right or wrong, not having shown itself a strong partisan of the projected change, found itself suddenly the object of the most violent attacks. The journals of every party, Whig or Tory, took part in the conflict.

We were no longer to view it as a union of such men as Davy, Wollaston, Young, Herschel, Kater, and Pond, but an assembly of individuals (I quote the words), "who obeyed a Bœotian influence." The *Nautical Almanac*, hitherto so renowned, was now declared to have become an object of shame to the English nation. If an error of the press were discovered, such as there must be in any collection of figures at all voluminous, the British navy, from the smallest bark up to the colossal three-decker, misled by an incorrect figure, would all together be engulfed in the ocean, &c.

It has been pretended that the principal promoter of these foolish exaggerations did not perceive such serious errors in the *Nautical Almanac* until after he had unsuccessfully attempted himself to obtain a place in the Board of Longitude. I know not whether the fact was so. In any case, I would not make myself the echo of the malicious commentaries to which it gave rise; I ought not to forget, in fact, that for many years past that member of the Royal Society to whom I allude has nobly devoted a part of his large fortune to the advancement of science. This commendable astronomer, like all men of science whose thoughts are concentrated on one sole object, fell into the error, which I do not pretend to excuse, of measuring through a magnifying glass the importance of the projects he had conceived; but that with which above all he must be reproached is, that he did not foresee that the hyperbolic language of his attacks would be taken literally; that he forgot that at all epochs and in all countries there are a great number of persons who having nothing to console them for their littleness, seize, as a prey, on all occasions of scandal, and under the mask of zeal for the public good enjoy the delight of being ignoble defamers of those of their contemporaries whose success has been proclaimed by fame. In Rome he whose office it was to insult the triumphant conqueror was altogether a slave; in London it was a member of the House of Commons, from whom the men of science received a cruel affront. An orator notorious for his prejudices, but who had hitherto vented his bitterness only against productions of French origin, attacked the most celebrated names in England, and retailed against them in open parliament puerile accusations, with a laughable gravity. Ministers whose eloquence was exercised for hours on the privileges of a rotten borough, did not pronounce a single word in favour of genius. The Board of Longitude was suppressed without opposition. The next day, it is true, the wants of an innumerable marine service made their imperative voice heard, and one of the men of science who had been displaced, the former Secretary of the Board, Dr. Young, found himself recalled to his old labours. Paltry reparation! Would the man of science feel less the separation from his illustrious colleagues,—would the man of feeling less perceive that the noble fruits of human intellect were subjected to tariff by the representatives of the country, in pounds, shillings, and pence, like sugar, pepper, or cinnamon?

The health of our colleague, which had already become somewhat precarious, declined from this sad epoch with fearful rapidity. Skilful physicians by whom he was attended soon lost hope. Young himself had a consciousness that his end was approaching, and saw it come with an admirable calmness. Until his last hour he occupied himself without intermission on an Egyptian dictionary then in the press, and which was not published till after his death. When his powers did not permit him any longer to sit up, or to employ a pen, he corrected the proofs with a pencil. One of the last acts of his life was to exact the suppression of a small publication written with talent, by a friendly hand, and directed against all those who had contributed to the destruction of the Board of Longitude.* Young died

* The whole account of the transactions connected with the abolition of the Board of Longitude must be received with some qualification. Arago writes on the subject in his usual vehement tone, and in the feeling in which the whole affair would naturally be viewed by a foreigner, perhaps not intimately acquainted with the minute points

surrounded by a family by whom he was adored, May 10, 1829, barely at the age of fifty-six. Examination showed that he suffered from ossification of the aorta.

of the case, and the somewhat different relative position occupied by the parties in England to that in which they might stand in France. It may be right very briefly to point out a few particulars in the case which are necessary for forming a correct impression of it. The Board of Longitude, originally instituted, as its name implied, for one specific object, which it was considered had been sufficiently attained, was in 1818 remodelled by Act of Parliament, when Dr. Young was appointed secretary to the Board and superintendent of the *Nautical Almanac;* the late Mr. F. Baily, whose eminence in astronomical science may perhaps be dated from that event, strongly pointed out the numerous defects of the *Nautical Almanac;* this led to some controversy of rather a sharp nature between himself and Dr. Young, who defended the existing system; other astronomers joined in the desire for these and even more extensive improvements, all which (with one slight concession) *were steadily opposed by Dr. Young.* Among these advocates for reform were several members of the Board itself, who urged them at its meetings. There was also a very prevalent impression, even among its own members, that the Board was not well constituted, and might have been capable of much better service to the nation if its functions were less restricted and the selection of its members placed on a better footing. In other quarters impressions unfavourable to its utility were prevalent; and it can hardly be matter of surprise that when the Board was itself divided in opinion, the public or the legislature should entertain doubts of its utility, or even hostile feelings towards it. What were the precise notions of the government, or the machinations by which they were influenced, it is impossible to say; but it is certain that in 1828, chiefly through the influence of Mr. Croker, its dissolution was determined upon and carried by Act of Parliament without any opposition being attempted. Instead, however, of an enlarged Board with increased powers, three scientific advisers of the Admiralty were appointed, of whom Dr. Young was one, retaining the superintendence of the *Nautical Almanac;* a system which has been since remodelled in accordance with the report of a committee appointed out of the Astronomical Society.

Dr. Young appears all along to have been affected only by the personal acrimony of some of the attacks upon himself in relation to the editorship of the *Nautical Almanac*, and not at all by any feeling for the Board of Longitude, as Arago would regard it.

I have not dwelt too long on the task imposed on me, if I have brought out, as I wished to do, the importance

That Board, as already observed, was divided against itself, and it therefore fell. It was never upheld on the only right ground. Neither the Board nor the friends of science sufficiently urged the strong and irresistible claims which they might have preferred to the government of the country, that "*a council of science*," with extended powers, properly selected and adequately remunerated, would be the appropriate adjunct of the government of a country all whose resources are so powerfully developed in exclusive dependence on the applications of science.

The government would thus have had the means of sound scientific advice constantly at hand, of which experience proves they are in daily want on every emergency; and which they obtain by asking the *gratuitous* services of men of science, and the crown would have possessed the means of making a graceful acknowledgment of the services, and paying a just tribute to the genius, of men devoted to the higher branches of the abstract sciences, which are of a nature incapable in themselves of affording any kind of remuneration, or in the ordinary course leading to any of those honours or preferments which await eminence in other professions.—*Translator*.

The reader may be referred for details of the questions here considered to the following documents:—

1. "Astronomical Tables and Remarks for 1822, published December, 1821," by F. Baily, Esq., with "Remarks on the present defective state of the *Nautical Almanac*."
2. A Reply to these Remarks appeared in Mr. Brande's *Quarterly Journal of Science*, April, 1822. (Attributed to Dr. Young.)
3. Practical Observations on the *Nautical Almanac*, &c., by Jas. South, F. R. S. 1822.
4. Reply to a Letter in the *Morning Chronicle* relative to the Government and Astronomical Science, &c. by the same. 1829.
5. Refutation of Misstatements, &c., in a paper presented to the Admiralty by Dr. T. Young, and printed by order of the House of Commons, by the same. 1829.
6. Further Remarks on the present defective state of the *Nautical Almanac*, &c., by F. Baily, Esq., F. R. S., &c. 1829.
7. Report of the Committee of the Astronomical Society relative to the improvement of the *Nautical Almanac*, adopted by the Council of the Society and approved and ordered to be carried into effect by the Lords Commissioners of the Admiralty, 1830. Memoirs of Astronomical Society, vol. iv. p. 447.

and novelty of the admirable law of interferences. Young is now placed before your eyes as one of the most illustrious men of science in whom England may justly take pride. Your thoughts, anticipating my words, may perhaps perceive already, in the recital of the just honours shown to the author of so beautiful a discovery, the peroration of this historical notice. These anticipations, I regret to say, will not be realized. The death of Young has in his own country created very little sensation. The doors of Westminster * Abbey, so easily accessible to titled mediocrity, remained shut upon a man of genius, who was not even a baronet. It was in the village of Farnborough, in the modest tomb of the family of his wife, that the remains of Thomas Young were deposited. The indifference of the English nation for

8. A motion was made in the House of Commons, February 23, 1829, for certain Returns respecting the Board of Longitude and the *Nautical Almanac*, &c.

The Returns were made and printed consisting of (1) "A Memorandum of a Statement made to the Chancellor of the Exchequer for reforming the *Nautical Almanac*, and establishment of a new Board of Longitude. (2) A Paper read at the Board, by J. Herschel, Esq. (3) A Report on a Memorandum, &c. by Thomas Young, M. D. In the last Dr. Young makes answer to what he considers objections raised in the "Memorandum," and also replies to those of Mr. Baily and Mr. South. Sir J. South's Pamphlet contains the Memorandum,—the objections raised or inferred by Dr. Young—his replies to them—all which are severely criticized.

At p. 60 is a curious account of some discussions at Sir H. Davy's soirée between Sir J. South and Dr. Young.

* The frequenters of Poets' Corner need not be reminded that literature and science are not excluded from their share of funereal honours in Westminster Abbey. M. Arago here, as in some other passages, may naturally be a little incorrect in referring to national usages. The *delay* which occurred in regard to Young's monument, is however not fully explained by Dean Peacock. (See *Life of Young*, p. 485.)—*Translator*.

those scientific labours which ought to add so much to its glory, is a rare anomaly, of which it would be curious to trace the causes. I should be wanting in frankness, I should be the panegyrist, not the historian, if I did not avow, that in general Young did not sufficiently accommodate himself to the capacity of his readers; that the greater part of the writings for which the sciences are indebted to him, are justly chargeable with a certain obscurity. But the neglect to which they were long consigned did not depend solely on this cause.

The exact sciences have an advantage over the works of art or imagination, which has been often pointed out. The truths of which they consist remain constant through ages without suffering in any respect from the caprices of fashion or the decline of taste: but thus, when once these researches rise into more elevated regions of thought, on how many competent judges of their merits can we reckon? When Richelieu let loose against the great Corneille a crowd of that class of men whom envy of the merit of others renders furious, the Parisians vehemently hissed the partisans of the despot Cardinal and applauded the poet. This reparation is denied to the geometer, the astronomer, or the physicist, who cultivate the highest parts of science. Those who can competently appreciate them throughout the whole extent of Europe never rise above the number of eight or ten. Imagine these unjust, indifferent, or even jealous, (for I suppose that *may* sometimes be the case,) and the public, reduced to believe on hearsay, would be ignorant that D'Alembert had connected the great phenomenon of precession of equinoxes with the principle of universal gravitation; that Lagrange had arrived at the discovery of the physical cause of the libration of the moon; that since the researches of Laplace, the acceleration of the motion of that luminary is found to be connected with a particular change in the form of the earth's orbit, &c. &c. The journals of science, when they are edited by men of recognized merit, thus acquire, on certain subjects, an influence which sometimes becomes fatal. It is thus I conceive that we may describe the influence which the *Edinburgh Review* has sometimes exercised.

Among the contributors to that celebrated journal at its commencement, a young writer was eminently distinguished, in whom the discoveries of Newton had inspired an ardent admiration. This sentiment so natural, so legitimate, unfortunately led him to misconceive the plausible, ingenious, and fertile character of the doctrine of interferences. The author of this theory had not, perhaps, always taken care to clothe his decisions, his statements, his critiques, with those more polished forms of expression the claims of which ought never to be neglected, and which moreover, became a matter of imperative duty when the question referred to the immortal author of the *Natural Philosophy* * [the *Principia ?*]

* It seems impossible to make this sentence intelligible unless we suppose the "immortal author" spoken of to be Newton, and by consequence that the title *Natural Philosophy* was a slip of the writer's pen, for *Principia*. Yet the supposition that the hostility of the *Edinburgh Review* was at all called forth by any want of courtesy towards Newton in the writings of Young is wholly unsupported by any thing in Young's papers, in which he cites the views of Newton with the greatest respect.—*Translator*.

Newton's support of the emission theory of light.—The authority of names can never be of any avail to the truly inductive philosopher,—his motto is emphatically "nullius in verba." But there has been always a propensity among writers on the subject to dwell on such authority, and to array great names on either side of any of those controverted points which have divided the scientific world. Perhaps where the question is purely one of opinion and refers simply to hypotheses,

The penalty of retaliation was applied to him with interest; the *Edinburgh Review* attacked the man of erudi-

upheld for what they are worth as such, the weight of a name may not be unworthy of due estimation; great experience and high genius may add value to a pure *hypothesis* though it could not to a positive *conclusion.* In regard to theories of light this has been conspicuously exemplified, and during a long continuance of controversial discussion it has been a matter of triumph to the opponents of the undulatory theory that the authority of Newton is on their side. And even Arago as well as some other supporters of it have spoken as if regretting that they were thus constrained to put themselves in antagonism to Newton. They have pictured two rival theories, the one headed by Newton and supported by Laplace, Biot, Brewster and Potter, the other upheld in opposition to them by Huyghens, Hooke, Euler, Young, Fresnel, Airy and all the Cambridge school.

But a very slight inquiry into the real facts entirely dispels this view of the case. In particular Dr. Young himself in proposing his theory, so far from opposing the Newtonian views, expressly endeavours to conciliate attention by claiming the weight of Newton's authority *on his own side:* thus in his paper " On the Theory of Light and Colours," (*Phil. Trans.* 1801,) he commences by highly extolling the optical researches of Newton, and then observes, "those who are attached, as they may be with the greatest justice, to every doctrine which is stamped with the Newtonian approbation, will probably be disposed to bestow on these considerations (*i. e.* his own views) so much the more of their attention as they shall appear to coincide more nearly with Newton's opinion." He then proceeds to examine in detail a number of passages from Newton's writings in which the theory of waves is distinctly upheld and even applied with some precision to the explanation of various phenomena of light, illustrated by their analogies to those of sound.

It is perfectly true that Newton in the actual investigation of several phenomena of light adopts other hypotheses than those of waves; and chiefly the idea of light (whatever may be its nature) being subject to certain attractions and repulsions,—to certain bendings when approaching near the edges of solid bodies,—to certain peculiar modifications or changes in its nature recurring periodically at certain minute intervals along the length of a ray,—to the idea of a ray having " sides " endued with different properties; in a word, a variety of conceptions, which he introduces for the purpose of giving some kind of imaginary physical representation of the *modus operandi* in each of the several curious

tion, the writer, the geometer, the experimenter, with a vehemence, with a severity of expression almost with-

experimental cases which he had examined. In all these there is no unity or community of principle,-there is at least nothing like the spirit of theory, no continual recurrence to one leading idea,—no perpetual appeal to any one principle however imaginary, but an attempt in each isolated case to frame something like an isolated hypothesis to suit it, and in some way to represent its phenomena though without any attempt to connect them with the others. It may perhaps be said that all these various suppositions agree in supposing light to be material, to be something emitted from the luminous source. But on a closer examination it seems far from certain that even this can be maintained. The only part of these investigations, perhaps, in which any thing very positive of this kind is distinctly introduced, is when Newton investigates the laws of refraction, on the express supposition of small molecules attracted by the molecules of the medium. But in this instance it has been truly observed, that at the time when Newton wrote, no mathematical method existed by which this kind of action could be reduced to calculation except those involving the action of attractive force. To give, then, a mathematical theory of ordinary reflexion and refraction he was necessitated to make use of this method. When he came to investigate those more recondite phenomena which he (very appropriately to their *apparent* nature) called "inflexion," the idea most naturally and obviously presented was, that some power or influence, analogous to attraction and repulsion, existing in the edge of an opaque body to bend out of their course rays passing very near it, and this might seem to imply the materiality of those rays. A kind of *alternating* action of this sort, which he imagined necessary to account for a part of the effect, would, however, hardly be reconcilable to the idea of direct emission. It would be a difficult matter to conceive particles darted through space with such inconceivable velocity as must belong to those of light, and yet stopping to wave about, in and out, as Newton expresses it, "like an eel," close to the edge of a body, by virtue of some mysterious influence which it exercises upon them.

Again: the theory of those alternating states, conditions, or "fits" as he termed them, at such minute intervals along the length of ray alternately putting it in a state to be reflected, and again to be transmitted by a transparent medium, seem very remote from the idea of a simple rectilinear progress of molecules through space following one another at immense intervals of distance though in inconceivably rapid

out example in scientific discussion. The public usually keeps on its guard when such violent language is addressed to it, but in this instance they adopted at the first onset the opinions of the journalist in which we cannot fairly accuse them of inconsiderateness. The journalist, in fact, was not one of those unfledged critics whose mission is not justified by any previous study of the subject. Several good papers, received by the Royal Society, had attested his mathematical knowledge, and had assigned him a distinguished place among the physicists to whom optical science was indebted: the profession of the bar in London had acknowledged him one of its shining luminaries; the Whig section of the House of Commons saw

succession in time. It would be easy to extend such remarks; but it will probably be seen, with sufficient evidence for our present purpose, that neither in profession nor in fact, can Newton's name be appealed to as at all an exclusive supporter of the material hypothesis of light; even if in other passages he had not distinctly referred to that of undulations. And of these references a large number are quoted from different portions of his writings, by Dr. Young, in the paper above cited. In some of these, while he admits the readiness with which the idea of waves represents the phenomena, he yet dwells on certain apparent objections which seemed to invalidate that idea.

Upon the whole it appears that the name of Newton can in no way be legitimately claimed as a partisan of either theory. Indeed, it is surprising that any claim of the kind could have been set up as regards the emission theory after his own distinct avowal:—

"'Tis true that from theory I argue the corporeity of light; but I do it without any absolute positiveness, as the word 'perhaps' intimates; and make it at most but a very plausible consequence of the doctrine, and not a fundamental supposition, nor so much as any part of it."—*Phil. Trans.* vol. x. 1675, p. 5086.

While in respect to either hypothesis it is sufficiently evident to those acquainted with his writings that he never *systematically* upheld either the one or the other; but from time to time, as each particular investigation seemed to require, he adopted the one or the other principle just as it seemed to give the more ready explanation of the point before him.—*Translator.*

in him an efficient orator who in parliamentary struggles was often the happy antagonist of Canning; this was the future President of the House of Peers,—the present Lord Chancellor.* How could opposition be offered to unjust criticisms proceeding from so high a quarter? I am not ignorant what firmness some minds enjoy in the consciousness of their being in the right; in the certainty that sooner or later truth will triumph; but I know also, that we shall act wisely in not reckoning too much on such exceptions. Listen, for example, to Galileo himself, repeating in a whisper after his abjuration, "E pur si muore!" and do not seek in these immortal words an augury for the future, for they are but the expression of the cruel vexation which the illustrious old man experienced. Young also, in writing a few pages which he published as an answer to the *Edinburgh Review,* showed himself deeply discouraged. The vivacity, the vehemence of his expressions, ill concealed the sentiment which oppressed him. In a word, let us hasten to say that justice, complete justice, was at length rendered to the great physicist. After several years the whole world recognized in him one of the brightest luminaries of the age. It is from France (and Young took pleasure in himself proclaiming it) that the first sign of this tardy reparation showed itself. I will add, that at an epoch considerably before the doctrine of interferences had made converts either in England or on the Continent, Young found within his own family circle one who comprehended it, and whose assent to it might well console him for the neglect of the public. The distinguished person whom I here point out to the notice of the physi-

* Lord Brougham, who held that office when this biography was written.

cists of Europe, will excuse me if I complete this indiscretion by stating the circumstances.

In the year 1816 I made a tour in England with my scientific friend M. Gay-Lussac. Fresnel had just then entered on his scientific career in the most brilliant manner, by the publication of his memoir on Diffraction. This work which, in our opinion, contained a capital experiment irreconcilable with the Newtonian theory of light, became naturally the first subject of our discussion with Dr. Young. We were astonished at the numerous qualifications which he put upon our praises of it, until at length he stated to us that the very experiment which we so much commended had been published, so long since as 1807, in his treatise on Natural Philosophy. This assertion did not seem to us well founded. It caused a long and minute discussion. Mrs. Young was present, without appearing to take any part in the conversation; but we imagined that the weak fear of being designated by the ridiculous sobriquet of bas-bleu rendered the ladies of England very reserved in the presence of foreigners; and our want of discernment did not strike us till the moment when Mrs. Young quickly quitted her place; we then began to attempt excuses to her husband, until we saw her reënter the room carrying under her arm a large quarto volume. This was the first volume of the *Natural Philosophy*. She placed it on the table, and without saying a word opened it at page 787, and pointed with her finger to a diagram in which the curvilinear route of the diffracted bands, on which the discussion turned, was theoretically established.

I trust I shall be pardoned these little details. Too numerous examples may almost have habituated the public to consider destitution, injustice, persecution, and misery as the natural wages of those who devote their vigils to the development of the human mind! Let us not then forget to point out the exceptions whenever they present themselves. If we wish that youth should give itself up with ardour to intellectual labours, let us show them that the glory attached to great discoveries allies itself, sometimes at least, with some degree of tranquillity and happiness. Let us even withdraw, if it be possible, from the history of science so many pages which tarnish its glory. Let us try to persuade ourselves that in the dungeons of the Inquisitors, a friendly voice had caused Galileo to hear some of the delightful expressions which posterity has kept sacred for his memory; that behind the thick walls of the Bastille, Fréret might yet have learned from the world of science, the glorious rank which it had reserved for him among the men of erudition whom France honours; that before going to die in an hospital, Borelli had found sometimes in the city of Rome a shelter against the inclemency of the atmosphere, and a little straw on which to lay his head; and lastly, that the great Kepler had not experienced the sufferings of hunger.

NOTE BY THE AUTHOR.

The Journals having done me the honour to mention sometimes the numerous testimonies of good will and friendship which Lord Brougham had shown me in 1834, as well in Scotland as in Paris, a word or two of explanation here seem indispensable. The éloge of Dr. Young was read at a public sitting of the Academy of Sciences, Nov. 26, 1832. At this period I had never had any personal acquaintance with the writer in the *Edinburgh Review*, and thus all charge of ingratitude must fall to the ground. But could you not, some might perhaps say, have suppressed entirely, when your paper was going to the press, all that related to so unfortunate a controversy? I could have done so, and in fact the idea had occurred to me; but I soon renounced it. I know too well the elevated feelings of my illustrious friend to fear that he will take offence at my frankness in regard to a question on which I have a profound conviction that the great extent of his genius has not preserved him from error. The homage which I render to the noble character of Lord Brougham in now publishing this passage of the éloge of Young without any modification, is, in my mind, sufficiently significant to render it needless to add a word more.

JAMES WATT.

BIOGRAPHY READ AT THE PUBLIC MEETING OF THE ACADEMY OF SCIENCES, ON THE 8TH OF DECEMBER, 1834.

Gentlemen,—After having waded through a long list of battles, assassinations, plagues, famines, catastrophes of all sorts presented by the annals of I know not what country, a philosopher exclaimed, "Happy the nation whose history is tedious!" Why ought we to add, in a literary point of view at least, "Unhappy the man on whom the duty falls to relate the history of a happy people!"

If the philosopher's exclamation loses none of its appositeness when applied to mere individuals, its counterpart characterizes with equal truth the position of some biographers.

Such were the reflections that occurred to me, whilst I was studying the life of James Watt, and collecting obliging communications from the relations, friends, and companions of the illustrious mechanic. His life, quite patriarchal, devoted to work, to study, and to meditation, will not afford us any of those striking events the recital of which, sprinkled with judgment among scientific details, relieves their weight. Still I will relate it, if but to show in what a humble position those projects were perfected, that were destined to raise the British nation to an unheard-of degree of power. I will especially endeavour to characterize, with extreme precision, the fruitful inventions which will for ever connect the name of Watt with the steam-engine. I foresee all the dangers of this line of conduct; I am aware that it may be said on going out of this room: We expected an historical eulogy, but we have only received a dry and arid *lesson*. Besides this, the reproach would not have weighed on me, if the *lesson* had been well understood. I will, therefore, exert every effort not to tire your patience; I will keep in mind that clearness is politeness in public speakers.

INFANCY AND YOUTH OF JAMES WATT.—HIS ADVANCEMENT TO THE APPOINTMENT OF ENGINEER TO THE UNIVERSITY OF GLASGOW.

James Watt, one of the eight Foreign Associates of the Academy of Sciences, was born at Greenock, in Scotland, the 19th of January, 1736. Our neighbours on the other side of the Channel, have the good sense to think that the genealogy of a respectable and industrious family, is quite as worthy of being preserved as the parchments of certain titled families that have become celebrated only by the enormity of their crimes and their vices. Thus I can say with certainty that the great grandfather of James Watt was an agriculturist, settled in the county of Aberdeen; that he was killed in one of Montrose's battles; that the conquering side, as was customary, (I was going to add, as is still customary in civil discords,) did not think death itself a sufficient expiation for the opinions in support of which the poor farmer had fought; that it punished the act in the person of the son, by confiscating his property; that the unfortunate child, Thomas Watt, was received by some distant relations; that in the entire insulation to which his difficult position condemned him, he assiduously devoted himself to deep studies; that in more tranquil times, he settled at Greenock, where he taught mathematics and the elements of navigation; that he resided at Crawford's Dyke, of which borough he was magistrate; and that finally he died in 1734, at the age of eighty-two.

Thomas Watt had two sons. The eldest, John, followed his father's profession at Glasgow. He died at the age of fifty (1737), leaving a chart of the Clyde,* which was published under the care of his brother James. This James, who was the father of the celebrated engineer, and for a long time treasurer of the municipal council of Greenock, as well as magistrate of the town, became remarkable in the performance of his duties by his ardent zeal, and an enlightened spirit of amelioration. He *combined*, (do not be alarmed; these three syllables, that have become a subject of general anathema in France, will not injure the memory of James Watt,) he *combined* three species of occupation; he was at once a seller of all sorts of nautical instruments † and stores, a

* This map is reëngraved in the *Memorials of Watt*, with an advertisement which ascribes its publication to James Watt, at Glasgow College; a MS. note on one copy, said to be in the handwriting of the Great Engineer, states that it was published by John Watt in 1760.—*Translator*.

† It may have been first owing to an examination of these instruments, that young Watt, in his eighteenth year, in conformity with his own desire, was apprenticed to a mathematical instrument-maker in London.—*Translator*.

builder, and a merchant; which unfortunately, about the close of his life, did not prevent certain commercial speculations from depriving him of a portion of the creditable fortune that he had gained before. He died at the age of eighty-four, in 1782.

James Watt, the subject of this essay, was born with a very delicate constitution. His mother, whose maiden name was Muirhead, gave him his first instruction in reading. He learned writing and ciphering from his father. He also attended the *Grammar School* of Greenock; and thus these humble Scotch seminaries are entitled, with just pride, to enroll the name of this celebrated engineer among the pupils that they have formed; as the College of La Flèche boasted of Descartes, as the University of Cambridge still cites Newton.

To be correct, I must add that frequent indispositions prevented young Watt from punctually attending the public school at Greenock; that during a great portion of the year he was confined to his room, and there devoted himself to study, without any out-door help. As is frequently the case with high intellectual faculties destined to yield great results, they began to develop themselves in retirement and solitude.

Watts was too sickly for his parents to think of urging him to assiduous occupation. They even left his amusements to his free choice. We shall see whether he abused this freedom.

A friend of Mr. Watt's one day found little James lying on the floor, and with a piece of chalk drawing all sorts of intersecting lines; whereupon he exclaimed—"Why do you allow that child to waste his time—send him to the public school!" Mr. Watt answered: "You might have spared us this hasty judgment; before condemning us, examine attentively what our son is doing." The apology soon followed; the boy, only six years old, was seeking the solution of a geometrical problem.

Prompted by an enlightened fondness, the father had early furnished the young scholar with a certain number of tools, and he made use of them with great ability; he took to pieces and put together again all the infantine toys that came into his hands; he continually made new ones. When older, he applied them to the construction of a small electrical machine; the bright sparks from which became a lively subject of amusement and surprise to all the playfellows of the poor invalid.

Watt, with an excellent memory, still would not perhaps have figured among the young prodigies of common schools; he would have refused to learn lessons like a parrot, because he felt an internal longing carefully to elaborate the intellectual elements which they presented to his mind. Nature had especially created him for meditation. The father, moreover, augured very favourably of the rising faculties of his son. Other less observant relations did not participate in these hopes; his grandmother, Mrs. Muirhead, said to him one day,— "James, I never saw such an idle young man as you are. Do take a book, and employ yourself usefully. Upwards of half an hour has elapsed without your saying a single word. Do you know what you have been doing all this time? You have taken off and replaced, and taken off again, the teapot lid; and you have alternately held in the steam that came out, first a saucer and then a spoon; you have busied yourself in examining and collecting together the little drops formed by the condensation of the steam, on the surface of the china and of the silver; is it not disgraceful to waste your time in this manner?"

In 1750, each of us in Mrs. Muirhead's position would probably have held the same language; but the world has advanced, and general knowledge has advanced with it; also, when I shall have presently explained, that the principal discovery of our associate consisted in a special manner of transforming steam into water, the reproaches of Mrs. Muirhead will appear quite in a different light; and little James watching the tea-pot, will be the great Engineer anticipating the important discoveries that were to immortalize him; every one will then perceive how remarkable it was that the words *condensation of steam* should so naturally have entered into an account of Watt's early childhood. Independently of this, I could not but think, from the singularity of the anecdote, that it deserved to be preserved. When an opportunity offers, let us prove to young people that Newton was not diffident only on that day when, to satisfy the curiosity of a high personage who desired to know how attraction had been discovered, he answered, *By constantly thinking of it!* Let us show to everybody, in the simple words of the immortal author of the *Principia,* the real secret of men of genius.

The love of anecdote that our associate showed so agreeably during upwards of half a century to all those around him, developed itself very early. The proof will be found in some lines that I am about to quote and translate from an unedited note given in 1798, by Mrs. Marion Campbell, a cousin and juvenile companion of the celebrated engineer.*

* I am indebted for this curious document to my friend Mr. James Watt, of Soho. Thanks to the deep veneration that he feels for the memory of his illustrious father, and thanks to the inexhaustible complaisance with which he listened to all my inquiries, I have been able to avoid several errors that have slipped into the most esteemed

"During a journey to Glasgow, Mrs. Watt entrusted her young son James to one of her friends. After a few weeks she returned to see him, but most assuredly not expecting the reception she met with. "Madam," said her friend, as soon as she saw her, "you must hasten to take James back to Greenock. I can no longer endure the state of excitement into which he throws me; I am harrassed by want of sleep. Every night, when the usual hour approaches for the family to retire to bed, your son adroitly contrives to raise a discussion, in the course of which he always finds means to introduce a story; this story is sure necessarily to engender a second, and a third, &c. And these tales, whether they be pathetic or comic, are so charming, so interesting, that the whole of my family listen to them with such attention, that a fly might be heard to fly. Thus, hours follow hours, without our being aware of it; but the next day I am ready to drop with fatigue. Dear madam, take your son home."

James Watt had a younger brother, John,* who, by deciding to follow his father's profession, left James the liberty of choosing any vocation; for according to Scotch customs, it suffices if one son adopts the paternal career. But it was difficult to say what vocation this would be, for the young student seemed to succeed equally well in whatever he tried.

The shores of Loch Lomond, already so celebrated by the reminiscences that they afford of the historian Buchanan, and of the illustrious inventor of Logarithms,

biographies, and from which I myself, deceived by verbal references too easily accepted, should otherwise have fallen into.

* He was lost in 1762, in one of his father's ships, on her passage from Greenock to America, aged twenty-three years.

developed his taste for the beauties of nature and for botany. Excursions to various mountains in Scotland made him feel that the inert crust of the globe is not less worthy of attention, and he became a mineralogist. James availed himself also of his frequent intercourse with the poor inhabitants of those picturesque districts, to learn their local traditions, their popular ballads, and their ignorant prejudices. When ill health confined him to his paternal roof, chemistry became the principal object of his experiments. Gravesande's *Elements of Natural History* initiated him into the thousands of wonders in general physics; finally, like all invalids, he devoured all the works on medicine and surgery that he could obtain. These latter sciences had awakened such a passion in the student, that he was detected one day carrying into his room the head of a child who had died of an unknown malady, for the purpose of dissecting it.

Still, Watt did not decide either in favour of botany, of mineralogy, of literature, of poetry, of chemistry, of physics, or of surgery, although he was so well prepared for each of those studies. In 1755 he went to London to place himself under Mr. John Morgan, a maker of mathematical and nautical instruments, in Finch Lane, Cornhill. The man, who was to cover England with motive powers by the side of which, as to their effects at least, the old colossal machine of Marly would seem a mere pygmy,—entered on the manual art of constructing with his own hands subtile, delicate, fragile instruments, those small but admirable reflecting sextants, to which nautical art owes its progress.

Watt did not remain above a year at Mr. Morgan's, and returned to Glasgow, where some heavy difficulties awaited him. Attached to their old privileges, the corporations of arts and of trades regarded the young artist from London as an intruder, and obstinately refused him permission to open even the most humble workshop. Every means of conciliation failing, the University of Glasgow interfered, and ceded to young Watt a small locality in their own buildings, allowing him to open a shop there and honouring him moreover with the title of their Engineer.* There still exist some small instruments of that epoch, of exquisite workmanship, made entirely by Watt's own hands. I will add that his son has lately placed before me the first essays of a steam-engine, and that they are truly remarkable by the high finish of the work, the firmness, the precision of the form. It was not then without reason, whatever may have been said of it, that Watt spoke with complacency of his own manual dexterity.

Perhaps you have some reason to think, that I carry my scruples rather far, in claiming for our associate a species of merit which cannot add to his glory. But I will acknowledge that I never intend to make a pedantic enumeration of the qualities with which superior men have been endowed, without recollecting that wretched general in the age of Louis XIV. who always carried one shoulder very high, because Prince Eugene of Savoy was rather deformed, and thought that this sufficed without his endeavouring to extend the likeness any farther.

Watt had scarcely reached his one and twentieth year when the University of Glasgow attached him to their

* This was not all. According to Stuart's Narrative, Watt picked up a practical acquaintance with machines from an industrious mechanic at Glasgow; a person "who was by turns a cutler and a whitesmith, a repairer of fiddles, a tuner of spinets, and a mender of fishing tackle,"—in a word, a very useful man at almost every thing.—*Translator*.

establishment. He had had as protectors, Adam Smith, author of the celebrated work on *The Wealth of Nations;* Black, whose discoveries relative to latent heat and carbonate of lime must place him in a distinguished rank among the most eminent chemists of the eighteenth century; Robert Simson, the celebrated restorer of the most important treatises by ancient geometers. These great men, however, thought at first that they had only delivered a good, zealous, and amiable workman from the overbearing corporations; but they soon after recognized in him a first-rate man, and bestowed on him their warmest friendship. The students in the University also esteemed it an honour to be admitted into Watt's intimacy. In short, *his shop*, yes, Gentlemen, his shop! became a sort of academy, where the illustrious men of Glasgow used to go to discuss the most delicate questions of art, of science, and of literature. I would not dare, I own, to pronounce what share this young workman of one and twenty took in these learned circles, if I could not depend on an unpublished paper by the most illustrious of the editors of the *British Encyclopedia.*

Robison says: "Although still a student, I had the vanity to think myself sufficiently advanced in my favourite subjects, mechanics and physics, when I was introduced to Watt; and I will acknowledge that I was not slightly mortified when I perceived how far superior the young workman was to me. . . . . Whenever any difficulty arrested us in the University, we used to run to our workman. When once excited, any subject became for him a text for serious study and discoveries. He never let go his hold, until he had entirely cleared up the proposed question; he either reduced it to nought, or obtained from it some net and substantial result. . . . .

One day, the desired solution seemed to require that Leupold's work on Machines should be read: Watt immediately learned German. On another occasion, and for a similar reason, he rendered himself master of the Italian language. . . . . The ingenuous simplicity of the young engineer immediately procured for him the good will of all who accosted him. Although I have lived much in the world, I must assert, that it would be impossible for me to cite a second example of so sincere and so general an attachment felt for a man of uncontested superiority. It is true that this superiority was veiled by the most amiable candour, and allied to a firm resolution to recognize every man's merit liberally. Watt was even inclined to assign things to the inventive spirit of his friends that were often only his own ideas dressed up in another form. I have all the more reason to assert his possessing this rare disposition, because I have myself experienced the effects of it."

You will have to decide, Gentlemen, whether it was not equally honourable to pronounce these closing words, as to have inspired them.

The deep and varied studies to which the circumstances of his singular position gave rise, never interfered with the young artist's professional work. He attended to this in the daytime; and devoted the night to theoretical researches. Relying on the resources of his imagination, Watt seemed to delight in difficult enterprises, and those to which he seemed least adapted. Will it be believed that he undertook to construct an organ, he who was totally insensible to the charms of music; he who had never been able even to distinguish one note from another, as *g* from *f*? Yet this enterprise was successfully carried out. We need scarcely add, that the new instrument presented essential improvements in the mechanical parts, in the regulators, in the method of appreciating the power of the wind; but it will excite astonishment to learn that its harmonic qualities were not less remarkable, and that they charmed professional musicians. Watt solved an important part of the problem: he arrived at the temperament assigned by a man learned in the mystery, in aid of the phenomenon of the vibrations then but ill understood; and which he could not have dived into, but in the profound though obscure work of Dr. Smith,* of Cambridge.

PRINCIPLES OF THE STEAM-ENGINE.

I have now reached the most brilliant portion of Watt's life, and also, I fear, the most difficult part of my task. The immense importance of the inventions of which I am about to treat, cannot be doubted for one moment; but I may not succeed in rendering them suitably appreciated, without entering into intricate numerical comparisons. In order that these comparisons, if they become essential, may be easily seized, I will present you, in the most compact manner possible, with the delicate notions of physics on which we shall have to rest them.

By the effect of simple changes of temperature, water may exist in three perfectly different conditions; in the solid state, in the liquid state, and in the aerial or gaseous state. Below zero on the scale of the centigrade thermometer, water becomes ice; at 100° it rapidly assumes the form of gas; in all the intermediary temperatures it remains fluid.

* Dr. Robert Smith's work, here alluded to, was intituled *Harmonics, or the Philosophy of Musical Sounds*, and printed in 1760. He was also the author of the well-known *System of Optics*.—*Translator*.

Careful observation of the instant of change from one of these conditions to another, leads to discoveries of the highest order, and which are keys to the economical appreciations of steam-engines.

Water is not necessarily hotter than any kind of ice; water may be kept at the temperature of zero without freezing; ice may remain at zero without melting; but while this water and this ice are both of the same temperature, are both at zero, it seems difficult to believe that they do not differ but by their physical properties; that no element, extraneous to the water so called, distinguishes the solid water from the fluid. A very simple experiment will clear up this mystery.

Mix a kilogram of water at zero with a kilogram of water at 79° centigrade; the two kilograms of the mixture will be at a temperature of 39° and a half; that is to say, at the mean of the two constituent fluids. The hot water preserves 39° and a half of its former heat, and has ceded 39° and a half to the cold water; this is very natural and might have been foreseen.

But let us repeat this experiment with one modification: instead of the kilogram of water at zero, let us take a kilogram of ice at the same temperature of zero. From the admixture of this kilogram of ice with the kilogram of water at 79°, there will result two kilograms of fluid water, because the ice bathed in the hot water cannot fail to melt and to preserve its former weight; but do not hastily attribute to the mixture, as in the preceding instance, a temperature of 39° and a half; for you would be mistaken; the temperature will be only zero; there will be no trace left of the 79° of heat which the hot water possessed: those 79° disintegrated the molecules of ice they have combined with them, but without heating them at all.

I do not hesitate to represent this experiment of Black's as one of the most remarkable in modern physics. Indeed, see the consequences to which it leads.

Water at zero, and ice at zero, differ in their internal constitution. The fluid contains, beyond what the solid body does, 79° of an imponderable body called *caloric.* Those 79° are so well hidden in the composition,—I was almost going to say in the aqueous amalgam, that the most sensitive thermometer does not reveal their existence. Heat then, imperceptible to our senses, imperceptible to the most delicate instruments, LATENT *heat,* for that is the name given to it, is one of the constituent principles of those bodies.

The comparison of boiling water, of water at 100° with the vapour that rises from it, and the temperature of which is also 100°, leads, though on a much grander scale, to analogous results. At the moment of the formation of steam of the temperature of 100°, the water at the same time imbibes an enormous quantity of heat in a *latent* form, in a form not sensible to the thermometer. When the steam resumes its fluid form, this latent heat is disengaged, and heats all bodies it meets with capable of absorbing it. If, for example, we occasion 5·35 kilograms of water at zero to be traversed by a single kilogram of steam at 100°, the steam will be entirely liquified. The 6·35 kilograms resulting from the mixture will be of the temperature of 100°. In the composition of one kilogram of steam then, a quantity of latent heat is absorbed that would raise a kilogram of water, provided the evaporation was prevented, from zero to 535° of the centigrade scale. This result will undoubtedly appear enormous, but it is certain ; the steam of water is created only on these conditions. Wherever a kilogram of water at 100° evaporates naturally or artificially, it must appropriate to itself, in order to be transformed, and it does attract from the surrounding bodies, 535° of heat. And these degrees, it cannot be too often repeated, are integrally restored by steam on whatever surfaces it is subsequently liquified. This ingenious proceeding is very ill understood, if it is supposed that the aqueous gas carries through the tubes where it circulates only the heat that is thermometrically sensible: the principal effects are due to the constituent heat, the hidden heat, the latent heat, which disengages itself at the moment when a contact with cold surfaces restores the steam from its gaseous to its fluid state.

Henceforward, then, we must place heat among the constituent principles of the steam of water. Heat is obtained only by burning wood or coal; steam therefore has a commercial value superior to that of water, by all the price of the combustible used in the act of creating steam. If the difference of the two values is very great, it must be attributed to the latent heat; for the thermometric or sensible heat has but a small share in it.

I may perhaps have occasion to enlarge, in the sequel, on some other properties of the steam of water. If I do not mention them at this moment, it is not that I attribute to this assembly the state of mind of certain scholars, who said one day to their Professor of Geometry,—"Why do you take so much trouble to demonstrate these theorems? We place entire confidence in you; give us your *word of honour* that it is true, and nothing more need be said!" But it is my duty not to abuse your patience; I have to keep in mind also, that by referring to special treatises, you can easily fill up the lacunæ that I have unavoidably left.

HISTORY OF THE STEAM-ENGINE IN ANCIENT TIMES.

Let us now endeavour to take the part of those nations and individuals, who appear to deserve to be quoted in the history of the steam-engine. Let us trace the chronological series of improvements made in this machine, from its first germs, which were very ancient, up to the discoveries by Watt. I enter on the subject with a firm inclination to be impartial, with a strong desire to render to each inventor the justice that is due to him, with a certainty of continuing a stranger to any consideration unworthy of the mission that you have given me, or unworthy of the majesty of science, or arising from national prejudices. I acknowledge, on the other hand, that I shall pay but little attention to the numerous decisions already come to, dictated by similar prejudices; that I shall allow myself still less, if possible, to be influenced by the bitter criticisms that no doubt await me, for the past is a mirror of the future.

A question well expressed is half solved. If this sensible axiom had been attended to, the discussions relative to the invention of the steam-engine would not assuredly have presented the symptoms of acrimony and violence with which they have been impressed till now. But the authors had blindly plunged into a defile that had no outlet, by wanting to find a sole inventor, in a case that requires us to distinguish several. The best informed watchmaker of the history of his art would be struck dumb, if he were asked in general terms, who was the inventor of watches? Though the question would not embarrass him much, if it referred separately to the moving power, to the various forms of escapement, or to the balance. And so it is with the steam-engine; it now presents the realization of several capital ideas, but each quite distinct, that could not have proceeded from one and the same source, and of which it is our duty carefully to seek out the origin and date.

If having made any use whatever of steam, as it has been asserted, gave a right to figure in its history, we ought to quote the Arabs in the first place; because from time immemorial, their principal food, the flour of maize, which they call *couscoussou*,* has been cooked by steam in cullenders placed over rustic boilers. Such an instance suffices to show up the ludicrous nature of the principle whence it results.

Our countryman Gerbert, the same who wore the tiara as Sylvester II., does he acquire more real claims when, about the middle of the ninth century, he made the tubes of an organ in the Cathedral of Rheims resound by means of steam from water? I think not; in the embryo Pope's instruments I perceive a current of steam substituted for a current of common air, to produce the usual musical phenomenon from the organ pipes; but by no means a mechanical effect, properly so called.

The first example of motion generated by steam is to be found in a toy still older than Gerbert's organ; in an eolipyle by Hero of Alexandria, the date of which is as far back as 120 B. C. Perhaps it may be difficult, not

* This *kùskùs*, or *cuscasou*, is a very nutritious dish; it consists of corn paste crumbled and put into an earthen cullender over a boiling pot in which meat or fowls, with ochra (*pisum ochrus*) and other vegetables, are stewing; and which is luted or stopped close round the junction. The contents of the cullender are therefore dressed by steam. How ancient this mode of cooking may be we know not, but the Arabs only go back to the flight in A.D. 622; about which time, as tradition has it, it was invented by Mahomet when his health required wholesome and savoury food.— *Translator*.

possessing any figure, to give a clear idea of the mode of action in this little apparatus; still I will attempt it.

When gas escapes in a certain direction from the vase in which it is contained, this vase by means of reaction will be inclined to move in a diametrically opposite direction. The recoil of a gun loaded with gunpowder is a similar agency; the gas engendered by the combustion of the saltpetre, the charcoal, and the sulphur, rushes into the air according to the direction of the gun; the reaction, produced in the rear, reaches the shoulder of the person who fires it; it is on the shoulder then that the recoil must act. To change the direction of the recoil, it would suffice to make the jet of gas issue in another direction. If the gun were closed at the end, and were pierced only by a lateral opening horizontally perpendicular to its direction, the gas from the powder would escape laterally and horizontally; therefore the recoil would act perpendicularly to the direction of the gun; and its force would be exerted on the arms and not on the shoulder. In the former instance, the recoil pushed the man who fired from the front to the rear, as if to upset him; in the second instance it would tend to turn him round on his own axis. Let the gun then be invariably fixed, and horizontally, to a vertical movable axis, and at the instant of being fired, it will alter its direction more or less, and it will also make the axis turn.

Continuing the same arrangements, let us suppose the rotatory vertical axis to be hollow, but closed at its upper end; let it rise from the base as a sort of chimney from the caldron where gas is engendered; let there be besides a free lateral communication between the interior of this axis and the interior of the gun's barrel, so that, after having filled the interior of the axis, the steam enters the gun barrel, and issues by the lateral horizontal opening. Except as to intensity, this steam in escaping will act like the gases disengaged from the powder in the barrel of the gun when closed at the end, and pierced laterally; only, we should not have but a mere shock as occurred in the instance of the sudden and harsh explosion from the gun; on the contrary, the rotatory motion will be uniform and continuous, like the cause which engenders it.

Instead of only one gun, or rather instead of merely one horizontal tube, let several be adapted to the vertical rotatory tube, and we shall have, with the exception of some slight differences, the ingenious apparatus of Hero of Alexandria.

Here we should, doubtless, have a machine in which the steam of water creates motion, and may produce mechanical effects of some importance; it would be truly a steam-engine. But let us hasten to add that it would have no real point of contact, either in its shape, or the moving power's mode of action, with the machines of that kind now in use. If ever the reaction of a current of steam becomes practically useful, we must, without hesitation, refer the idea back to Hero; though at present the rotatory eolipyle can only be quoted here as carving on wood is cited in the history of printing.*

* These reflections are applicable also to the project that Branca, an Italian architect, published at Rome, in 1629, in a work entitled *Le Machine*, and which consisted in generating a rotatory movement by directing the steam issuing out of an eolipyle as breathings, or in a current, or on the pallets of a wheel. If, contrary to all probability, steam is some day usefully employed in the simple form of blowing, Branca, or the author, now unknown, from whom he may have borrowed the idea, will take the first rank in the history of this new species of machines. Relative to the machines of the present day, the claims of Branca would be quite null.

HISTORY OF THE STEAM-ENGINE IN RECENT TIMES.

In our manufacturing machines, in our packet-boats, in our railways, the motion results directly from the *elasticity* of steam. It is therefore of importance to seek where and how the idea of this power first arose.

Neither the Greeks nor the Romans were ignorant that the steam of water can acquire a prodigious mechanical power. They already explained, by the aid of the sudden evaporation of a certain quantity of this fluid, the frightful earthquakes which in a few seconds hurl the ocean beyond its natural limits; which overturned from their very foundations the most solid monuments of human labour; which suddenly create dangerous rocks in the midst of deep seas; and which heave up high mountains in the very centre of continents.

Whatever may be said of it, this theory of earthquakes does not show that its authors had devoted themselves to appreciations, to experiments, to exact measurements. No one now ignores that at the moment when the incandescent metal flows into the founder's moulds of earth or plaster, a few drops of any fluid contained in them would suffice to occasion dangerous explosions. Notwithstanding the progress of science, modern founders do not always avoid such accidents; how then could the ancients entirely keep clear of them? Whilst they cast thousands of statues, splendid ornaments of their temples, of their public places, of their gardens, of the private dwellings of Athens and of Rome, misfortunes must have occurred; the artisans discovered the immediate cause; the philosophers, on the other hand, following out the spirit of generalization, which was the characteristic of their schools, saw in them miniatures, or true images, of Etna's eruptions.

All this may be true, without having the least importance in the history that now occupies us. I have not even insisted, I acknowledge, so much on these slight lineaments of ancient science relative to the power of steam, but in order to live at peace, if possible, with the Daciers of both sexes, with the Dutens of our own epoch.*

Both natural and artificial powers, before becoming really subservient to the use of man, have almost always been adopted for objects of superstition. Nor will the steam of water be an exception to the general rule.

The chronicles informed us that on the banks of the Weser, the god of the ancient Teutones sometimes indicated his displeasure to them by a sort of thunder-clap, which was immediately followed by a cloud that filled the sacred area. The image of their god Bustérich, found, it is said, in some excavations, clearly reveals the way in which the pretended prodigy was obtained.

The statue was of metal. The hollow head contained an amphora of water. Wooden plugs closed the mouth and a hole above the forehead. Some charcoal, adroitly placed in the cavity of the cranium, gradually warmed

* For the same reason, I cannot dispense with here relating an anecdote, which, notwithstanding its romantic style, and containing what we now know to be contrary to the way in which steam acts, still shows the high opinion that the ancients had formed of this mechanical agent. It is related that Anthemius, Justinian's architect, occupied a house next door to that of Zeno, and to annoy that orator, who was his declared enemy, he placed in the ground floor of his own house several cauldrons containing water; that from an opening made in the lid of each of these there proceeded a flexible tube, which was conducted into the party-wall and up to the beams that supported the floors in Zeno's house; in short, that those floors heaved as if there had been a violent earthquake, as soon as fire was applied to the boilers.

the fluid. Soon the steam that was generated made the tompions fly out with a great report; then it escaped in two violent jets, and formed a thick cloud between the god and his stupefied worshippers. It would appear that in the middle ages some monks thought the invention a good prize, and that the head of Bustérich has not acted before assembled Teutones only.*

In order to meet with useful notions on the properties of steam, after the first glimpses given by the Greek philosophers, we are obliged to pass over an interval of twenty centuries. It is true that then some precise, conclusive, and irresistible experiments follow upon conjectures devoid of proofs.

In 1605, Flurence Rivault, gentleman of the bed-chamber to Henry IV., and preceptor to Louis XIII., discovers, for example, that a shell or bomb, if made thick and containing water, when placed on the fire after *being well closed*, (so as to prevent the steam from expanding freely in the air in proportion as it is generated, will sooner or later explode. The power of steam is here found characterized by a clear and, to a certain degree, sensitive proof, with numerical appreciations; but it is still presented to us as a terrible means of destruction.†

* Hero of Alexandria attributed the sounds, the objects of so much controversy, issuing from the statue of Memnon when the rays of the rising sun shone upon it, to the passage, through certain openings, of a current of steam that the solar heat was deemed to have produced at the expense of the fluid with which the Egyptian priests, it is said, provided the interior of the pedestal of the Colossus. Solomon de Caus, Kircher, &c., have gone so far as to wish to discover the special arrangements by which the theocratic fraud took possession of credulous imaginations; but all these suppositions lead us to think that they have not guessed right, even if there be, in this respect, any thing to guess.

† If any learned man were to think that by stopping at Flurence

Some eminent minds did not stop short at this meagre reflection. They conceived that mechanical forces, as well as human passions, must become useful or injurious, according as they are well or ill directed. In the special instance of steam, the simplest arrangement suffices to adapt this redoubtable elastic power to productive labour; which, according to all appearances, shakes the earth from its very foundations, which surrounds the furnace of the statuary with real dangers, and which shatters the thickest bomb into a hundred fragments!

In what state does this projectile exist before its explosion? The lower part contains some very hot water, *but still fluid;* the rest of the cavity is filled with steam. This steam, it being the characteristic trait of all gaseous substances, exerts its action equally in every direction: it presses with similar intensity on the water and on the metallic envelope that contains it. Let us apply a tap to the lower part of the bomb. As soon as it is open, the water, being urged by the steam, will rush out with extreme swiftness. If the tap opens into a tube, which, after curving round the exterior of the shell, rises up vertically, the water, being forced to change its course, will rise up in the tube in proportion to the elasticity of the steam; or, for it is the same thing though in other words,

Rivault I have not gone back far enough; if he were to borrow a quotation from Alberti, who wrote in 1411; if, according to that author, he were to tell us that from the beginning of the fifteenth century, the lime-burners feared much for themselves and their kilns, from the explosion of pieces of limestone fortuitously containing some cavities, I should answer that Alberti himself was ignorant of the real cause of those terrible explosions, for he attributed them to the *air* in the small cavities being transformed into *steam* by the action of flame. I must remark, in conclusion, that a piece of limestone, accidentally hollow, would not have afforded the means of numerical appreciation of which Rivault's experiment seems susceptible.

the water will rise in proportion to its temperature. The only limits of the ascending movement will be the resistance of the walls of the apparatus.

For our bomb let us substitute a thick metal caldron, of vast capacity, and nothing will prevent our carrying large quantities of fluid to indefinite heights by the simple action of steam; we shall have constructed, in the full meaning of the word, a steam-engine capable of emptying or exhausting.

You now know the invention which France and England have disputed upon, as formerly seven towns of Greece claimed respectively the honour of having been the cradle of Homer. On the other side of the Channel the honour is assigned to the Marquis of Worcester, of the illustrious house of Somerset. On this side of the Straits, we feel that it belongs to a humble engineer,* almost entirely forgotten in biographical works; to Solomon de Caus, born at Dieppe, or in its environs. Let us cast an impartial glance on the claims of these two competitors.

Worcester, deeply implicated in the political intrigues of the latter years of the reigns of the Stuarts, was confined in the tower of London.

"Que faire en pareil gîte, à moins que l'on ne songe?"
What could we do in such a bed but dream?

* The term "un humble ingénieur" is hardly applicable, for De Caus was, before the year 1612, engineer and architect to Louis XIII., King of France; he then entered the service of the Elector Palatine, who married the daughter of James I., with whom he came to England, and was employed by the Prince of Wales in ornamenting Richmond Gardens. His work was entitled *Les Raisons des Forces Mouvantes, avec diverses Machines tant utiles que plaisantes.* In Partington's Lectures on the Steam Engine, he quotes a book by *Isaac* De Caus, "natif de Dieppe;" it is named *Nouvelle Invention de lever l' Eau plus haut que sa source, avec quelques Machines mouvantes par le moyen de l'Eau;* it is a folio volume without date or place.—*Translator.*

Now one day, according to tradition, the lid of the saucepan, in which his dinner was being cooked, suddenly rose. Worcester then considered the strangeness of the phenomenon that he had just witnessed. The thought now occurred to him that the same power which had raised the lid might become, under certain circumstances, a useful and convenient motive power. After recovering his liberty, he described, in 1663, in a book entitled *Century of Inventions*,* the means by which he intended to realize his idea. The essential part of these means, as far at least as they can be understood, is the bomb half filled with a fluid, and the vertically ascending tube, as we just now described.

This bomb, this same tube, are drawn in the *Reason of Moving Forces*, a work by Solomon de Caus. There, the idea is presented clearly, simply, and without any pretension. Its origin has nothing romantic in it; it is not connected with the events of civil war, nor with a celebrated state prison, nor even with the rising of the lid of a prisoner's saucepan; but, what is of infinitely more importance in a question of priority, it is, by its publication, forty-eight years older than the *Century of Inventions*, and forty-one years anterior to Worcester's imprisonment.

Thus reduced to a comparison of dates, the debate seemed to be brought to a close. Indeed, how maintain that 1615 had not preceded 1663? But those persons whose principal aim was to expel any French name from this important chapter of the history of the sciences, immediately changed their ground, as soon as they had

* It is expressly stated on the title-page of this pamphlet, that it was written in the year 1655, though not published till 1663.—*Translator*.

occasioned the *Reasons of Moving Forces* to be disinterred from their dusty shelves. Without hesitation they pulled down their former idol; the Marquis of Worcester was sacrificed to the desire of annulling the claims of Solomon de Caus; the bomb placed on a burning brazier with its ascending tube, ceased at last to be the true germ of the present steam-engine!*

As to myself, I do not grant that the man was of no utility who, reflecting on the enormous elasticity of steam when greatly heated, was the first to perceive that it might be used to raise great quantities of water to all imaginable heights. I cannot admit that no mention is due of the engineer who was also the first to describe a machine adapted to realizing such effects. Let us not forget that we cannot judge soundly of the merit of an invention, without transferring ourselves in imagination to the epoch in which it was made; without expelling from our mind for the time all the knowledge that subsequent centuries have poured in upon us. Let us imagine an ancient mechanic, Archimedes, for example, consulted on the means of raising the water contained in a vast, closed, metallic recipient, to a great height. He would certainly speak of great levers, of single or multiplied pulleys, of a windlass, perhaps of his ingenious screw; but what would be his surprise if to solve the problem some one would be content with a fagot and a match?

* In *Les Raisons des Forces Mouvantes*, it is evident that De Caus ascribes the force which shivered the shell entirely to the air; and he seems to consider that the force of the air proceeded from the water which exhaled in it. M. Arago cannot be borne out in saying, of those who do not arrive at his conclusions, that "*d'écarter tout nom Français*" was their principal thought. We know not to whom he alludes in assigning such a base motive, but the assertion infringes greatly on the impartiality which he promised us.—*Translator*.

Well, I must ask, should we dare to refuse the epithet of invention to a proceeding at which the immortal author of the earliest and true principles of statics and hydrostatics would have been astonished? The apparatus of Solomon de Caus, that metallic envelop in which an almost indefinite motive power is created by the aid of a fagot and a match, will always figure nobly in the history of the steam-engine.*

It is very doubtful whether Solomon de Caus, or Worcester ever had their apparatus made. This honour belongs to an Englishman,† to Captain Savery.‡. I compare

* It has been printed that G. B. Porta had given in his *Spiritali*, in 1606, nine or ten years before the publication of Solomon de Caus's work, the description of a machine intended to raise water by means of the elastic power of steam. I have elsewhere shown that the learned Neapolitan does *not speak, either directly or indirectly, of a machine* in the passage alluded to; that his aim, that his only aim, was to determine experimentally the relative volumes of water and of steam; that in the small physical apparatus employed for this purpose, according to the very words of the author, the steam could not raise the water more than a few centimetres (some inches); that in the whole description of the experiment, there is not a single word implying the idea that Porta knew the power of this agent, and the possibility of applying it to the production of a useful machine.

Is it thought that I ought to have quoted Porta, at least on account of his researches on the transformation of water into steam? But I should then say that the phenomenon had already been studied with attention by Professor Besson of Orleans, about the middle of the sixteenth century, and that one of the treatises of that mechanic in 1569, contains a special essay on determining the relative volumes of water and steam.

† Bonnain says that, after Kircher's death, a model was found in his museum of a machine which that enthusiastic writer had described in 1656, and which differed from that of Solomon de Caus only in one respect—the motive steam was engendered in a vessel totally distinct from that containing the water to be elevated.

‡ Thomas Savery was a sailor, but, not being in the Royal Navy, is styled Esquire Savery in the Royal Society correspondence. Nor is our author quite right in supposing this was the first engine. The

the machine constructed by that engineer in 1698, to that of his predecessors, although he introduced some essential modifications into it; that, amongst others, of generating the steam in a separate vessel. Although it may signify little relative to principle whether the steam be generated from the same water that is to be elevated and in the same caldron where it is to act, or from a separate vessel to be admitted at will through a tube of communication furnished with a tap above the fluid that is to be expelled, it is not so in practice. Another alteration, still more useful and worthy of special mention, equally due to Savery, will be more appropriately treated of in the article that we shall devote in the sequel to the labours of Papin and Newcomen.

Savery had entitled his work *The Miner's Friend.* But the miners did not show themselves sensible of his politeness. With only one exception, none of them ordered his machine. They have been used only to distribute water through various parts of palaces and country houses, parks and gardens; recourse has been had to them only to overcome a difference of levels of twelve or fifteen metres. We must keep in mind, however, that the danger of explosion would have been very great, if the immense power had been given to this apparatus that the inventor asserted they could bear.

Marquis of Worcester did actually make an "apparatus" to *drive water up by fire;* and Cosmo de Medici, Grand Duke of Tuscany, describes in his *Diary* that he saw it in operation at Vauxhall, in the year 1656,—"went beyond the palace of the Archbishop of Canterbury, to see an hydraulic machine invented by my Lord Somerset, Marquis of Worcester. It raises water more than forty geometrical feet by the power of one man only; and in a very short space of time will draw up four vessels of water through a tube or channel not more than a span in width." Savery's engine was an improvement upon this by the introduction of a vacuum.—*Translator.*

Notwithstanding the incompleteness of Savary's practical success, this engineer's name deserves to hold a very distinguished place in the history of the steam-engine. Those persons whose life has been devoted to speculative exertions, are little aware of the distance there is between the project, apparently the most studied, and its realization. Not that I presume to say, with a celebrated German Professor, that Nature always exclaims *no, no!* when we wish to raise a corner of the veil with which she covers herself; but, in following up the same metaphor, it may be permitted to assert that the enterprise increases in difficulty, in delicacy, and in uncertainty, in proportion as it requires the united efforts of more artists, and the employment of more material elements; in these various respects, and considering the nature of the epoch, no one can have felt himself more unfavourably situated than Savery.

MODERN STEAM-ENGINE.

I have spoken hitherto of steam-engines, the resemblance of which to those that now bear that name may be more or less contested. We shall now treat of the *modern steam-engine*, of that which is in use in our manufactories, in our boats, at the entrance of nearly all our wells and mines. We shall see it created, then enlarge and develop itself, sometimes by the inspiration of clever men, sometimes by the prickings of necessity, for necessity is the mother of genius.

The first name that we shall meet in this new period is that of Denis Papin. It is to Papin that France will owe the honourable rank that she may claim in the history of the steam-engine. Still the highly legitimate pride, which these successes inspire us with, will not be unmixed. We shall find the claims of our countrymen nowhere but in foreign collections; his principal works will be published beyond the Rhine; his liberty will be menaced by the revocation of the edict of Nantes; it will be in a painful exile that he will temporarily enjoy that privilege of which studious men are most jealous, tranquillity of mind. Let us hasten to throw a veil over the deplorable results of our civil discords; let us forget that fanaticism was attached to the religious opinions of the physicist of Blois and return to mechanics; in this respect at least the orthodoxy of Papin has never been disputed.

There are two things to be considered in every machine; on one hand the moving power, on the other the arrangement, more or less complicated, of the fixed and movable parts, and by the aid of which the moving power transmits its action to the resistance. At the height to which mechanical knowledge has now attained, the success of a machine intended to produce great effects, depends chiefly on the moving power, on the way of applying it, and economizing its action. And therefore it was to produce an economical moving power capable of making the piston of a large cylinder oscillate constantly, that Papin devoted his life. Then to obtain from the oscillations of the piston the power required to turn the stones of a corn mill, the cylinders of a flatting mill, the paddle-wheels of a steamboat, the bobbins of a spinning mill: to raise the heavy hammer that strikes with redoubled blows enormous masses of incandescent iron, on its coming out of the reverberating furnace; to cut thick bars of metal with the two jaws of the shears, as we cut ribbon with sharp scissors: those are, I repeat it, so many problems of a very secondary order, and that would not puzzle the commonest engineers. We may employ ourselves, therefore, exclusively with the means by the aid of which Papin proposed to induce his oscillating motion.

Let us imagine a large vertical cylinder, open at top, and its base resting on a metallic table, pierced with a hole that a cock can either close or open at will.

Introduce a piston into this cylinder, that is to say, a circular plate, filling it entirely but movable, that shall exactly close it. The atmosphere will rest with all its weight on the upper surface of this species of diaphragm, and will push it from the top to the bottom. The portion of atmosphere that occupies the lower part of the cylinder will tend, by reaction, to produce an inverse movement. This second force will be equal to the first if the tap is open, because gas presses equally in all directions. The piston will thus find itself urged by two opposite forces, which will equalize each other. It will descend, however, though only by reason of its gravity. A counterpoise, slightly heavier than the piston, will suffice to raise it, on the contrary, up to the summit of the cylinder, and keep it there. Suppose the piston to have reached this extreme position. Let us seek the means to make it descend from thence *with great force*, and carry it up again.

Let us imagine after having shut the lower cock, we succeed in *suddenly* annihilating all the air contained in the cylinder,—in a word, to render it a vacuum. A vacuum once made, the piston not receiving any pressure but from the external atmosphere which presses it from above, *will descend rapidly*. On this movement being achieved, the cock will be opened. The air will thereby return underneath to counterbalance the upper atmosphere. As at the beginning, the counterpoise will make the piston remount to the cylinder, and all the various parts of the apparatus will be found in their initial state. A second evacuation, or, if we like it better, a second annihilation of the internal air, will again make the piston fall, and so on.

The true moving power in this arrangement would be the weight of the atmosphere. Let us hasten to undeceive those who would think that they found in the facility with which we walk, and even run through the air, an index of the weakness of this motive power. With a cylinder of two metres in diameter, the effort made by the piston of the pump in descending, the weight that it could raise to an equal height with the cylinder at each of these oscillations, would be 35,000 kilograms. This enormous power, frequently renewed, may be obtained by a very simple apparatus, if we discover a prompt and economical method of alternately generating and destroying the atmospheric pressure at will, in a metal cylinder.

This problem was solved by Papin. Its beautiful and great solution consists in substituting an atmosphere of steam for the common atmosphere; by replacing the latter with a gas which at 100 centigrade degrees has exactly the same elastic force, but with the important advantage, not possessed by the atmosphere, that the power of aqueous gas is very soon destroyed on its temperature being lowered, that it ends by almost entirely disappearing if sufficiently cooled. I should equally well characterize Papin's discovery, and in few words, if I said, that he proposed to use the steam of water to make a vacuum in large spaces; and that this is besides a prompt and economical method.*

* An English engineer, deceived no doubt by some imperfect translation, asserted not long since that the idea of employing the steam of

The machine in which our countryman was the first to combine the elastic force of steam with the property possessed by this vapour of annihilating itself by cooling, he never made on a large scale. His experiments were always made with simple models. The water intended to generate the steam was not even contained in a separate vessel; enclosed in the cylinder, it rested on the metal plate that closed the orifice at the bottom. It was this plate that Papin heated directly, to transform the water into steam; it was from the same plate that he took away the fire when he wished for condensation to be effected. Such a proceeding, barely allowable in an experiment intended to verify the correctness of a principle, would evidently be still less admissible if the piston were required to move with some celerity. Papin, whilst saying that success might be attained " by various constructions easy to imagine," does not indicate any of them. He leaves to his successors both the merit of applying his fruitful idea, and that of inventing the details, which alone could ensure the success of the machine.

In our early researches respecting the employment of steam, we have had to quote—ancient philosophers of Greece and Rome; one of the most celebrated mechanics of the Alexandrian school; a pope; a gentleman of the court of Henri IV.; a hydraulist, born in Normandy (in that province fruitful in great men, that has enriched the national Pleiad with Malherbe, Corneille, Poussin, Fontenelle, Laplace, and Fresnel); a member of the

water in one and the same machine, as an elastic power and as a rapid means of forming a vacuum, belonged to Hero. On my side I have proved, unanswerably, that the Alexandrian mechanic had never thought of steam; that in his apparatus the alternate movement was to result only from the dilatation and the condensation of air, arising from the intermittent action of the solar rays.

House of Lords; an English engineer; finally, a French doctor, of the Royal Society of London;* for, we must acknowledge it, Papin, almost always exiled, was only a correspondent of our Academy. Now, however, simple artisans, mere workmen, will enter the list. All classes of society will thus have concurred towards the creation of a machine by which the whole world was to benefit.

In 1705, fifteen years after the publication of Papin's first memoir in the *Acts of Leipzig*, Newcomen and Cawley, one of them a hardware man, the other a glazier at Dartmouth, in Devonshire, constructed (be pleased to observe that I did not say projected, for the difference is great), constructed a machine intended to effect drainage, and in which there was a separate caldron for generating the steam. This machine, as well as Papin's small model, has a vertical metal cylinder, closed at the bottom, open at the top, with a well-adjusted piston, intended to travel from end to end, both rising and falling. Both in the one apparatus and in the other, when the steam can freely reach the base of the cylinder, fill it, and thus counterbalance the pressure of the external atmosphere, the ascending movement of the piston is effected by a

* The ingenious Dr. Denis Papin was intimately connected with the Royal Society and its illustrious president, Newton, since he held the office of curator to that body, on a salary of forty pounds per annum. It is to be regretted that the funds of the Society, then, were so low that some of Papin's offered experiments seem to have hung fire, on account of the expenses amounting to fifteen pounds! Newton reported favourably on the proposal; and Papin said, "I am fully persuaded that Esquire Savery is so well-minded for the public good that he will desire, as much as anybody, that this may be done." It is a singular incident in the history of the wonderful engine, that though Papin invented the safety-valve, he did not apply it to his steam-machine.—*Translator*.

counterpoise. In the English machine, in short, in imitation of Papin's, as soon as the piston has reached its maximum of ascent, the steam that had tended to push it there is refrigerated; thus a vacuum is created throughout the space that the piston had traversed, and the external atmosphere forces it to descend again.

To obtain the requisite refrigeration, we already know that Papin contented himself with removing the chafing-dish that heated the base of the little metallic cylinder. Newcomen and Cawley had recourse to an arrangement far preferable in every respect: they poured an ample quantity of cold water into the circular space contained between the outer surface of the cylinder of their machine and the internal surface of a second rather larger cylinder, which served as an envelop to the first. The cold was gradually communicated through all the thickness of the metal, and lastly reached the steam itself.*

Papin's machine, thus perfected as to the manner of cooling or condensing the steam, excited the proprietors of mines to the highest pitch. It spread rapidly through several counties of England, and rendered great service. The slowness of its movements, the necessary consequence of the tardiness with which the steam cooled and lost its elasticity, was still a subject of great regret. Chance fortunately indicated a very simple way of obviating this impediment.

At the beginning of the eighteenth century the art of casting metallic cylinders, and of hermetically sealing

* Savery had already adopted throwing cold water on the *exterior surface* of a metal vase, to condense the steam within it. This was the origin of his partnership with Newcomen and Cawley; yet we must not forget that Savery's patent, his machines, and the work in which he describes them, are posterior by several years to Papin's memoirs.

them by means of movable pistons, was still in its infancy. Wherefore in Newcomen's early engines, the piston was covered with water intended to fill up the vacancies between the circumference of this movable piece and the surface of the cylinder. To the great surprise of the manufacturers, one of their engines began one day to oscillate much faster than usual. After many examinations it was ascertained that on that day the piston was pierced, that some cold water fell into the cylinder by little drops, and that by passing through the steam, they annihilated it rapidly. From this fortuitous incident may be dated the entire abandonment of all exterior refrigeration, and the adoption of a watering pot, to shed a *shower of cold water* throughout the capacity of the cylinder at the instant of the piston's descent. The alternate up and down motion now acquired all the desired swiftness.

But let us see whether there was not another equally important improvement effected also by chance.

Newcomen's first engine required the most uninterrupted attention from the person who had to open and shut the cocks either to introduce the steam into the cylinder, or to throw in the cold shower intended to condense it. It happened on a certain day that this person was young Henry Potter.* The companions of this child were then at play, and their exclamations of joy tantalize him severely. He longs to go and join them; but the task entrusted to him would not allow of half a minute's absence. His mind becomes excited; strong passion awakes his genius: he discovers relative connections of which he had never dreamt before. Of the

* The name of this play-loving and ingenious boy appears to have been *Humphrey* Potter.—*Translator*.

two taps, the one was to be opened at the moment when the beam, that Newcomen had been the first to introduce to such good purpose in his engines, had completed the descending oscillation, and it must be shut exactly at the opposite oscillation. The management of the second tap must be the exact contrary. The positions of the balance and of the taps are necessarily dependent on each other. Potter seizes on this fact: he perceives that the beam may impress on the other pieces all the motion that the play of the engine required, and instantly realizes his conception. Several cords are fastened to the handles of the taps; the opposite ends Potter ties to portions of the beam suitably selected; thus the purchase which this exercises on certain cords while rising, and those that it exercises on others in descending, supplant the manual efforts; for the first time the engine works by itself; for the first time no other workman is seen near it but the stoker, who from time to time goes to keep up the fire under the boiler.

For the cords of young Potter, the constructors soon substituted rigid vertical rods fixed to the beam and furnished with several pegs which pressed the heads of the several taps or valves either downwards or upwards. The rods themselves have been exchanged for other combinations; but however humiliating such an acknowledgment may be, all these inventions are mere modifications of the mechanism suggested to a child by the wish to join his little companions at play.

WATT'S LABOURS IN THE STEAM-ENGINE.

In physical cabinets we find a good many machines on which industry had founded great hopes, though the expense of their manufacture, or that of keeping them at work, has reduced them to be mere instruments of demonstration. This would have been the final fate of Newcomen's machine, in localities at least not rich in combustibles, if Watt's efforts, of which I must now present you with an analysis, had not come in to give it an unhoped-for degree of perfection. This perfection must not be considered as the result of some fortuitous observation, or of a single inspiration of genius; the inventor achieved it by assiduous labour, by experiments of extreme delicacy and correctness. One would say that Watt had adopted as his guide that celebrated maxim of Bacon's—"To write, speak, meditate, or act, when we are not sufficiently provided with *facts* to stake out our thoughts, is like navigating without a pilot along a coast strewed with dangers, or rushing out on the immense ocean without compass or rudder."

In the collection belonging to the University of Glasgow, there was a little model of a steam-engine by Newcomen that had never worked well. The Professor of Physics, Anderson, desired Watt to repair it. In the hands of this powerful workman the defects of its construction disappeared; from that time the apparatus was made to work annually under the inspection of the astonished students. A man of common mind would have rested satisfied with this success. Watt, on the contrary, as usual with him, saw cause in it for deep study. His researches were successively directed to all the points that appeared likely to clear up the theory of the machine. He ascertained the proportion in which water dilates in passing from a state of fluidity into that of vapour; the quantity of water that a certain weight of coal can convert into vapour; the quantity and weight of steam expended at each oscillation by one of Newcomen's engines of known dimensions; the quantity of cold water that must be injected into the cylinder to give a certain force to the piston's descending oscillation; and finally the elasticity of steam at various temperatures.

Here was enough to occupy the life of a laborious physicist, yet Watt found means to conduct all these numerous and difficult researches to a good termination, without the work of the shop suffering thereby. Dr. Cleland wished, not long since, to take me to the house, near the port of Glasgow, whither our associate retired on quitting his tools, to become an experimenter. It was razed to the ground! Our anger was keen but of short duration. Within the area, still visible of the foundations, ten or twelve vigorous workmen appeared to be occupied in sanctifying the cradle of modern steam-engines; they were hammering with redoubled blows various portions of boilers, the united dimensions of which certainly equalled those of the humble dwelling that had disappeared there. On such a spot, and under such circumstances, the most elegant mansion, the most sumptuous monument, the finest statue, would have awakened less reflection than those colossal boilers.

If the properties of steam are still present to your mind, you will perceive at a glance, that the economic working of Newcomen's engine seems to require two irreconcilable conditions. When the piston descends, the cylinder is required to be cold, otherwise it meets some steam there, still very elastic, which retards the operation very much, and diminishes the effect of the external atmosphere. Then, when steam at the temperature of 100° flows into that same cylinder and finds it cold, the steam restores its heat by becoming partially fluid, and until the cylinder has regained the temperature of 100°, its elasticity will be found considerably attenuated; thence will ensue slowness of motion, for the counterpoise will not raise the piston until there is sufficient spring contained in the cylinder to counterbalance the action of the atmosphere; thence there will also arise an increase of expense, for, as I have already said, the price of steam is very high. No doubt will remain on the immense importance of this economical consideration, when I shall have stated that the Glasgow model at each oscillation expended a volume of steam several times larger than that of the cylinder. The expense of steam, or, what comes to the same thing, the expense of fuel, or, if we like it better, the pecuniary cost of keeping on the working of the machine, would be several times less if the successive heatings and coolings, the inconveniences of which have just been described, could be avoided.

This apparently insolvable problem was solved by Watt in the most simple manner. It sufficed for him to add to the former arrangement of the engine a vessel totally distinct from the cylinder, and communicating with it only by a small tube furnished with a tap. This vessel, now known as *the condenser*, is Watt's principal invention. Notwithstanding my earnest wish to abridge, I feel that I must explain its mode of action.

If there be a free communication between a cylinder full of steam and a vessel containing neither steam nor air, the steam from the cylinder will partly and very rapidly pass into the empty vessel; the passage will only cease when the elasticity becomes equal in both. Let us suppose that by an abundant and constant injection of water, the whole capacity and the sides of the vessel be kept constantly cold, then the steam will condense as soon as it enters; all the steam which before filled the cylinder will be gradually annihilated; the cylinder will thus be cleared of steam without its sides being in the least cooled, and the fresh supply of steam, with which it will require to be filled, will not lose any of its elasticity.

The *condenser* attracts to itself all the steam contained in the cylinder, partly because it contains some cold water, and partly because is contains no elastic fluids; but as soon as some steam has been condensed, those two conditions on which success depended have disappeared; the condensing water has become hot by absorbing the latent caloric of the steam; a considerable portion of steam has been generated at the expense of that hot water; the cold water contained besides some atmospheric air which must have been disengaged during its heating. If this hot water was not carried away after each operation, together with the steam and the air contained in the condenser, in the end no effect would be produced. Watt, therefore, attains this triple purpose by the aid of a common pump, called an air-pump, and the piston of which carries a rod suitably attached to the beam worked by the engine. The power intended to keep the air-pump in motion, diminishes by that much the power of the engine; but it is only a small portion of the loss that was occasioned, in the old arrangement, by the steam being condensed on the refrigerated surface of the body of the engine.

Still another invention by Watt deserves a word, the advantages of which will become evident to everybody.

When the piston descends in Newcomen's engine, it is by the weight of the atmosphere. The atmosphere is cold, hence it must cool the sides of the metal cylinder, which is open at the top, in proportion as it expands itself over their entire surface. This cooling is not compensated during the whole ascension of the piston, without the expense of a certain quantity of steam. But there is no loss of this sort in the engines modified by Watt. The atmospheric action is totally eliminated by the following means:—

The top of the cylinder is closed by a metal cover, only pierced in the centre by a hole furnished with greased tow stuffed in hard, but through which the rod of the piston has free motion, though without allowing free passage either to air or steam. The piston thus divides the capacity of the cylinder into two distinct and well-closed areas. When it has to descend, the steam from the caldron reaches freely the upper area through a tube conveniently placed, and pushes it from top to bottom as the atmosphere did in Newcomen's engine. There is no obstacle to this motion, because whilst it is going on, only the base of the cylinder is in communication with the condenser, wherein all the steam from that lower area resumes its fluid state. As soon as the piston has quite reached the bottom, the mere turning of a tap suffices to bring the two areas of the cylinder, situated above and below the piston, into communication with each other, so that both shall be filled with steam of the same degree of elasticity, and the piston being thus equally acted upon, upwards and downwards, ascends again to the top of the cylinder, as in Newcomen's atmospheric engine, merely by the action of a slight counterpoise.

Pursuing his researches on the means of economizing steam, Watt also reduced the result of the refrigeration of the external surface of the cylinder containing the piston, almost to nothing. With this view he enclosed the metal cylinder in a wooden case of larger diameter, filling the intermediate annular space with steam.*

Now the engine was complete. The improvements effected by Watt are evident; there can be no doubt of their immense utility. As a means of drainage, then, you would expect to see them substituted for Newcomen's comparatively ruinous engines. Undeceive yourselves: the author of a discovery has always to contend against those whose interest may be injured, the obstinate partisans of every thing old, and finally, the envious. And these three classes united, I regret to acknowledge it, form the great majority of the public. In my calculation I even deduct those who are doubly influenced to avoid a paradoxical result. This compact mass of opponents can only be disunited and dissipated by time; yet time is insufficient, it must be attacked with spirit and unceasingly; our means of attack must be varied, imitating the chemist in this respect,—he learning from experience, that the entire solution of certain amalgams requires the successive application of several acids. Force of character and perseverance of will, which in the long run disintegrate the best woven intrigues, are not always found conjoined with creative genius. In case of need, Watt would be a convincing proof of this. His capital invention—his happy idea on the possibility

* It is the cylinder and piston that constitute the eminent virtue of the engine, the steam being only the *agent* employed to work the pump, so to speak. Every modification, therefore, which can promote the action of this most convenient and powerful agent is a crucial advantage. It is, therefore, that the vast improvements made by Watt —not only in working the piston-rod in the aperture of the stuffing-box, but also in promoting the uniform warmth of the cylinder by a jacket or outer casing—brought the steam-engine substantially to its present rank.—*Translator.*

of condensing steam in a vessel separate from the cylinder in which the mechanical action goes on—was in 1765. Two years elapsed without his scarcely making an effort to apply it on a large scale. His friends at last put him in communication with Dr. Roebuck, founder of the large works at Carron, still celebrated at the present day. The engineer and the man of projects enter into partnership; Watt cedes two thirds of his patent to him. An engine is constructed on the new principles: it confirms all the expectations of theory; its success is complete. But in the interim, Dr. Roebuck's affairs receive various checks. Watt's invention would undoubtedly have restored them: it would have sufficed to borrow money; but our associate felt more inclined to give up his discovery and change his business. In 1767, while Smeaton was carrying on some triangulations and levellings between the two rivers of the Forth and the Clyde, forerunners of the gigantic works of which that part of Scotland was to be the theatre, we find Watt occupied with similar operations along a rival line crossing the Lomond passage. Later, he draws the plan of a canal that was to bring coals from Monkland to Glasgow, and superintends the execution of it. Several projects of a similar nature, and, among others, that of a navigable canal across the Isthmus of Crinan, which Mr. Rennie afterwards finished; some deep studies on certain improvements in the ports of Ayr, Glasgow, and Greenock; the construction of the Hamilton and Rutherglen bridges; surveys of the ground through which the celebrated Caledonian Canal was to pass, occupied our associate up to the end of 1773. Without wishing at all to diminish the merit of these enterprises, I may be permitted to say that their interest and importance was chiefly local, and to assert that neither their conception, direction, nor execution required a man called James Watt.

If I were to forget my duties as the mouthpiece of the Academy, and endeavour more to make you smile than try to relate useful truths, I should find matter here for a striking contrast. I might cite this or that author who, at our weekly meetings, labours loudly to communicate some little remarks, some trifling reminiscence, some little note, conceived and got up the previous evening; I might represent him cursing his destiny, because some clause in the rules, or the order of insertion of some author, an earlier riser than himself, occasions his lecture to be deferred for a week, allowing him the guarantee, during the whole of that cruel week, of his *sealed paquet* being deposited in our archives. On the other hand, we should see the inventor of a machine destined to form an epoch in the annals of the world, undergo without a murmur the stupid contempt of capitalists, and during eight years bend his superior genius down to surveys, plans, and minute levellings; to troublesome items of clearing or filling in, and to toises of masonry. Let us confine ourselves to supposing that Watt's philosophy led to serenity of character, moderation in desires, to true modesty. But so much indifference, however noble the cause may have been, should have its just limit. It is not without ample motive that society severely reprobates those of its members who withdraw from circulation the heaps of gold contained in their iron chests. Are we less culpable if we deprive our country, our fellow-citizens, our century, of the treasures, a thousand times more precious, resulting from the exercise of mind; if we keep to ourselves immortal inventions, sources of the most noble, of the purest enjoyments of intellect; if we do not reward the creators of mechanical combinations, which would multiply the products of industry to infinity; who would weaken, to the benefit of civilization and humanity, the effect of the difference of position; who would some day allow the rudest manufactories to be examined without finding, in any part of them, the distressing spectacle of fathers of families and children of both sexes assimilated to brutes, advancing precipitately to their tombs?

In the early part of 1774, after contending with Watt's indifference, his friends put him into communication with Mr. Boulton, of Soho, near Birmingham; an enterprising active man, gifted with various talents.* The two

* In the notes which accompanied the last edition of Professor Robison's Essay on the Steam-engine, Watt expressed himself in the following terms relative to Mr. Boulton: "The friendship that he bore me ended only with his life. The friendship that I bore him leads me to feel it my duty to avail myself of this opportunity, the last, probably, that will be offered me, to say how much I was indebted to him. It is to the earnest encouragement held out to me by Mr. Boulton, to his taste for scientific discoveries, and to the sagacity with which he applied them to the progress of the arts; it is also to the intimate knowledge he possessed of manufacturing and commercial affairs, that I attribute, in great measure, the success with which my efforts have been crowned."

Mr. Boulton had already had a manufactory for several years at Soho, when the partnership began which has rendered his name so inseparable from that of Watt. This establishment, the first that had been formed on so large a scale in England, is still quoted for its elegant architecture. Boulton used to make there all sorts of work in steel, in plated articles, in silver, in *or moulu;* even to astronomical clocks, and paintings on glass. During the last twenty years of his life, Boulton occupied himself with improving the coining of money. By the combination of some operations invented in France, with new presses and an ingenious application of the steam-engine, he contrived to unite an exceeding rapidity of performance with perfection of work. It was Boulton who executed for the English Government the recoining of the whole copper currency in the United Kingdom.

friends applied to Parliament for a prolongation of privilege; since Watt's Patent, dated 1769, had only a few more years to run. The bill gave rise to the most animated discussion. The celebrated mechanic wrote as follows to his aged father: "This business could not be carried on without great expense and anxiety. Without the aid of some warm-hearted friends, we should not have succeeded, for several of the most powerful people in the House of Commons were opposed to us." It seemed to me interesting to search out to what class of society these Parliamentary persons belonged, to whom Watt alluded, and who refused to the man of genius a small portion of the riches that he was about to create. Judge of my surprise, when I found the celebrated Burke at their head! Is it possible then that men may devote themselves to deep studies, possess knowledge and probity, exercise to an eminent degree oratorical powers that move the feelings, and influence political assemblies, yet sometimes be deficient in plain common sense? Now, however, owing to the wise and important modifications introduced by Lord Brougham in the laws relative to patents, inventors will no longer have to undergo the annoyances with which Watt was teased.

As soon as Parliament had granted a prolongation of twenty-five years to Watt's patent, he and Boulton together began the establishments at Soho, which have

The economy and correctness of this great work rendered counterfeiting almost impossible. The numerous executions with which the towns of London and Birmingham had been annually afflicted till then, entirely ceased. It was on this occasion that Dr. Darwin exclaimed in his *Botanical Garden*, "If at Rome a civic crown was awarded to those who had saved the life of a single fellow-citizen, did not Boulton deserve to be covered with crowns of oak by us?"

Mr. Boulton died in 1809, at the age of eighty-one years.

become the most useful school in practical mechanics for all England. The construction of draining pumps of very large dimensions was soon undertaken there, and repeated experiments showed that, with equal effect, they saved three quarters of the fuel that was consumed by Newcomen's previous engines. From that moment the new pumps were spread through all the mining counties, especially in Cornwall. Boulton and Watt received as a duty the value of one third of the coal saved by each of their engines. We may form an opinion of the commercial importance of the invention from an authentic fact; in the Chace-water Mine alone, where three pumps were at work, the proprietors found it to their advantage to buy up the inventor's rights for the annual sum of 60,000 francs (£2,400). Thus in one establishment alone, the substitution of the *condenser* for internal injection, had occasioned an annual saving in fuel of upwards of 180,000 francs (£7,000).*

Men are easily reconciled to paying the rent of a house, or the price of a farm. But this good-will disappears when an *idea* is the subject treated of, whatever advantage, whatever profit, it may be the means of procuring. Ideas! are they not conceived without trouble or labour? Who can prove but that with time the same might not have occurred to everybody? In this way days, months, and years of priority would give no force to a patent!

Such opinions, which I need not here criticize, had obtained a footing from mere routine, as decided. Men

* Here it must be borne in mind that a principal method of insuring a return for their outlay, was their manufacturing steam-engines on the most extensive scale, with a degree of accuracy never before applied in the production of large machinery; and this was so fully accomplished, that all other engines were superseded.—*Translator.*

of genius, the *manufacturers of ideas*, it seemed, were to remain strangers to material enjoyments; it was natural that their history should continue to resemble a legend of martyrs!

Whatever may be thought of these reflections, it is certain that the Cornwall miners paid the dues that were granted to the Soho engineers with increased repugnance from year to year. They availed themselves of the very earliest difficulties raised by plagiarists, to claim release from all obligation. The discussion was serious; it might compromise the social position of our associate; he therefore bestowed his entire attention to it, and became a lawyer. The long and expensive lawsuits that resulted therefrom, but which they finally gained, would not deserve to be now exhumed; but having recently quoted Burke as one of the adversaries to our great mechanic, it appears only a just compensation here to mention that the Roys, Mylnes, Herschels, Delucs, Ramsdens, Robisons, Murdocks, Rennies, Cummings, Mores, Southerns, eagerly presented themselves before the magistrates, to maintain the rights of persecuted genius. It may be also advisable to add, as a curious trait in the history of the human mind, that the lawyers (I shall here prudently remark that we treat only of the lawyers of a neighbouring country), to whom malignity imputes a superabundant luxury in words, reproached Watt, against whom they had leagued in great numbers, for having invented nothing but ideas. This, I may remark in passing, brought upon them before the tribunal, the following apostrophe from Mr. Rous: * "Go,

* Mr. Rous, who acted as counsel for the patentees, published his speech in the form of a pamphlet. In the text we have reproduced the English from a version of M. Arago's French, an unsatisfactory

gentlemen, go and rub yourselves against those untangible combinations, as you are pleased to call Watt's engines—against those pretended abstract ideas; they will crush you like gnats, they will hurl you up in the air out of sight!"

The persecutions which a warm-hearted man meets with, in the quarters where strict justice would lead him to expect unanimous testimonies of gratitude, seldom fail to discourage, and to sour his disposition. Nor did Watt's good humour remain proof against such trials. Seven long years of lawsuits had excited in him such a sentiment of indignation, that it occasionally showed itself in severe expressions; thus he wrote to one of his friends:—"What I most detest in this world are plagiarists. The plagiarists! They have already cruelly assailed me; and if I had not an excellent memory, their impudent assertions would have ended by persuading me that I have made no improvement in steam-engines. The bad passions of those men to whom I have been most useful—would you believe it? have gone so far as to lead them to maintain that those improvements, instead of deserving this denomination, have been highly prejudicial to public wealth."

practice arising from necessity; for, in his full acquaintance with our writings, he is exuberant in quotations without always giving chapter and verse; and, moreover, many of the cited passages are from letters and other manuscript documents. In the instance before us, the keen satire of Rous was in asking the opposite party whether it could be seriously contended that Watt's invention, which, during the space of nearly thirty years, had been admired in all Europe as the greatest *practical* advance ever made in the *arts*, was a mere *abstract* discovery in *science*; and, he observed, that if those who thus pleaded were to approach the *untangible substance*, as they were pleased to call it, with the same ignorance of its nature that they thus affected, they would be crushed before it like flies, leaving no trace of their existence.—*Translator*.

Watt, though greatly irritated, was not discouraged. His engines were not, in the first place, like Newcomen's, mere pumps, mere draining pumps. In a few years he transformed them into universal motive powers, and of indefinite force. His first step in this line was the invention of a *double-acting engine* (*à double effet*).

To conceive the principle of it, let my report of the *modified engine* of which I have already treated (page 391,) be consulted. The cylinder is closed; the external air has no access to it; it is steam pressure, and not atmospheric, that makes the piston descend; the ascending movement is due to a simple counterpoise, because at the moment when this takes place, the steam, being enabled to circulate freely from the higher to the lower portions of the cylinder, presses equally on the piston in both directions. Every one will hence see, that the modified engine, or Newcomen's, has power only during the descending oscillation of the piston.

A very simple change remedied this serious defect, and produced the *double-acting engine.*

In the engine known under this name, as well as in the one which we denominated the modified engine, the steam from the boiler, when the mechanic wishes it, goes freely above the piston and presses it down without meeting any obstacle; because at that same moment, the lower area of the cylinder is in communication with the condenser. This movement once achieved, and a certain cock having been opened, the steam from the caldron can enter only below the piston, and elevates it; the steam above it, which had produced the descending movement, then goes to regain its fluid state in the condenser, with which it has become, in its turn, in free communication. The contrary arrangement of the cocks replaces all things in their primitive state, as soon as the piston has regained its maximum height. Thus similar effects are reproduced indefinitely.

The motive power is here, as explained above, exclusively steam; and the engine, except by the inequality arising from the weight of the piston, has the same power whether the piston be ascending or descending. This is the reason why, from the moment of its appearance it was justly called *a double-acting engine.*

To render this new motive power of easy and convenient application, Watt had to overcome other difficulties: it was requisite to find the means of establishing a *rigid communication* between the inflexible rod of the piston oscillating in a straight line and a beam that oscillated circularly. The solution which he gave of this important problem is perhaps his most ingenious invention.

Among the constituent parts of a steam-engine, you have, no doubt, remarked a certain articulated parallelogram. With each double oscillation it develops and contracts itself, with the smoothness of motion,—I had almost said with the grace,—that charms us in the gestures of a consummate actor. Follow attentively with your eye its various transformations, and you will find it subject to the most curious geometrical conditions; that *three* of the summits of the parallelogram's angles describe arcs of circles in space, whilst the *fourth,* the summit of the angle that raises and lowers the piston-rod, moves very nearly in a straight line. The immense utility of the result strikes mechanics less than the simplicity of means by which Watt obtained it.*

* We here give Watt's words in relating the experiment of this articulated parallelogram (*this beautiful arrangement is called parallel mo-*

Power is not the only element of success in industrial works. Regularity of action is not less important; but what regularity could be expected from a motive power engendered by fire fed by shovels full, and the coal itself of various qualities; and this under the direction of a workman, sometimes not very intelligent, almost always inattentive? The motive steam will be more abundant, it will flow more rapidly into the cylinder, it will make the piston work faster in proportion as the fire is more intense. Great inequalities of movement then appear to be inevitable. Watt's genius had to provide against this serious defect. The throttle-valves by which the steam issues from the boiler to enter the cylinder are not constantly open. When the working of the engine accelerates, these valves partly close; a certain volume of steam must therefore occupy a longer time in passing through them, and the acceleration ceases. The aperture of the valves, on the contrary, dilates when the motion slackens. The pieces requisite for the performance of these various changes connect the valves with the axes which the engine sets to work, by the introduc-

tion—Translator): "I was myself surprised at the regularity of its action. When I saw it work for the first time, I felt truly all the pleasure of novelty, as if I was examining *the invention of another man.*"

Smeaton, who was a great admirer of Watt, did not believe, however, that it could in practice become a general and economical means of impressing *directly* rotatory motion to axes. He maintained that steam-engines would always be more serviceable in pumping water direct. This fluid having reached a suitable height, was then to be thrown into the trough, or on to the pallets of common hydraulic wheels. In this respect the prophecies of Smeaton were not realized. Yet, in 1834, on visiting the establishment of Mr. Boulton at Soho, I saw an old steam-engine still employed to raise water from a large pool, and pour it into the troughs of a great hydraulic wheel, when the season being very dry the water-power was insufficient.

tion of an apparatus, the principle of which Watt discovered in the regulator of the sails of some flour-mills: this he named the *governor;* which is now called the *centrifugal regulator.* Its efficacy is such, that a few years ago in the cotton-spinning manufactory of a renowned mechanic, Mr. Lee, there was a clock set in motion by the engine of the establishment, and it showed no great inferiority to a common spring clock.

Watt's regulator, and an intelligent use of the revolving principle,—that is the secret, the true secret, of the astonishing perfection of the industrial products of our epoch; this is what now gives to the steam-engine a rate entirely free from jerks. That is the reason why it can, with equal success, embroider muslins and forge anchors, weave the most delicate webs and communicate a rapid movement to the heavy stones of a flour-mill. This also explains how Watt had said, fearless of being reproached for exaggeration, that to prevent the comings and goings of servants, he would be served, he would have gruel brought to him, in case of illness, by tablets connected with his steam-engine. I am aware it is supposed by the generality of people, that this suavity of motion is obtained only by a loss of power; but it is an error, a gross error: the saying, "much noise and little work," is true not only in the moral world, but is also an axiom in mechanics.

A few words more and we shall reach the end of our technical details.

Within these few years, great advantage has been found in not allowing a free access of steam from the boiler into the cylinder, during the *whole* time of each oscillation of the engine.* This communication is inter-

* This constituted Watt's celebrated expansion engine, so named

rupted, for example, when the piston has reached one third of its course. The two remaining thirds of the cylinder's length are then traversed by virtue of the acquired velocity, and especially by the *detention* of the steam. Watt had already indicated such an arrangement.* Some very good judges esteem the economical importance of the *steam-detent* as equal to that of the condenser. It seems certain that since its adoption, the Cornwall engines give unhoped-for results ; that with one bushel of coals they equal the labour of twenty men during ten hours. Let us keep in mind, that in the coal districts a bushel of coals only costs ninepence, and it will be demonstrated that over the greater part of England, Watt reduced the price of a man's day's work, a day of ten hours' labour, to *less than a sou (one half-penny,)* of our money.†

because the small portion of steam already admitted, then expanded till the piston had reached the end of the cylinder.—*Translator.*

* The principle of the steam detention had been neatly expressed in a letter from Watt to Dr. Small dated 1769, it was put in practice in 1776, at Soho, and also in 1778 at the *Shadwell water works*, from economical considerations. The invention, and the advantages expected from it, are fully described in the patent of 1782.

† At a moment when so many people are interested in direct rotation engines, I should be unpardonably neglectful if I did not say that Watt had both thought of them, as proved in his patents, and had made some. Watt abandoned those engines, not because they would not work, but because, in an economical point of view, they appeared to him decidedly inferior to the double-acting engines, and to those with rectilinear oscillations.

There are few inventions, large or small, amongst those of which the steam-engine offers us such an admirable assemblage, that have not been developed from some of Watt's early ideas. Follow up his labours, and besides the important points which we have minutely detailed, you will see him propose engines without condensation, engines in which the steam, after having acted, is allowed to escape into the open air, for those localities where it would be difficult to procure an abundance of cold water.

Numerical valuations make us appreciate so well the importance of his inventions, that I cannot resist the desire to present two more improvements. I borrow them from one of the most celebrated correspondents of the Academy, from Mr. John Herschel.

The ascent of Mont Blanc, starting from the valley of Chamouni, is justly considered as the hardest work that a man can accomplish in two days. Thus, the maximum mechanical work of which we are capable, in twice twenty-four hours, is measured by transporting the weight of our body to the elevation of Mont Blanc. This work, or its equivalent, would be accomplished by a steam-engine in the course of burning one kilogram of coal. Watt has, therefore, ascertained that the daily power of a man does not exceed what is contained in half a kilogram of coal (1 lb. Avs.).

Herodotus records that the construction of the great pyramid of Egypt employed one hundred thousand men during twenty years. The pyramid consists of calcareous

The detent intended to be used in engines having several cylinders, will also figure among the projects of the Soho engineer. He suggests the idea of perfectly water-tight pistons, though consisting entirely of pieces of metal. It was Watt also who first had recourse to mercurial gauges to appreciate the elasticity of the steam, both in the boiler and in the condenser; who imagined a simple and permanent gauge, by the aid of which, and at a glance, the height of the water in the boiler can be known; and who, to prevent this level from ever varying to an inconvenient extent, connected the movements of the feeding-pump with those of a float, which, when required, was placed in an opening of the lid of the engine's principal cylinder, forming a little *indicator*, so combined as to show exactly the law of the steam's consumption relative to the piston's position, &c. If time permitted, I would show Watt not less clever, or less fortunate, in his endeavours to improve the boilers, to diminish the loss of heat, and to burn completely the torrents of black smoke that escape from common chimneys, however high they may be carried.

stone; its volume and its weight can be easily calculated; its weight has been found to be about 5,900,000 kilograms (nearly 5000 tons).

To elevate this weight to thirty-eight metres, which is the pyramid's centre of gravity, it would require to burn 8,244 hectolitres of coal (cubic metres). Our neighbours have some foundries where they consume this quantity every week.

MACHINES CONSIDERED RELATIVE TO THEIR EFFECT ON THE WELFARE OF THE WORKING CLASSES.*

Many persons, without doubting the genius of Watt, look on the inventions for which the world is indebted to him, and on the impulse that they have given to industrial labours, as a social misfortune. If we believed them, the adoption of each new machine inevitably adds to the troubles and miseries of labourers. Those won-

* In writing this chapter it seemed to me that I might unscrupulously avail myself of many documents that I had collected, either in various conversations with my friend Lord Brougham, or works that he himself has published, or that have appeared under his patronage.

If I were to attend to the criticisms that have been printed after the reading of this Biography, by trying to combat the opinion that machines are injurious to the labouring classes, I should be attacking an old prejudice that has no longer any foundation, a mere phantom. I would not ask more than to be able to believe it, for then I would very willingly suppress all my arguments, bad or good. Unfortunately some letters frequently sent me by excellent workmen, either as an academician or as a deputy; unfortunately, moreover, the recent and *ex-professo* dissertations of several economists, leave me no doubt as to the necessity of still saying, of repeating in every shape, that machines have never been the true and permanent cause of the sufferings of one of the most numerous and most interesting of the classes of society; that their destruction would aggravate the present state of things; and that it is by no means in that direction that a remedy would be found for the evils which I warmly compassionate.

derful mechanical combinations that we are accustomed to admire for the regularity and harmony of their movements, for the power and delicacy of their effects, would be instruments of injury; the legislator ought to proscribe them with a just and implacable rigour.

Conscientious opinions, especially when they are connected with praiseworthy sentiments of philanthropy, have a claim to an attentive examination. I add, that on my part this is an imperious duty. I should have neglected, indeed, the argument by which the labours of our illustrious academician are shown to be most worthy of public estimation, if, far from acceding to the prejudices of certain minds against the improvement of machines, I did not point out such works to the attention of well-meaning men, as the most powerful, the most direct, the most efficacious means of rescuing workmen from cruel sufferings, and calling them to partake of a crowd of benefits, which seemed to be regarded as the exclusive appanage of riches.

When we have to select one of two diametrically opposite propositions; when the one being true, the other must be false, and when nothing seems at first sight to be able to dictate a rational choice, geometers seize on these contrary propositions; they follow up their details carefully through all their ramifications; they make their last logical results rise up: now the ill-stated proposition, and that one only, seldom fails to lead, by wire-drawing, to some results that a clear intellect could not admit. Let us try for a moment the method of examination that Euclid often uses, and which is so justly designated by the epithet of *mode of reducing to absurdity*.

The adversaries of machines would wish to annihilate them, or at least to restrain their propagation,—to reserve, say they, more employment for the working classes. Let us, for a moment, take up this position, and the anathema will be found to extend far beyond machines properly so called.

From the beginning we shall be led, for example, to tax our ancestors with great improvidence. If instead of founding, if instead of persevering in extending the city of Paris on the two banks of the Seine, they had established it in the middle of the plain of Villejuif, for centuries back the water-carriers would have formed the most occupied, the most numerous, the most important portion of the population. Well, Messrs. Economists, set to work in favour of the water-carriers. To make the Seine deviate from its course is not an impossibility; propose this undertaking; open a subscription immediately to leave Paris dry, and the general laugh will show you that the *mode of reducing to absurdity** has some good in it, even in political economy; and in their plain sense, the workmen themselves will tell you that the river has created the immense capital in which such resources are found; and that, without it, Paris would perhaps still be a Villejuif.

Good Parisians had hitherto congratulated themselves on the vicinity of those inexhaustible quarries where successive generations go to dig out materials for the construction of their temples, their palaces, their private dwellings. A mere illusion! The new political economy will prove to you that it would have been eminently advantageous if the plaster, the freestone, and rubble had

* This "méthode de réduction à l'absurde" is the *reductio ad absurdum*, or arguing *ex absurdo*, of logicians and mathematicians; in which the truth of a proposition is proved by showing that the contrary is unreasonable.—*Translator*.

been found only near Bourges for example. On this hypothesis, compute on your fingers the number of workmen that would have been required to bring to the site of the capital all the stone that during five centuries has been worked up by architects, and you will find a truly prodigious result: and however little the new ideas may smile upon you, you may go into ecstasies at your ease on the happiness that such a state of things would have shed on the proletaries.

Let us venture some doubts, although I know very well that the Vertots of our day perfectly resemble the Rhodian historian, *when their seat is made,* ("*quand leur siége est fait.*")

The capital of a powerful kingdom, not very distant from France, is traversed by a majestic river, which even men-of-war ascend under full sail. The surrounding country is furrowed in all directions by canals which carry heavy burdens at a very small freightage. A regular network of routes, admirably kept up, lead to all the most distant parts of that territory. To these gifts of nature and of art, this capital, which of course every one has already named, unites *an advantage* of which Paris is deprived; the quarries of building-stone are not at its gates, they lie at a distance. There then the Utopia of the new economists is realized. Will they not now count up by hundreds of thousands, perhaps by millions, the quarrymen, the boatmen, the carters, the labourers incessantly employed, digging out, carrying away, preparing the building-stone for the construction of the immense number of edifices with which that capital is annually enriched? We will leave them to count at their ease. There has happened in that city what would have happened in Paris if it had been devoid of its rich quarries;

stone being very dear, it is not used;* brick is the general substitute.

Millions of workmen are now executing, both on the surface of the earth and in its bowels, immense works which could not possibly be undertaken, if certain machines were proscribed. Two or three examples will suffice to render this truth palpable.

The carrying off the water that rises daily in the galleries of the Cornish mines alone, requires the power of 50,000 horses, or of 300,000 men. I ask you whether the pay of 300,000 workmen would not absorb all the benefit of the undertaking?

Does the question of the expense and the benefit appear to be too delicate? Other considerations will lead to the same result.

The working of one Cornish mine alone, comprised under the name of the *Consolidated Mines*, requires a steam-engine equal to upwards of three hundred horses constantly in harness, and each twenty-four hours it realizes the work of one thousand horses. Need I fear any contradiction if I assert that there are no means of making upwards of three hundred horses, or two thousand or three thousand men, labour simultaneously and to good purpose around the confined mouth of the shaft of a mine? To proscribe the steam-engine of the *Consolidated Mines* would be to reduce to inaction the great number of workmen that the engine renders it possible to employ there; it would be the same as declaring that the copper and tin of Cornwall shall remain buried there for ever, under a mass of earth, of rock, and of water several hundred meters in thickness. The thesis brought

* This is a very incorrect expression, and might mislead a Parisian *badaud.—Translator.*

into this last form will certainly have few defenders; but what signifies the form when the substance is evidently the same?

If from labours that require an immense development of power, we were to pass on to the examination of various industrial products, which, from the delicacy of their materials and the regularity of their forms, have been placed among the wonders of art, the insufficiency, the inferiority, of our organs compared with ingenious mechanical combinations, would equally strike all minds. Where is there, for instance, so clever a spinner as to draw a thread from one pound of cotton wool fifty-three leagues long, as is done by the machine called the *mule-jenny?*

I am not ignorant of what certain moralists have preached on the inutility of muslins and laces and gossamer net, in the weaving of which this fine thread is used; but it suffices for me to remark, that the most perfect mule-jenny spins under the constant inspection of a great many workpeople; that the only requisite they care for is, to manufacture goods that will sell; in short, that if luxury is an evil, a vice, or even a crime, it is the buyers who are to blame, and not the poor proletaries, whose existence, I believe, would be very uncertain if they themselves endeavoured to manufacture for the ladies woollen stuffs instead of fashionable *tulle.*

Now let us quit remarks on details, and dive down to the very bottom of the question.

Marcus Aurelius said: "We must not receive the opinions of our fathers as children would, for the mere reason that they were our fathers' opinions." This maxim, though assuredly a very just one, ought not to prevent us from thinking, or at least from presuming, that those opinions against which no criticism has ever been pronounced from the commencement of societies, are conformable to reason and to general advantage. Well, on the question so much debated, relative to the utility of machines, what was the unanimous opinion of antiquity? Its ingenious mythology will inform us; the founders of empires, the legislators, the conquerors of tyrants who oppressed their country, received the title of *demi-gods* only; but it was among the gods themselves that they placed the inventors of the spade, the sickle, and the plough.

I already hear our adversaries, on account of the extreme simplicity of the instruments that I have cited, boldly refuse them the name of machines, unwilling to regard them as any thing but *tools;* and ensconce themselves obstinately behind this distinction.

I might answer that such a distinction is puerile; that it would be impossible to say precisely where the tool ends and the machine begins; but it is better worth remarking that in the pleadings against machines nothing has ever been said of their greater or less complication. If they are repudiated, it is because with their aid one man can do the work that would otherwise require several men; now would any one dare to maintain that a knife, a gimblet, a file, a saw, do not confer great facility of operation on the hand that uses them; that the hand thus strengthened would not do the work of a great many hands armed only with their nails?

The workmen, seduced by the detestable theories of some of their pretended friends, did not stop at the sophisticated distinction between tools and machines; they wandered over certain counties of England, in 1830, vociferating the cry of *down with the machines!*

Rigorous logicians, they broke in the farms, the sickle intended to reap the corn, the flail that was to beat the corn, the sieve by the aid of which the corn is winnowed. And, in fact, are not the sickle, the flail, and the sieve means for shortening labour? The spade, the hoe, the plough, the seedsower, could not find grace in the eyes of this blinded horde; and if any thing surprises me, it is that in their fury they spared the horses, a sort of machine comparatively cheap to keep, and each of which could do daily as much work as six or seven men.

Political economy has fortunately obtained a place among the sciences of observation. The substitution of machines for animated beings has been so often tried during many years past, that people cannot hereafter but perceive the general results amidst some accidental irregularities. These results are as follows:

By sparing manual labour, machines enable us to manufacture at a cheaper rate; the effect of this cheapness in an increased demand, such an increased demand (so vivacious is our desire to be well off) that notwithstanding the most inconceivable lowering of price, the money value of the totality of the merchandise produced, surpasses each year what it was before the improvement; the number of workmen employed by each branch of industry increases with the introduction of means for manufacturing expeditiously.

This last result is exactly contrary to what is wished for by those who hate machines. At first sight it may appear paradoxical, yet we shall soon see it proved by a rapid examination of the most confirmed industrial facts.

When, three centuries and a half ago, the printing machine was invented, copyists used to furnish books to the very small number of rich men who could indulge in this expensive fancy. One of these copyists being able by the aid of the new proceeding to do the work of two hundred, there were not wanting men in that epoch who dubbed the new invention as *infernal*, as about to reduce to inaction, in a certain rank of society, nine hundred and ninety-five men out of one thousand. But let us now place the real result by the side of the sinister prediction.

Manuscript books were very little in demand; printed books, on the contrary, on account of their low price, were sought after with the most lively eagerness. It was found necessary incessantly to reproduce the Greek and Roman authors. New ideas, new opinions occasioned a multitude of new books to arise; some of eternal interest, others inspired by passing events. At last it was calculated that in London, before the invention of printing, the book trade employed only two hundred men, now they are counted by twenty thousand.

And how much more would it be if, laying aside the confined, and I might say material, point of view that I have had to select, we were to estimate printing by its moral and intellectual phases; if we were to examine the influence that it exerted on public manners, on the diffusion of public knowledge, on the progress of human reason; if we were to work out the enumeration of the many books for which we are indebted to printing, that the copyists would certainly have disdained, and in which genius yet goes daily gathering the elements of its fruitful conceptions? But I must keep in mind that at present we have only to treat of the number of workmen employed by each branch of industry.

That of cotton offers even more demonstrative results

than is done by printing. When Arkwright, an ingenious barber of Preston, (who, by the way, left each of his children two or three millions of francs of income,) rendered it both useful and profitable to substitute revolving cylinders for the fingers of the women who used to spin, the annual product of the cotton manufacture in England did not exceed 50,000,000 francs (2,000,000*l.*), now it exceeds 900,000,000 francs (36,000,000*l.*). In the county of Lancaster alone, they annually deliver to the calico manufacturers a quantity of yarn that 21,000,000 clever spinners could not accomplish with only the aid of the rock and spindle. Moreover, although in the art of spinning mechanical means have been pushed, we may say, to their utmost degree of perfection, 1,500,000 people now find occupation there, where, before the inventions of Arkwright and of Watt, there were only 50,000.*

A certain philosopher exclaimed, in a deep fit of despondency, "Nothing new is published in the present day, unless we call new that which has been forgotten." If the philosopher alluded only to errors and prejudices, he spoke truth. Time has been so fruitful in this line, that no one can any more claim priority. For example, the pretended modern philanthropists have not the merit (if there be any merit in it) of inventing the systems that I am examining. Rather look at that poor William Lea (*Lee*), working the first stocking-frame in the presence of James I. The mechanism appeared admirable; why was he repulsed? It was under the pre-

* Mr. Edward Baines, author of a much esteemed work on the British cotton manufactures, has had the whimsical curiosity to learn what length of thread is annually used in weaving the cotton manufactures. This entire length he finds to be equal to *fifty-one times the distance of the sun from the earth!* (fifty-one times thirty-nine millions of post leagues, or about two thousand millions of such leagues.)

text that the working class would suffer. France showed herself equally short-sighted: William Lea found no encouragement there, and he was reduced to die in a hospital; like so many other men of genius, who have had the misfortune of being too much a-head of their age!

Besides this, we should be very much mistaken if we supposed the body of knitters very numerous, to whom William Lea fell a victim. In 1583, it was only people of high rank and fortune who wore stockings. The middle class substituted for this portion of modern dress narrow stripes of variously coloured cloths. The rest of the population (nine hundred and ninety-nine out of a thousand) walked bare-legged. In consequence of the extremely low price of stockings in the present day, there is not above one man in a thousand who cannot afford to buy them. Hence an immense number of workmen, in every part of the world, is now employed in this branch of manufacture.*

If it be deemed necessary I will add, that at Stockport, the substitution of steam power for manual labour in weaving looms, has not prevented the workmen from increasing by one third in a few years.

We must now deprive our adversaries of their last re-

* This is certainly an epochal point of great interest in domestic manufacture. The bandaged stocking is of a very remote date, and is found in all the Saxon figures of our missals and monuments; it was in common use among the peasantry of Europe even during the fifteenth century. Henry VIII., it appears, wore silk stockings, and Queen Elizabeth refused to wear any others, whence they came into vogue. These seem to have been brought from abroad; but in 1564, William Rider, an apprentice on London Bridge, borrowed a pair of knit worsted stockings from Mantua, took the hint, and made a pair exactly like them, which he presented to the Earl of Pembroke. And these are the first pair of worsted stockings known to be knit in England: the prototype of millions upon millions.—*Translator.*

source; we must not leave them the power of saying that we have only cited *old* branches of industry. I will, therefore, now remark how much they were, not long since, deceived in their lugubrious forebodings relative to engraving on steel. A copper plate, they said, will not give above two thousand impressions. A steel plate, by yielding a hundred thousand without being worn, would replace fifty copper plates. Will not these numbers prove that the greater part of the former engravers (forty-nine out of fifty) will feel obliged to abandon their profession, to change their graver for the trowel or the hoe, or beg charity in the public streets?

For the twentieth time, prophets of evil, be pleased not to forget in your lucubrations, the principal element of the problem which you undertake to solve! Think of the insatiable desire to be well off, that Nature has implanted in the human heart; remember that one wish is no sooner satisfied, than it immediately gives rise to another wish; that our appetites of every sort increase with the cheapness of the objects adapted for their indulgence, and to a degree that defies the creative powers of the most powerful machines.

But to return to the engravings. An immense majority of the public did without them when they were dear; their price decreases, and all the world seeks for them. They have become the necessary ornament of the best books; to middling books they give some chance of sale. There are no almanacs even now, but what the old hideous figures of Nostradamus, by Matthew Laensberg, are replaced by picturesque views which, in a few seconds, transport our immovable citizens from the shores of the Ganges to those of the Amazon, from the Himalayas to the Cordilleras, from Pekin to New York. Look also at those engravers, whose ruin was so piteously announced to us; never were they either more numerous or more occupied.

I am going to bring forward some irrefragable facts. They will render it impossible, I think, to maintain that among the inhabitants of this earth, such, at least, as Nature has created, the use of machines can bring on the result of a diminution of the number of workmen employed in each sort of industry. Other customs, other habits, other passions, might, perhaps, have led to an entirely different result; but I leave such a text to those who may be tempted to write treatises on political economy for the use of the inhabitants of the Moon, or of Jupiter, or of Saturn.

Placed in a much more confined theatre, I ask myself whether, after having sapped the very foundations of the system maintained by the adversaries of machines, it can be still requisite to cast a glance at some criticisms of detail. Need we remark, for example, that the poor's rate, that bleeding wound in the British nation, that wound which some people pretend to trace to the abuse of machines, dates from the reign of Elizabeth, from a period anterior by two centuries to the labours of Arkwright and of Watt?

You will at least acknowledge, they say to us, that the fire-machines, the mule-jennies, that the machines used for carding, for printing, &c., objects of your predilection, have not prevented pauperism from increasing and propagating itself. This fresh avowal will cost me but little. Did any one recommend machines as a universal panacea? Was it ever maintained that they would have the unheard-of property of discarding error and passion from political assemblies? that they would direct the counsellors of princes to the paths of wisdom, of moderation, of humanity? Was it ever pretended that they would turn Pitt from unceasingly meddling in the affairs of neighbouring countries? from annually raising enemies to France in every part of Europe?* from paying them large subsidies, in short, from loading England with a debt of many hundred millions? There, there is the reason why the poor's-rate has increased so fast, and so prodigiously. Machines have not, and could not, produce this evil. I dare even assert that they much diminish it; and I will prove it in a few words. The county of Lancashire carries on more manufactures than any other in England. It is there that we find the cities of Manchester, Preston, Bolton, Warrington, and Liverpool; it is in that county that machines were most quickly and most generally introduced. Well, let us distribute the entire annual amount of the poor-rates of Lancashire among the whole of its population; in other words, let us learn what would be the quotient for each individual; and we shall find a result nearly three times smaller than the mean of all the other counties! You see, numbers are pitiless towards the inventors of theories.

Moreover, let not these large words of poor-rates make us believe, on the faith of some declaimers, that the labouring classes among our neighbours are entirely devoid of

* It is to be regretted that our author should allow his prejudices, which we happen personally to know were very strong, thus again to run him off the rail, and forget his promise to enter upon "*ce sujet avec la ferme volonté d'être impartial.*" While he assails "Pitt" he contrives to omit the provocation and necessity of the case: but assuredly it was not Pitt who broke loose, and among other wild and unprecedented phantasies, invited all the nations of Europe to demolish their governments. Yet what has all this to do with James Watt?—*Translator.*

resources and foresight. A work of recent date has shown, that in England alone (Ireland and Scotland being thus left aside), the capital belonging to mere workmen, that has been deposited in the savings' banks, amounts to nearly four hundred millions of francs (16,000,000*l.*). The verification of property in all the principal towns is not less instructive.

One principle only has remained uncontested, amidst all the animated debates to which political economy has given rise : and this is, that population increases with general comfort, and that it diminishes rapidly in times of scarcity.* Let us place facts by the side of the principle. Whilst the mean population of England was increasing during the last thirty years 50 per cent., Nottingham and Birmingham, two of the most industrial cities, presented a still larger augmentation, to the amount of 25 and even 40 per cent.† Finally, Manchester and Glasgow, which occupy the first rank in the whole British empire, from the number, the size, and the importance of the machines that they employ, saw their population, in the same period of the last thirty years, increase from 150 to 160 per cent. This was three or four times more than in the agricultural counties and towns not possessing manufactories.

Such numbers speak for themselves. No sophistry, no false philanthropy, no efforts of eloquence, can resist them.

* Ireland is an exception to this rule, the cause of which is well known; and I shall have occasion to recur to it.

† This sentence would have been clearer, had the author, instead of "*accroissements de* 25 *et de* 40 *pour* 100 *plus considérables encore*," said 75 and even 90 per cent.; because he means 25 added to the above 50, and 40 added to the 50 per cent.,—since he gives them as instances of larger augmentations.—*Translator.*

Machines have given rise to a particular kind of objection, which I must not pass over in silence. At the time of their introduction, at the time when they begin to take the place of manual labour, certain classes of workmen suffer from the change. Their honourable, their laborious industry, is almost suddenly annihilated. Even those who under the old system were the cleverest, being sometimes devoid of the qualities required in the new operations, remain unemployed. They seldom succeed all at once in adapting themselves to a new kind of labour.

These reflections are just and true. I will add that the bad consequences pointed out by them must often recur: some caprice in the fashions even, suffice to produce deep misery. If I do not conclude from thence that the world ought to remain stationary, God forbid that in wishing the general interests of society to advance, I would have it remain deaf to the individual sufferings caused by this temporary advance! Authority, always on the watch relative to new inventions, seldom fails to catch them by fiscal measures. Would it be expecting too much from it, were it asked to allow the first contributions levied on genius to be devoted to opening some special workshops where the artisans who had been suddenly dispossessed of their occupation should, for a time, find employment consonant to their powers and their knowledge? This method has sometimes been found successful; it would then only remain to generalize it. Humanity makes it a duty, and sound policy counsels it; besides which, some terrible events, of which history preserves the recollection, would also recommend this method on the part of economy.

The objections of theorists who feared that the progress

of mechanics would reduce the working class to complete inaction, have been followed by others quite of a different character, and on which it appears indispensable to dwell for a moment.

By suppressing all efforts of strength in manufactories, machines allow of a great number of children of both sexes being called in. Some industrial and some avaricious parents often abuse this power. The time devoted to work is most unreasonably long. For the daily pay of eight or ten centimes, some minds are devoted to eternal stupidity, which a few hours of study would have rendered fruitful; limbs are condemned to be rickety, that required open air, and exercise in the wholesome rays of the sun for their development.

To ask a legislator to put an end to this hideous exhaustion of the poor by the rich; to solicit measures for combating the demoralization which is the usual consequence of numerous gatherings of young work-people; to try to introduce and distribute certain machines among the cottages, so that, according to the seasons, agricultural labours might be interspersed with the industrial;—this would be an act of humanity, an act of patriotism; this would show a knowledge of the present requirements of the working classes. But to persist in executing laboriously and expensively, by hand, works that machines can perform in a twinkling and at a low price, would but assimilate proletaries to brutes. To ask daily efforts from them which ruin their health, and which science can procure a hundredfold by the action of wind, of water, or of steam, would be going in the contrary direction to the wished-for result: this would be devoting the poor to nudity; reserving exclusively for the rich a host of enjoyments, which at present are shared by everybody: this, in short, would be, from sheer inconsiderateness, going back to the age of ignorance, to barbarity, and to misery.

It is time to quit this subject, although I am far from having exhausted it. I shall not assuredly have triumphed over a crowd of inveterate and systematic prejudices: but I may hope, at least, that my pleading will obtain the concurrence of those thousands of idlers in the capital, whose life is passed in proportioning a taste for pleasures with their bad health. In a few years, thanks to Watt's discoveries, all these Sybarites, incessantly impelled by steam along railways, can rapidly visit the various regions of the kingdom. They can go the same day to see the fleet get under weigh at Toulon; breakfast at Marseilles on the succulent roach of the Mediterranean; at noon plunge their enervated limbs in the mineral waters of Bagnères; and return at night, by way of Bordeaux, to the ball or the opera! Do you doubt this? I shall say that my itinerary only supposes a rate of twenty-six leagues per hour; that several trials of steam carriages have realized a velocity of fifteen leagues; that Mr. Stephenson, in short, the celebrated engineer of Newcastle, offers to construct steam-engines two and a half times more rapid: engines that will accomplish forty leagues per hour!

PRESS FOR COPYING LETTERS.—HEATING BY STEAM.—COMPOSITION OF WATER.—BLEACHING BY THE AID OF CHLORINE.—ESSAY ON THE PHYSIOLOGICAL EFFECTS THAT MAY RESULT FROM BREATHING VARIOUS GASES.

When Watt went to reside at Soho, Birmingham counted Priestley among the inhabitants of its vicinity,—Priestley, and his name alone says all; Darwin the author of the *Zoonomia*, and of a celebrated poem entitled *The Loves of the Plants;* Withering, a distinguished physician and botanist; Keir, a chemist well known by his notes to his translation of Macquer, and by an interesting memoir on the crystallization of glass; Galton, author of an elementary treatise on Ornithology; Edgeworth, author of various works justly appreciated, and father of the so celebrated Maria. These learned men soon became friends of the illustrious mechanic, and most of them formed, with him and Boulton, an association called the *Lunar Society*. Such a whimsical appellation gave rise to many mistakes: it only meant that they met on the evening of full moon, a time of the month chosen by preference, in order that the members might see their way home.

Each sitting of the Lunar Society was, for Watt, a fresh opportunity for showing the remarkable fecundity of invention with which Nature had endowed him. Darwin said one day to his companions, "I have imagined a certain double pen, a pen with two beaks, by the aid of which we may write every thing in duplicate; and thus at once give the original and the copy of a letter." Watt almost immediately replied: "I hope to find a better solution of the problem. I will work out my ideas to-night, and will communicate them to you to-morrow." The next day the copying press was invented, and even a small model allowed already of an opinion being formed of its effects. This instrument, so useful and so generally adopted in all the English counting-houses, has recently received some modifications, an honour claimed by many workmen; but I can assert that the present form was actually described and drawn in 1780, in the patent of our associate.

Warming by steam was more recent by three years. Watt adopted it in his own house in 1783. We must acknowledge that this ingenious method is found indicated in the *Philosophical Transactions* for the year 1745 by Colonel Cooke;* but the idea passed away unheeded. At all events, Watt will not have the honour only of reviving it: he was the first to apply steam; it was his calculations on the extent of surface requisite for the warming of halls of various sizes, that in the beginning served as a guide to the greater part of the English engineers.

If Watt had only produced, in the course of his long life, the separate condenser for the steam-engine, the detent for regulating the steam, and the articulated parallelogram, he would still occupy one of the highest places among the small number of men whose life marks an epoch in the history of the world; but his name seems to me to be splendidly connected with the greatest and the most important discovery in modern chemistry: the discovery of *the components of water*. My assertion may be daring, for the numerous works in which this essential point of the history of the sciences is treated *ex professo*, have forgotten Watt. I hope, however that you will follow my discussion without prejudice; that you will not allow yourselves to be deterred from the examina-

* I read in a work by Mr. Robert Stuart that Sir Hugh Platte had an idea, before Colonel Cooke, of the possibility of applying steam to warming dwellings. In the *Garden of Eden* by that author, published in 1660, something is said to that effect for preserving plants through the winter in the green-house. Sir Hugh Platte proposes placing lids, made of tin or of any other metal, over the saucepans in which the viands are being cooked, and then to certain openings in these lids to adapt tubes, by which the heating steam may be led wherever it is desired.

tion, by some authorities which are not however so numerous as might be supposed; that you will not refuse to remark how few authors in the present day refer back to original sources; how disagreeable they find it to disturb the dust of libraries; and, on the contrary, how convenient to feed on the erudition of other people, to reduce the composition of a book to the mere work of editing. But the promise that I hold of your confidence in me, has appeared of more weight. I have pressed into my service a number of printed memoirs, the whole of a voluminous authentic correspondence still in manuscript; and if after fifty years I come to claim for Watt an honour that has been inconsiderately granted to one of his most illustrious countrymen, it is because it has seemed to me beneficial to show that in the heart of academies, truth is sure to shine out sooner or later, and that in matters of discovery, there is never any prescription.

The theory of the four pretended elements, fire, air, water, and earth, the varied combinations of which were to produce all known bodies, is one of the numerous legacies that have come down to us from the brilliant philosophy which, through several centuries, dazzled and misled some of the noblest intellects. Van Helmont was the first who shook, though slightly, one of the principles of this ancient theorem, by pointing out to the attention of chemists, various permanently elastic fluids, several sorts of air, that he called *gases*, the properties of which differed from those of common air, from those of the elemental air. Boyle's and Hooke's experiments raised more serious difficulties still: they prove that common air, necessary to respiration and to combustion, undergoes remarkable changes in the course of those two phenomena, and exhibits changes of properties which imply the notion of composition. The numerous observations at Hales; the successive discoveries of carbonic acid by Black, of hydrogen by Cavendish; of nitrous acid, of oxygen, of muriatic acid, of sulphurous acid, and of ammonia by Priestley, definitively banished the old idea of there being a unique and elementary air; that being among the almost constantly false conceptions hazarded by people, who have the audacity to think themselves called upon, not to discover, but to guess the course of nature.

Amidst so many remarkable incidents, water had still preserved its character as an element. The year 1776 * was at last signalized by one of those observations that were to lead to the upsetting of this general belief. It must be acknowledged that we must also assign the same year for the singular efforts made by the chemists, not to surrender to the natural results of their experiments. The observation of which I wish to speak belongs to Macquer.

That judicious chemist having placed a white porcelain saucer over the flame of hydrogen gas which was burning tranquilly out of the mouth of a bottle, remarked that this flame was not accompanied by any smoke properly so called; that it deposited no soot; that the part of the saucer which was *licked* by the flame was, on the contrary, evidently covered by small drops of a fluid resembling water, and which, after verification, was found to be pure water. This was certainly a singular result. Observe carefully, it was in the midst of the flame, on that part of

* It was in this year, 1776, according to Priestley, that Volta fired inflammable air by the electric spark: the experiment of Macquer appears to have been made two years afterwards.—*Translator*.

the saucer which was *licked* by it, as Macquer says, that the little drops of water were deposited. The chemist, however, did not dwell upon this fact; he was not surprised at what it contains of surprising: he simply cites it without any commentary; he does not perceive that he was touching a great discovery with his finger.

Should genius then, in the sciences of observation, be reduced to the faculty of asking, at appropriate times, *why?*

The physical world enrolls volcanoes that have never made but one eruption. It is the same in the intellectual world; for there are men who, after a flash of genius, entirely disappear from the history of science. Such was Warltire, whom I am here led to cite by the chronological order of dates for a truly remarkable experiment. At the commencement of the year 1781, this physicist imagined that an electric spark could not pass through certain gaseous mixtures without occasioning some decided changes in them. So novel an idea, unsuggested by any previous analogy, but of which such happy applications have since been made, would have merited for its author, I think, some honourable mention on the part of the historians of science. Warltire was wrong as to the changes that electricity would create, but fortunately for him he did foresee that an explosion would accompany them. It was therefore that he made the experiment in a metallic vase, having enclosed some air and some hydrogen in it.

Cavendish soon repeated Warltire's experiment. The *positive date* of his repetition (I call thus all dates resulting from an authentic deposit, or an academical lecture, or a printed paper) is anterior to the month of April 1783, since Priestley cites Cavendish's observations in a memoir of the 21st of that month. The citation besides informs us only of one circumstance; it is, that Cavendish had obtained *water* by the detonation of a mixture of oxygen and hydrogen, a result already proved by Warltire.

In his April memoir, Priestley added a remarkable circumstance to those which resulted from the experiments of his predecessors, for he proved that the weight of the water deposited on the sides of the vase at the moment of the oxygen's and hydrogen's detonation, is the sum of the weight of both the gases.

Watt, to whom Priestley communicated this important result, immediately saw in it, with the penetration of a superior mind, that water is not a simple body.

He therefore wrote to his illustrious friend: "What are the products of your experiments, *water*, *light*, and *heat*? Are we not then authorized from hence to conclude that water is a union of oxyen and hydrogen gas, deprived of a portion of their latent or elementary heat; that oxygen is water deprived of its hydrogen but united to latent heat and light?"

"If light be only a modification of heat, or only a circumstance attendant on its manifestation, or a component part of hydrogen, oxygen gas must be water deprived of its hydrogen, but united to some latent heat."

This passage, so clear, so neat, so methodical, is extracted from a letter by Watt, of the 26th of April, 1783. The letter was communicated by Priestley to several learned men in London, and referred immediately after to Sir Joseph Banks, President of the Royal Society, to be read at a meeting of that learned society. Some circumstances, which I suppress because they are irrelevant to our present purpose, retarded the reading by a year; but the letter remained in the archives of the Society.* It is inserted in the seventy-fourth volume of the *Philosophical Transactions*, under its true date of the 26th of April, 1783. It is found there inserted in a letter from Watt to De Luc, dated 26th of November, 1783, distinguished by inverted commas, applied by the Secretary of the Royal Society.

I do not ask for indulgence on this profusion of details, it will be perceived that a minute comparison of dates could alone bring the whole truth to light; and that the subject is one of those discoveries that do most honour to the human mind.

Among the pretenders to this fruitful discovery, we are now going to see arise the two greatest chemists boasted of by France and England. Everybody must have already named to themselves Lavoisier and Cavendish.

The date of the public reading of the memoir in which Lavoisier detailed his experiments, in which he developed his views on the production of water by the combustion of oxygen and hydrogen, is posterior by two months to Watt's letter (already analyzed) being deposited in the archives of the Royal Society of London.

The celebrated memoir by Cavendish, entitled *Experiments on Air*, is more recent still; it was read the 15th of January, 1784. It might excite reasonable surprise

* To this diffident and philosophical document we refer the reader; in it Watt states that he feels great reluctance to lay his thoughts "before the public in their present indigested state, and without having been able to bring them to the test of such experiments as would confirm or refute them." M. Arago, in rendering portions of the paper, resorts to the exact chemical language of the present day; whence he uses *hydrogène* for inflammable air and phlogiston, and *oxygène* for dephlogisticated air.—*Translator.*

that facts so well authenticated should have become the subject of such an earnest polemical dispute, if I did not hasten to lay before you a circumstance that I have not mentioned before. Lavoisier declared, in positive terms, that Blagden, Secretary of the Royal Society of London, was present at his first experiments on the 24th of June, 1783, and that "he informed him that Cavendish, having already tried in London to burn hydrogen gas in closed vessels, had obtained a very sensible quantity of water."

Cavendish also repeated in his memoir, the communication made by Blagden to Lavoisier. According to him, it was more detailed than the French chemist had acknowledged. He said, that the information included the conclusion to which the experiments led, that is to say, the theory of water being a compound.

Blagden, being called to account, wrote in the Journal of Creil, in 1786, to confirm the assertion made by Cavendish.

If we believe this, the experiments of the Academician of Paris would not have been more than a simple verification of those made by the English chemist. He assures us that he announced to Lavoisier, that the water obtained in London was precisely equal in weight to the sum of the weight of the two gases that had been burned. And Blagden finally adds: "*Lavoisier told the truth, but not all the truth.*"

Such a reproach is severe; but if it were well founded, should I not diminish its weight very much, if I were to show that excepting Watt, all those whose names figure in this story more or less exposed themselves?

Priestley details some experiments as if they were his own, and it results from them that the water engendered by the detonation of a mixture of oxygen and hydrogen, weighs exactly the same as the two gases burnt. Some time after, Cavendish claims this result as his own, and insinuates that he had communicated it verbally to the Birmingham chemist.

Cavendish infers from this similarity of weight, that water is not a simple body; yet he makes no mention of a memoir deposited in the archives of the Royal Society, in which Watt developed the same theory. It is true, that at the day of publication the name of Watt is not forgotten; but it was not in the archives that the celebrated engineer's labours could be seen: they are declared to have become known, by a recent reading, at the public meeting. At the present day, however, it is perfectly agreed that this reading followed, by several months,* that of the memoir in which Cavendish alludes to it.

On reaching the field of this serious discussion, Blagden announces his firm intention to elucidate every thing, to correct every thing. And in fact he did not draw back from any accusation, from any inquiry into dates, as long as the object was to insure to his patron and friend, Cavendish, a priority above the French chemist. But as soon as his explanations concerned two of his countrymen, they became vague and obscure. He says: "In the spring of 1783, Mr. Cavendish showed us that he was led to conclude from his experiments, that water is nothing but oxygen deprived of its phlogiston (that is to say, deprived of its hydrogen). *About the same time*, the news reached London, that Mr. Watt, of Birmingham, had been led by some observations to a similar result." This expression, *about the same time*, to speak in Mr.

* This delay, it should be observed, was in consequence of Watt's own request; his reason for so doing is shown in the note to page 432. —*Translator*.

Blagden's own style, would not be *all the truth*. *About the same time* decides nothing: questions of priority might depend on weeks, on days, on hours, on minutes. To be clear and precise, as had been promised, he should have said whether the verbal communication made by Cavendish, to several members of the Royal Society, preceded or followed the arrival in London of the news of Watt's experiments. Can it be supposed that Blagden would not have explained himself on a fact of this importance, if he could have quoted an authentic date in favour of his friend.

To render the complication complete, the correctors of the press, the compositors, the printers, of the *Philosophical Transactions*, all took part in this affair. Several dates are incorrectly given. On the separate copies of his memoir which Cavendish distributed among various learned men, I perceive an error of a whole year.* By a sad fatality, for it is a real misfortune unwillingly to give rise to painful and undeserved suspicions, not one of these numerous errors of the type was favourable to Watt! God forbid that I should mean, by these remarks, to criminate the literary probity of the illustrious philosophers whose names I have cited: they only prove that in matters of discovery, strict justice is all that ought

* Our author must have been excited here, for he thinks that not only the high-minded Cavendish and Blagden, but even the printers of the papers, were in a conspiracy against Watt; and, though he calls God to witness that he means nothing against their probity, he makes a very bold insinuation that they were leagued against truth. The separate copies of Cavendish's paper, pulled off for private distribution, were dated 1783 instead of 1784; as soon as the error was discovered, means were taken to correct it. Such an accidental error occurs in Watt's own communication in the seventy-fourth volume of *Transactions;* it being there said to have been read in April, 1784, though stated to have been written in November, 1784.—*Translator*.

to be expected from a rival or competitor, however eminent his reputation may already be. Cavendish could scarcely listen to people on business, when they went to consult him about the investment of his twenty-five or thirty millions (*a million sterling or more*) ; but you now know whether he felt equally indifferent about experiments. It would not be requiring too much, then, if the historians of science were not to receive, as available titles to property, any but written titles ; perhaps, I ought rather to say, any but published titles. Then, and only then, would those quarrels end, which are continually recommencing, by which national vanity generally suffers ; then the name of Watt would resume in the history of chemistry the high post that is his due.

When the solution of a question of priority, like the one we have been discussing, is founded on the most attentive examination of printed memoirs, and on a minute comparison of dates, it assumes the character of a real demonstration. Still I feel myself bound to give a rapid glance at the various difficulties to which some very good intellects appear to me to have attached importance.

How can it be admitted, I have been asked, that in the midst of an immense whirlpool of commercial affairs, that preoccupied by a multitude of lawsuits, that obliged to provide by daily inventions against the difficulties of a rising manufactory, Watt could find the time to follow the progress of chemistry step by step, to make fresh experiments, to propose explanations which the masters of the science themselves would not have thought of ?

To this difficulty I shall make a short but conclusive reply : I hold in my hands the copy of an active correspondence principally relative to chemical topics, that Watt kept up during the years 1782, 1783, and 1784, with Priestley, Black, De Luc, the engineer Smeaton, Gilbert Hamilton (of Glasgow), and Fry (of Bristol).

The following is an objection that appears more specious ; it arises from a deep knowledge of the human heart.

The discovery of the composition of water, advancing step by step with the admirable inventions that are united in the steam-engine, can we suppose that Watt would, from inconsiderateness, or at least without showing any displeasure, allow himself to be despoiled of the honour which it would eternally shed on his name ?

This reasoning has the defect of erring completely at its very basis. Watt never yielded the share that legitimately belonged to him in the discovery of the composition of water. He had his memoir carefully printed in the *Philosophical Transactions.* A detailed note authentically proved the date of the presentation of the various paragraphs of that writing. What could, what ought, a philosopher of Watt's character to do, otherwise than patiently await the day of retribution ? However, a piece of awkwardness on the part of De Luc had well nigh dragged our associate from his forbearance. The Genevese physician, after having warned the illustrious engineer of the inexplicable absence of his name from the first edition of Cavendish's Memoir, and after having described this omission in terms which the high renown of both parties does not allow me to repeat, writes to his friend : "I should almost advise you, considering your position, to extract practical results from your discoveries, for the sake of your purse."

These words offended Watt's high mind ; he replied : "If I do not immediately claim my rights, you must impute it to an indolence of disposition, which leads me to feel it easier to bear with injustice, than to struggle for redress. And as to considerations of pecuniary interest, they are of no value in my estimation. Besides which, my future depends on the encouragement that the public may be inclined to grant me, and not at all on that of Mr. Cavendish or of his friends."

Ought I to fear, that I have attached too much importance to the theory that Watt imagined for explaining Priestley's experiments? I think not. Those who would refuse a rational consent to this theory, because it now seems the inevitable result of facts, must forget that the finest discoveries achieved by the human mind have been, above all, remarkable for their simplicity. What did Newton* himself do, when, repeating an experiment that had been known already for fifteen centuries, he discovered white light? He gave so natural an interpretation of this experiment, that it now seems impossible to offer any other; he says—"All that is obtained, by any proceeding whatever, from a pencil of white light, must have been contained in it in a state of mixture. The glass prism possesses no creative property. If the paral-

* This is barely in point; some of the phenomena of colours were certainly known before the advent of Newton, but that *princeps philosophorum* formed the prismatic spectrum itself, by which the spaces occupied by the successive colours were accurately defined, the colours submitted to a similar analysis, and the white light re-formed; thus ascertaining and proving that light, instead of being homogeneous as had been supposed, was actually a heterogeneous mixture of differently refrangible rays. Nor do we quite quadrate with the lengthy discussion before us, since we do not consider the case—*in rê* the beautiful composition of water—to be conclusively established. To those readers who are interested in so crucial a point in scientific history, we recommend a perusal of Vernon Harcourt's remarkable address to the British Association at Birmingham, in 1839; it being alike free from reckless assertion, and that hot nationality which warps judgment.—*Translator*.

lel ray, infinitely diluted with the solar light that falls on the first surface, issues from the second surface, diverging and with a sensible breadth, it is because the glass separates that which, in the white pencil, was by its nature unequally refrangible." These words are nothing but a literal translation of the known experiment of the prismatic solar spectrum. This translation, however, had escaped an Aristotle, a Descartes, a Robert Hooke.

Without departing from the subject, let us come to some arguments which will lead in a still more direct line to the point. The theory conceived by Watt of the composition of water reaches London. If it had been according to the ideas of those times, as simple, as self-evident as it appears to us now, the counsel of the Royal Society would not have failed to adopt it : but its strangeness made them doubt the correctness of Priestley's experiments. They went so far as to laugh at it, said De Luc, *as at the explanation of the golden tooth.*

A theory, the conception of which did not present any difficulty, would certainly have been despised by Cavendish. But recollect with what eagerness, under the inspiration of that man of genius, Blagden claimed the priority of it against Lavoisier.

Priestley, to whom a great part of the honour of Watt's discovery belonged,—Priestley, whose affectionate sentiments for the celebrated engineer cannot be doubted, wrote to him, under date of the 29th April, 1783,—"Look with surprise and indignation at the drawing of an apparatus, by the aid of which I have *irrevocably undermined your beautiful hypothesis.*"

In conclusion, an hypothesis at which they laughed in the Royal Society ; which made Cavendish emerge from his habitual reserve ; which Priestley, laying all self-love aside, endeavoured to upset, deserves to be registered in the history of science as a great discovery, whatever opinion we may entertain of it at the present day, owing to knowledge that has become common.*

The art of bleaching by means of chlorine, that beautiful invention of Berthollet's, was introduced into England by James Watt, after the journey he made to Paris about the end of 1786. He constructed all the requisite apparatus, directed its establishment, presided at the first trials; and then confided to Mr. Macgregor, his father-in-law, the management of the new art. Notwithstanding the solicitations of the illustrious engineer, our celebrated countryman *had obstinately refused*† to become a partner in an enterprise which offered no unfavourable chance, and the profits of which, it seemed, must become very great.

Scarcely had they discovered, during the second half of the last century, the numerous gaseous substances, which now act so important a part in the explanation of chemical phenomena, when they thought of rendering them useful in medicine. Dr. Beddoes followed up this idea with sagacity and perseverance. Private subscriptions even enabled him to establish a *Pneumatic Institu-*

* Lord Brougham was present at the public meeting, where, in the name of the Academy of Sciences I paid this tribute of gratitude and admiration to Watt's memory. On his return to England he collected some valuable documents, and again studied the historical question to which I have devoted so much space, with the superiority of perception which is familiar to him, with the scrupulousness, in some measure justiciary, which might be expected from a former Lord Chancellor of Great Britain. I owe to a degree of kindness, of which I feel the full value, the advantage of being able to offer the public the hitherto unpublished researches of my illustrious co-academician. See the end of this *éloge*.

† This expression is correct, however fabulous it may now appear.

tion at Clifton, near Bristol, where the therapeutic properties of all the gases were to be carefully studied. The Pneumatic Institution had for some time the advantage of being under the direction of the young Humphry Davy, who was then entering on his scientific career. It could boast also of having James Watt as one of its founders. The celebrated engineer did more: he imagined, described and executed, in his manufactory at Soho, the apparatus which generated the gases; and he administered it to the patients. I have found several editions of his Memoir treating of these researches* under the several dates of 1794, 1795, 1796.

Our associate's attention was attracted to this subject, in consequence of his being cruelly deprived of several friends and relations before the usual age, by diseases of the chest. It was chiefly the *lésion* of the respiratory organs that Watt thought might be treated by the aid of the specific properties of the new gases. He also expected some advantage from the action of the impalpable molecules, of iron, and of zinc, which hydrogen carries along with it when prepared in a certain way. I will finally add, that among the numerous medical notes published by Dr. Beddoes, and announcing results more or less decisive, there is one signed John Carmichael, relative to the radical cure of hæmoptysis in a servant, Richard Newberry, who was made at certain times to breathe a mixture of steam and carbonic acid by Watt himself. Although I am quite aware of my utter incom-

* It was especially the illness of his daughter, and the delicate health of his younger son, that led Watt to interest himself so deeply on this head. His work was entitled a *Description of a Pneumatic Apparatus, with Directions for procuring the Factitious Airs.—Translator.*

petence on such a subject, may I not be permitted to regret that a treatment which counted a Watt and a Jenner among its adherents, has been entirely abandoned, although no series of experiments can be cited in manifest opposition to those of the Pneumatic Institution at Clifton? *

WATT IN PRIVATE LIFE.—DETAILS OF EVENTS AND OF HIS DISPOSITION. — HIS DEATH. — NUMEROUS STATUES ERECTED TO HIS MEMORY.—REFLECTIONS.

Watt had married, in 1764, his cousin, Miss Miller. She was an accomplished person, of superior mind, and whose never failing sweetness and cheerfulness of disposition soon raised the celebrated engineer from the indolence, the melancholy and the misanthropy that a nervous illness and the injustice of man threatened to render fatal. But for Miss Miller, Watt would probably never have made his beautiful inventions public. Four children, two boys and two girls, were the fruit of this marriage. Mrs. Watt died at the birth of a third boy, who did not survive. Her husband was then busy in the north of Scotland, with the plans for the Caledonian Canal. Why should I not be permitted to transcribe here with all their originality some lines from the journal to which he committed daily his most private thoughts, his fears, his hopes! Why should I not show him to you, after his misfortune, stopping on the sill of the door of his house where his *sweet welcomer* no longer awaited

* Twenty years before the establishment of the Pneumatic Institution at Bristol, Watt already applied his chemical and minerological knowledge to improving the products of a pottery that he had established at Glasgow together with some friends, and of which he continued a partner to the end of his life.

him; unable to reënter those rooms, where he was no longer to find *the comfort of his life!* Perhaps so true a picture of deep grief would silence those systematic spirits who—without pausing at the thousands of striking contrary instances—deny that the qualities of the heart are possessed by any man whose intellect has been nurtured with the fruitful, the sublime, the imperishable truths of the exact sciences.

After remaining for some years a widower, Watt had again the happiness to find in Miss Mac Grigor a companion worthy of him by the variety of her talents, the soundness of her judgment, and the energy of her character.*

At the expiration of the patent granted him by Parliament, Watt, at the beginning of 1800, retired entirely from business.

His two sons succeeded him. Under the sensible direction of Mr. Boulton junior and the two young Messrs. Watt the manufactory at Soho prospered, and exhibited new and important developments. Even now it occupies the first rank in England among the establishments for constructing large machines. The second of the two sons, Gregory Watt, became known to the world in a brilliant manner, by his literary compositions, and by his geological labours. He died at the age of twenty-seven, in 1804, of a disease of the chest. This sad event overthrew the illustrious engineer. The tender attentions of his family and of his friends with difficulty succeeded in restoring some degree of calm to his broken heart. This very justifiable grief seems to

* Mrs. Watt (Mac Grigor) expired 1832, at a very advanced age. She had endured the grief of surviving the two children that resulted from her marriage with Mr. Watt.

explain the almost absolute silence which Watt maintained during the several latter years of his life. I am far from denying that it was without influence; but what occasion is there to seek for extraordinary causes, when already, under date of 1783, we read in a letter from Watt to his friend Dr. Black: "Recollect well, that I have no desire to entertain the public with the experiments which I have made;"—when we also meet elsewhere, these very singular words in the mouth of a man who has filled the world with his renown: "I know only two pleasures, idleness and sleep." This sleep, however, was very light; and let us add, that the least excitement sufficed to rouse him from his favourite idleness. All the objects that were presented to him gradually received from him a mental suggestion of change of form, of nature, or of construction, which would have rendered them capable of important applications. These conceptions, for want of opportunities of being produced, were lost to the world.* The following anecdote will explain my ideas.

A company at Glasgow had erected large buildings and powerful engines on the right bank of the Clyde, intended to carry water to all the houses in the town. When this work was completed, they perceived that there existed on the opposite shore a spring, or rather a natural filter, which gave the water evidently superior qualities.

* There can be no doubt that Watt was deeply affected by his melancholy bereavement; but his mental energy was never impaired by it, nor his interest in science and literature weakened. Indeed there seems to be but little recollection of the lengthy silence above alluded to. The anecdote which follows respecting the lobster's tail, which he imitated on a large scale by a sort of ball-and-socket movement, shows that his inventive powers were still bright and fertile in 1811. —*Translator*.

To change the site of the establishment, could not even be proposed; they therefore thought of leading a fixed conduit-pipe all across the river, along the bottom, the mouth of which should always be in the midst of portable water; but the construction of the wood-work to support such a pipe, on its muddy, changeable, and uneven bed, always covered with several metres of water, seemed to require too heavy an outlay. Watt was consulted. His solution was all ready; having some days before seen a lobster on the table, he sought and found how mechanism might, with the aid of some iron, form a series of articulations, which should have all the flexible mobility of the tail of crustacea; he therefore proposed an articulated conduit-pipe, susceptible of bending itself to all the present and future inflections of the bed of the river. According to the plans and designs of Watt, therefore, the Glasgow Company ordered this iron lobster-tail to be made, sixty centimetres (nearly two feet) in diameter, and above three hundred metres (1000 feet, English) in length; and its success was complete.

Those who had the happiness of being personally acquainted with him, do not hesitate to assert that, in his own house, the qualities of his heart shone even above those of the philosopher. An infantine candour, the greatest simplicity of manners, a love of justice carried beyond every scruple, an inexhaustible benevolence, these are the virtues that have given rise to indelible recollections both in Scotland and England. Watt, although so moderate and so gentle, became irritated when in his presence an invention was not assigned to its true author; especially when any low flatterer wished to enrich him at other men's expense. In his eyes, scientific discoveries were the highest of all property.

Whole hours of discussion did not seem too much to him, if the object was to do justice to diffident inventors, either robbed by plagiarists, or only forgotten by an ungrateful public.

Watt's memory might be cited as prodigious, even by the side of all that is related of this faculty in some highly endowed men. Its extent, however, was its least merit; it imbibed all that was of any value; and it entirely rejected, almost instinctively, the superfluities that it would have been useless to preserve.

The variety of knowledge possessed by our academician would be truly incredible, if not attested by many eminent men. Lord Jeffrey, in an eloquent biographical notice, happily characterized, both the strong and subtle intelligence of his friend, when he compared it to the elephant's trunk, so wonderfully organized, that the animal uses it with equal facility either to "pick up a pin" or "to rend an oak."

Sir Walter Scott speaks of his countryman in the following terms, in the preface to *The Monastery* :— *

"It was only once my fortune to meet him, whether in body or in spirit it matters not. There were assembled about half a score of our Northern Lights. . . . . Amidst this company stood Mr. Watt, the man whose genius discovered the means of multiplying our national resources to a degree perhaps even beyond his own stupendous powers of calculation and combination; bringing the treasures of the abyss to the summit of the earth; giving the feeble arm of man the momentum of an Afrite; commanding manufactures to rise, as the rod of the prophet produced water in the desert; affording the means of dispensing with that time and tide which wait for no man; and of sailing without that wind which defied the commands and threats of Xerxes himself. This potent commander of the elements, the abridger

* We have thought it better to give the whole passage from Sir Walter Scott, than to reproduce it from our author's French; nor have we adopted his omissions.—*Translator*.

of time and space, this magician whose cloudy machinery has produced a change on the world, the effects of which, extraordinary as they are, are perhaps only now beginning to be felt, was not only the profound man of science, the most successful combiner of powers and calculator of numbers as adapted to practical purposes, was not only one of the most generally well informed, but one of the best and kindest of human beings.

"There he stood, surrounded by the little band I have mentioned of northern literati, men not less tenacious, generally speaking, of their own fame and their own opinions than the National Regiments are supposed to be jealous of the high character which they have won upon service. Methinks I yet see and hear what I shall never see or hear again. In his eighty-fifth (*eighty-third?*) year, the alert, kind, benevolent, old man had his attention at every one's question, his information at every one's command.

"His talents and fancy overflowed on every subject. One gentleman was a deep philologist—he talked with him on the origin of the alphabet as if he had been coeval with Cadmus; another, a celebrated critic—you would have said the old man had studied political economy and belles-lettres all his life; of science it is unnecessary to speak, it was his own distinguished walk. And yet, Captain Clutterbuck, when he spoke with your countryman, Jedediah Cleishbotham, you would have sworn he had been coeval with Claver'se and Burley, with the persecutors and persecuted, and could number every shot the dragoons had fired at the fugitive covenanters. In fact we discovered that no novel of the least celebrity escaped his perusal, and that the gifted man of science was as much addicted to the productions of your native country (the land of Utopia aforesaid), in other words, as shameless and obstinate a peruser of novels as if he had been a very milliner's apprentice of eighteen."

If our associate had wished it, he could also have made himself a name among novelists. Among his intimate friends he seldom failed to improve on the terrible, moving, or burlesque anecdotes that he heard related. The minute details of his recitals, the proper names with which he strewed them; the technical descriptions he gave of the castles, the country houses, the forests, the caverns, to which the scene was successively transferred, gave to these impromptus such an air of veracity, that one could not entertain the slightest sentiment of distrust. One day however, Watt was at a loss how to extricate his characters from the labyrinth into which he had imprudently thrown them. One of his friends perceived, by the uncommon number of pinches of snuff he took, that the narrator wished thereby to excuse frequent pauses, and gain time for reflection. He therefore addressed this indiscreet question to him: "Are you perhaps relating to us a story of your own creation?" "That doubt astonishes me," wittily replied the old man; "during the twenty years that I have had the happiness of passing my evenings with you, I have done nothing else! It is possible that they really wished to represent me as emulous of Robertson or of Hume, whilst all my ambition was limited to follow, however far behind, the steps of Princess Scheherazade in the *Thousand and One Nights!*"

Each year, during a very short visit to London, or to other towns at a less distance from Birmingham, Watt examined minutely all the novelties that had appeared since his preceding visit. I do not except even the sight of the industrious fleas or the puppet-shows; for the illustrious engineer went to them with all the delight of a school-boy. While perusing, even at the present day, the itinerary of these annual excursions, we should find luminous traces of Watt's presence. At Manchester for example, we should see the hydraulic ram serving, according to his own proposition, to raise the water of condensation from a steam-engine up to the reservoir feeding the caldron.

Watt generally resided on an estate near Soho called Heathfield, which he acquired about the year 1790. The filial veneration of my friend Mr. James Watt, for every thing connected with his father's memory, procurred for me, in 1834, the satisfaction of finding the library and the furniture at Heathfield in the same state in which the illustrious engineer left them. Another property on the picturesque banks of the river Wye, in Wales, offers to the tourist numerous proofs of the enlightened taste both of Watt and of his son, by the improvement of the roads, by the plantations, and by agricultural labours of all kinds.

Watt's health had become stronger with his years. His intellectual faculties continued in full vigour to his last moments. He thought at one time that they were declining, and adhering to the thought expressed on the seal that he had selected (an eye surrounded by the word *Observare*), he determined to clear up his doubts by self-observation; accordingly, when above seventy, we see him seeking the kind of study to which he should best have recourse for a trial, and distressed that no subject was new to him. He recollects at last that there is an Anglo-Saxon language, that it is a difficult language, and the Anglo-Saxon becomes the desired experimental means, —the facility which he finds in rendering himself master of it, proves to him how unfounded his apprehensions were.

Watt devoted his last days to the construction of a machine for copying promptly either statues or sculpture of any size with mathematical fidelity. This machine, of which we hope the arts will not be deprived, must have been well advanced. Many of its productions—already very satisfactory—may be seen in various private collections in Scotland and in England. The illustrious engineer had presented them in joke, as the first essays of a young artist entering the eighty-third year of his age.

It was not permitted to our associate to see the end of this eighty-third year. From the very beginning of the summer of 1819, some alarming symptoms defied all the powers of medicine. Watt himself was not deceived. He said to the numerous friends who visited him—"I am moved by the attachment that you show me, I hasten to thank you for it, as you see me arrived at my last illness." His son did not appear to him sufficiently resigned; whereupon he each day sought a new reason by which to point out to him with gentleness and tenderness, "all the motives of consolation that he might derive from the circumstances under which the inevitable event was about to occur." This sad event did in fact take place on the 25th of August, 1819.

Watt was buried by the side of the parish church of Heathfield, near Birmingham, in the county of Stafford. Mr. James Watt, whose distinguished talents, and whose noble sentiments delighted his father's heart for nearly twenty-five years, erected a splendid Gothic monument to him, and it now greatly adorns Handsworth Church.* In the centre there stands an admirable statue by Chantrey, the exact representation of the old man's noble features.

A second statue, also of marble, from the hands of the same sculptor, has been placed by filial piety in one of the halls of the brilliant university where, during his youth, the then unknown artist, though harassed by the corporation, received such flattering and well-deserved encouragement. Nor has Greenock forgotten that Watt

* To a general reader this paragraph might convey an ambiguity; Watt died in his house at Heathfield, at the age of eighty-three years and seven months; and his remains are deposited in the chancel of the adjoining parochial church of Handsworth, near those of his excellent friend Miss Boulton.—*Translator.*

was born there. The inhabitants have subscribed for a statue of the illustrious mechanic, to be placed in a fine library, built on a piece of ground generously given by Sir Michael Shaw Stewart; and there will be gathered the books that the town possessed, and the collection of scientific works that Watt had presented to the town during his life. This building has already cost 3500*l.* sterling (upwards of 87,000 frs. of our money), a considerable expense for which the liberality of Mr. Watt, Junior, has provided. A grand colossal statue in bronze, on a beautiful granite base, now adorns one of the angles of George's Square, at Glasgow; proving to all beholders, how much that capital of Scotch industry prides itself in having been the cradle of Watt's discoveries. Finally,* the gates of Westminster Abbey opened at the imposing voice of a host of subscribers; and a colossal statue of our co-academician, of Carrara marble, a masterpiece of Chantrey's, the pedestal bearing an inscription by Lord Brougham, has become within these few years one of the principal ornaments of the English Pantheon. Doubtless a little coquetry was necessary to bring together the illustrious names of Watt, Chantrey, and Brougham on the same monument; but I can see nothing to blame in it: glory to the people who thus seize every opportunity of honouring their great men!

This inscription by Lord Brougham, put on the pedestal of the statue of our *confrère*, appears to us to be worthy of a place in these pages, devoted to the memory of one of the greatest geniuses that ever illustrated science and industry; we will reproduce it then literally, a translation shall follow:—

* Two years ago a statue of Watt was erected in Edinburgh.—*Translator.*

NOT TO PERPETUATE A NAME
WHICH MUST ENDURE WHILE THE PEACEFUL ARTS FLOURISH,
BUT TO SHOW
THAT MANKIND HAVE LEARNT TO HONOUR THOSE
WHO DESERVE THEIR GRATITUDE,
THE KING,
HIS MINISTERS, AND MANY OF THE NOBLES
AND COMMONERS OF THE REALM,
RAISED THIS MONUMENT TO
JAMES WATT,
WHO DIRECTING THE FORCE OF AN ORIGINAL GENIUS
EARLY EXERCISED IN PHILOSOPHIC RESEARCH,
TO THE IMPROVEMENT OF
THE STEAM-ENGINE,
ENLARGED THE RESOURCES OF HIS COUNTRY,
INCREASED THE POWER OF MAN,
AND ROSE TO AN EMINENT PLACE
AMONG THE MOST ILLUSTRIOUS FOLLOWERS OF SCIENCE
AND THE REAL BENEFACTORS OF THE WORLD.
BORN AT GREENOCK, MDCCXXXVI,
DIED AT HEATHFIELD, IN STAFFORDSHIRE, MDCCCXIX.*

There are, actually counted, five large statues erected in a short time to the honour of Watt. Must we acknowledge it?—this homage of filial piety, of public gratitude, has excited the ill-humour of some narrow minds, who, remaining stationary themselves, think they can arrest the march of centuries. If we believe them, some military men, some magistrates, some ministers (I must confess they have not dared to say all the ministers), would have a right to statues. I know not whether Homer, Aristotle, Descartes, Newton would appear to these new Aristarchi deserving of a bust; assuredly they would refuse the most unassuming medal to the Papins, the Vaucansons, the Watts, the Arkwrights, and other mechanics, unknown, perhaps, in a certain world, but

* The French translation, for obvious reasons, is omitted.—*Translator.*

whose renown will go on increasing from age to age with the progress of knowledge. When such heresies are brought forward in open daylight, we ought not to disdain combating them. It is not without reason that the public has been called a sponge of prejudices; now prejudices are like noxious weeds, the slightest effort suffices to extirpate them on their first appearance; but, on the other hand, they resist if they are allowed time to grow, to expand, to seize by their numerous organs all that is suited to their nature.

If this discussion should wound the self-love of some people, I must remark that it has been provoked. Have the learned men of our own times uttered complaints at not seeing any of the great authors, whose inheritance they cultivate, figure in those long ranges of colossal statues, which authority pompously raises on our bridges and in our public squares? Do they not know that their monuments are fragile, that storms upset and destroy them, that frost suffices to spoil their outlines, and to reduce them to amorphous blocks?

Their sculpture and their painting is the press. Thanks to that admirable invention, when the works which science or imagination produces possess real merit, they may defy time and political revolutions. Neither the exigencies of the Exchequer, nor the inquietudes and terrors of despots, could prevent those productions from penetrating beyond the best-guarded frontiers. A thousand ships will carry them, in various shapes, from one hemisphere to the other. They will be read in Iceland and in Van Diemen's Land at the same time. They will be read at evening meetings in the humble cottage, they will be read in brilliant assemblies in palaces. The author, the artist, the engineer are known, appreciated, by the whole world, by that which there is in man of most noble, of most elevated: by the soul, by the thoughts, by the intellect. How foolish must that man be who, placed on such a theatre, should be detected in wishing that his lineaments were preserved by the chisel of a David,* to be some day exposed to the glances of idlers taking their walk. Such honours, I repeat it, need not be envied by the learned man, by the author, or by the artist; but they ought not, on any account, to allow themselves to be declared unworthy of them. Such, at least, have been the thoughts that lead me to submit the following discussion to your judgment.

Is it not a truly strange circumstance, that these vain pretensions that I am combating should have been raised merely on account of these five statues, not one of which cost a single obolus to the public treasury? Far from me, however, to take advantage of this inconsiderateness. I prefer taking the question in a more general point of view, such as it was laid down: the pretended pre-eminence of arms over letters, over science, over art; for we must not deceive ourselves—if magistrates and administrators have been mentioned together with military men, it was only as a passport.

The shortness of the time allowed me for this discus-

* It is uncertain whether the noted Jacques Louis David, or Pierre Jean David is here meant; for though the former is generally known as a painter only, he proposed to construct a huge colossus in honour of the people, out of the ruins of royal statues; and of this he made a model. But we could have wished that our author's taste had prevented his intruding the truisms in this and in the tirade which follows; at least, the biography of the enriched and greatly honoured Watt hardly appears to be a fit peg whereon to hang so laboured a declamation. Even now, one of the finest line-of-battle ships in the British fleet is the JAMES WATT; still, we admit, the best records of an eminent man are certainly his works.—*Translator.*

sion, imposes on me the duty of being methodical. In order that my sentiments may not be mistaken, I will at once declare aloud that independence, that national liberty, are in my opinion the greatest possible good; that to defend them against foreigners, or against internal enemies, is our first duty; and that to have defended them at the cost of our blood, is the highest title to public gratitude. Raise, raise splendid monuments to the memory of the soldiers who fell on the glorious ramparts of Mayence, on the immortal fields of Zurich, of Marengo, and certainly my offering shall not be waited for; but do not require me to do violence to my reason, to the sentiments that Nature has implanted in the human heart; do not hope that I will ever consent to place all military services on the same level.

What Frenchman possessed of a heart, even in the reign of Louis XIV., would have sought for an example of courage either among the scenes of cruelty in the Dragonnades, or among the whirlwinds of flame that devoured the towns, the villages, and the rich country of the Palatinate?

Not long since, after a thousand prodigies of patience, of cleverness, of bravery, our valiant soldiers penetrated into the half-destroyed Saragossa, and reached the door of a church where the preacher was still making the ears of the resigned crowd ring with these magnificent words: "Spaniards, I am going to celebrate your funerals!" I know not, but I think that at such a moment the true friends of our national glory, comparing the various merits of the conquerors and the vanquished, would willingly perhaps have inverted the address!

But I consent to your laying aside the question of morality. Submit the personal claims of some gainers of battles to the crucible of a conscientious analysis; believe me, that even if you make an equitable partition by chance (a sort of ally for whom one always makes allowance, as being dumb), many pretended heroes will appear to you very unworthy of that pompous title.

If it were found requisite, I would not recoil from a detailed examination; I, who in a purely academic career, can have had but little opportunity of collecting correct documents on such a subject,—I could, for example, cite in our own annals a recent battle, a battle gained, the official report of which describes it as having been foreseen and calmly prepared, with the most consummate ability; but which, in reality, was the result of a sudden rush on the part of the soldiers, without any order from the Commander-in-Chief to whom the honour was assigned, without his having been there, without his having known of it!

To escape from the commonplace reproach of incompetence, I will call on some military men themselves to aid in supporting the philosophic thesis which I maintain. It will be seen what enthusiastic and enlightened appreciators they were of intellectual labours; it will be seen that in their inner mind, these never held a second rank. Obliged to restrict myself, I will try to make high renown supply the deficiency of number and novelty: I will cite Alexander, Pompey, Cæsar, and Napoleon!

The Macedonian conqueror's admiration of Homer is historical. Aristotle at his desire undertook the task of revising the text of the Iliad. That corrected copy became a cherished book; and when, in the centre of Asia, amidst the spoils of Darius, a magnificent casket was found, enriched with gold, pearls, and precious stones, which seemed to excite the covetousness of his highest officers, the conqueror of Arbela exclaimed: "Let that be reserved for me; it shall contain my Homer. It is the best and most faithful counsellor I have in my military affairs. Besides, it is but just that the richest production of art should preserve the most precious work of the human mind."

The sacking of Thebes had already shown, still more clearly, the unlimited respect and admiration that Alexander entertained for letters. Only one family out of that populous city escaped death and slavery: this was the family of Pindar. Only one house remained intact amidst the ruined temples, palaces, and private dwellings: this was the house where Pindar was born, not Epaminondas!

When Pompey, after finishing the war against Mithridates, went to visit the celebrated philosopher Posidonias, he prohibited the lictors from knocking at the door with their sticks, as was the custom. Thus, says Pliny, were the fasces of the man who had seen the East and the West prostrated before him, lowered before the humble dwelling of a learned man!

Cæsar, who may also be claimed as a man of letters, allows us to perceive, in at least twenty places in his immortal Commentaries, what rank was occupied in his own esteem by the various faculties with which nature had so liberally endowed him. How brief he is, how rapid in relating combats and battles! See, on the contrary, whether he thinks any detail superfluous in the description of the temporary bridge by means of which his army crossed the Rhine. It is because success depended here on the conception, and the conception was exclusively his own.

It has also been already remarked, that the part which

Cæsar by preference attributed to himself in the events of the war, that of which he seems to have been most proud, was a moral influence. *Cæsar harangued his army*, is constantly the first phrase with which he begins, when describing a battle gained. And *Cæsar did not arrive soon enough to talk to his soldiers, to exhort them to conduct themselves well*, is the general accompaniment of the recital of a surprise or of a momentary repulse. The *general* frequently undertakes to efface himself in the presence of the *orator*. And the judicious Montaigne remarks : "His language, truly, in many places, does him notable service !"

Meantime, without transition, without even insisting on the well-known exclamation of Frederic the Great: "*I would rather have written the Century of Louis XIV. by Voltaire, than have gained a hundred battles.*" I come to Napoleon. As we must hasten on, I will not recall the celebrated proclamations, written under the shade of the Egyptian Pyramids by the *Member of the Institute*, Commander-in-Chief of the army of the East; nor the treaties of peace, in which monuments of art or of science were the price of the vanquished people's ransom; nor the profound esteem which the general, become emperor, never ceased to feel for the Lagranges, the Laplaces, the Monges, the Berthollets, nor the riches nor the honours which he showered down upon them. An anecdote, little known, will lead more directly to my aim.

Everybody remembers the decennial prizes. The four classes of the Institute had sketched out rapid analyses of the progress made in the sciences, letters, and arts. The presidents and the secretaries were to be called in succession to read them to Napoleon, in the presence of the great dignitaries of the empire, and the Council of State.

On the 27th of February, 1808, it came to the turn of the French Academy. As may be easily supposed, the assembly on that day was even more numerous than usual: who does not think himself a judge in matters of taste? Chenier reads. He is listened to with attentive silence: but all at once he is interrupted by the emperor, who, putting his hand on his heart, his body leaning forward, his voice affected by a visible emotion, exclaimed: "It is too much, too much, Gentlemen, you overpower me; words fail me in which to express my gratitude!"

I leave you to imagine the deep surprise of the many courtiers who witnessed this scene; those men who from flattery to flattery had come at last to say to their master, and without his appearing astonished at it: "When God had created Napoleon, he felt the want of repose!"

But what then were the words that went so exactly, so directly to the heart of Napoleon? These words were the following:—

"In camps where, far from the calamities of the interior, national glory was unalterably preserved, another style of eloquence arose, unknown until then to modern nations. We must even acknowledge, that when we read in ancient authors harangues from the most renowned leaders, we are often tempted to admire only the talent of the historians in them. But here, it is impossible to doubt; the monuments exist: history has only to collect them together. It was from the armies of Italy that those beautiful proclamations emanated, in which the conqueror of Lodi and of Arcoli, created at the same time a new system of warfare, and a new style of military eloquence, of which he will for ever remain the model."

On the 28th of February, the day after the celebrated sitting that I have just described, the *Moniteur*, with its *known fidelity*, published an answer from the emperor to Chenier's discourse. It was cold, laconic, unmeaning; it had, in short, all the characteristics that other people would say are those of an official document. As to the incident that I recorded, there was no allusion to it; a wretched concession to predominant opinions, to the susceptibilities of a military etiquette! The master of the world, to use Pliny's expression, ceding for a moment to his inward feeling, had not the less bowed his fasces to the literary title awarded to him by an Academy.

These reflections on the comparative merits of the man of letters and the man of arms, although not chiefly suggested by what is said, by what is done under our ocular experience, would not be inapplicable to the country of James Watt. I travelled not long since through England and Scotland. The good will with which I was received, authorized questions on my part, as dry, as pointed, as direct, as might, under other circumstances, have come only from the president of a commission of inquiry. Already fully preoccupied with the obligation I should be under, at my return, to give a judgment on the illustrious mechanic; already feeling uneasy at the solemn character of the meeting before which I am speaking, I had prepared the following question: "What do you think of the influence that Watt had on the riches, on the power, and on the prosperity of England?" I do not exaggerate in saying that I addressed this question to upwards of a hundred persons belonging to all classes of society, to all varieties of political opinions, from the most violent radicals to the most obstinate conservatives. The answer was always the same; every one placed the services of our academician above all comparison; each man quoted, besides, the discourses pronounced at the meeting in which the Westminster statue was voted, as the faithful and unanimous expression of the sentiments of the English nation. What did these discourses say?

Lord Liverpool, Prime Minister of the Crown, calls Watt, "one of the most extraordinary men that England ever produced, one of the greatest benefactors to the human race." He declared that "his inventions have augmented the resources of his country and of the whole world, to an incalculable degree." Then, considering the question in a political point of view, he added,—"I have lived at a time, when the success of a war depended on the possibility of pushing our fleets out of port without loss of time; contrary winds prevailed during whole months, and would have entirely upset the intentions of government. Thanks to the steam-engine, such difficulties have disappeared for ever." *

"Direct your attention," Sir Humphry Davy exclaimed, "to the metropolis of this powerful empire, to our towns, to our villages, to our arsenals, to our manufactories; examine our subterranean cavities, and the works accomplished on the surface of the globe; contemplate our rivers, our canals, the seas which bathe our shores; you will everywhere find proofs of the eternal benefits conferred by that great man."

The illustrious President of the Royal Society also

* It should be observed that during the wars of which Lord Liverpool had any cognizance, steam had not been applied to this purpose. —*Translator*.

said: "The genius exerted by Watt in his admirable inventions, has contributed more to show the practical utility of science, to enlarge the power of man over the material world, to multiply and to spread the conveniences of life, than the efforts of any other man of modern times." Finally, Davy does not hesitate to place Watt above Archimedes!

Then Huskisson, Minister of the Board of Trade, divesting himself for a moment of the character (*qualité*) of an Englishman (?), proclaims, that compared in their bearings on the happiness of the whole human species, Watt's inventions would still appear to him to deserve the *highest admiration.* He explains in what manner the economy of labour, the indefinite multiplication and cheapness of industrial products, contribute to excite and to spread knowledge. He said: "The steam-engine is not only, in the hands of man, the most powerful instrument they use to alter the face of the physical world; it acts also as a moral and irresistible lever for pushing on the great cause of civilization."

From this point of view, Watt appeared to him in a distinguished rank among the benefactors of humanity. As an Englishman he does not hesitate to say that without Watt's creations the British nation could not have stood the immense expenses of its recent war with France.

The same idea may be observed in the discourse of another member of Parliament, in that of Sir James Mackintosh: see whether he expresses himself in less positive terms. "It was the inventions of Watt that enabled England to sustain the severest, the most dangerous conflicts that she was ever engaged in." Everything considered, Mackintosh declares, without hesitation, that "no man has had more evident claim than Watt to the homage of his country, to the respect and veneration of future ages."

I will now give some numerical estimates, some numbers, which to my mind are more eloquent still than the several passages which I have been quoting.

Mr. Boulton, junior, announced that in the year 1819, the manufactory of Soho alone had already made Watt's engines equal to the labour of a hundred thousand horses; that the saving arising from the substitution of these machines for animal power amounted to seventy-five millions of francs (three millions sterling) per annum. In England and Scotland at that time, there existed upwards of ten thousand steam-engines. They did the work of five hundred thousand horses, or of between three and four millions of men; with an annual saving of three or four hundred millions of francs (twelve or sixteen millions sterling). And these results must by this time be more than doubled.

I have thus abridged what was thought of Watt by the ministers, the statesmen, the learned men, and the industrial men—the best able to appreciate him. Gentlemen, the creator of six or eight millions of workmen, indefatigable and assiduous workmen, among whom authority will never have to repress combination or riot, workmen on five centimes per day (one half-penny); this man, who, by brilliant inventions, gave England the means of maintaining a desperate struggle, during which its very nationality was at stake, this new Archimedes, this benefactor of the whole human race, whose memory will be blessed by future generations—what was done to honour him during his life?

The peerage is in England the first of its dignities, its

highest reward. You will naturally suppose that Watt was made a peer.

Such a thing was not even thought of!

To speak honestly, so much the worse for the peerage, which would have been honoured by the name of Watt!

Such a neglect, however, in a nation so justly proud of its great men, might well astonish me. And when I inquired the cause, what do you think they answered? "The dignities of which you speak are reserved for officers of the army and navy, for influential orators in the House of Commons, for members of the nobility. *It is not the fashion* (I do not invent, I quote precisely,) it is not the custom, to grant them to learned men, to literary men, to artists, to engineers!" I know well that it was not the fashion under Queen Anne, since Newton was not made a peer of England.* But after a century and a half of progress in science and in philosophy, when each of us during the short course of his life has seen so many wandering kings cast off, proscribed, succeeded on their thrones by soldiers without genealogy, sons of their sword, was it not allowable to think that it had become obsolete to divide men into folds; that none would any longer say to their faces, as in the inflexible code of the Pharaohs—"Whatever be your services,

* The whole truth should have been told. Newton, though unfortunately not made a peer, was never hidden under a bushel. He was knighted by Queen Anne, and *courted* by King George I. and by the Princess of Wales, afterwards Queen Caroline. He was President of the Royal Society, a Member of Parliament, a Master of the Mint; and at his interment the pall was supported by the Lord High Chancellor, the Dukes of Montrose and Roxburgh, and the Earls of Pembroke, Sussex, and Macclesfield. Moreover, our author seems to have excluded the host of lawyer-peers from the class "learned men."—*Translator.*

your virtues, your knowledge, not one of you shall overstep the boundary of your caste;" that a foolish custom, in short, since such a custom exists, should no longer blot the institutions of a great nation!

Let us trust to the future. A time will come when the science of destruction will bow before the arts of peace; when the genius which multiplies our powers, which creates new products, which spreads comfort among masses of people, will occupy that place in the general esteem of mankind, that reason and good sense assign to it already.

Watt will then appear before the grand jury of the two worlds. Every one will see him, aided by his steam-engine, penetrate in a few weeks into the bowels of the earth to depths where, before him, we could not have arrived without a century's most painful efforts; he will dig spacious galleries there, and will clear them in a few minutes of the immense volumes of water that used to inundate them daily; he will drag from a virgin soil the inexhaustible riches that nature deposited there.

Uniting delicacy with power, Watt will twist with equal success the enormous strands of the colossal cable by which the man-of-war moors itself in the midst of the chafed ocean—and the microscopic filaments of that lace, of that aerial web, which forms so favourite a portion of the various dresses introduced by fashion.

A few oscillations of this same machine will restore to agriculture vast swamps; thus fertile countries will be rescued from the periodical and fatal miasma that used to be fostered there by the burning summer-suns.

The great mechanical powers that we used to have to seek in mountainous regions, at the foot of large waterfalls, now, thanks to Watt's discovery, will arise at will, in a compact form, and without annoyance in the midst of towns, in every floor of a house.

The intensity of this power will vary according to the will of the mechanic; it will not depend as formerly on the most inconstant of natural causes: on atmospheric meteorology.

The various branches of a manufactory can be united in one common area, and under one roof.

The industrial products, whilst undergoing improvement, will also be reduced in price.

The population well-fed, well-dressed, well-warmed, will increase rapidly; it will cover every part of the territory with elegant habitations; even those parts that might justly be called the steppes of Europe, and which from the aridity of ages seemed to be condemned to remain the exclusive domain of wild beasts.

In a few years hamlets will become important cities: in a few years boroughs, such as Birmingham, where there used to be scarcely thirty streets, will rise to be ranked among the largest cities, the handsomest and the richest of a powerful kingdom.

Installed on board ship, the steam-engine will replace a hundredfold the efforts of the triple, of the quadruple banks of rowers, from whom our ancestors required a degree of labour classed among the punishments of the worst criminals.

By the aid of a few tons of coals, man will conquer the elements; he will laugh at calms, at contrary winds, at storms.

Passages from one country to another will become more rapid; the time of the steamboat's arrival can be foretold as correctly as that of a public land conveyance; you will no more go to the sea-shore for weeks, or even whole months, your heart a prey to cruel anguish, seeking with an anxious eye along the horizon, for the uncertain glimpse of the ship that is to restore to you a father, a mother, a brother, or a friend.

To conclude, the steam-engine, dragging in its train some thousands of travellers, will run along the railways much faster than the best blood horse bearing only his light jockey along the race-course.

There, Gentlemen, is a very brief sketch of the benefits bequeathed to the world by the machine, the germs of which Papin had deposited in his works, and which, after so many ingenious efforts, Watt has brought to an admirable perfection.* Posterity certainly will not weigh

* A translator should not, perhaps, enter the lists, but he may intrude a remark. It is difficult to opine why our author should bestir himself so eagerly to give Watt the composition of water, and yet impair his grand claim to universal homage by foisting in the names of Rivault, De Caus, and others as inventors: the early engines were mere toys and pumps, and therefore foreign to the marvellous and almost animated machine which is now in use. Some of Watt's excogitations and contrivances, the product of lengthy intellectual struggles, are slurred over, while others are not even alluded to; and the difficulties he had to combat with in metallurgy are altogether omitted.

We ought to be cautious in attaching an undue value to mere sagacious surmises, unsupported by legitimate proof; for notions may arise without being brought to bear; and simultaneous ideas may be formed without the parties being indebted to each other. M. Arago cannot tell whether De Caus actually made an engine; but surely he ought, as a self-constituted historical umpire, to have consulted the published *Travels of Cosmo III.* (*Grand Duke of Tuscany*) *in England, in the reign of Charles II.*, and he would there have found that the Marquis of Worcester actually did make one (*see note to page* 378). Now for all that is admirable in the structure of the mighty piece of mechanism, and really marvellous in its application, Watt was not a mere improver, but a highly-gifted inventor. We therefore insist that, to all its useful intents and purposes, the present STEAM-ENGINE is a British production. Thus in transcendental science, although preceding and

them with other labours that have been too much vaunted; and whose real influence at the tribunal of reason, will always remain circumscribed to a circle of a few individuals, and a short compass of years.

They used formerly to appeal to the age of Augustus, then to the age of Louis XIV. Some eminent minds have already maintained that it would be justice to speak of the age of Voltaire, of Rousseau, of Montesquieu. As to myself, I do not hesitate to announce, that when to the immense services already rendered by the steam-engine, all the wonders are added that it still promises, grateful nations will also speak of the ages of Papin and of Watt!

ACADEMICAL TITLES WITH WHICH WATT WAS INVESTED.

A biography of Watt, intended to make part of our collection of memoirs, would certainly be incomplete if it did not contain a list of the academical titles with which the illustrious engineer was invested. This list, moreover, will occupy only a few lines:—

contemporary philosophers had made conjectures on the subject that did not differ widely from truth, Newton, by an inductive ascent through a train of abstruse investigations to its principle, and thereby detecting and expounding its laws, is justly recognized as the author of the sublime hypothesis of GRAVITATION. Who will deny to Herschel the merit of discovering the planet Uranus, since Flamsteed had previously observed it as a star? Or still later, because some philosophers thought that there might exist a planet exterior to Uranus, who would deny the palm to those whose energies were awakened by the orbital tremblings of that outer body to the splendid discovery of Neptune? In reality, De Caus, Worcester, and Papin may be placed with respect to Watt, as Gilbert, Kepler, and Hooke are to Newton; or as Lambert, De Zach, and Bode will be to Le Verrier and Adams.—*Translator.*

Watt became:

Fellow of the Royal Society of Edinburgh	. in 1784;
Fellow of the Royal Society of London	. in 1785;
Fellow of the Society of Batavia	. in 1787;
By a spontaneous and unanimous vote, the Senate of the University of Glasgow awarded to Watt the honorary degree of Doctor of Laws	. in 1806;
Correspondent of the Institute .	. in 1808;
The Academy of Sciences of the Institute paid Watt the highest honour there is in its awards, by naming him one of its eight Foreign Associates .	. in 1814.

APPENDIX.

RETRANSLATION OF AN HISTORICAL NOTE BY LORD BROUGHAM, ON THE DISCOVERY OF THE COMPOSITION OF WATER.

THERE is no doubt that in England, at least, the researches respecting the composition of water originated in Warltire's experiments related in the fifth volume of Priestley.* Cavendish cites them expressly as having given him the idea of his work (*Phil. Trans.* 1784, p. 126). Warltire's experiments consisted in the combustion of a mixture of oxygen and hydrogen, by means of the electric spark, and in closed vessels. Two results were reported therefrom: 1. a perceptible loss of weight; 2. the precipitation of some humidity on the sides of the vessels.

Watt inadvertently said in the note to page 332, of his Memoir (*Phil. Trans.* 1784), that the aqueous precipitation was observed for the first time by Cavendish; but Cavendish himself declares, p. 127, that Warltire had perceived the slight aqueous deposit, and quotes on this subject Priestley's fifth volume. Cavendish could not ascertain any loss of weight. He remarks that Priestley's essays *had led him to the same result*,† and adds that the humidity which was deposited con-

* Warltire's letter, dated Birmingham, 18th April, 1781, was published by Dr. Priestley in the second volume of his *Experiments and Observations relating to various branches of Natural Philosophy, with a continuation of the Observations on Air*, forming, in short, the fifth volume of the *Experiments and Observations on different Kinds of Air*, published at Birmingham in 1781.—(*Note by Mr. Watt, jun.*)

† The note by Mr. Cavendish to p. 127, seems to imply that Priest-

tained no impurity (literally no particle of soot or of *sooty matter*). After a great number of trials, Cavendish perceived that if a mixture of common and of inflammable air is ignited, a mixture formed of 1000 measures of the former and 423 of the latter, "about one fifth of the common and nearly the

ley had not perceived any loss of weight; but I do not find this assertion anywhere in the Memoirs of the Birmingham chemist.

Warltire's earliest experiments on the combustion of gas were made in a copper globe which weighed 398 grammes, and the volume was 170 centilitres. The author wished " to decide whether heat is, or is not heavy."

Warltire first describes the method of mixing the gases, and of adjusting the scales; he then says, "I always carefully weighed the vessel filled with common air, so that the difference of weight after the addition of the inflammable air enabled me to judge whether the mixture had been effected in the desired proportions. The passage of the electric spark rendered the globe hot. After it had cooled by exposure to the air of the room, I suspended it again on the scales. I always found a loss of weight, but there were differences between one experiment and another. The mean loss was 129 milligrammes."

Warltire continues as follows: "I have exploded my airs in glass vessels since I saw you recently do so yourself (Priestley), and I have observed, AS YOU DID, that however dry and clean the vessel might be before the explosion, it was afterwards covered with dew and a black *sooty substance.*"

In comparing all these claims, does not the merit of having first perceived the dew belong to Priestley?

In the few remarks that Priestley has added to his correspondent's letter, he confirms the loss of weight, and adds, " Still, I do not think that the bold opinion of the latent heat of bodies entering as a sensible part of their weight, can be admitted without making experiments on a larger scale. If that is confirmed it will be a very remarkable fact, and one that will do infinite credit to Warltire's sagacity."

And Priestley continues, " We must say also, that at the moment when he (Warltire) saw the dew on the interior surface of the closed glass vessel, he said that it confirmed an opinion which he had long entertained, the opinion that common air parts with its humidity when it is phlogisticated."

It is evident then that Warltire explained the dew by the simple mechanical precipitation of the hygrometric water contained in cammon air.—(*Note by Mr. Watt, jun.*)

whole of the inflammable air lose their elasticity, and *form by their condensation* the dew that covers the glass. . . . . On examining the dew, Cavendish found that it consisted of pure water. . . . . He thence concluded that nearly all the inflammable air and about one sixth of the common air *are turned into pure water*."

In a similar way, Cavendish burned a mixture of inflammable air, and dephlogisticated air (or hydrogen and oxygen); the fluid that was precipitated was always more or less acid, according as the gas burned with the inflammable air contained more or less phlogiston. The acid thus engendered was nitric acid.

Mr. Cavendish ascertained that nearly the whole of the inflammable air and the dephlogisticated air are *converted into pure water*; also, that if those airs could be obtained in a perfectly pure state, the whole would be *condensed*. If common air and inflammable air do not yield any acid when they are burnt, it is, according to our author, because the heat is not then intense.

Cavendish declares that his experiments, except in as far as they relate to the acid, were made in the summer of 1781, and that Priestley was aware of them. He adds, "One of my friends *gave some account* of them to Lavoisier, in the course of last spring (the spring of 1783), and also of the result that I had inferred from them, that is to say, that dephlogisticated air is water deprived of its phlogiston. But at that time, Lavoisier was so far from thinking that such a opinion was legitimate, that until the moment when he determined to repeat the experiments himself, he felt some difficulty in believing that nearly the whole of the two airs could be converted into water."

The friend alluded to in the preceding passage was Dr., since become Sir Charles Blagden. It is a remarkable circumstance, that this passage in the work of Mr. Cavendish should not have formed part of the original Memoir that was presented to the Royal Society. The Memoir seems to be written in the author's own handwriting; but the paragraphs

134 and 135 were not there at first; they are added, and an indication is given as to where they belong; the writing is no longer that of Cavendish; these additions are in the handwriting of Blagden. And it must have been he who gave all the relative details to Lavoisier, for it is not said that Cavendish held any direct correspondence with him.

The date of the reading of Cavendish's Memoir was the 15th of January, 1784. The volume of the *Philosophical Transactions*, of which this Memoir forms a part, did not appear till about six months after.

Lavoisier's Memoir (*volume of the Academy of Sciences for* 1781)* had been read in November and December, 1783. Various additions were made to it afterwards. The publication took place in 1784.

This Memoir contained a description of the experiments of June, 1783, at which Lavoisier announces that Blagden was present. Lavoisier adds, that this English physicist informed him "that Cavendish having already burnt inflammable air in closed vessels, had obtained a very sensible quantity of water;" but he nowhere says that Blagden informed him of the conclusions that Cavendish had inferred from those same experiments.

Lavoisier declares, in the most express manner, that the weight of the water is equal to that of the two gases that were ignited, unless, contrary to his own opinion, a sensible weight be assigned to the heat and to the light that were disengaged during the experiment.

This account does not agree with that of Blagden, which, according to all probability, was written as a refutation to Lavoisier's relation, after the reading of Cavendish's Memoir, and before the volume of the Academy of Sciences had reached England. This volume appeared in 1784, and assuredly it could not have reached London, either when Cavendish read his paper to the Royal Society, or still less when he wrote it. We must remark, besides, that in the passage of Cavendish's

* The date 1781 appears to be a clerical error for 1784.—*Translator*.

manuscript Memoir, in the handwriting of Blagden, there is only one communication of experiments alluded to: one communication to Priestley. The experiments are there said to have been made in 1781; but there is no mention of the date of the communication. Nor are we informed whether the conclusions inferred from those experiments, and which, according to Blagden, were communicated by him to Lavoisier in the summer of 1783, were equally included in the communication made to Priestley. This chemist, in his Memoir written before the month of April, 1783, read in June of the same year, and quoted by Cavendish, says nothing of the theory of the latter, although he quotes experiments.

Several propositions flow from the preceding facts:—

1. Cavendish, in the Memoir that was read to the Royal Society the 15th of January, 1784, describes the capital experiment of the combustion of the oxygen and hydrogen in closed vessels, and cites water as the product of this combustion;

2. In the same Memoir Cavendish deduces from these same experiments that the two forementioned gases are transformed into water;

3. In an addition by Blagden, made with the consent of Cavendish, the date of the summer of 1781 is assigned to the experiments of the latter; a communication to Priestley is quoted, without specifying the epoch, without mentioning conclusions, without stating even when those conclusions occurred to the mind of Cavendish. This must be regarded as a *most material* omission;

4. In one of the additions made to the Memoir by Blagden, Cavendish's conclusion is related in the following words: Oxygen gas is water deprived of its phlogiston. This addition is posterior to the arrival of Lavoisier's Memoir in England.

It may moreover be remarked, that in another edition to Cavendish's Memoir, written by the hand of that chemist, and which is certainly posterior to the arrival of Lavoisier's Memoir in England, Cavendish distinctly asserts for the first time, as in Lavoisier's hypothesis, that water is a compound of oxygen and hydrogen. Perhaps no essential difference will be found between this conclusion and the one which Cavendish had asserted before, that oxygen gas is water deprived of its phlogiston, for to render them identical it will suffice to look upon phlogiston as hydrogen; but to say of water that it consists of oxygen and hydrogen, is, certainly embracing a neater and less equivocal conclusion. I add, that in the original part of his Memoir, in that which was read to the Royal Society before the arrival of Lavoisier's Memoir in England, Cavendish thinks it more correct to consider inflammable air as phlogisticated water than as pure phlogiston."—(P. 140, *Phil. Trans.* for 1784.)

Now let us see what part Watt acted. The dates will here be of importance.

It appears that Watt wrote a letter to Dr. Priestley, on the 26th of April, 1783, in which he discusses the experiment of igniting the two gases in closed vessels, and that by it he came to the conclusion that water is composed of dephlogisticated air and phlogiston, both of them deprived of a part of their latent heat.*

Priestley deposited the letter in the hands of Sir Joseph Banks, with a request that it should be read at one of the earliest meetings of the Royal Society. But Watt afterwards wished the reading to be deferred, in order to have time to see how his theory agreed with some of Priestley's recent ex-

* We may feel quite safe in deducing from the inedited correspondence of Watt, that he had already formed his theory on the composition of water in December, 1782, and probably earlier. At all events, in his Memoir of the 21st of April, 1783, Priestley declares that, before his own experiments, Watt had entertained the idea that steam might be transformed into permanent gases.—(P. 416, *Phil. Trans.* 1783.)

Watt himself, in his Memoir (p. 335, *Phil. Trans.* 1784), declares that, during several years, he had entertained an opinion that air is a modification of water, and he makes known in detail the experiments and the reasonings on which this opinion rested.—(*Note by Mr. Watt, junior.*)

periments. In short, the letter was not read till April, 1784.* This letter was incorporated by Watt in a Memoir addressed to Deluc, dated 26th Nov. 1783.† Many new observations, and new reasonings, were introduced into this Memoir, although nearly the whole of the original letter was preserved in it, and in the printing it was distinguished from the additions by inverted commas. The important deduction, previously quoted, will be found in the part thus marked. We read also that the letter was communicated to several Fellows of the Royal Society when it reached Priestley in April, 1783.

In Cavendish's Memoir, such as it was when read, there was no allusion to Watt's theory; but it is mentioned in an addition, entirely in the handwriting of Cavendish, posterior to the reading of Watt's letters, (*Phil. Trans.* 1784, p. 140.) In this addition Cavendish gives his reasons for not liking to render his conclusions complicated as Watt did, with considerations relative to the disengagement of latent heat; but it leaves us in doubt on the question as to whether the author was ever aware of the letter to Priestley of April, 1783, or whether he only saw the letter dated 26th of November, 1783, and read the 29th of April, 1784; on which it is requisite to remark that the two letters appeared in the *Philosophical Transactions* united in one. The letter to Priestley of the 26th April, 1783, remained some time (two months according to Watt's Memoir,) in the hands of Sir Joseph Banks and other Fellows of the Royal Society, during the spring of 1783. This is what we learn from the circumstances related in the note at p. 330. It seemed difficult to suppose that Blagden, Secretary of the

* The letter to Priestley was read the 22d of April, 1784.

† Undoubtedly the Genevese physicist, then in London, received it at the time. It remained in his hands until Watt heard of the reading of Cavendish's Memoir at the Royal Society. From that moment my father made all possible arrangements for the Memoir addressed to Deluc and the letter of the 26th of April, 1783, addressed to Dr. Priestley, being read immediately at the Royal Society. This reading, claimed by Watt for the Memoir addressed to Deluc, was dated 29th of April, 1784.—(*Note by Mr. Watt, jun.*)

Society, did not see the Memoir. Sir Joseph Banks must have given it to him, since he intended it to be read at the meeting, (*Phil. Trans.* 1784, p. 330, note.) Let us add that as the letter was preserved in the archives of the Society, it was in charge of Blagden, the Secretary. Would it be possible to suppose that the person whose hand wrote the remarkable passage already quoted, relative to a communication made to Lavoisier, in June, 1783, of the conclusions that Cavendish had come to, would not have told Cavendish that Watt had come to those conclusions at the latest in April, 1783? The conclusions are identical, with the mere difference that Cavendish calls dephlogisticated air water deprived of its phlogiston, and that Watt affirms water to be a union of dephlogisticated air and phlogiston.

We must remark that in Watt's theory there is the same uncertainty, the same vagueness, which we have already observed in that of Cavendish, and that it also proceeds from the use of the term phlogiston, which was not well defined.* In Cavendish we cannot decide whether phlogiston is merely inflammable air, or whether this chemist is not rather inclined to consider a combination of water and phlogiston as inflammable air. Watt says expressly, even in his Memoir of the 26th November, 1783, and in a passage that does not form part of the April letter in 1783, that inflammable air, according to his ideas, contains a small quantity of water and a great deal of elementary heat.

These expressions from two such eminent men, should be regarded as indicating a certain degree of hesitation, relative to the composition of water. If Watt and Cavendish had had a precise idea that water results from the union of two gases

* In a note to his Memoir of the 26th of November, 1783 (p. 331), we read the following remark by Watt: "Anterior to Dr. Priestley's experiments, Kirwan had proved, by some ingenious deductions borrowed from other facts, that inflammable air is in all probability the true phlogiston in an aerial form. Kirwan's arguments appear to me perfectly convincing; but it seems more suitable to establish this point of the question by direct experiments."

deprived of their latent heat, from the union of the bases of inflammable air and of dephlogisticated air; if this idea had been accompanied in their minds by as much clearness as in that of Lavoisier, they would certainly have avoided the uncertainty and obscurity which I have pointed out.*

As far as relates to Watt, the following are the new facts that we have succeeded in establishing.

1. There is no proof that anybody had given, in a written document, anterior to Watt, the present theory of the composition of water.

2. Watt established this theory during the year 1783, in

* At the foot of p. 333, of the *Transactions* (for 1784), in a part of his April letter, 1783, printed in italics, Watt said: "Are we not then authorized to conclude that water is composed of dephlogisticated air and phlogiston deprived of part of their latent or elementary heat; that dephlogisticated air, or pure air, is composed of water deprived of its phlogiston and united to elementary heat and light; that heat and light are contained in it in a latent state, since they do not affect either the thermometer or the eye? If light is only a modification of heat, or a peculiarity in its existence, or a constituent part of inflammable air, then pure or dephlogisticated air is composed of water deprived of its phlogiston, and united to some elementary heat."

Is not this passage as clear, precise, and intelligible as Lavoisier's conclusions?—(*Note by Mr. Watt, jun.*)

The obscurity complained of by Lord Brougham in the theoretical conceptions of Watt and of Cavendish appears to me unfounded. In 1784 they knew how to prepare two permanent and very dissimilar gases. Those two gases were by some distinguished as pure air and inflammable air; by others as dephlogisticated air and phlogiston; by others, finally, as oxygen and hydrogen. By the combination of dephlogisticated air and phlogiston, they generated water weighing as much as the two gases. Thenceforward water was no longer a simple body; it was composed of dephlogisticated air and phlogiston. The chemist who deduced this conclusion might have false ideas on the internal nature of phlogiston without its casting any uncertainty on the merit of his first discovery. Has it been even now *mathematically demonstrated* that hydrogen (or phlogiston) is an elementary body; that it is not, as Watt and Cavendish for a time supposed, the combination of a radical with a little water?—(*Note by M. Arago.*)

more distinct terms than Cavendish did in his Memoir read to the Royal Society in January, 1784. By noticing also the disengagement of latent heat in the operation, Watt added very much to the clearness of his conception.

3. There is no proof, there is not even any assertion whence it would result, that the *theory* of Cavendish (Blagden calls it *conclusion*) was communicated to Priestley previously to Watt's delivering his ideas in the letter of the 26th of April, 1783; and still more, nothing leads one to suppose, especially after reading Watt's letter, that he had ever heard any thing relative to the composition of water either from Priestley or from any other person.

4. Watt's theory was known by the Fellows of the Royal Society *several* months before the conclusions of Cavendish had been committed to paper; *eight* months before the Memoir of that chemist was presented to that same Society. We can go farther, and deduce from facts and dates now before us, that Watt was the first to speak of the composition of water; that if any one was anterior to him, there is no proof of it.

5. Finally, a repugnance to abandon the doctrine of phlogiston, a sort of timidity in separating from an opinion so long established, so deeply rooted, prevented Watt and Cavendish from rendering complete justice to their own theory; whilst Lavoisier, who had broken through those trammels, was the first to present the new doctrine in all its perfection.*

It might be very possible that without knowing any thing of their respective labours, Watt, Cavendish, and Lavoisier had nearly at the same time made the great step of concluding from experiment, that water is the product of a combination

* No one ought to have expected from Watt, writing and publishing for the first time, exposed to the cares of an immense manufactory and of commercial affairs equally extensive, that he could vie with the eloquent and practised pen of Lavoisier; but the substance of his theory (see p. 333 of his Memoir) seems, at least to me, who in truth may not perhaps be an impartial judge, as luminous and as remarkable in expression as the conclusions of the illustrious French chemist.—(*Note by Mr. Watt, jun.*)

of the two gases so often quoted. Such is, in short, with more or less distinctness, the conclusion that the three learned men presented.

It now remains to consider Blagden's declaration, from which Lavoisier might have learned the theory of Cavendish, even before he had made his principal experiment. Blagden inserted this declaration in Cavendish's own Memoir; * it was published in the *Philosophical Transactions*, and it does not appear that Lavoisier ever contradicted it, however irreconcilable it was with his own recital.

Notwithstanding all Blagden's susceptible jealousy in favour of the priority of Cavendish, there has not been on his part a single allusion from which one might deduce that, before publishing his own, Watt had heard of his competitor's theory.

We will not be so positive relative to the question of Cavendish having had some knowledge of Watt's labours, before arranging the conclusions in his own Memoir. To maintain that Cavendish was not ignorant of Watt's conclusions, we might remark how very improbable it was that neither Blagden nor any one else to whom those conclusions were known, had ever mentioned them to him. It might also be said that Blagden, even in those portions of the Memoir that were written in his own hand, and intended to claim the priority for Cavendish against Lavoisier, nowhere affirms that the theory of Cavendish was conceived before the month of April, 1783, although in another addition to his friend's original Memoir there is a quotation relative to Watt's theory.

Since the question as to the epoch when Cavendish drew conclusions from his experiments, is enveloped in great obscurity, it may be of some utility to inquire what were this

* A letter to Professor Crell, in which Blagden gave a detailed account of the discovery, appeared in the *Annalen* of 1786. It is remarkable that in this letter, Blagden says that he communicated to Lavoisier the opinions of Cavendish *and of Watt*, and that this latter name figures here for the first time in the confidential verbal recitals of the Secretary of the Royal Society.—(*Note by Mr. Watt, jun.*)

chemist's habits when he communicated his discoveries to the Royal Society.

A Committee of that Society, to which Gilpin belonged, made a series of experiments on the formation of nitric acid. This Committee, placed under the direction of Cavendish, sought to convince those who doubted of the composition of the acid in question, incidentally indicated in the Memoir of January, 1784, and afterwards more at length in a Memoir of June, 1785. The experiments were made between the 6th of December, 1787, and the 19th of March, 1788. The date of the reading of Cavendish's Memoir was the 17th of April, 1788. The reading and the printing then occurred within less than a month of the completion of the experiments.

Kirwan presented his objections to Cavendish's Memoir relative to the composition of water, on the 5th of February, 1784. Cavendish's answer was read on the 4th of the following March.

The experiments on the density of the earth occupied the interval between the 5th of August, 1797, and the 27th of May, 1798. The date of the reading of that Memoir was the 27th of June, 1798.

In the Memoir on the eudiometer, the experiments quoted were made in the latter half of 1781, but the Memoir was not read till January, 1783. Here the interval was greater than in the preceding communications. From the nature of the subject, however, it is probable that the author undertook fresh experiments in 1782.

Every thing renders it probable that Watt conceived his theory in the course of a few months or even of a few weeks prior to April, 1783. It is certain that this theory was considered by him as his property, for he did not allude to any anterior or analogous communication; nor does he say that he had heard of Cavendish having come to similar conclusions.

We cannot believe that Blagden would have heard no mention of Cavendish's theory prior to the date of Watt's letter, if that theory had actually preceded the letter, and that he would not have been eager to point out this circumstance in the additions that he made to his friend's Memoir.

It is well finally to remark, that Watt depended entirely on Blagden's taking care to correct the proofs, and attending to every thing else that could relate to the printing of his Memoir. This is proved by a letter, still existing, addressed to Blagden. Watt saw his Memoir only after it had been printed.

The notes by Mr. Watt, jun., made part of a manuscript which was sent me by Lord Brougham; and it is at the express request of my illustrious co-academician that I have had them printed as a useful commentary on his work.

NOTE BY W. FAIRBAIRN, F.R.S., F.G.S.

In writing his historical eulogy of James Watt, the distinguished French philosopher has allowed his partiality for his countrymen to overstep the boundaries within which an impartial writer should be restrained. To associate Dr. Papin as a coadjutor of Watt in the discovery and invention of the steam-engine, is to give to the former a degree of prominence to which he is certainly not entitled; and it is much to be regretted, that men in so high a position as Arago, with minds so imbued with the love of truth, and the desire to award to individual merit the praise justly due to labours in the field of discovery, should be so biassed by love of country as to endeavour to curtail the merits, and to divide the honour which exclusively belongs to one who has done more for practical science, and for the great family of mankind, than any other person since the days of Newton.

Papin was contemporary with Newton, and laboured in the same field as Savery, in experiments on the effects of steam as a motive power; but we have yet to learn that that power was ever applied by him to the organic parts of an engine, calculated to overcome the resistance of a load, such as the propulsion of machinery or the raising water from mines. The discovery of an element of power is a totally different thing to its application through the organic parts of a machine. The first is the result of experimental research in the laboratory; the second is the result of toilsome labour in the workshop, in the actual production of a machine; merit for the former belongs to Dr. Papin, for the latter, exclusively to Newcomen and James Watt.

Savery constructed an engine for raising water upon the principle of condensation. It consisted of two vessels,—a boiler and a condenser, if we may so term them, the latter being connected by pipes with the water in the mine and the reservoir to which it was to be raised. Under the boiler a fire was lighted, and the steam was allowed to fill the condenser; the connection with the boiler was then cut off, and a jet of cold water thrown into the condenser, which at once created a vacuum; the pressure of the atmosphere now forced the water from a depth not exceeding 30 feet in the mine, into the condenser, where it was retained by a valve. Steam from the boiler then forced the water from the condenser upwards through the pipe to the reservoir above, and as soon as it was again filled with steam, the process was repeated. This slow and tedious operation was regulated by hand, but that could only be done under the limits stated above, and with an enormous consumption of fuel. This was the apparatus adopted by Savery, but we have no satisfactory information that Dr. Papin ever constructed an engine worked by steam; his attempts were made on models which were never usefully applied; and Dr. Hooke, in his correspondence with Newcomen and the Royal Society, pointed out the absurdity and fallacy of the air-pipes and pistons, which he proposed as a means of raising water from mines. The only real inventor, antecedent to Watt, was Newcomen, who introduced the open top cylinder, and the reciprocating motion of the piston and beam. The apparatus antecedent to this scarcely deserved the name of *engine*, still less should it be considered the parent of the modern steam-engine. Newcomen's engine first acquired the character of an automaton (however rudely formed) from the ingenious application of the boy Potter, while its subsequent developments, far surpassing in number and importance all that had preceded, are exclusively due to James Watt. Newcomen invented the engine as it was when Watt repaired the far-famed model belonging to the Glasgow University—a mere pumping machine; Watt made it a source of motive power capable of application in every situation and for every kind of work; and it was in his hands that it received the name and properties it now possesses, as the most extraordinary invention of all time.

Arago arrogates to Papin the merit as if his discoveries had led to the mechanical arrangements of the steam-engine, or to the invention of condensation in a separate vessel. Now it is evident that Watt was not in any way indebted to him, even for a hint in the attainment of these results. Papin was not even capable of devising the mechanical arrangements of an engine, as it issued from the hands of Watt; and even Newcomen's was so rude an attempt, that the present steam-engine may be safely considered as the exclusive invention of James Watt.

It is highly interesting and exceedingly curious to trace the progressive developments of this machine, as it acquired, by slow but certain stages, its present proportions and power. The constant study, unwearied application, and experimental research which distinguished every step made in advance, will, to the end of time, uphold the name, and exhibit the untiring energy, of the man who produced so important—so various results.

It is unbecoming in a great man and a great nation to attempt to drag forward competitors where no competition exists, —where, in fact, the inventor stands alone as the benefactor of the human race. If Watt had done no more than the introduction of his condenser, whereby he gained one of the greatest steps towards making the engine what it is, quadrupled its power, and gave to it the docility and powers of adaptation of almost animal existence,—if he had done no more than this, he was entitled to a world's gratitude, and to all the honours of an original inventor. But it was not this that marked the fertility of his mind, but the perfection of his engine by an organization which has made it so powerful and yet so perfect, which has given it a smoothness of action and almost vital adaptability to every kind of work, and which will ever excite the admiration of every mind conversant with the beauty of mechanical design.

So valuable an invention did not escape constant piracy. Engines began to be erected on the principles of separate condensation, which not only infringed the patent rights, but from their miserable construction brought discredit on engines as a class; so that Boulton and Watt were compelled at last, however reluctantly, to commence a long series of legal proceedings, which at length fully established the validity of their patent.

To show the progress that was made in the construction of engines, and the immense importance of their manufacture, we quote from a recent work on the *Mechanical Inventions of James Watt*, by James Muirhead, Esq., the number of engines constructed at Soho.

"*Memorandum.*

Soho Foundry, 16th March, 1854.

"The number and power of the engines made by Messrs. Boulton, Watt, and Co., to the date January, 1824, were thus reckoned by the late Mr. Boulton and Mr. Creighton (one of his assistants at Soho) :—

Engines.	Nominal Horse-power.	Power of living Horses required to do the same work.
283 for pumping and blowing	11,247 × 4	44,988
805 rotative . . .	12,618 × 3	37,854
76 boat engines . .	2,080 × 3	6,240
1,164	25,945	89,082

"And between January 1824 and January 1854, the numbers are the following:—

34 for pumping and blowing	2,403 × 4	9,612
164 rotative . . .	7,517 × 3	22,551
243 boat engines . .	15,358 × 3	46,074
441	25,278	78,237

"Giving the following total numbers:—

1,164	25,945	89,082
441	25,278	78,237
1,605	51,223	167,319

"The first engine seems to have been made for Bedworth, in 1776."

It will be noticed that for pumping engines the nominal horse-power is multiplied by four to give the real horse-power required to do the same work in the same time; and this is on the supposition that a horse can work only six hours a day, whilst the engine can work twenty-four. But in rotative engines an allowance has been made in the above table for loss of power in the action of the crank, &c. as compared with the direct action in the other case, and the nominal horse-power is multiplied by three only.

Perhaps it would be more accurate to suppose that a horse can work for eight hours out of the twenty-four; but at the same time to multiply the nominal horse-power by two, because each indicated horse-power of the engine = 33,000 lbs. raised one foot high per minute, is at least twice as much as its nominal power, or twice as much as an ordinary horse could work up to. We shall then find that it would require no less than 250,974 living horses to perform the work of the engines constructed by Messrs. Boulton and Watt up to January 1854.

One of Watt's fellow labourers should hardly be passed over in any statement connected with the steam-engine; we allude to the late Mr. William Murdock, whose vast practical knowledge was employed in carrying out the designs of Watt for upwards of half a century. Mr. Murdock directed the application of the new steam-engines to drain the water of the Cornish mines. In order to adapt that moving power to exhausting pumps, and to establish the system in mines of extreme depth inundated by appalling quantities of water, great skill in practical mechanics was requisite. Mr. Murdock showed that he had sufficient resources of genius and wisdom of experience to triumph over every difficulty. He was the introducer of the system of lighting by coal gas, and for his paper on that subject sent to the Royal Society he received the Rumford gold medal. He was also the patentee of some new methods of constructing steam-engines, &c., and his suggestions often enriched the Soho machinery. We have therefore great pleasure in bearing testimony to the merits of one of our first practical mechanics, the able assistant and coadjutor of James Watt.

W. F.

THE END.

A LIST OF BOOKS

PUBLISHED BY

TICKNOR AND FIELDS.

Sir Walter Scott.

ILLUSTRATED HOUSEHOLD EDITION OF THE WAVERLEY NOVELS. In portable size, 16mo. form. Price 75 cents a volume.

The paper is of fine quality; the stereotype plates are not old ones repaired, the type having been cast expressly for this edition. The Novels are illustrated with capital steel plates engraved in the best manner, after drawings and paintings by the most eminent artists, among whom are Birket Foster, Darley, Billings, Landseer, Harvey, and Faed. This Edition contains all the latest notes and corrections of the author, a Glossary and Index; and some curious additions, especially in "Guy Mannering" and the "Bride of Lammermoor;" being the fullest edition of the Novels ever published. *The notes are at the foot of the page*,—a great convenience to the reader.

Any of the following Novels sold separate.

WAVERLEY, 2 vols.
GUY MANNERING, 2 vols.
THE ANTIQUARY, 2 vols.
ROB ROY, 2 vols.
OLD MORTALITY, 2 vols.
BLACK DWARF, LEGEND OF MONTROSE, } 2 vols.
HEART OF MID LOTHIAN, 2 vols.
BRIDE OF LAMMERMOOR, 2 vols.
IVANHOE, 2 vols.
THE MONASTERY, 2 vols.
THE ABBOT, 2 vols.
KENILWORTH, 2 vols.
THE PIRATE, 2 vols.
THE FORTUNES OF NIGEL, 2 vols.
PEVERIL OF THE PEAK, 2 vols.
QUENTIN DURWARD, 2 vols.
ST. RONAN'S WELL, 2 vols.
REDGAUNTLET, 2 vols.
THE BETROTHED, THE HIGHLAND WIDOW, } 2 vols.
THE TALISMAN, TWO DROVERS, MY AUNT MARGARET'S MIRROR, THE TAPESTRIED CHAMBER, THE LAIRD'S JOCK. } 2 vols.
WOODSTOCK, 2 vols.
THE FAIR MAID OF PERTH, 2 vols.
ANNE OF GEIERSTEIN, 2 vols.
COUNT ROBERT OF PARIS, 2 vols.
THE SURGEON'S DAUGHTER, CASTLE DANGEROUS, INDEX AND GLOSSARY. } 2 vols.

Thomas De Quincey.

Confessions of an English Opium-Eater, and Suspiria de Profundis. With Portrait. 75 cents.

Biographical Essays. 75 cents.

Miscellaneous Essays. 75 cents.

The Cæsars. 75 cents.

Literary Reminiscences. 2 vols. $1.50.

Narrative and Miscellaneous Papers. 2 vols. $1.50.

Essays on the Poets, &c. 1 vol. 16mo. 75 cents.

Historical and Critical Essays. 2 vols. $1.50.

Autobiographic Sketches. 1 vol. 75 cents.

Essays on Philosophical Writers, &c. 2 vols. 16mo. $1.50.

Letters to a Young Man, and other Papers. 1 vol. 75 cents.

Theological Essays and other Papers. 2 vols. $1.50.

The Note Book. 1 vol. 75 cents.

Memorials and other Papers. 2 vols. 16mo. $1.50.

Alfred Tennyson.

Poetical Works. With Portrait. 2 vols. Cloth. $2.00.

Pocket Edition of Poems Complete. 75 cents.

The Princess. Cloth. 50 cents.

In Memoriam. Cloth. 75 cents.

Maud, and other Poems. Cloth. 50 cents.

Charles Reade.

Peg Woffington. A Novel. 75 cents.

Christie Johnstone. A Novel. 75 cents.

Clouds and Sunshine. A Novel. 75 cents.

'Never too late to mend.' 2 vols. $1.50.

White Lies. A Novel. 1 vol. $1.25.

Propria Quæ Maribus and The Box Tunnel. 25 cts.

Henry W. Longfellow.

POETICAL WORKS. In two volumes. 16mo. Boards. $2.00.
POCKET EDITION OF POETICAL WORKS. In two volumes. $1.75.
POCKET EDITION OF PROSE WORKS COMPLETE. In two volumes. $1.75.
THE SONG OF HIAWATHA. $1.00.
EVANGELINE: A TALE OF ACADIE. 75 cents.
THE GOLDEN LEGEND. A POEM. $1.00.
HYPERION. A ROMANCE. $1.00.
OUTRE-MER. A PILGRIMAGE. $1.00.
KAVANAGH. A TALE. 75 cents.
THE COURTSHIP OF MILES STANDISH. 1 vol. 16mo. 75 cents.
Illustrated editions of EVANGELINE, POEMS, HYPERION, THE GOLDEN LEGEND, and MILES STANDISH.

Oliver Wendell Holmes.

POEMS. With fine Portrait. Boards. $1.00. Cloth. $1.12.
ASTRÆA. Fancy paper. 25 cents.

William Howitt.

LAND, LABOR, AND GOLD. 2 vols. $2.00.
A BOY'S ADVENTURES IN AUSTRALIA. 75 cents.

Charles Kingsley.

TWO YEARS AGO. A New Novel. $1.25.
AMYAS LEIGH. A Novel $1.25.
GLAUCUS; OR, THE WONDERS OF THE SHORE. 50 cts.
POETICAL WORKS. 75 cents.
THE HEROES; OR, GREEK FAIRY TALES. 75 cents.
ANDROMEDA AND OTHER POEMS. 50 cents.
SIR WALTER RALEIGH AND HIS TIME, &c. $1.25.

Nathaniel Hawthorne.

TWICE-TOLD TALES. Two volumes. $1.50.
THE SCARLET LETTER. 75 cents.
THE HOUSE OF THE SEVEN GABLES. $1.00.
THE SNOW IMAGE, AND OTHER TALES. 75 cents.
THE BLITHEDALE ROMANCE. 75 cents.
MOSSES FROM AN OLD MANSE. 2 vols. $1.50.
TRUE STORIES FROM HISTORY AND BIOGRAPHY. With four fine Engravings. 75 cents.
A WONDER-BOOK FOR GIRLS AND BOYS. With seven fine Engravings. 75 cents.
TANGLEWOOD TALES. Another "Wonder-Book." With Engravings. 88 cents.

Barry Cornwall.

ENGLISH SONGS AND OTHER SMALL POEMS. $1.00.
DRAMATIC POEMS. Just published. $1.00.
ESSAYS AND TALES IN PROSE. 2 vols. $1.50.

James Russell Lowell.

COMPLETE POETICAL WORKS. In Blue and Gold. 2 vols. $1.50.
POETICAL WORKS. 2 vols. 16mo. Cloth. $1.50.
SIR LAUNFAL. New Edition. 25 cents.
A FABLE FOR CRITICS. New Edition. 50 cents.
THE BIGLOW PAPERS. A New Edition. 63 cents.

Coventry Patmore.

THE ANGEL IN THE HOUSE. BETROTHAL.
" " " " ESPOUSALS. 75 cts. each.

Charles Sumner.

ORATIONS AND SPEECHES. 2 vols. $2.50.
RECENT SPEECHES AND ADDRESSES. $1.25.

John G. Whittier.

POCKET EDITION OF POETICAL WORKS. 2 vols. $1.50.
OLD PORTRAITS AND MODERN SKETCHES. 75 cents.
MARGARET SMITH'S JOURNAL. 75 cents.
SONGS OF LABOR, AND OTHER POEMS. Boards. 50 cts.
THE CHAPEL OF THE HERMITS. Cloth. 50 cents.
LITERARY RECREATIONS, &c. Cloth. $1.00.
THE PANORAMA, AND OTHER POEMS. Cloth. 50 cents.

Alexander Smith.

A LIFE DRAMA. 1 vol. 16mo. 50 cents.
CITY POEMS. 1 vol. 16mo. 63 cents.

Bayard Taylor.

POEMS OF HOME AND TRAVEL. Cloth. 75 cents.
POEMS OF THE ORIENT. Cloth. 75 cents.

Edwin P. Whipple.

ESSAYS AND REVIEWS. 2 vols. $2.00.
LECTURES ON LITERATURE AND LIFE. 63 cents.
WASHINGTON AND THE REVOLUTION. 20 cents.

George S. Hillard.

SIX MONTHS IN ITALY. 1 vol. 16mo. $1.50.
DANGERS AND DUTIES OF THE MERCANTILE PROFESSION. 25 cents.
SELECTIONS FROM THE WRITINGS OF WALTER SAVAGE LANDOR. 1 vol. 16mo 75 cents.

Robert Browning.

POETICAL WORKS. 2 vols. $2.00.
MEN AND WOMEN. 1 vol. $1.00.

Henry Giles.

Lectures, Essays, &c. 2 vols. $1.50.
Discourses on Life. 75 cents.
Illustrations of Genius. Cloth. $1.00.

William Motherwell.

Poems, Narrative and Lyrical. New Ed. $1.25.
Posthumous Poems. Boards. 50 cents.
Minstrelsy, Anc. and Mod. 2 vols. Boards. $1.50.

Capt. Mayne Reid.

The Plant Hunters. With Plates. 75 cents.
The Desert Home: or, The Adventures of a Lost Family in the Wilderness. With fine Plates. $1.00.
The Boy Hunters. With fine Plates. 75 cents.
The Young Voyageurs: or, The Boy Hunters in the North. With Plates. 75 cents.
The Forest Exiles. With fine Plates. 75 cents.
The Bush Boys. With fine Plates. 75 cents.
The Young Yagers. With fine Plates. 75 cents.
Ran Away to Sea: An Autobiography for Boys. With fine Plates. 75 cents.

Goethe.

Wilhelm Meister. Translated by *Carlyle.* 2 vols. $2.50.
Faust. Translated by *Hayward.* 75 cents.
Faust. Translated by *Charles T. Brooks.* $1.00.

Rev. Charles Lowell.

Practical Sermons. 1 vol. 12mo. $1.25.
Occasional Sermons. With fine Portrait. $1.25.

Rev. F. W. Robertson.

SERMONS. First Series. $1.00.
" Second " $1.00.
" Third " $1.00.
" Fourth " $1.00.
LECTURES AND ADDRESSES ON LITERARY AND SOCIAL TOPICS. $1.00.

R. H. Stoddard.

POEMS. Cloth. 63 cents.
ADVENTURES IN FAIRY LAND. 75 cents.
SONGS OF SUMMER. 75 cents.

George Lunt.

LYRIC POEMS, &c. Cloth. 63 cents.
JULIA. A Poem. 50 cents.
THREE ERAS OF NEW ENGLAND. $1.00.

Philip James Bailey.

THE MYSTIC, AND OTHER POEMS. 50 cents.
THE ANGEL WORLD, &c. 50 cents.
THE AGE, A SATIRE. 75 cents.

Anna Mary Howitt.

AN ART STUDENT IN MUNICH. $1.25.
A SCHOOL OF LIFE. A Story. 75 cents.

Mary Russell Mitford.

OUR VILLAGE. Illustrated. 2 vols. 16mo. $2.50.
ATHERTON, AND OTHER STORIES. 1 vol. 16mo. $1.25.

Josiah Phillips Quincy.

LYTERIA: A DRAMATIC POEM. 50 cents.
CHARICLES: A DRAMATIC POEM. 50 cents.

Grace Greenwood.

GREENWOOD LEAVES. 1st & 2d Series. $1.25 each.
POETICAL WORKS. With fine Portrait. 75 cents.
HISTORY OF MY PETS. With six fine Engravings. Scarlet cloth. 50 cents.
RECOLLECTIONS OF MY CHILDHOOD. With six fine Engravings. Scarlet cloth. 50 cents.
HAPS AND MISHAPS OF A TOUR IN EUROPE. $1.25.
MERRIE ENGLAND. A new Juvenile. 75 cents.
A FOREST TRAGEDY, AND OTHER TALES. $1.00.
STORIES AND LEGENDS. A new Juvenile. 75 cents.

Mrs. Crosland.

LYDIA: A WOMAN'S BOOK. Cloth. 75 cents.
ENGLISH TALES AND SKETCHES. Cloth. $1.00.
MEMORABLE WOMEN. Illustrated. $1.00.

Mrs. Jameson.

CHARACTERISTICS OF WOMEN.	Blue and Gold.		75 cents.
LOVES OF THE POETS.	"	"	75 cents.
DIARY OF AN ENNUYÉE	"	"	75 cents.
SKETCHES OF ART, &c.	"	"	75 cents.
STUDIES AND STORIES.	"	"	75 cents.

Mrs. Mowatt.

AUTOBIOGRAPHY OF AN ACTRESS. $1.25.
PLAYS. ARMAND AND FASHION. 50 cents.
MIMIC LIFE. 1 vol. $1.25.
THE TWIN ROSES. 1 vol. 75 cents.

Mrs. Howe.

PASSION FLOWERS. 75 cents.
WORDS FOR THE HOUR. 75 cents.
THE WORLD'S OWN. 50 cents.

Alice Cary.

POEMS. 1 vol. 16mo. $1.00.
CLOVERNOOK CHILDREN. With Plates. 75 cents.

Mrs. Eliza B. Lee.

MEMOIR OF THE BUCKMINSTERS. $1.25.
FLORENCE, THE PARISH ORPHAN. 50 cents.
PARTHENIA. 1 vol. 16mo. $1.00.

Samuel Smiles.

LIFE OF GEORGE STEPHENSON: RAILWAY ENGINEER. $1.25.

Blanchard Jerrold.

DOUGLAS JERROLD'S WIT. 75 cents.
LIFE AND LETTERS OF DOUGLAS JERROLD. $1.00.

Mrs. Judson.

ALDERBROOK. By *Fanny Forrester*. 2 vols. $1.75.
THE KATHAYAN SLAVE, AND OTHER PAPERS. 1 vol. 63 cents.
MY TWO SISTERS: A SKETCH FROM MEMORY. 50 cents.

Trelawny.

RECOLLECTIONS OF SHELLEY AND BYRON. 75 cents.

Charles Sprague.

POETICAL AND PROSE WRITINGS. With fine Portrait. Boards. 75 cents.

Mrs. Lawrence.

LIGHT ON THE DARK RIVER: OR MEMOIRS OF MRS. HAMLIN. 1 vol. 16mo. Cloth. $1.00.

www.ingramcontent.com/pod-product-compliance
Lightning Source LLC
LaVergne TN
LVHW021320110826
845150LV00003B/622

9781425556631